A TEXT BOOK OF

COMMUNICATION SYSTEM-II

For

Semester - V

THIRD YEAR DEGREE COURSE IN ELECTRONICS / ENGINEERING ELECTRONICS AND TELECOMMUNICATION ENGINEERING

As Per New Revised Syllabus of North Maharashtra University, Jalgaon,
June 2013-2014

G. R. PATIL
M.E. (Electronics)
Associate Professor,
E & TC Department
Army Institute of Technology
Dighi, PUNE.

COMMUNICATION SYSTEM - II

ISBN 978-93-5164-111-7

First Edition : September, 2015

© : **Author**

The text of this publication, or any part thereof, should not be reproduced or transmitted in any form or stored in any computer storage system or device for distribution including photocopy, recording, taping or information retrieval system or reproduced on any disc, tape, perforated media or other information storage device etc., without the written permission of Author with whom the rights are reserved. Breach of this condition is liable for legal action.

Every effort has been made to avoid errors or omissions in this publication. In spite of this, errors may have crept in. Any mistake, error or discrepancy so noted and shall be brought to our notice shall be taken care of in the next edition. It is notified that neither the publisher nor the author or seller shall be responsible for any damage or loss of action to any one, of any kind, in any manner, therefrom.

Published By :
NIRALI PRAKASHAN
Abhyudaya Pragati, 1312, Shivaji Nagar,
Off J.M. Road, PUNE – 411005
Tel - (020) 25512336/37/39, Fax - (020) 25511379
Email : niralipune@pragationline.com

Printed By :
REPRO INDIA LTD.
50/2 T.T.C. MIDC,
Industrial Area, Mahape, Navi Mumbai
Tel - (022) 2778 2011

DISTRIBUTION CENTRES

PUNE

Nirali Prakashan
119, Budhwar Peth, Jogeshwari Mandir Lane
Pune 411002, Maharashtra
Tel : (020) 2445 2044, 66022708, Fax : (020) 2445 1538
Email : niralilocal@pragationline.com

Nirali Prakashan
S. No. 28/25, Dhyari,
Near Pari Company, Pune 411041
Tel : (020) 24690204 Fax : (020) 24690316
Email : bookorder@pragationline.com

MUMBAI
Nirali Prakashan
385, S.V.P. Road, Rasdhara Co-op. Hsg. Society Ltd.,
Girgaum, Mumbai 400004, Maharashtra
Tel : (022) 2385 6339 / 2386 9976, Fax : (022) 2386 9976
Email : niralimumbai@pragationline.com

DISTRIBUTION BRANCHES

NAGPUR
Pratibha Book Distributors
Above Maratha Mandir, Shop No. 3, First Floor,
Rani Jhansi Square, Sitabuldi, Nagpur 440012,
Maharashtra, Tel : (0712) 254 7129

BENGALURU
Pragati Book House
House No. 1, Sanjeevappa Lane, Avenue Road Cross,
Opp. Rice Church, Bengaluru – 560002.
Tel : (080) 64513344, 64513355,
Mob : 9880582331, 9845021552
Email: bharatsavla@yahoo.com

JALGAON
Nirali Prakashan
34, V. V. Golani Market, Navi Peth, Jalgaon 425001,
Maharashtra, Tel : (0257) 222 0395
Mob : 94234 91860

KOLHAPUR
Nirali Prakashan
New Mahadvar Road,
Kedar Plaza, 1st Floor Opp. IDBI Bank
Kolhapur 416 012, Maharashtra. Mob : 9850046155

CHENNAI
Pragati Books
9/1, Montieth Road, Behind Taas Mahal, Egmore,
Chennai 600008 Tamil Nadu, Tel : (044) 6518 3535,
Mob : 94440 01782 / 98450 21552 / 98805 82331, Email : bharatsavla@yahoo.com

RETAIL OUTLETS

PUNE

Pragati Book Centre
157, Budhwar Peth, Opp. Ratan Talkies,
Pune 411002, Maharashtra
Tel : (020) 2445 8887 / 6602 2707, Fax : (020) 2445 8887

Pragati Book Centre
Amber Chamber, 28/A, Budhwar Peth,
Appa Balwant Chowk, Pune : 411002, Maharashtra,
Tel : (020) 20240335 / 66281669
Email : pbcpune@pragationline.com

Pragati Book Centre
676/B, Budhwar Peth, Opp. Jogeshwari Mandir,
Pune 411002, Maharashtra
Tel : (020) 6601 7784 / 6602 0855

PBC Book Sellers & Stationers
152, Budhwar Peth, Pune 411002, Maharashtra
Tel : (020) 2445 2254 / 6609 2463

MUMBAI
Pragati Book Corner
Indira Niwas, 111 - A, Bhavani Shankar Road, Dadar (W), Mumbai 400028, Maharashtra
Tel : (022) 2422 3526 / 6662 5254, Email : pbcmumbai@pragationline.com

Preface ...

This book is written for Third Year Electronics and Telecommunication Engineering Course of North Maharashtra University. It is written strictly as per the revised syllabus of North Maharashtra University for the subject 'Communication System - II'.

The objective of this book is to provide understanding of the various aspects of digital communication through examples and illustrations.

Communication System is used almost in every information transmission and are growing at an exponential rate.

This book explains the basic concepts of Communication System. Various types of Communication Systems are discussed in detail with their performance analysis. The working of these systems is explained with extensive waveforms and mathematical treatment wherever necessary is also given. Number of Solved Problems are also given to strengthen the concepts.

To understand the concepts explained in the book the students are required to have the knowledge of Parseval's Theorem, Random Variables, Waveform Coding.

The author is thankful to Shri. Dineshbhai Furia, Shri. Jignesh Furia, Shri. P. M. More, Mr. Malik Shaikh, Mrs. Roshan Shaikh and other Staff of Nirali Prakashan for bringing out this book in the shortest possible time.

Any constructive criticism and suggestions will be appreciated by the author for enhancing the utility of this book.

Pune   **Authors**

Syllabus ...

Unit I : Spectra, Probability and Random Variables (9L, 16M)
   (a)   Basic Signal Processing Operation in Digital Communication
   (b)   Power Density Spectrum, Energy Spectral Density
   (c)   Parseval's Theorem, Rayleigh Energy Theorem
   (d)   Probability and Sample Space
   (e)   Random Variables, Random Process and Probability Function
   (f)   Probability Models

Unit II : Waveform Coding and Baseband Shaping for Data Transmission (8L, 16M)
   (a)   Pulse Code Modulation (PCM) and PCM with Noise.
   (b)   Delta Modulation
   (c)   Digital Multiplexing
   (d)   Discrete PAM Signals and Power Spectra of Discrete PAM Signals
   (e)   ISI and Nyquist's Criterion for Distortion less Baseband Binary Transmission
   (f)   Eye Pattern

Unit III : Digital Modulation Techniques (9L, 16M)
   (a)   Digital Modulation Formats
   (b)   Coherent Binary Modulation Techniques
   (c)   Coherent Quadrature Modulation Techniques
   (d)   Noncoherent Binary Modulation Techniques
   (e)   M-ary Modulation Techniques
   (f)   Bit Vs. Symbol Error Probability and Synchronization

Unit IV : Information and Detection Theory (8L, 16M)
   (a)   Uncertainty, Information and Entropy
   (b)   Source Coding Theory
   (c)   Huffman Coding and Discrete Memoryless Channels
   (d)   Mutual Information, Channel Capacity and Channel Coding Theory
   (e)   Differential Entropy and Mutual Information
   (f)   Channel Capacity Theorem

Unit V : Channel Coding (8L, 16M)
   (a)   Coding Introduction, Error Probability with repetition in the Binary Symmetric Channel
   (b)   Linear Block Codes
   (c)   Algebraic Codes
   (d)   Automatic Repeat Request

***

Contents ...

Unit I : Spectra, Probability and Random Variables   1.1 - 1.40

Unit II : Waveform Coding and Baseband Shaping for Data Transmission   2.1 - 2.52

Unit III : Digital Modulation Techniques   3.1 - 3.64

Unit IV : Information and Detection Theory   4.1 - 4.62

Unit V : Channel Coding   5.1 - 5.70

***

Unit I

SPECTRA, PROBABILITY AND RANDOM VARIABLES

1.1 Basic Signal Processing Operation in Digital Communication

Fig. 1.1 shows the basic operations in digital communication system. The source and the destination are the two physically separate points. When the signal travels in the communication channel, noise interferes with it. Because of this interference, the smeared or disturbed version of the input signal is received at the receiver. Therefore, the signal received may not be correct. That is errors are introduced in the received signal. Thus the effects of noise due to the communication channel limit the rate at which signal can be transmitted. The probability of error in the received signal and transmission rate are normally used as performance measures of the digital communication system.

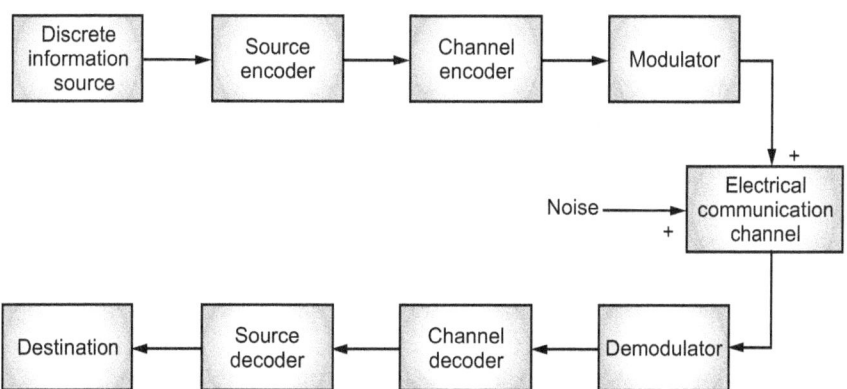

Fig. 1.1: Basic Digital Communication System

1. Information Source:

The information source generates the message signal to be transmitted. In case of analog communication, the information source is analog. In case of digital communication, the information source produces a message signal which is not continuously varying with time. Rather the message signal is intermittent with respect to time. The examples of discrete information sources are data from computers, teletype etc. Even the message containing text is also discrete. The analog signal can be converted to discrete signal by sampling and quantization. In sampling, the analog signal is chopped off at regular time intervals. Those chopped samples from a discrete signal.

The discrete information sources have the following important parameters:

(a) **Source alphabet:** These are the letters, digits or special characters available from the information source.

(b) **Symbol rate:** It is the rate at which the information source generates source alphabets. It is normally represented in symbols/sec unit.

(c) **Source alphabet probabilities:** Each source alphabet from the source has independent occurrence rate in the sequence. For example, letters A, E, I etc. occur frequently in the sequence. Thus, probability of the occurrence of each source alphabet can become one of the important property which is useful in digital communication.

(d) **Probabilistic dependence of symbols in a sequence :** The information carrying capacity of each source alphabet is different in a particular sequence. This parameter defines average information content of the symbols. The entropy of a source refers to the average information content per symbol in long messages. Entropy is defined in terms of bits per symbol. Bit is the abbreviation for binary digit. The source information rate is thus the product of symbol rate and source entropy i.e.

Information rate = Symbol rate × Source entropy

(Bits/sec)   (Symbols/sec)   (Bits/Symbol)

The information rate represents minimum average data rate required to transmit information from source to the destination.

2. Source Encoder and Decoder:

The symbols produced by the information source are given to the source encoder. These symbols cannot be transmitted directly. They are first converted into digital form (i.e. Binary sequence of 1's and 0's) by the source encoder. Every binary '1' and '0' is called a bit. The group of bits is called a codeword. The source encoder assigns codewords to the symbols. For every distinct symbol there is a unique codword. The codeword can be of 4, 8, 16 or 32 bits length. As the number of bits are increased in each codeword, the symbols that can be represented are increased.

For example, 8 bits will have 2^8 = 256 distinct codewords. Therefore, 8 bits can be used to represent 256 symbols, 16 bits can represent 2^{16} = 65536 symbols and so on. In both of the above examples the number of bits in every codeword is same throughout. That is 8 in first case and 16 in next case respectively. This is called fixed length coding. Fixed length coding is efficient only if all the symbols occur with equal probabilities in a statistically independent sequence. In the practical situations, the symbols in the sequence are statistically dependent and they have unequal probabilities of occurrence. For example, let us assume that the symbol sequence represents the percentage marks of the students. The 02%, 08%, 20%, 98%, 99% etc. symbols will have minimum probability of occurrence. But 60%, 55%, 70%, 75% will have more probability. For such symbols normally variable length codewords are assigned. More bits (More length) are assigned to rarely occurring symbols and less bits are assigned to frequently occurring symbols. Typical source encoders are pulse code modulators, delta modulators, vector quantizers etc. We will come across these codewords in detail in the subsequent chapters. Source encoders have the following important parameters.

(a) **Block size:** This gives the maximum number of distinct codewords that can be represented by the source encoder. It depends upon maximum number of bits in the codeword. For example, the block size of 8 bits source encoder will have $2^8 = 256$ codewords.

(b) **Codeword length:** This is the number of bit used to represent each codeword. For example, if 8 bits are assigned to every codeword, then codeword length is 8 bits.

(c) **Average data rate:** It is the output bits per second from the source encoder. The source encoder assigns multiple number of bits to every input symbol. Therefore, the data rate is normally higher than the symbol rate.

Therefore, the data rate is normally higher than the symbol rate. For example, symbols/sec and the length of codeword is 8 bits. Then let us consider that the symbols are given to the source encoder at the rate of 10.

$$\text{Date rate} = \text{Symbol rate} \times \text{Codeword length}$$
$$= 10 \times 8 = 80 \text{ bits}$$

Information rate is the minimum number of bits per second needed to convey information from source to destination as stated earlier. Therefore Optimum data rate is equal to information rate. But because of practical limitations, designing such source encoder is difficult. Hence average data rate is higher than information rate and hence symbol rate also,

(d) **Efficiency of the encoder:** This is the ratio of minimum source information rate to the actual output data rate of the source encoder.

At the receiver, some decoder is used to perform the reverse operation to that of source encoder. It converts the binary output of the channel decoder into a symbol sequence. Both variable length and fixed length decoders are possible. Some decoders use memory to store codewords. The decoders and encoders can be synchronous or asynchronous.

3. **Channel Encoder and Decoder:**

At this stage we know that the message or information signal is converted in the form of binary sequence (i.e. 1's and 0's). The communication channel adds noise and interference to the signal being transmitted.

Therefore, errors are introduced in the binary sequence received at the receiver. Hence errors are also introduced in the symbols generated from these binary codewords. To avoid these errors, channel coding is done. The channel encoder adds some redundant binary bits to the input sequence. These redundant bits are added with some properly defined logic. For example, consider that the codeword from the source encoder is three bits long and one redundant bit is added to make it 4-bit long. This 4th bit is added (either 1 or 0) such that number of 1's in the encoded word remain even (also called even parity). Following table gives output of source encoder, the 4th bit depending upon the parity, and output of channel encoder.

Table 1.1: Even parity coding

Output of source encoder			Bit to be added by channel encoder for even parity	Output of channel encoder			
b_3	b_2	b_1	b_0	b_3	b_2	b_1	b_0
1	1	0	0	1	1	0	0
0	1	0	1	0	1	0	1
0	0	0	0	0	0	0	0
1	1	1	1	1	1	1	1
:	:	:	:	:	:	:	:

Observe in the above table that every codeword at the output of channel encoder contains "even" number of 1's. At the receiver, if odd number of 1's are detected, then receiver comes to know that there is an error in the received signal. The channel decoder at the receiver is thus able to detect error in the bit sequence, and reduce the effects of channel noise and distortion. The channel encoder and decoder thus serve to increase the reliability of the received signal. The extra bits which are added by the channel encoders carry no information, rather, they are used by the channel decoder to detect and correct errors if any. These error correcting bits may be added recurrent, after the block of few symbols or added in every symbol as shown in Table 1.1. The example of parity coding given above is just illustrative. There are many advanced and efficient coding techniques available.

The coding and decoding operation at encoder and decoder needs the memory (storage) and processing of binary data. Because of microcontrollers and computers, the complexity of encoders and decoders is nowadays very much reduced. The important parameters for channel encoder are:

(a) The method of coding used.
(b) Coding rate, which depends upon the redundant bits added by the channel encoder.
(c) Coding efficiency, which is the ratio of data rate at the input to the data rate at the output of encoder.
(d) Error control capabilities, i.e. detecting and correcting errors.
(e) Feasibility or complexity of the encoder and decoder.

The time delay involved in the decoding is also an important parameter for channel decoder.

4. Digital Modulators and Demodulators:

Whenever the modulating signal is discrete (i.e. binary codewords), then digital modulation techniques are used. The carrier signal used by digital modulators is always continuous sinusoidal wave of high frequency. The digital modulators maps the input binary sequence of 1's and 0's to analog signal waveforms. If one bit at a time is to be transmitted, then digital modulator signal is $s_1(t)$ to transmit binary '0' and $s_2(1)$ to transmit binary '1'. For example, consider the output of digital modulator shown in Fig. 1.2.

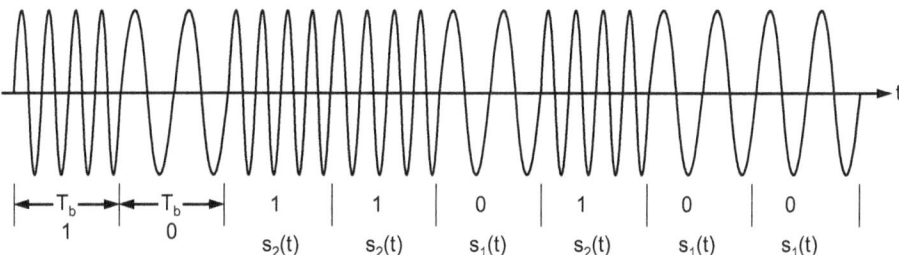

Fig. 1.2: Frequency modulated output of a digital modulator

The signal $s_1(t)$ has law frequency compared to signal $s_2(t)$. It is frequency modulation (FM) in two steps corresponding to binary symbols '0' and '1'. Thus even though the modulated signal appears to be continuous, the modulation is discrete (or in steps). Single carrier is converted into two waveforms $s_1(t)$ and $s_2(t)$ because of digital modulation.

If the codeword contains two bits and they are to be transmitted at a time, then there will be $M = 2^2 = 4$ distinct symbols (or codewords). These four codewords will require four distinct waveforms for transmission. Such modulators are called M-ary modulators. Frequency Shift Keying (FSK), Phase Shift Keying (PSK), Amplitude Shift Keying (ASK), Differential Phase Shift Keying (DPSK), Minimum Shift Keying (MSK) are the examples of various digital modulators. Since these modulators use continuous carrier wave, they are also called digital CW modulators.

In the receiver, the digital demodulator converts the input modulated signal to the sequence of binary bits. The most important parameter for the demodulator is the method of demodulation. The other parameters for the selection of digital modulation method are,

(a) Probability of symbol or bit error.
(b) Bandwidth needed to transmit the signal.
(c) Synchronous or asynchronous method of detection and
(d) Complexity of implementation.

5. Communication Channel:

As we have seen in the preceding sections, the connection between transmitter and receiver is through communication channel. We have seen that the communication can take place through wirelines, wireless or fiber optic channels. The other media such as, optical disks, magnetic tapes and disks etc. can also be called as communication channel, because they can also carry data through them. Every communication channel has got some problems. Following are the common problems associated with the channels :

(a) **Additive noise interference:** This noise is generated due to internal solid state devices and resistors etc. used to implement the communication system.

(b) **Signal attenuation:** It occurs due to internal resistance of the channel and fading of the signal.

(c) **Amplitude and phase distortion:** The signal is distorted in amplitude and phase because of non-linear characteristics of the channel.

(d) **Multipath distortion:** This distortion occurs mostly in wireless communication channels. Signals coming from different paths tend to interfere with each other. There are two main resources available with the communication channels. These two resources are -

   (i) **Channel Bandwidth:** This is the maximum possible range of frequencies that can be used for transmission. For example, the bandwidth offered by wireline channels is less compared to fibre optic channels.

   (ii) **Power in the transmitted signal:** This is the power that can be put in the signal being transmitted. The effect of noise can be minimized by increasing the power. But this cannot be increased to very high value because of the equipment and other constraints. For example, the power in the wireline channel is limited because of the cables.

The power and bandwidth limit the data rate of the communication channel. As we know, the fiber optic channel transports light signals from one place to another just like a metallic wire carriers an electric signal. There is no current or metallic conductor in optical fibre. The optical fibre has the following advantages:

(a) Very large bandwidths are possible.

(b) Transmission losses are very small.

(c) Electromagnetic interference is absent.

(d) They have small size and weight.

(e) They offer ruggedness and flexibility.

(f) Optical fibres are low cost and cheap.

Satellites essentially perform wireless communication. Mainly satellites are repeaters. Broad area coverage is the main advantage of satellites. The power requirement is also less, since solar energy is used by satellites. Global communication is very easily possible through satellite channel. The interference on satellite channels is present but it is minimum.

1.2 Signal Energy and Energy Spectral Density

The energy E_g of a signal g(t) is defined as,

$$E_g = \int_{-\infty}^{\infty} |g(t)|^2 \, dt \qquad \ldots (1.1)$$

From Rayleigh's energy theorem, we know,

$$E_g = \int_{-\infty}^{\infty} |g(t)|^2 \, dt = \int_{-\infty}^{\infty} |G(f)|^2 \, df \qquad \ldots (1.2)$$

The above equation allows us to determine the signal energy from either the time domain specifications g(t) or frequency domain specification G(f) of the same signal.

Energy Spectral Density:

Equation (1.2) can be interpreted as energy of the signal g(t) is the result of contribution of a spectral components of frequency f and is proportional to $|G(f)|^2$.

Consider a bandpass filter of bandwidth Δf and the signal is passed through it.
Since, $\qquad Y(f) = H(f) G(f)$
Energy of the signal which is output from the filter will be,

$$E_y = \int_{-\infty}^{\infty} |H(f) G(f)|^2 \, df$$

Since, $\qquad H(f) = 1 \quad ; \quad$ Over Δf, where $\Delta f \to 0$
$\qquad \qquad \qquad = 0 \quad ; \quad$ elsewhere
$\qquad E_y = 2|G(f)|^2 \, df$

Thus, $2|G(f)|^2 \, df$ is the energy contributed by spectral components in two narrow bands each of width $\rightleftharpoons f$.

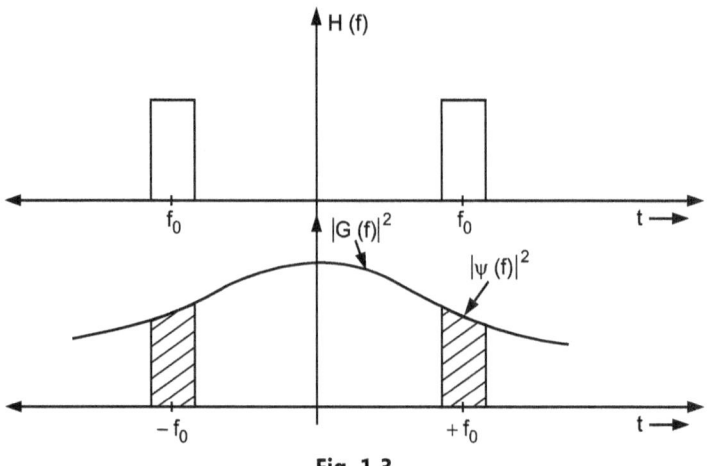

Fig. 1.3

Therefore, we interpret $|G(f)|^2$ as energy per unit bandwidth (Hz) of spectral components g(t) centred around f. Actually energy contributed per unit bandwidth is $2|G(f)|^2$ because both positive and negative frequency components combine to form the components in Δf. However, for convenience we consider only one sided component.

The energy per unit bandwidth is called Energy Spectral Density (ESD) denoted as,

$$\psi_g(f) = |G(f)|^2$$

∴
$$E_g = \int_{-\infty}^{\infty} \psi_g(f)\, df$$

Essential Bandwidth:
The bandwidth B is called essential bandwidth if we suppress the signal spectrum with little effect on signal energy (say 95% and above).

Properties of ESD:
(1) The total area under ESD function is equal to energy of the signal.

$$E = \int_{-\infty}^{\infty} \psi_g(f)\, df$$

(2) If a signal with ESD $\psi_g(f)$ is passed through an LTI system having transfer function h(t), then output energy,

$$\psi_y(f) = |H(f)|^2 \psi_x(f)$$

Proof:
$$\psi(f) = H(f) X(f)$$
$$|Y(f)|^2 = |H(f)|^2 |X(f)|^2$$
$$\psi_y(f) = |H(f)|^2 \psi_x(f)$$

(3) Autocorrelation function $R_y(\tau)$ and energy spectral density function form Fourier transfer pair.
$$R_g(\tau) \rightleftharpoons \psi_g(f)$$

(4) ESD is a non-negative real valued function of frequency
$$\psi_g(f) \geq 0 \quad \text{for all } f$$

(5) The energy spectral density of real valued energy signal g(t) is an even function of frequency
$$\psi_g(-f) = \psi_g(f)$$

1.3 Signal Power and Power Spectral Density (PSD)

For a power signal, a meaningful measure of its size is its power as its time average of signal energy over infinite time interval.

i.e.
$$P_g = \lim_{T \to \infty} \frac{1}{T} \int_{-T/2}^{+T/2} g^2(t)\, dt$$

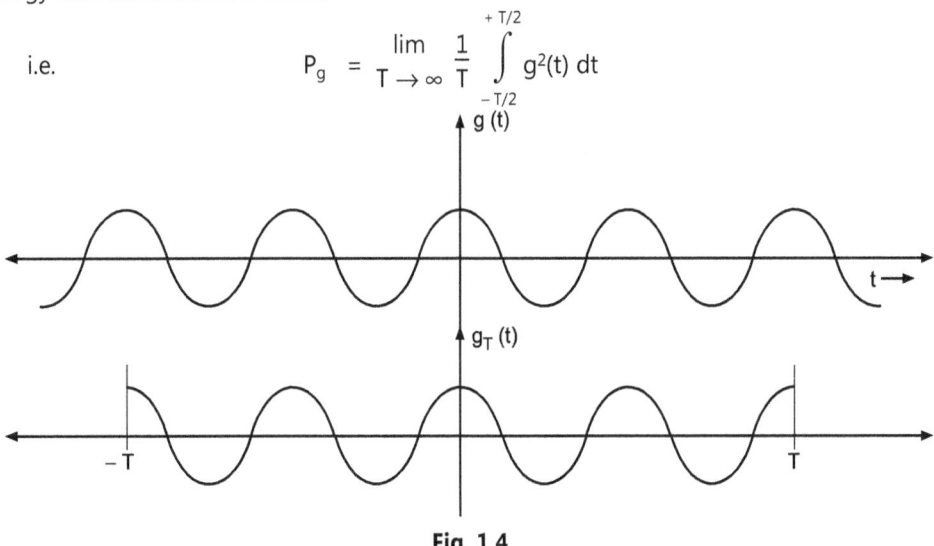

Fig. 1.4

For the truncated signal $g_T(t)$ we can write,
$$P_g = \lim_{T \to \infty} \frac{E_{gT}}{2T}$$

which relates power and energy.

If
$$g_T(t) \rightleftharpoons G_T(f)$$

then,
$$E_{gT} = \int g_T^2(t)\,dt = \int |G_T(f)|^2\,df$$

$$\therefore \quad P_g = \lim_{T \to \infty} \frac{E_{gT}}{T} = \lim_{T \to \infty} \left[\int |G_T(f)|^2\,df \right]$$

$$= \int_{-\infty}^{\infty} \lim_{T \to \infty} \frac{|G(f)|^2}{2T}\,df$$

Thus, $\lim_{T \to \infty} \frac{|G(f)|^2}{2T}$ is called power spectral density and is denoted as $S_g(f)$.

$$\therefore \quad S_g(f) = \lim_{T \to \infty} \frac{|G_T(f)|^2}{2T}$$

As in case of ESD, PSD is also positive, real and even function of f.

Properties of PSD:

1. The area under PSD is equal to average power of the signal.
2. If $|H(f)|^2$ is power gain of linear time invariant system then output power spectral density.
$$S_g(f) = |H(f)|^2 S_x(f)$$
3. The autocorrelation function $R_g(\tau)$ and PSD $S_g(f)$ form a Fourier transform pair.
$$R_g(\tau) \rightleftharpoons S_g(f)$$
4. $S_g(f) \geq 0$
5. $S_g(-f) = S_g(f)$

Signal Power is its Mean Square Value:

$$P_g = \lim_{T \to \infty} \int_{-\infty}^{\infty} g^2(t)\,dt$$

This equation shows that the signal power is average mean of its squared values. In other words, P_g is the means square value of g(t).

Interpretation of PSD:

Because PSD is a time average of ESD of g(t), we can show that $S_g(f)$ represents power per unit bandwidth.

Example 1.1:

Find energy spectral density of:
(a) exponential pulse,
(b) sinc pulse.

Solution: (a) Exponential Pulse:

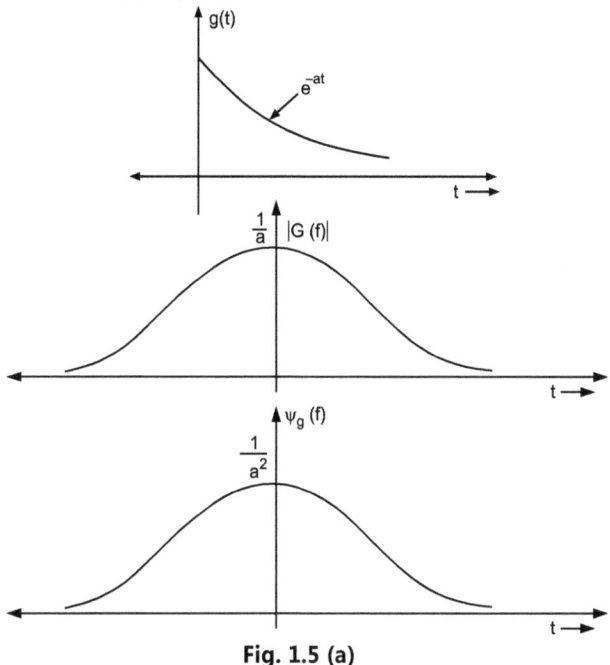

$$g(f) = e^{-at} u(t)$$

$$G(f) = \frac{1}{a + j2\pi f}$$

$$|G(f)| = \frac{1}{\sqrt{a^2 + 4\pi^2 f^2}}$$

$$|G(f)|^2 = \frac{1}{a^2 + 4\pi^2 f^2}$$

Fig. 1.5 (a)

(b) Sinc Pulse:

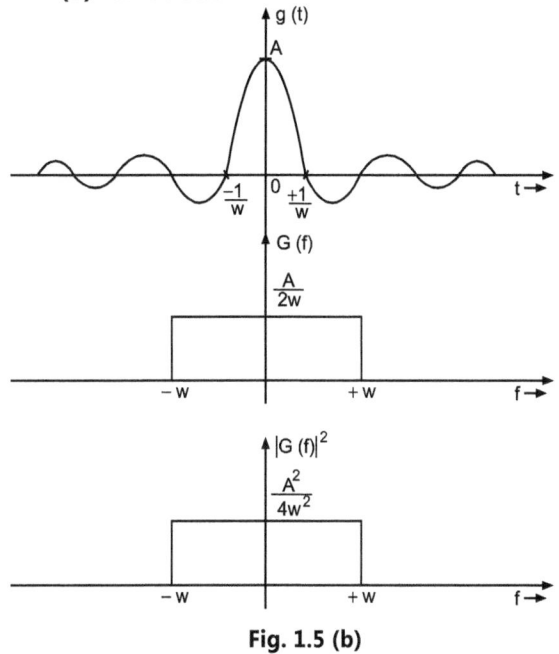

$$g(t) = A \operatorname{sinc}(2wt)$$

$$G(f) = \frac{A}{2w} \operatorname{rect}\left(\frac{f}{2w}\right)$$

$$|G(f)|^2 = \frac{A^2}{4w^2} \operatorname{rect}^2\left(\frac{f}{2w}\right)$$

$$E = \frac{A^2}{2w}$$

Fig. 1.5 (b)

Example 1.2:

A rectangular pulse of unit amplitude and unit duration is passed through an ideal low pass filter of bandwidth B. Find ESD of output signal and energy.

$$H(f) = +1 \quad ; \quad -B \leq f \leq B$$
$$= 0 \quad ; \quad |f| > B$$

Solution:

$$\text{rect}(t) \rightleftharpoons \text{sinc}(f)$$
$$x(t) = \text{rect}(t)$$
$$X(f) = \text{sinc}(f)$$
$$\psi_x(f) = \text{sinc}^2(f)$$

$$\therefore \quad \psi_y(f) = |H(f)|^2 \psi_x(f)$$

$$= \begin{cases} \psi_x(f) & ; \quad -B \leq f \leq B \\ 0 & ; \quad |f| > B \end{cases}$$

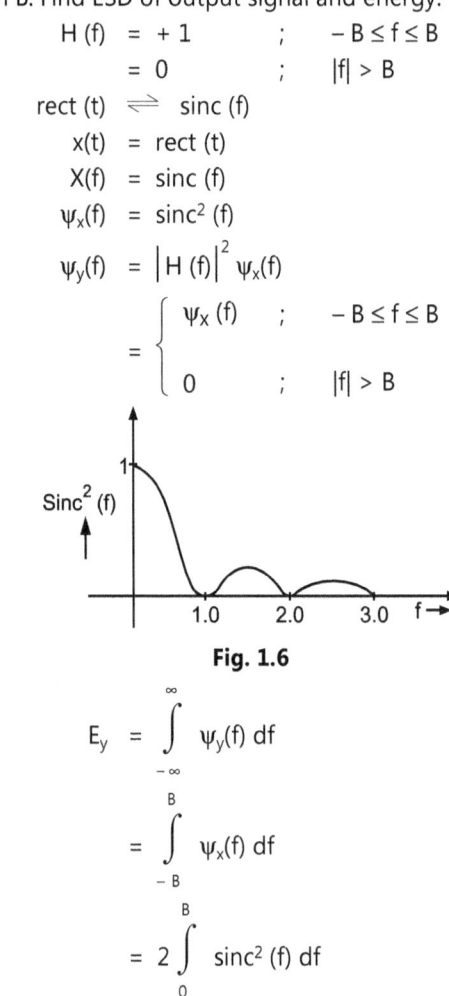

Fig. 1.6

$$E_y = \int_{-\infty}^{\infty} \psi_y(f)\, df$$

$$= \int_{-B}^{B} \psi_x(f)\, df$$

$$= 2 \int_{0}^{B} \text{sinc}^2(f)\, df$$

1.4 Parseval's Theorem

If x(t) is the periodic power signal with Fourier coefficients X(k), then average power in the signals is given by $\sum_{k=-\infty}^{\infty} |X(k)|^2$ i.e.,

$$\text{Power, } P = \sum_{k=-\infty}^{\infty} |X(k)|^2 \qquad \ldots (1.3)$$

Proof: The power in the signal x(t) is given as,

$$P = \frac{1}{T} \int_{-T/2}^{T/2} |x(t)|^2 \, dt = \frac{1}{T} \int_{-T/2}^{T/2} x(t) \, x^*(t) \, dt \qquad \ldots (1.4)$$

We have, $\quad x(t) = \sum_{k=-\infty}^{\infty} X(k) \, e^{jk\omega_0 t} \qquad$ By synthesis equation

$\therefore \quad x^*(t) = \left[\sum_{k=-\infty}^{\infty} X(k) \, e^{jk\omega_0 t} \right]^* \qquad$ By taking conjugates on both sides

$$= \sum_{k=-\infty}^{\infty} X^*(k) \, e^{-jk\omega_0 t}$$

Putting above expression of x*(t) in equation (1.4),

$$P = \frac{1}{T} \int_{-T/2}^{T/2} x(t) \sum_{k=-\infty}^{\infty} X^*(k) \, e^{-jk\omega_0 t} \, dt$$

Here, $\int_{-T/2}^{T/2} = \int_{<T>}$ i.e. integration over one period of x(t). Interchanging the order of summation and integration,

$$P = \sum_{k=-\infty}^{\infty} X^*(k) \cdot \frac{1}{T} \int_{<T>} x(t) \, e^{-jk\omega_0 t} \, dt = \sum_{k=-\infty}^{\infty} X^*(k) \, X(k)$$

$$= \sum_{k=-\infty}^{\infty} |X(k)|^2$$

Significance: Power of the signal can be obtained by squaring and adding the magnitudes of Fourier coefficients.

1.5 Rayleight's Theorem

Statement: Energy of the signal can be obtained by interchanging its energy spectrum.

$$E = \int_{-\infty}^{\infty} |x(t)|^2 \, dt = \frac{1}{2\pi} \int_{-\infty}^{\infty} |X(\omega)|^2 \, d\omega = \int_{-\infty}^{\infty} |X(f)|^2 \, df \qquad \ldots (1.5)$$

Proof:
$$E = \int_{-\infty}^{\infty} |x(t)|^2 \, dt = \int_{-\infty}^{\infty} x(t) x^*(t) \, dt \qquad \ldots (1.6)$$

The Fourier Transform states that,

$$x(t) = \frac{1}{2\pi} \int_{-\infty}^{\infty} X(\omega) e^{j\omega t} d\omega$$

Adding conjugate of both the sides,

$$x^*(t) = \frac{1}{2\pi} \int_{-\infty}^{\infty} X^*(\omega) e^{-j\omega t} d\omega$$

Putting above expression for $x^*(t)$ in equation (1.),

$$E = \int_{-\infty}^{\infty} x(t) \left[\frac{1}{2\pi} \int_{-\infty}^{\infty} X^*(\omega) e^{-j\omega t} d\omega \right] = \frac{1}{2\pi} \int_{-\infty}^{\infty} X^*(\omega) \int_{-\infty}^{\infty} x(t) e^{-j\omega t} d\omega$$

$$= \frac{1}{2\pi} \int_{-\infty}^{\infty} X^*(\omega) \cdot X(\omega) d\omega = \frac{1}{2\pi} \int_{-\infty}^{\infty} |X(\omega)|^2 d\omega$$

Now, $\omega = 2\pi f$, $d\omega = 2\pi df$. Hence, above equation becomes,

$$E = \int_{-\infty}^{\infty} |X(f)|^2 df$$

1.6 Concept of Probability

Random or non-deterministic signals are described in terms of their statistical properties. Probability theory is a mathematical tool which allows us to describe or specify these signals.

1.6.1 Important Definitions

1. **Random Experiment:** An experiment whose outcome cannot be predicted.
2. **Events:** A set of outcomes of random experiment meeting some specification.
3. **Sample Space (S):** It is a collection of all possible separately identifiable outcomes of random experiment.
4. **Element/Sample Point:** Each outcome of random experiment belonging to sample space.
5. **Probability:** If N (A) is the number of occurrences of the event A of a random experiment, while we conduct N independent trials of this experiment, then the function

$$P(A) = \lim_{N \to \infty} \frac{N(A)}{N} \quad \ldots (1.7)$$

is called probability of A.

6. **Compliment (A^c):** It is an event containing all elements not in A.
7. **Union ($A \cup B$):** It is an event containing all sample points in A and B.
8. **Intersection ($A \cap B$):** It is an event containing sample points common to both A and B.
9. **Mutually exclusive events:** If A and B are such that $A \cap B = \phi$, then A and B are said to be disjoints or mutually exclusive events.
10. When A and B are not mutually exclusive then,
$$P(A \cup B) = P(A) + P(B) - P(AB) \qquad \ldots (1.8)$$
where, P (AB) is probability of joint event A and B also denoted as $P(A \cap B)$.

Example 1.3:

A coin is tossed three times in succession. What is the probability of obtaining exactly two heads?

Solution: The sample space contains $2^3 = 8$ elements

$$S = \{HHH, \underline{HHT}, \underline{HTH}, HTT, \underline{THH}, THT, TTH, TTT\}$$

The event: exactly two heads are obtained contains 3 elements (3_{C_2}).

∴ P (Obtaining exactly two heads) = $\dfrac{3}{8}$

Example 1.4:

Two dice are thrown. Find the probability that sum on the dice is less than 3.

Solution: There are total 36 sample points in the sample S.

The event sum obtained is less than 3 contains points $\{(1, 2), (2, 1), (1, 1), (1, 1)\} = 4$ points.

∴ Probability that sum obtained is less than 3 is = $\dfrac{4}{36} = \dfrac{1}{9}$

1.6.2 Conditional Probability

If the probability of one event is influenced by another. e.g. drawing of cards in succession, then we denote such probability as P(B|A). It is called conditional probability and denotes probability of B given that A has occurred. It is defined as,

$$P(B|A) = \dfrac{P(AB)}{P(A)} \qquad P(A) \neq 0 \qquad \ldots (1.9)$$

Also,

$$P(A|B) = \dfrac{P(AB)}{P(B)} \qquad P(B) \neq 0 \qquad \ldots (1.10)$$

∴

$$P(A|B) = \dfrac{P(A) \cdot P(B|A)}{P(B)} \qquad \ldots (1.11)$$

$$P(B|A) = \dfrac{P(B) \cdot P(A|B)}{P(A)} \qquad \ldots (1.12)$$

(1.11) and (1.12) are known as **Baye's rule.**

If the conditional probability P(B|A) is equal to elementary probability of B.

i.e.   P(B|A) = P(B)

then,   P(AB) = P(A) P(B)

∴   P(A|B) = P(A)

Thus, if A and B are such that occurrence of one event does not depend on another then they are said to be statistically independent or disjoint.

While finding probability of successive trials we can use following important result. It is called Bernoulli's trials.

If P is probability of success of certain event A, then (1 – P) will probability of failure of that event. The probability of getting k successes in n trials is given by,

$$P(k \text{ success in n trials}) = {}^nC_k \, p^k \, (1-p)^{n-k}$$

If $B_1, B_2, B_3, ..., B_n$ are mutually exclusive events and event A occurs when any one of $B_1, B_2, B_3, ..., B_n$ occurs then,

$$P(B_i|A) = \frac{P(B_i) \, P(A|B_i)}{\Sigma \, P(B_i) \, P(A|B_i)}$$

This relation is also called Baye's rule.

Example 1.5:

Two factories produce identical clocks. The production of first factory is 10,000 units of which 100 are defective. The second factory produces 20,000 of which 300 are defective. What is the probability that particular defective clock was produced in first factory?

Solution: Let $A \cap B_1$ be the event that clock produced by first factor is defective.

∴ $P(A|B_1) = \dfrac{100}{10000} = \dfrac{1}{100}$

Let $A|B_2$ be the event that clock produced by second factory is defective.

∴ $P(A|B_2) = \dfrac{300}{20000} = \dfrac{3}{200}$

Assume that $P(B_1) = P(B_2) = \dfrac{1}{2}$

where, B_1 – Event that clock is produced by 1ˢᵗ factory.

and B_2 – Event that clock is produced by 2ⁿᵈ factor.

∴   Probability that the particular defective clock produced in first factor will be

$$P(B_1|A) = \frac{P(B_1) \times P(A|B_1)}{P(B_1) \, P(A|B_1) + P(B_2) \, P(A|B_2)}$$

$$= \frac{\frac{1}{2} \times \frac{1}{100}}{\frac{1}{2} \times \frac{1}{100} + \frac{1}{2} \times \frac{3}{200}}$$

$$= \frac{2}{5}$$

1.7 Sample Space

Before proceeding for the axiomatic approach, we define the sample space, event and axioms of probability. A physical experiment is the basic to the probability theory. A single performance of the experiment is called a trial for which there is an outcome. We are mainly interested in mathematical modelling of the experiment. Consider an experiment of rolling a die and observing the number that shows up. There are six numbers that can be shown up. These six numbers are all the possible outcomes in the experiment. If the rolling of the die is unbiased we know that each outcome is equally likely to occur. Therefore, likelyhood of any one occurring is 1/6. We understand that, this experiment is governed by two sets. One is the set of all the possible outcomes and the other is the set of likely hoods of outcomes.

The set of all possible outcomes in any given experiment is called the sample space, it is denoted by S. This is an important set for a given experiment. Different experiments form different sample spaces. Sample space S is a universal set for a given experiment. Every experiment is governed by the sample space. Every possible outcome is an element of the sample space. Sample space can be discrete or continuous.

In the die experiment we referred to, the sample space consists of six elements, they are discrete and countable. Such sample space is called discrete and countable. The sample space can be discrete and countably infinite. For example, S is the sample space for the experiment 'choose a positive even number' that is S = {2, 4, 6, 8, ………}. This sample space consists of infinite number of elements, but they are countable.

Consider another sample space S of an experiment defined by **'choose any number between 1 and 10'**. It consists of uncountably infinite number of elements. Such a sample space is called continuous. Another experiment 'spin the pointer and measure the final angle θ with reference 0°, the pointer may stop at any θ between 0° and 360°. Therefore, the sample space consists of uncountable infinite elements. The sample space of this is another example for the continuous sample space.

1.7.1 Event

In most of the applications, we may not be directly interested in all the possible outcomes. We may be interested in some of the outcomes or the nature of the outcomes of the experiment. In the experiment of rolling a die, we might be more interested in the even number or odd number that shows up. We define an event to deal such cases.

An event is defined as a subset of the sample space. As an event is a set, all the definitions and laws of set theory are applicable to the event. We can have 2^N number of events defined for an experiment, where N is the number of elements in the sample space S of that particular experiment. For the experiment rolling of die, we can define 2^6 events, such as 'the number showing up is even', 'number showing up is one', 'number showing up is six' etc.

As in case of sample space, events may be discrete or continuous. The event 'number showing up is even' is a discrete and finite event in case of rolling a die experiment.

In experiment of 'choose an odd integer', the sample space of this experiment consists of countably infinite number of elements. An event defined for this experiment as 'the number is prime' in the experiment of 'choosing an integer'. This event will be discrete but infinite.

An event can be continuous, for example in case of the experiment, 'choose any number between 1 and 5' the event may be defined as 'the number is between 3.5 and 4'. This event is uncountably infinite, which is said to be a continuous event.

In the spinning of the pointer experiment the event can be defined as the 'final angle θ is between 90 and 135'. This event is continuous, because it consists of uncountably infinite elements. Event can be discrete for a continuous sample space. For example, 'the angle θ is 45°' in case of spinning of the pointer experiment.

1.7.2 Definition of Probability and Axioms

A non-negative number is assigned to each event defined on the sample space. This number is called probability. Therefore, the probability is a function of the events defined and it is denoted by P (A). P (A) stands for 'probability of occurrence of event A'.

The assignment of the probability is based on three axioms. Let A be any event defined on a sample space S. Then the first two axioms are,

    Axiom 1 : $\quad\quad\quad\quad P(A) \geq 0$ ... (1.13)

    Axiom 2 : $\quad\quad\quad\quad P(S) = 1$ ... (1.14)

The first axiom is only due to the fact that, we are interested in working with positive numbers. The second axiom implies that the sample space itself is an event. If there are N events A_n, n = 1, 2, 3, ..., N where N may be infinite, defined on sample space S, and having the property that any of the two events are mutually exclusive that is,

$$A_m \cap A_n = \phi$$

for all m ≠ n, then the third axiom is,

$$P\left(\bigcup_{n=1}^{N} A_n\right) = \sum_{n=1}^{N} P(A_n) \text{ if } A_m \cap A_n = \phi \text{ for all } m \neq n\ 1, 2, 3, ... N, \text{ with N is possibly infinite.}$$

    ... (1.15)

This axiom implies that the probability of the event equal to the union of any number of mutually exclusive events is equal to the sum of the individual event probabilities.

Suppose in experiment of spinning of a pointer on a wheel of chance that is labelled from 1 to 360 slots. On each trail of the experiment, the pointer stops at any one of the slots x. Outcome in this experiment is the number of the slot at which pointer stops. Set of all the possible outcomes is sample space S = {0 < x ≤ 360}. Let an event A is defined as the 'pointer stopping between any two numbers $x_2 \geq x_1$'. The probability of the event should be $P(A) = \frac{x_2 - x_1}{360}$, it satisfies the axiom for all x_2 and x_1 because $x_2 \geq x_1$. It satisfies the second axiom when x_2 is 360 and x_1 is 0 in the event A.

Now suppose, we break the wheel's periphery into N contiguous segments $A_n = \{x_{n-1} < x \leq x_n\}$, where $x_n = \frac{n(360)}{N}$, n = 1, 2, 3, ..., N, with $x_0 = 1$. Then,

$P(A_n) = \frac{1}{N}$ and for any N,

$$P\left(\bigcup_{n=1}^{N} A_n\right) = \sum_{n=1}^{N} P(A_n) = \sum_{n=1}^{N} \frac{1}{N}$$

$$= 1 = P(S) \text{ which satisfies the third axiom.} \quad \ldots (1.16)$$

Let an event K defined as the 'pointer stops at angle 45°'. Since the sample space consists of uncountably infinite number of elements, the probability of event P (K) is zero. It is true because N → ∞. Thus, probability of a discrete event defined on a continuous sample space is zero. It implies that the events can occur even if the probability of that event is zero. It can be understood from this experiment that the pointer can stop at any angle, but it may never stop at the same precise angle again. The infinite sample space has only one discrete event therefore, its probability is zero. This event is not an impossible event which has no elements. It may so happen that the events with probability may not occur.

The three axioms of probability completely describe the experiment and mathematically model the experiment. Thus, an experiment is defined mathematically by three points.

1. Sample space assignment.
2. Definition of events of interest.
3. Assignment of probabilities of each event, such that all the three axioms are satisfied.

1.8 Random Variables

The outcome of a random experiment may be numerical or non-numerical e.g. in rolling of die it is numerical whereas, in tossing of a coin it is non-numerical. We need to assign a real number to mathematically represent the outcome of experiment. This real number can be assigned using some convenient rule. e.g. in tossing of coin we can assign – 1 to head and 1 to tail. In general, if there are m sample points $\lambda_1, \lambda_2, \lambda_3, ..., \lambda_m$, then we can assign a real number $X(\lambda_i)$ to the sample point λ_i. Here, X is a function that maps sample points into real number $x_1, x_2, x_3, ..., x_n$. (Note that m may not be equal to n). Thus, we have a random variable which takes on values $x_1, x_2, x_3, ..., x_n$. The probability of a Random variable taking a value x_i is $p_X(x_i)$.

Thus, random variable is defined as

1. A real valued function defined over a sample space.
2. A real valued function whose domain is sample space and whose range is some set of real numbers.

1.8.1 Discrete Random Variable

A random variable that takes finite number of values is known as discrete random variable. Let us take some examples.

Example 1.6:
1. Experiment: A coin is tossed three times in succession.
2. Sample space: {HHH, HHT, HTH, THH, HTT, THT, TTH, TTT}
3. Random variable: Number of heads
4. $\therefore$ $\quad S = \{3, 2, 2, 2, 1, 1, 1, 0\}$

    $\therefore$ Random variable X can take 4 values.
5. 0, 1, 2, 3 denoted as x_1, x_2, x_3, x_4.

$$\therefore p_X(x_1) = \frac{1}{8} \quad p_X(x_2) = \frac{3}{8} \quad p_X(x_3) = \frac{3}{8} \quad p_X(x_4) = \frac{1}{8}$$

Example 1.7:
1. Experiment: Throwing of a die.
2. Sample space $S = \{1, 2, 3, 4, 5, 6\}$
3. Random variable X = Number obtained

$$X = \{1, 2, 3, 4, 5, 6\}$$
$$\quad\quad x_1 \; x_2 \; x_3 \; x_4 \; x_5 \; x_6$$

4. $p_X(x_1) = p_X(x_2) = p_X(x_3) = p_X(x_4) = p_X(x_5) = p_X(x_6) = \frac{1}{6}$

Conditional Probabilities:

If X and Y are two random variables, then the conditional probability of $X = x_i$ given $Y = y_j$ is denoted by

$$P_{X|Y}(x_i|y_j)$$

We also have
$$P_{XY}(x_i, y_j) = P_{X|Y}(x_i|y_j) \cdot P_Y(y_j)$$
$$= P_{Y|X}(y_j|x_i) P_X(x_i)$$

$\therefore$
$$\sum_i P_{XY}(x_i, y_j) = \sum_i P_{X|Y}(x_i|y_j) P_Y(y_j)$$
$$= P_Y(y_j) \sum_i P_{X|Y}(x_i|y_j)$$
$$= P_Y(y_j)$$

Similarly,
$$p_X(x_i) = \sum_j P_{XY}(x_i, y_j)$$

where, $p_X(x_i)$ and $P_Y(y_j)$ are called marginal probabilities.

Example 1.8:

Over a binary communication channel, the symbol 0 is transmitted with probability 0.4 and 1 is transmitted with probability 0.6. It is given that probability of detecting error given 0 is transmitted is 10^{-6} and probability of detecting error given 1 is transmitted is 10^{-4}. Determine error probability of channel.

Solution: Let $p(e, x_i)$ denote the joint probability that error is detected when x_i is transmitted.

$\therefore$
$$p(e) = p(e, x_1) + p(e, x_2)$$

where, $x_1 = 0$ and $x_2 = 1$.

But
$$p(e, x_1) = p(x_1) \cdot p(e|x_1) = 0.4 \times 10^{-6}$$
$$p(e, x_2) = p(x_2) \cdot p(e/x_2) = 0.6 \times 10^{-4}$$

$\therefore$
$$p(e) = 0.604 \times 10^{-4}$$

1.8.2 Discrete Probability Distribution

Let X be a discrete random variable taking values $x_1, x_2, x_3, \ldots, x_m$. These values are assumed to be in ascending order.

Let $p_X(X = x_j) = p_X(x_j)$ $\quad j = 1, 2, 3, \ldots, m$

Then $p_X(x_j)$ is probability distribution function (PDF).

There is another important function called Cumulative Distribution Function (CDF) defined as "Probability that random variable X takes values less than or equal to x.

i.e.
$$F_X(x_i) = p_X(X \le x_i)$$

Example 1.9:

Find the CDF for the random experiment of obtaining number of heads when 3 coins are tossed in succession.

Solution: Random variable $X = \{x_1 = 0, x_2 = 1, x_3 = 2, x_4 = 3\}$

$$p_X(0) = \frac{1}{8} \quad p_X(1) = \frac{3}{8} \quad p_X(2) = \frac{3}{8} \quad p_X(3) = \frac{1}{8}$$

$$F_X(0) = \frac{1}{8} \qquad F_X(1) = \frac{1}{8} + \frac{3}{8} = \frac{1}{2}$$

$$F_X(2) = \frac{1}{8} + \frac{3}{8} + \frac{3}{8} = \frac{7}{8} \qquad F_X(3) = \frac{1}{8} + \frac{3}{8} + \frac{3}{8} + \frac{1}{8} = 1$$

The plot of $p_X(x)$ and $F_X(x)$ is shown in Fig. 1.7.

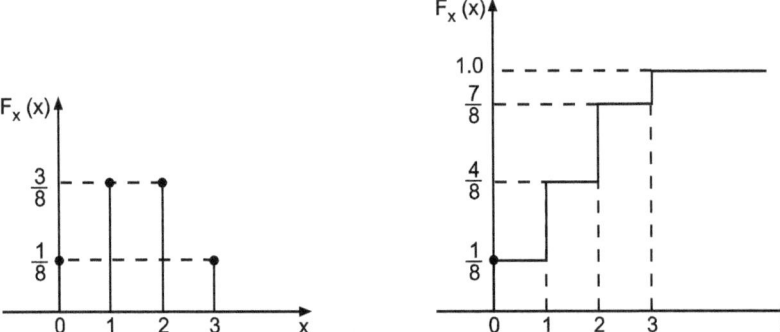

Fig. 1.7: PDF and CDF for Example 1.

Properties of CDF:
1. $0 \leq F_X(x) \leq 1$
2. $F_X(\infty) = 1$
3. $F_X(-\infty) = 0$
4. $F_X(x_1) \leq F_X(x_2)$ if $x_1 \leq x_2$
5. $P(x_1 \leq x \leq x_2) = F_X(x_2) - F_X(x_1)$

1.8.3 Continuous Random Variable

A continuous random variable can assume only value in a certain interval. There will be infinite number of possible values that this random variable can take. Hence, more meaningful quantity in case of continuous random variable will not be $p_X(X = x_i)$ but $p(x \leq x \leq X + \Delta x)$. Therefore, CDF will describe this more suitably.

The CDF for the interval $x \leq X \leq x + \Delta x$ will be $F_X(x + \Delta x) - F_X(x)$. Now, from property 5 of CDF listed above we can write:

$$p(x < X \leq x + \Delta x) = F_X(x + \Delta x) - F_X(x)$$

We can write using Taylor series equation, if $\Delta x \to 0$.

$$F_X(x + \Delta x) \cong F_X(x) + \frac{dF_X(x)}{dx} \cdot \Delta x$$

$$\therefore \lim_{\Delta x \to 0} \frac{dF_X(x)}{dx} \cdot \Delta x = F_X(x + \Delta x) - F_X(x) = p(x \leq X \leq x + \Delta x)$$

We designate a function called Probability density.

$$\frac{dF_X(x)}{dx} = p_X(x)$$

$$\therefore F_X(x) = \int_{-\infty}^{x} p_X(x)\, dx$$

and $p(x_1 \leq x \leq x_2)$
$$= F_X(x_2) - F_X(x_1)$$
$$= \int_{-\infty}^{x_2} p_X(x_2)\, dx - \int_{-\infty}^{x_1} p_X(x)\, dx$$
$$= \int_{x_1}^{x_2} p_X(x)\, dx$$

A typical CDF and PDF curves are plotted in Fig. 1.8.

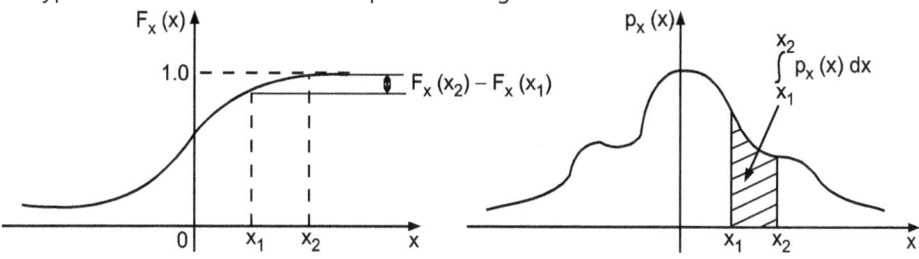

Fig. 1.8: CDF and PDF plots for Continuous RV

Example 1.10:

Given $F_X(x) = \begin{cases} 0 & ; \quad x \leq 0 \\ kx^2 & ; \quad 0 < x \leq 10 \\ 100k & ; \quad x > 10 \end{cases}$

Find: (i) k, (ii) $P(x \leq 5)$, (iii) $P(5 \leq x \leq 7)$

Solution: We know,

$$p_X(x) = \frac{d}{dx} F_X(x)$$

$$\therefore \quad p_X(x) = 0 \quad ; \quad x \leq 0$$
$$= 2kx \quad ; \quad x < x \leq 10$$
$$= 0 \quad ; \quad x > 10$$

(i) Now, $\int_{-\infty}^{\infty} p_X(x)\, dx = 1$

$$\therefore \int_{-\infty}^{0} p_X(x)\, dx + \int_{0}^{10} p_X(x)\, dx + \int_{10}^{\infty} p_X(x)\, dx = 1$$

$$0 + \int_{0}^{10} 2k x\, dx + 0 = 1$$

$$\therefore \int_{0}^{10} 2k x\, dx = 1$$

$$2k \left[\frac{x^2}{2}\right]_{0}^{10} = 1$$

$$2k \times \frac{100}{2} = 1$$

$$k = \frac{1}{100}$$

(ii) $\quad p_X(x \leq 5) = \int_{-\infty}^{5} p_X(x)\, dx$

$$= \int_{-\infty}^{0} p_X(x)\, dx + \int_{0}^{5} p_X(x)\, dx$$

$$= 0 + \int_{0}^{5} 2 \times \frac{1}{100} \times x\, dx$$

$$= \frac{25}{100} = \frac{1}{4}$$

(iii) $\quad P(5 \leq x \leq 7) = F_X(7) - F_X(5)$

$$= \int_{-\infty}^{7} p_X(x)\,dx - \int_{-\infty}^{5} p_X(x)\,dx$$

$$= \frac{1}{100} \times (7)^2 - \frac{1}{100} \times (5)^2$$

$$= \frac{24}{100} = \frac{6}{25}$$

1.8.4 Joint Distribution

If there are two random variables X and Y, then we define CDF $F_{XY}(x, y)$ as

$$F_{XY}(x, y) = P(X \leq x \text{ and } Y \leq y)$$

and the joint PDF as

$$p_{XY}(x, y) = \frac{\partial^2}{\partial x \partial y} F_{XY}(x, y)$$

Just like single variable PDF we can write

$$\lim_{\substack{\Delta x \to 0 \\ \Delta y \to 0}} p_{XY}(x, y)\,\Delta x\,\Delta y = p(x < X \leq x + \Delta x, y < Y \leq y + \Delta y)$$

$$= p_{XY}(x, y)$$

The two variable X and Y are observed jointly over the interval $(x, x + \Delta x)$ and $(y, y + \Delta y)$ respectively.

The probability of jointly observing X over (x_1, x_2) and Y over (y_1, y_2) is given by

$$p(x_1 < x \leq x_2, y_1 < y \leq y_2) = \int_{x_1}^{x_2} \int_{y_1}^{y_2} p_{XY}(x, y)\,dx\,dy$$

The marginal probabilities $p_X(x)$ and $p_Y(y)$ are given by

$$p_X(x) = \int_{-\infty}^{\infty} p_{XY}(x, y)\,dy$$

and

$$p_Y(y) = \int_{-\infty}^{\infty} p_{XY}(x, y)\,dx$$

The concept of conditional probability densities can also be applied to discrete Random Variables.

The conditional PDF $p_{X|Y}(x|y_j)$ is PDF of X given that Y has a value y_j. It means $p_{X|Y}(x|y_j) \cdot \Delta x$ is probability of observing x over the range $(x, x + \Delta x)$ given $Y = y_j$.

The Baye's rule can be extended here as

$$p_{X|Y}(x|y) \cdot p_Y(y) = p_{XY}(x, y)$$
$$p_{Y|X}(y|x) \cdot p_X(x) = p_{XY}(x, y)$$

and
$$p_{X|Y}(x|y) = \frac{p_{Y|X}(y|x) \, p_X(x)}{p_Y(y)}$$

Continuous random variables are said to be independent if

$$p_{X|Y}(x|y) = p_X(x)$$
and
$$p_{Y|X}(y|x) = p_Y(y)$$
$$\therefore \quad p_{XY}(x, y) = p_X(x) \, p_Y(y)$$

1.9 Standard Probability Distribution Models

There are certain standard probability distribution models available for analysis of Random phenomenon occurring in practice. There are two categories of these models depending on whether the random variable is discrete or continuous.

(1) Binomial Distribution:

It is used to describe an integer valued discrete random variable associated with repeated trials i.e. the number of times an event with probability p occurs in n independent trials.

In a sequence of n independent trials the occurrence of event (say A) k times is given by

$$P_X(x = k) = {}^nC_k \, p^k \, (1-p)^{n-k}$$

where, p is the probability of occurrence of event A.

$$\therefore \quad p_X(x \leq n) = F_X(x) = \sum_{k=0}^{n} {}^nC_k \, p^k \, (1-p)^{n-k}$$

For Binomial distribution

$$\text{Mean value } m_X = np$$
$$\text{Variance } \sigma_X^2 = np(1-P)$$

(2) Poisson Distribution:

It again describes integer-valued Random Variable associated with respected trials. It corresponds to number of times an event occurs in an interval with very small probability in very large number of trials.

i.e. As n → ∞ and p → 0

$$p(X = k) = \frac{(np)^k \times e^{-np}}{k!}$$

$$= \frac{\lambda^k e^{-\lambda}}{k!}$$

where, $\lambda = np$

Here, $m_X = np$

$\sigma_X^2 = np(1-p) = np$

(3) Uniform Distribution:

It describes Random variable which is distributed uniformly in an interval as shown in Fig. 1.9.

$$p_X(x) = \frac{1}{b-a} \quad ; \quad a \leq x \leq b$$

$$= 0 \quad ; \quad \text{Otherwise}$$

The PDF and CDF are plotted in Fig. 1.3. The mean value for this distribution is

$$m_X = \frac{1}{a+b}$$

The standard deviation is

$$\sigma_X = \sqrt{\frac{(b-a)^2}{12}}$$

(4) Gaussian Distribution:

When many small fluctuating components of system contribute to a random phenomenon then, it can be described by Gaussian PDF. Many random phenomenon in practice follow this distribution e.g. thermal noise.

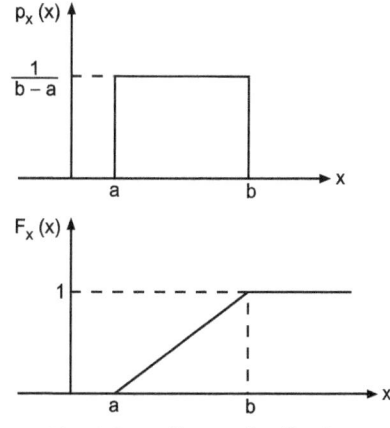

Fig. 1.9: Uniform Distribution

A Gaussian random variable X is continuous random variable with mean m_X and variance σ_X^2 whose PDF is given by

$$p_X(x) = \frac{1}{\sqrt{2\pi \sigma_X^2}} e^{-(x-m_X)^2/\sigma_X^2} ; \quad -\infty < x < \infty$$

It is plotted in Fig. 1.10 along with CDF.

Mean value of this distribution = m_X

Standard deviation = σ_X

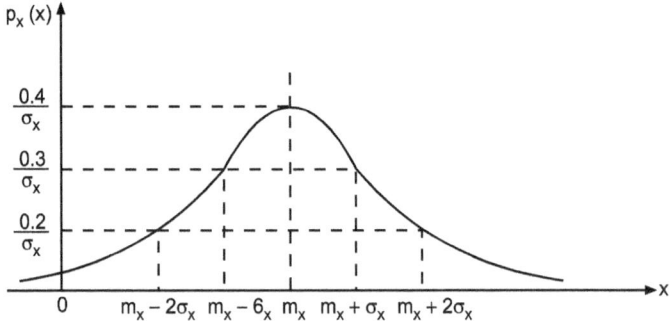

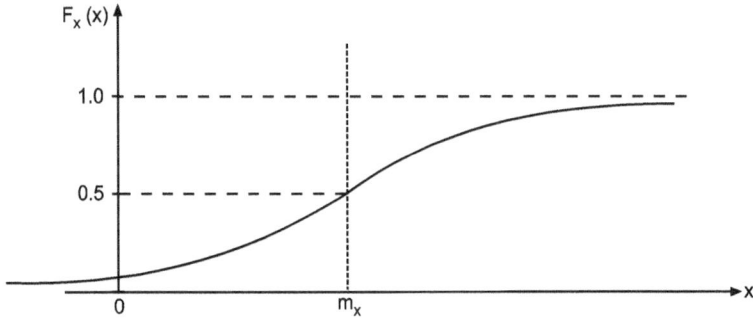

Fig. 1.10: PDF and CDF of Gaussian Distribution

(5) Rayleigh Distribution:

It describes a continuous random variable R derived from two Gaussian random variables X and Y, which have zero mean and same variance $x^2 + y^2$.

It is given by

$$p_R(r) = \frac{r^2}{\sigma^2} e^{-r^2/2\sigma^2} \quad ; \quad r \geq 0$$
$$= 0 \quad ; \quad r < 0$$

Also,
$$p_\phi(\theta) = \frac{1}{2\pi} \quad ; \quad 0 \leq \phi \leq 2\pi$$
$$= 0 \quad ; \quad \text{Otherwise}$$

where, $r = \sqrt{x^2 + y^2}$ and $\phi = \tan^{-1}\left(\frac{y}{x}\right)$.

The distribution (PDF) is shown in Fig. 1.11.

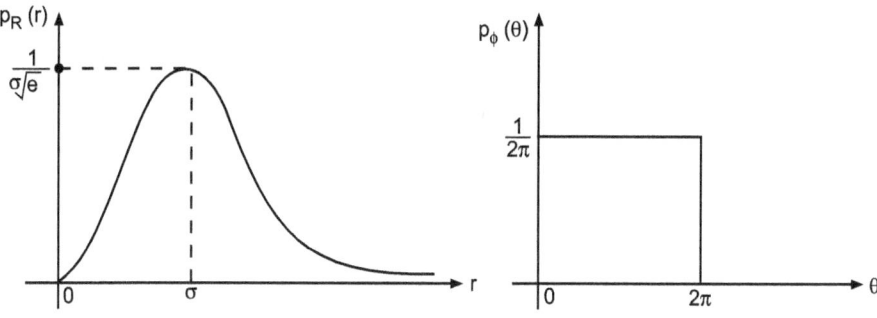

Fig. 1.11

The mean value is given by

$$m_R = \sqrt{\frac{\pi}{2}}\sigma$$

The variance is given by

$$\sigma_R = \left(2 - \frac{\pi}{2}\right)\sigma^2$$

1.10 Cumulative Probability Distribution Function (C.D.F.)

The function $P(X \leq x)$ is called cumulative probability distribution function (CDF) and denoted by $F_X(x)$.

∴ $\quad F_X(x) = P(X \leq x) \quad -\infty < x < \infty \qquad$ ... (1.17)

and argument x can be any real number ranging from $-\infty$ to $+\infty$. The subscript X identifies random variable whose characteristics determine the function $F_X(x)$, argument x defines the event $X \leq x$ so x is not a r.v.

1.10.1 Properties of C.D.F.

$F_X(x)$ represents a probability, it must be bounded by,

$$0 \leq F_X(x) \leq 1 \qquad ... (1.18)$$

When we defined random variable, the condition for X to be random variable is that $P(X = -\infty)$, $P(X = \infty)$ is zero. Therefore, probability of X being less than $P(X \leq -\infty) = 0$.

∴ $\quad F_X(-\infty) = 0 \qquad$ ... (1.19)

Similarly, $\quad F_X(\infty) = 1, \qquad$ ... (1.20)

Since, $P(X \leq \infty)$, if $X \leq \infty$ all the points on the real axis, whatever the points may be for particular r.v. X, every point is $x \leq \infty$.

$$F_X(\infty) = 1 \qquad \ldots (1.21)$$

The complementary events $X \leq x$ and $X > x$ encompasses the entire real line, so

$$P(X > x) = 1 - F_X(x) \qquad \ldots (1.22)$$

which is illustrated in the Fig. 1.12.

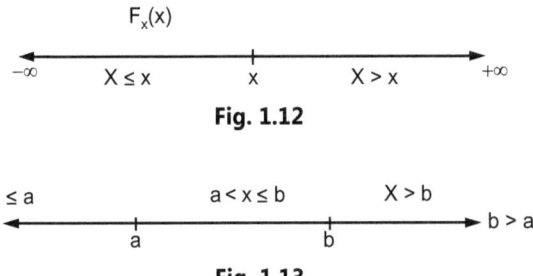

Fig. 1.12

Fig. 1.13

$X \leq a$, $a < X \leq b$, $X > b$ encompasses the whole real line therefore, it is as shown in the Fig. 1.13.

$$P(X \leq a) + P(a < X \leq b) + P(X > b) = 1$$

Here,
$$P(X \leq a) = F_X(a)$$
$$P(X > b) = 1 - F_X(b)$$

$$\therefore F_X(a) + P(a < X \leq b) + X - F_X(b) = 1$$

$$P(a < X \leq b) = F_X(b) - F_X(a) \qquad \ldots (1.23)$$

where, $\qquad b > a$

and also, $\qquad F_X(b) \geq F_X(a) \qquad$ for $b > a \qquad \ldots (1.24)$

We can list all the properties of C.D.F. discussed.

(1) $F_X(-\infty) = 0$

(2) $F_X(\infty) = 1$

(3) $0 \leq F_X(x) \leq 1$

(4) $F_X(a < X \leq b) = F_X(b) - F_X(a)$ $b > a$

(5) $F_X(b) \geq F_X(a)$ $b > a$

(6) $F_X(x_k) = \sum_{i=1}^{k} P_X(x_i)$ where $P_X(x_1) = P(X = x_i)$ frequency function of $X = x_i \qquad \ldots (1.25)$

Cumulative probability distribution function is plotted in the Fig. 1.14.
For example, throwing a die for $X(S) = s^2$.

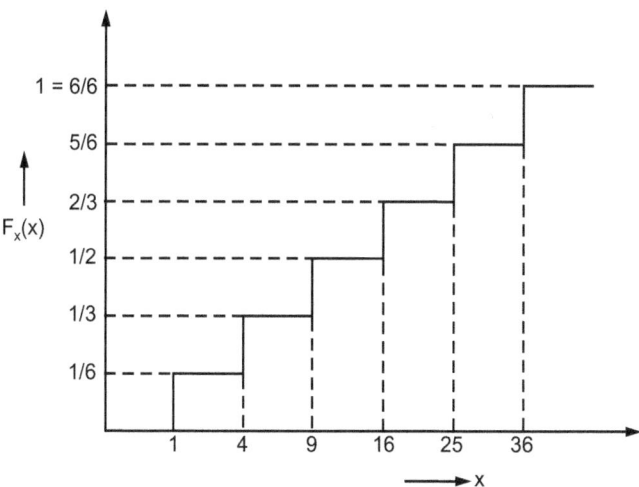

Fig. 1.14: Cumulative Distribution Function

Mathematically the stair case type of $F_X(x)$ is written, with the help of unit step functions as,

$$F_X(x) = \sum_{i=1}^{N} P(x_i)\, u(x - x_i) \quad \ldots (1.26)$$

Similarly, for continuous random variable, the C.D.F. will be a continuous curve. For instance in the example of $X(\theta) = \cos\theta$, a random variable defined for a spinning pointer, for every point between $-1 \leq x \leq 1$ is possible outcome.

Continuous random variable has an uncountably infinite number of possible values, the chance of observing $X = a$ is vanishingly small, that $P(X = a) = 0$. Therefore, frequency functions have no meaning for continuous random variables. However, events such as, $X \leq a$ or $a < X \leq b$ may have non-zero probability values. $F_X(x)$ still provides useful information in case of continuous random variable. But more commonly, the continuous random variable is described by probability density function.

1.11 Probability Density Function (P.D.F.)

P.D.F. is defined by,
$$f_X(x) = \frac{dF_X(x)}{dx} \quad \ldots (1.27)$$

and it is denoted by $f_X(x)$.

$f_X(x)$ exists if derivative $F_X(x)$ exists. For discrete random variables the $F_X(x)$ is stair case type as illustrated in the Fig. 1.14. For this kind of $F_X(x)$, we represent $f_X(x)$ with the help of delta functions to represent the unit impulse train points as shown in the Fig. 1.15. Unit step and delta functions are related by,

$$\delta(x) = \frac{du(x)}{dx} \text{ or} \qquad \text{... (1.28)}$$

$$u(x) = \int_{-\infty}^{x} \delta(\lambda) \, d\lambda \qquad \text{... (1.29)}$$

Equation,
$$F_X(x) = \sum_{i=1}^{N} P(x_i) \, u(x - x_i)$$

$$\frac{d F_X(x)}{dx} = \sum_{i=1}^{N} P(x_i) \, \delta(x - x_i) \qquad \text{... (1.30)}$$

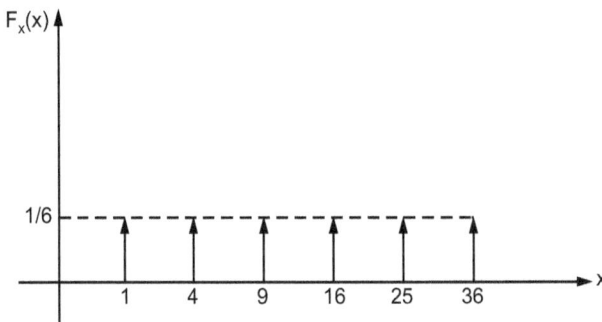

Fig. 1.15

$$f_X(x) = \frac{dF_X(x)}{dx}$$

we can get $F_X(x)$ from $f_X(x)$ as,

$$F_X(x) = \int_{-\infty}^{x} f_X(\lambda) \, d\lambda$$

λ is a dummy variable.

1.11.1 Properties of P.D.F.

1. $0 \leq f_X(x)$ for all x. ... (1.31)

   Probability is non-negative number.

2. $\int_{-\infty}^{+\infty} f_X(x) \, dx = 1$ ... (1.32)

   $f_X(x)$ has unit area.

3. $F_X(x) = \int_{-\infty}^{x} f_X(\lambda) \, d\lambda$ ... (1.33)

4. $P(a < X \leq b) = \int_{a}^{b} f_X(x) \, dx$. ... (1.34)

1.12 Random Processes

- Random signals that occur in communication system are functions of time. They are called random processes.
- Random process is an extension of the concept of Random variable.
- In case of random variable, we map the outcome of random experiment into a number.
- Random signals like noise however are to be described as a function time.
- This random variable that is function of time is called **random process** or **stochastic process**.
- For example, noise voltages generated by number of identical resistors due to thermal electron motion. This voltage is random in nature. But it has to be denoted as function of time as v(t). Such random variable which is function of time is called random process.
- Let us look into this in more detail so that we can specify the random process mathematically. Fig. 1.16 shows thermal noise waveforms produced by large number of resistors.

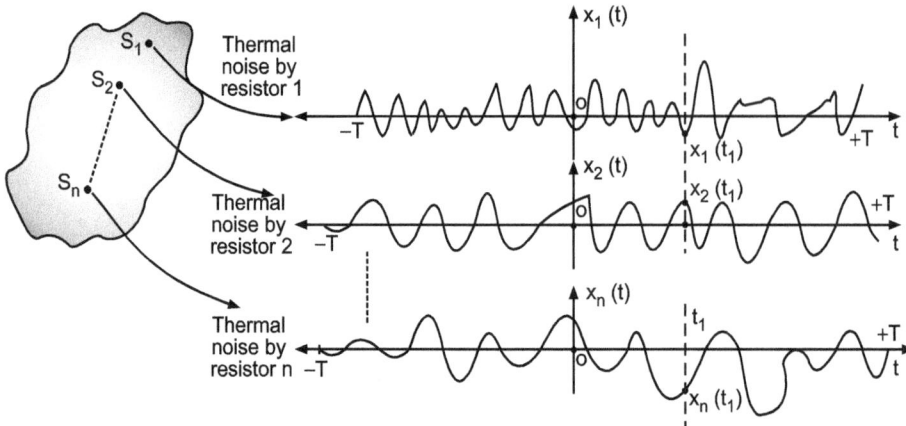

Fig. 1.16: Thermal Noise Generated by n Identical Resistors

- The sample space S as shown in figure consists of n different waveforms.
- We assign a function $X(t, v_i)$ to each sample point (waveform).
- The collection of all such sample functions is called an **ensemble.**
- For simplification, let us denote $X(t, v_i)$ as $x_i(t)$.

    i.e. $\qquad\qquad x_i(t) \equiv X(t, v_i)$

    Thus, $x_1(t)$ represents first sample point.

    $x_2(t)$ represents second sample point and so on.

- The random process consisting of sample functions $X(t, v_i)$ or $x_i(t)$ is denoted as $X(t, v)$ or simply as $X(t)$.
- Thus, $X(t)$ is a random process consisting of sample functions $x_1(t), x_2(t), ..., x_n(t)$.
- Now, let us look into another way of representing random process.
- For this refer Fig. 9.1. For a time t, inside the observation interval $-T$ to $+T$, we have a set of voltages $x_1(t_1), x_2(t_1), x_3(t_1), ..., x_n(t_1)$. Similarly, we can have number of sets like this at time $t_2, t_3, ...$. Each set will now constitute a random variable. Thus, random process $X(t)$ consists of ensemble of random variables $\{x_1(t_j), x_2(t_j), x_3(t_j), ..., x_n(t_j)\}$; where, $j = 1, 2, 3, ..., \infty$.
- Thus, random process $X(t)$ can also be thought as an ensemble of following random variables.

    Random Variable 1 : $X(t_1) = \{x_1(t_1), x_2(t_1), x_3(t_1), ..., x_n(t_1)\}$

    Random Variable 2 : $X(t_2) = \{x_1(t_2), x_2(t_2), x_3(t_2), ..., x_n(t_2)\}$

Random Variable 3 : $X(t_3) = \{x_1(t_3), x_2(t_3), x_3(t_3), ..., x_n(t_3)\}$

$$\vdots$$
$$\vdots$$

so on upto ∞.

- This second view of random process is useful for analysis of random process.
- Let us now summarise the difference between Random Variable and Random Processes.

Random Variable	Random Processes
1. Outcome of random experiment is mapped into a number.	1. Outcome of random experiment is mapped into waveform that is function of time.
2. Random variable is a collection of sample points.	2. Random process is a collection is infinite number of random variables.
3. e.g. Tossing of a coin thrice and number of heads noted.	3. e.g. Thermal noise generated by resistors.

Now, we will consider some more examples of Random process.

1. We record temperature of a city every day. The temperature recorded on one day (24 hours) will constitute a sample function. An ensemble of such sample functions will constitute a random process. There will be infinite number of sample functions in this random process.
2. We record the output of binary signal generator over an interval 0 to $5T_b$ where, T_b is bit duration. There will be an ensemble of 32 sample functions (waveforms). This ensemble will also be random process. It has finite number of sample functions.
3. An information source such a speech generates time varying signals whose contents are not known in advance. Here, random process will provide natural way to model information.
4. Reflection of radio waves from different layers of the ionospheres that make long-range broadcasting possible. Due to randomness of the reflection, the received signal can be modeled as random process.

1.12.1 Mathematical Definition of Random Process

- One important aspect that needs to be emphasised here is that, the random process X(t) will also have a probability associated with an observation of one of the sample functions of the random process.

- Thus, randomness is associated with the uncertainty as to which sample function (waveform) will occur in a given trial. Hence, we define the random process as below.

> **Definition :**
>
> *A random process X(t) is defined as an ensemble of time functions together with probability rule that assigns a probability to any meaningful event associated with an observation of one of the sample functions of X(t).*

- Here, meaningful event associated with an observation of sample function can be some statistical parameter. Thus, we need some quantitative measure to specify the random process.
- Consider an example of random process, $X(t) = A \cos(2\pi f_c t + \phi)$, where, ϕ is uniformly distributed over $(0, 2\pi)$.
- This analytical expression describes the random process completely.
- But this may not be always possible. In situation, where ensemble is obtained experimentally, we must find some quantitative measure that will specify the random process.
- Random process as we have seen earlier is a collection of random variables, which are generally dependent. We need joint Probability Distribution Functions (PDF) of these random variables.
- Let $x(t_1)$ be a random variable generated by observing all sample functions of X(t) at $t = t_1$.
- Let $x(t_2)$ be a random variable generated by observing all sample functions of X(t) at $t = t_2$ and so on upto $x(t_n)$.
- Then, the random process X(t) can be specified in terms of its joint PDF as

    $p_{X(t_1) X(t_2) X(t_3) ... X(t_n)} (x_1, x_2, x_3, ..., x_n)$ for all n (upto ∞).

    or

    $p_{X_1, X_2, ..., X_n} (x_1, x_2, ... x_n; t_1, t_2 ... t_n)$

- Determining these PDFs is a difficult task. But most of the times we have to deal with first or second order statistics only.
- A complete statistical description of a random process X(t) is known if for any integer n and any choice and $(t_1, t_2, t_3 ... t_n)$ the joint PDF of $X(t_1), X(t_2), X(t_3) ... X(t_n)$ is given.
- A process X(t) is described by its mth order statistics if for all $n \leq m$ and all $(t_1, t_2, t_3 ... t_n)$ the joint PDF of $X(t_1), X(t_2), X(t_3) ... X(t_n)$ is given.

- Thus, to specify a random process we need ensemble statistics, which will give you idea of which sample function will occur in a given trial.

1.12.2 Classification of Random Processes

- Till now we have seen two methods to describe random process : (i) Analytical and (ii) Statistical.
- Statistical description can be complete description or n^{th} order description.
- Second order statistical description may be adequate to describe a random process if not we can go for higher order description.

Depending on ensemble statistics the random processes can be classified as

(i)   Stationary process
(ii) Non-stationary process
(iii) Wide-sense (or weakly) Stationary Process
(iv) Ergodic Process

1.12.2.1 Stationary Process

- A random process X(t) is called stationary, if its statistical characteristics do not change with shift of time origin. In other words, statistical characterisation of the stationary random process is time invariant.
- The processes whose statistical properties are time independent are called **Stationary processes**.
- If $x(t_1), x(t_2), ..., x(t_n)$ are random variables obtained by observing the random process at time $t_1, t_2, ..., t_n$. The joint probability density function of this set of random variables is given by

$$p_{X(t_1) X(t_2) ... X(t_n)}(x_1, x_2, ..., x_n)$$

- If we shift all observation times a fixed time τ, we obtain another set of random variables $x(t_1 + \tau), x(t_2 + \tau) x(t_3 + \tau), ..., x(t_n + \tau)$. The observation times are $t_1 + \tau, t_2 + \tau, ..., t_n + \tau$. Let the joint probability density function of this set of random variables be

$$p_{X(t_1 + \tau) X(t_2 + \tau), ..., X(t_n + \tau)}(x_1, x_2, ..., x_n)$$

- The random process X(t) is said to be **strictly stationary**, if

$$p_{X(t_1) X(t_2), ..., X(t_n)}(x_1, x_2, ..., x_n)$$
$$= p_{X(t_1 + \tau) X(t_2 + \tau), ..., X(t_n + \tau)}(x_1, x_2, ..., x_n)$$

... (1.35)

For all time shifts, all n and all possible choices of observation times $t_1, t_2, ..., t_n$.

- Thus, a random process X(t) initiated at t = −∞ is strictly stationary if joint probability density function of any set of random variables obtained by observing random process X(t) is invariant with respect to the location of origin t = 0.
- What this means is, if we determine $p_{X(t_1)}(x_1)$ i.e. PDF of Random Variable $X(t_1)$ and shift the origin by τ and determine $p_{X(t_1 + \tau)}(x_1)$ the two PDFs must be same for stationary random process.

  i.e. for n = 1 in equation (1.35) for all τ,

  $$p_{X(t)}(x) = p_{X(t + \tau)}(x) = p_X(x) \qquad \text{... (1.36)}$$

  Similarly,

  for n = 2 and $\tau = -t_1$

  $$p_{X(t_1) X(t_2)}(x_1, x_2) = p_{X(0) X(t_2 - t_1)}(x_1, x_2) \qquad \text{... (1.37)}$$

  For all t_1 and t_2

- Thus, second order distribution function of a stationary random process depends only on time difference between the observation times t and t + τ.

Mean:

- Mean value for random process is defined as

$$m_{X(t)} = \overline{X(t)} = E[X(t)] = \int_{-\infty}^{\infty} x\, p_{X(t)}(x)\, dx$$

- For stationary process from equation (1.36)

$$p_{X(t)}(x) = p_{X(t + \tau)}(x) = p_X(x)$$

  for all τ

  i.e. $\qquad p_{X(t_1)}(x) = p_{X(t_2)}(x) = ... = p_{X(t_n)}(x) \qquad \text{... (1.38)}$

  ∴ $\qquad m_{X(t_1)} = m_{X(t_2)} = ... = m_{X(t_n)} = m_X \qquad \text{... (1.39)}$

- Hence, mean of a stationary random process is constant.

Autocorrelation:

- Autocorrelation for random process is defined as,

$$R_X(t_1, t_2) = \int_{-\infty}^{\infty} \int_{-\infty}^{\infty} x_1 x_2\, p_{X(t_1) X(t_2)}(x_1, x_2)\, dx_1\, dx_2$$

- For a stationary process from equation (1.37),

$$p_{X(t_1)X(t_2)}(x_1, x_2) = p_{X(0)X(t_2-t_1)}(x_1, x_2)$$

$$\therefore \quad R_X(t_1, t_2) = R_X(t_2 - t_1) \quad \text{for all } t_1 \text{ and } t_2$$

$$= R_X(\tau)$$

where, $\quad t_2 = t_1 + \tau \quad$ ... (1.40)

- Thus, Autocorrelation function can also be written as,

$$R_X(\tau) = E[X(t)X(t+\tau)] \quad ... (1.41)$$

- Hence, autocorrelation function of a stationary process depends only on the observation time difference $t_2 - t_1$.

Autocovariance:

- For a random process it is specified as,

$$C_X(t_1, t_2) = E[(X(t_1) - m_{X(t_1)})(X(t_2) - m_{X(t_2)})]$$

- For stationary process it is given by,

$$C_X(t_1, t_2) = R_X(t_2 - t_1) - m_X^2 \quad ... (1.42)$$

- The **non-stationary process** is the random process whose ensemble statistics depends on time.

- Example of stationary process is noise process because its statistical parameters do not change with time.

- Example of non-stationary process can be temperature of a city. Its ensemble statistics depends on time.

- The two conditions listed above for mean and autocorrelation for stationary process are not sufficient to guarantee that random process is strictly stationary.

- If the two conditions are satisfied by any process then it is called wide-sense stationary or weakly stationary.

- For a process to be strictly stationary condition 9.7 needs to be satisfied.

- Strictly stationarity is a very strong condition that only a few processes may satisfy.

1.12.2.2 Wide-Sense or Weakly Stationary Process

- As discussed earlier a random process may not be strictly stationary but if it satisfies the two condition for mean and autocorrelation given by equations (1.39) and (1.40), then it is called Wide-sense or weakly stationary process.

- The two conditions are listed below.

    (i) $m_{X(t_1)} = m_{X(t_2)} = m_{X(t_3)} = \ldots = m_{X(t_n)} = m_X$ i.e. $m_{X(t)}$ is independent of t.

    (ii) $R_X(t_1, t_2) = R_X(t_2 - t_1) = R_X(\tau)$ i.e. $R_X(t_1, t_2)$ depends on the time difference $\tau = t_1 - t_2$ and not on t_1 and t_2 individually.

- All stationary processes are wide-sense stationary but converse is not necessarily true.

EXERCISE

1. Define random processes. Explain random processes with example.
2. What is stationary process?
3. Explain wide sense stationary process with example.
4. Explain probability distribution models.
5. Explain random variables.
6. Write short note on P.S.D. and E.S.D.

***

Unit II

WAVEFORM CODING
AND
BASEBAND SHAPING FOR DIGITAL TRANSMISSION

2.1 Pulse Code Modulation (PCM)

We can transmit analog signal in digital format. The different methods of doing this are Pulse Code Modulation (PCM), Differential Pulse Code Modulation (DPCM), Delta Modulation (DM), Adaptive Delta Modulation (ADM), Adaptive Delta Modulation (ADM), Linear Predictive Coding (CPC), etc.

Pulse Code Modulation (PCM) is a method of converting an analog signal into digital form. The information contained in instantaneous samples of analog signal is represented by digital words in a serial bit stream. It is a digital pulse modulation technique. It is also a waveform coding technique. It is a simple technique in which the same information is sampled and quantized to one of the L levels. Each quantized level is digitally encoded into v-bits.

2.1.1 PCM Generation and Reconstruction

When analog signal is converted into digital format, the two basic operations required are:
- (i) Time Discretization
- (ii) Amplitude Discretization.

Sampling operation does time discretization, whereas amplitude discretization can be achieved using quantization. The quantized amplitudes are converted into sequence of symbols (usually binary). They are called codewords. The general block diagram of a PCM system is shown in Fig. 2.1 (a).

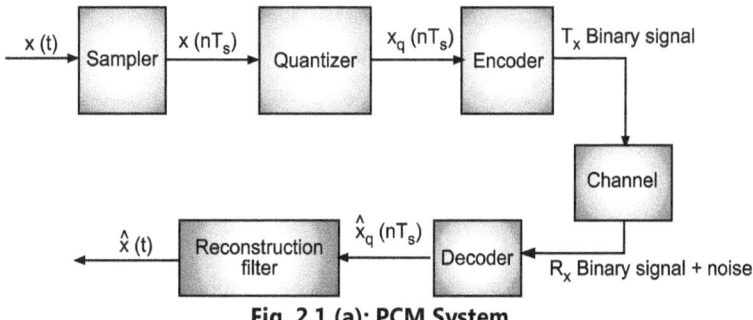

Fig. 2.1 (a): PCM System

x(t) is analog information signal to be transmitted. It is sampled at intervals $t = nT_s$ to given $x(nT_s)$ by sampler block. The quantizer converts each sample to one of the pre-selected set of finite number of amplitudes. The encoder represents the quantized samples by v-bit codeword. The bits are transmitted over channel and received by the receiver.

The decoder converts v-bit codewords into corresponding samples. The reconstruction filter interpolates the samples to recover the analog information $\hat{x}(t)$ which will be approximately same version of x(t). Now, let us go into more details of the PCM systems and see what additional things are required. More detailed block diagram is shown in Figs. 2.1 (b) and (c).

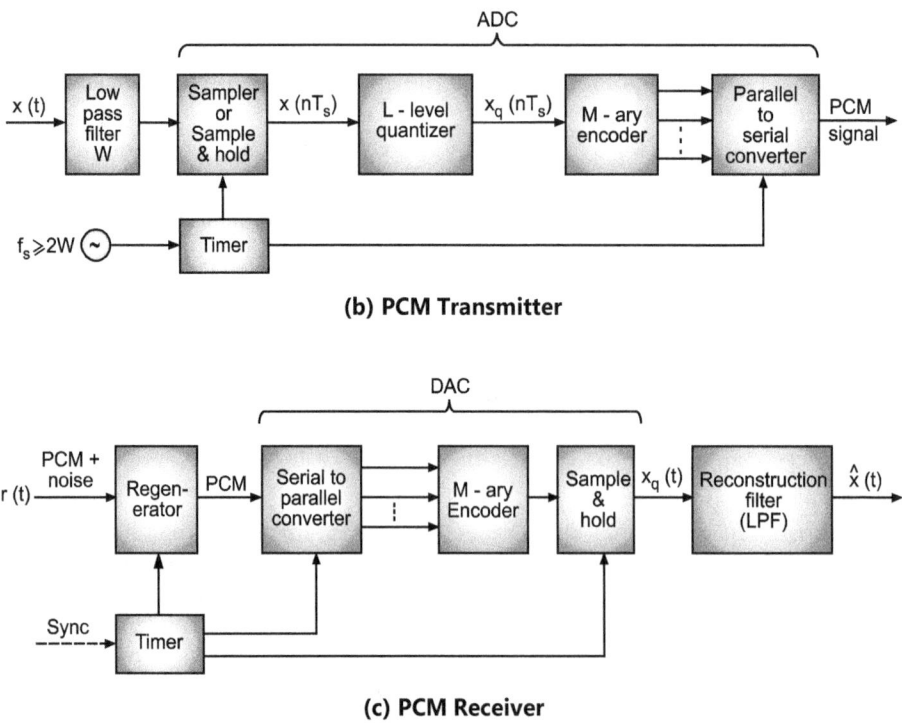

(b) PCM Transmitter

(c) PCM Receiver

Fig. 2.1

2.1.1.1 Low Pass Filter

In order to convert an analog signal into digital form, we need to first sample the signal. In order to avoid the effect of aliasing resulting form sampling under, we need to limit the signal in bandwidth.

Hence, we pass the signal which is time limited and hence having infinite bandwidth through a low pass filter. This filter is also called **antialias filter.**

2.1.1.2 Sampling

The low pass filtered analog signal is sampled with sampling rate slightly above Nyquist rate ($f_s > 2W$). This will create a guard band to facilitate use of practical low pass filter for reconstruction. The sampling operation generates a flat-top PAM signal as shown in Fig. 2.2.

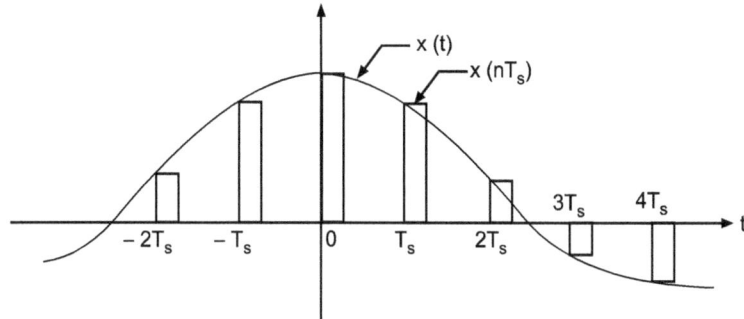

Fig. 2.2: Sampling Process

2.1.1.3 Quantizing

Sampling process gives rise to train of samples with amplitude depending on the instant of sampling. If the message signal x (t) ranges from + A to – A, there will be infinite levels x (nT_s) assumes between this range.

In order to convert the samples into bit stream, we need to limit the number of levels of sampled signal. For this the amplitude range (– A, A), is divided to finite number of levels and the sampled amplitude is approximated to nearest possible level.

This process is called quantizing. It is shown in Fig. 2.3. This means original continuous signal is approximated by a signal having discrete amplitudes from an available set.

Thus, amplitude quantization is the process of transforming sample amplitude x (nT_s) at t = nT_s into a discrete amplitude x_q (nT_s) taken from finite set of amplitudes. The quantization process is assumed to be less memory and instantaneous. Memory less means the quantization of current sample does not depend on its past values.

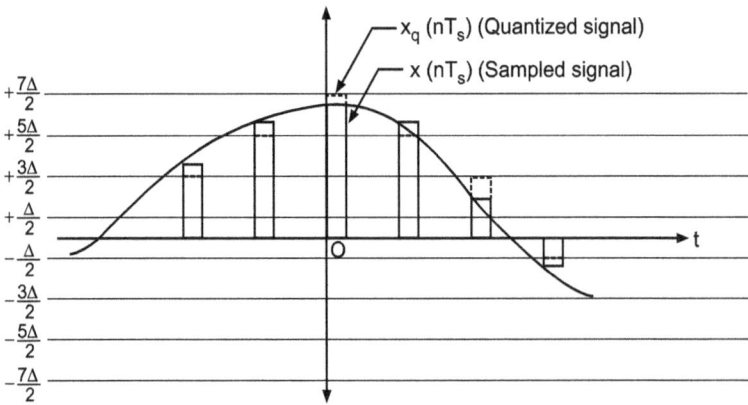

Fig. 2.3: Quantization Process

Let L be total number of amplitude levels used in a quantizer. There will be L decision level or decision thresholds. The input X (nT_s) is transformed into X_q (nT_s) which is called representation level or reconstruction level. Thus, the output of quantizer will be one of the L representation levels.

The difference between two adjacent representation levels is called quantum or step size (Δ). Quantizer can be of uniform or non-uniform type. In uniform quantizer the representation levels are uniformly spaced.

In non-uniform quantizer the approximated levels are spaced non-uniformly. The quantizer characteristics can be midtread or midrise type. The input-output characteristics of these types of quantizers are shown in Fig. 2.4 (a) and (b).

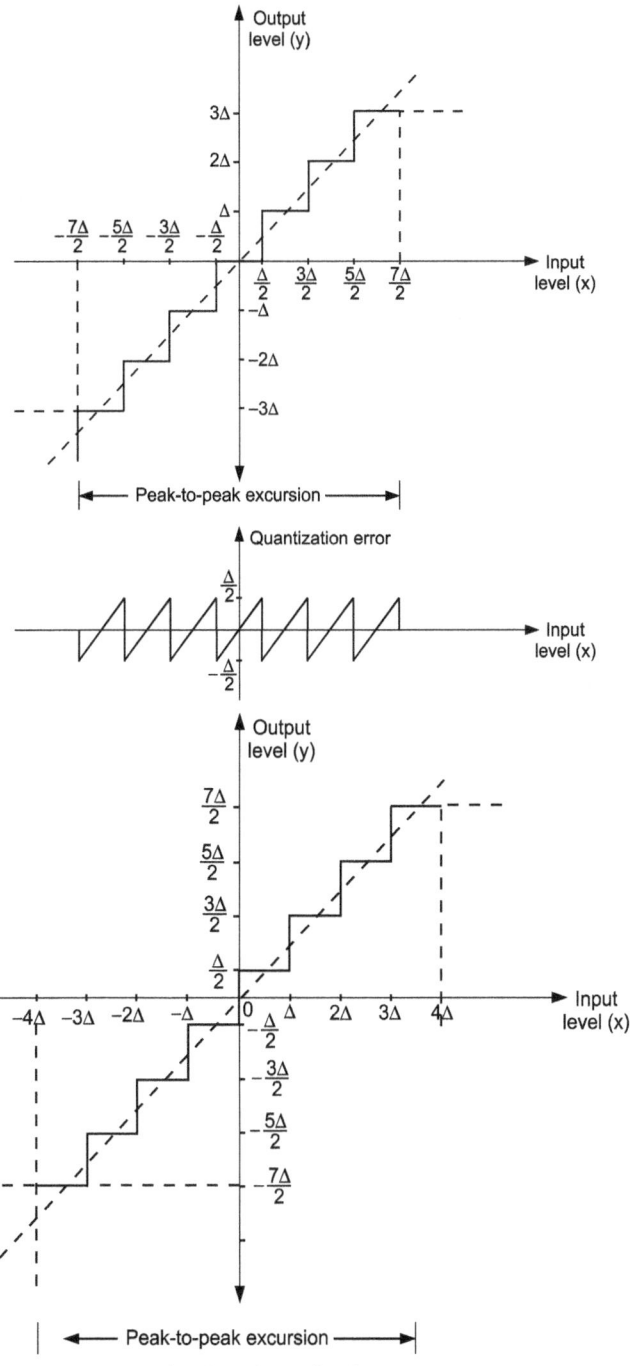

Fig. 2.4: Quantization Types

The input signal level to quantizer is represented by x and output level is y. The error signal which is difference between input and output is shown for midtread type quantizer. The error will always be less than or equal to Δ/2.

Fig. 2.5 illustrates the quantization error resulting from quantization process.

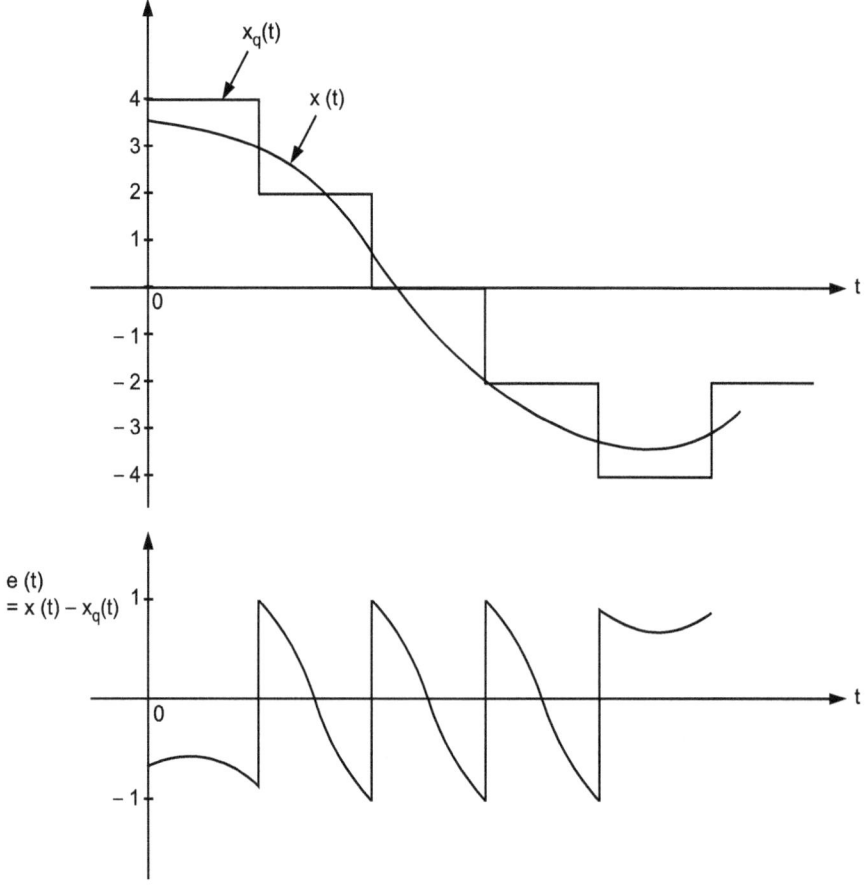

Fig. 2.5

The signal x(t) is input to the quantizer with quantization levels, 0, ±2, ±4. The quantized signal $x_q(t)$ is output from the quantizer. The error signal $e(t) = x(t) - x_q(t)$ is random signal hence termed as quantization noise. Note that the quantization process shown in Fig. 2.3 was for the case if the input quantizer is set of equispaced samples of x(t).

In that case, output was also sequence of equispace samples. It can be implemented using digital processor. The quantization process shown in Fig. 2.5 uses Analog to Digital Converter (ADC).

Comparison of Midrise and Midtread Quantizer:
When there is no input (zero input level) to quantizer the output of midtread will be zero whereas midrise output will be $\pm \Delta/2$. This situation can arise in telephony when there is silence in speech or handset is covered for some purpose.

The average noise power during zero input condition in will be $\Delta^2/4 \left[\frac{1}{2}\left(\frac{\Delta}{2}\right)^2 + \frac{1}{2}\left(-\frac{\Delta}{2}\right)^2 \right]$ in case of midrise and it will be zero for midtread. Hence, midtread is better in terms of performance. The number of quantization levels in case of midrise will be even and for midtread will be odd. But for encoding these levels should be even.

2.1.1.4 Encoding

The quantized signal $x_q(nT_s)$ can be converted into digital format. This process is called encoding. The signal can be encoded using any one of the following techniques. It is one-to-one representation of quantized samples by using code elements or symbols.

(i) **Binary Code:** It represents each quantized amplitude into 0's and 1's.
(ii) **Ternary Code:** It represents each quantized level into three levels.
(iii) **M-ary Code:** It represents each quantized amplitude into M levels (more than 3).

However, maximum advantages over the effect of noise in transmission medium is obtained by using a binary code. It is because binary symbols withstand relatively high level of noise and are easy to regenerate. There are several ways to establish one-to-one correspondence between representation level and code word. For example, we can use an encoder which makes n sequential comparisons to generate n-bit code word.

The level is compared with a voltage obtained by a combination of reference voltages proportional to $2^7, 2^6, 2^5, ..., 2^0$. Hence, if we are using 3-bit PCM, then we can have $2^3 = 8$ quantization levels into which we have to divide the signal amplitudes – A_{max} to $+ A_{max}$. The quantized output can be encoded in 3-bit format as follows:

Quantized Level	Encoder Output
$- A_{max} \left(-\frac{7\Delta}{2} \right)$	000
$- 3A_{max}/4 \left(-\frac{5\Delta}{2} \right)$	001
$- 2A_{max}/4 \left(-\frac{3\Delta}{2} \right)$	010

Quantized Level	Encoder Output
$-A_{max}/4 \left(-\dfrac{\Delta}{2}\right)$	011
$+A_{max}/4 \left(+\dfrac{\Delta}{2}\right)$	100
$+2A_{max}/4 \left(+\dfrac{3\Delta}{2}\right)$	101
$+3A_{max}/4 \left(+\dfrac{5\Delta}{2}\right)$	110
$+A_{max} \left(+\dfrac{7\Delta}{2}\right)$	111

The number of bits required for encoding a sample depends on number of quantization levels. If there are L quantization levels, then number of bits required for encoding a sample will be $\log_2 L$. In other words, if we use v bits for encoding there will be 2^v quantization levels.

i.e. $\boxed{L = 2^v}$ or $\boxed{v = \log_2 L}$ ... (2.1)

Consider the following example shown in Fig. 2.6.

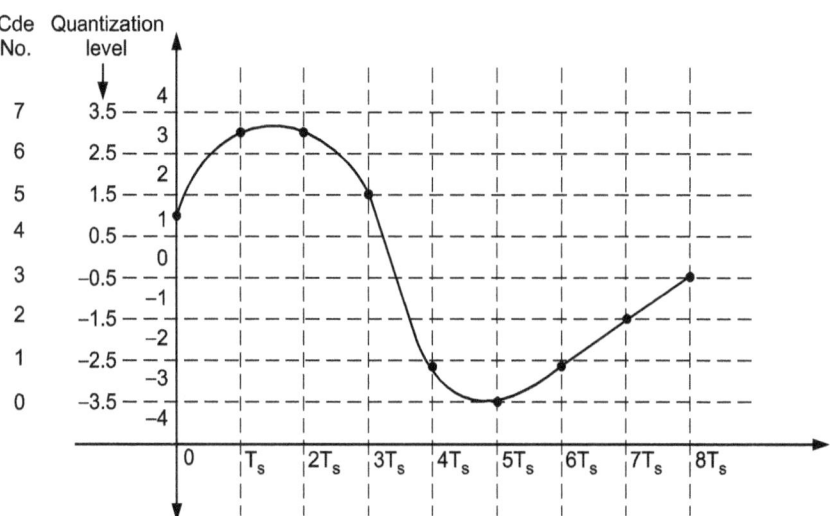

Fig. 2.6: Encoding

Natural sample values	1	2.8	2.9	1.5	−2.9	−3.3	−2.6	−1.6	−0.7
Quantized values	1.5	2.5	2.5	1.5	−2.5	−3.5	−2.5	−1.5	−0.5
Code number	5	6	6	5	1	0	1	2	3
PCM output	101	110	110	101	001	000	001	010	011

2.1.1.5 Regeneration

The most important feature of PCM system lies in ability to control distortion and noise.
This is achieved by reconstructing the PCM signal by means of chain of regenerative repeaters located at sufficiently close spacing. It consists of circuit which reshapes the distorted signal into clean pulses.

Fig. 2.7 shows block diagram of regenerative repeaters.

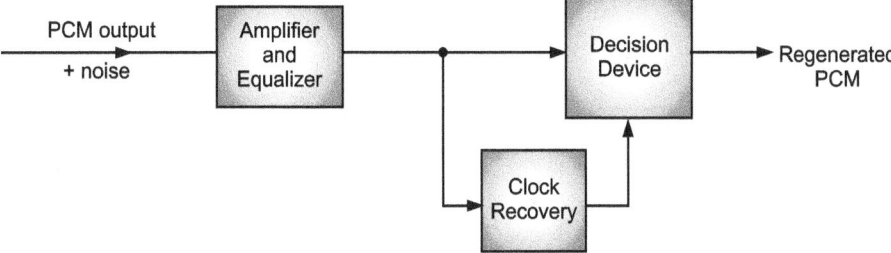

Fig. 2.7: Regenerative Repeater

The three basic functions performed by regenerative repeater are:
   (i) Equalization
   (ii) Clock Recovery (Timing)
   (iii) Decision-making.

When the PCM signal is transmitted through channel it undergoes amplitude and phase distortion. Equaliser is used to compensate for these distortions.

The receiver pulses are to be sampled at every bit duration to recover the clock from them for timing purpose. The clock recovery circuit or timing circuit does this.

The decision device is used to decide in every bit interval, the received bit (1/0) based on received sample of the pulse and preset threshold.

2.1.1.6 Decoding

The first operation in the receiver is to regenerate the received pulses (1's and 0's). These pulses are regrouped into code words and decoded into quantized signal. The decoding process involves generating a pulse whose amplitude is linear sum of 1's and 0's in the codeword (similar to binary to decimal conversion). This process is also called Digital to Analog Conversion (DAC).

2.1.1.7 Reconstruction Filters

The decoded output (DAC output) is staircase waveform. A low pass filter whose cut-off frequency is equal to message bandwidth W Hz is used to smoothen out the DAC output.

2.1.1.8 Bandwidth Requirement of PCM
- How much bandwidth is required for transmission of PCM signal ?
- If the signal bandwidth is W Hz, then it requires to be sampled at a rate 2W samples per second.

If each sample is encoded into v bits then the bit rate i.e. number of bits per second will be,

Bit rate (r) = Number of samples per second × Number of bits per sample

∴ $r = f_s \times v$

∴ $\boxed{r = vf_s}$ ... (2.2)

Therefore, bandwidth needed for PCM will be,

$$\boxed{B_T = \frac{1}{2} \times r = \frac{1}{2} vf_s}$$ ... (2.3)

The minimum bandwidth requirement for transmission of PCM signal will be when $f_s = 2W$

∴ $\boxed{(B_T)_{min} = \frac{1}{2} v \times 2W = v \times W}$ ... (2.4)

Example 2.1: An analog signal with maximum frequency 3 kHz is transmitted using binary PCM. The number of quantization levels used are 16. Find minimum bandwidth requirement.

Solution: Given: W = 3 kHz

Number of quantization levels = L = 16

∴ Sampling rate f_s = 2 × W

= 2 × 3 = 6 kHz

Since, $L = 2^v$

Number of bits per sample (v) = $\log_2 L$

= $\log_2 16$

= 4

∴ Bit rate of this system

$r = v \times f_s$

= 4 × 6 kHz

= 24 kbps

Minimum bandwidth required

$(B_T)_{min} = \frac{1}{2} \times v \times 2W$

= $\frac{1}{2} \times 24$

= 12 kHz

2.1.2 Quantization Noise

The process of quantization introduces quantization error in the PCM signal. This is because sampled output is approximated to nearest level. If signal x (t) is sampled at a rate $\frac{1}{T_s}$ then x (nT_s) will be the sample at $t = nT_s$. Let us say that it is approximated to x_q (nT_s) after quantization. The error difference $q = x(nT_s) - x_q(nT_s)$ is called quantization noise.

Quantizer output for a typical input signal is shown in Fig. 2.8 (a). The plot of quantization error alongwith the quantized signal is shown in Fig. 2.8 (b).

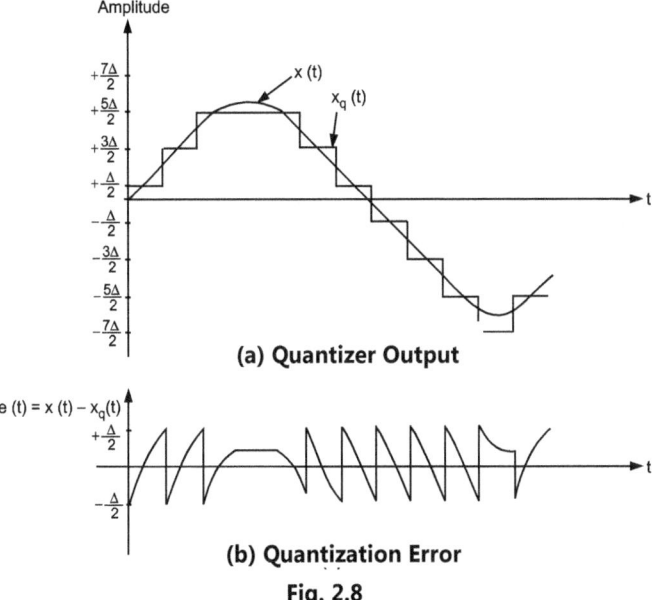

(a) Quantizer Output

(b) Quantization Error

Fig. 2.8

It can be seen from the quantization error graph that the quantization error takes on any value between $+\Delta/2$ and $-\Delta/2$. Thus, it is uniformly distributed random variable with zero mean. Let us denote this variable as Q. The probability density function for Q is plotted in Fig. 2.9.

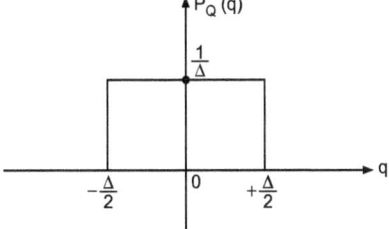

Fig. 2.9: PDF of Quantization Error

Hence,
$$P_Q(q) = \begin{cases} \dfrac{1}{\Delta} & ; \ -\dfrac{\Delta}{2} \le q \le +\dfrac{\Delta}{2} \\ 0 & ; \ \text{Otherwise} \end{cases} \quad \ldots (2.5)$$

The variance can be calculated as,

$$\begin{aligned}
\sigma_Q^2 &= \int_{-\Delta/2}^{\Delta/2} q^2 \, P_Q(q) \, dq \\
&= \int_{-\Delta/2}^{\Delta/2} q^2 \times \frac{1}{\Delta} \, dq \\
&= \frac{1}{\Delta} \left[\frac{q^3}{3} \right]_{-\Delta/2}^{\Delta/2} \\
&= \frac{\Delta^2}{12} \qquad \ldots (2.6)
\end{aligned}$$

This variance is mean square value of quantization noise. Since mean value is zero, ($E[X^2] = \sigma_X^2 - m_X^2$). Hence, this is quantization noise power.

∴ Quantization noise power,

$$\boxed{P_{Nq} = \frac{\Delta^2}{12}}$$

Let us consider an input whose amplitude ranges from $-A_{max}$ to $+A_{max}$. Assuming uniform quantizer of midrise type, step size is given by,

$$\Delta = \frac{2 A_{max}}{L} \quad \ldots (2.7)$$

where, L is the number of representation levels.
Let v be number of bits per sample.

∴ $\qquad L = 2^v$
or $\qquad v = \log_2 L$

∴ $$\Delta = \frac{2 A_{max}}{2^v} \quad \ldots (2.8)$$

Hence, quantization noise will be,

∴ $$P_{Nq} = \frac{\Delta^2}{12} = \frac{4 A_{max}^2}{2^{2v} \times 12} = \frac{A_{max}^2}{3L^2}$$

$$\boxed{P_{Nq} = \frac{A_{max}^2}{3 \times 2^{2v}}} \quad \ldots (2.9)$$

Therefore, the output signal-to-noise ratio of uniform quantizer will be,

$$\left(\frac{S}{N}\right)_0 = \frac{P_s}{P_{Nq}}$$

$$\boxed{\left(\frac{S}{N}\right)_0 = \left(\frac{3 P_s / 2}{A_{max}^2}\right) \times 2^{2v}} \qquad \ldots (2.10)$$

This equation shows that signal-to-noise ratio is proportional to bits per sample v. This is obvious from the fact that more number of bits per sample will increase number of levels which in turn will decrease step size.

But then this will require more bandwidth as, $B_T = \frac{1}{2} v f_s$.

If input signal is a sinusoidal signal, then signal power is,

$$P_s = \frac{A_{max}^2}{2}$$

∴
$$\left(\frac{S}{N}\right)_0 = \frac{3 \times A_{max}^2 / 2}{A_{max}^2} \times 2^{2v}$$

$$\left(\frac{S}{N}\right)_0 = \frac{3}{2} 2^{2v} \qquad \ldots (2.11)$$

or
$$\left(\frac{S}{N}\right)_0 = \frac{3L^2}{2}$$

∴
$$\left(\frac{S}{N}\right)_0 \text{ in dB} = 10 \log_{10}\left(\frac{3}{2} 2^{2v}\right)$$

$$= 10 \log_{10} \frac{3}{2} + 10 \log_{10} 2^{2v}$$

$$= 1.8 + 20 \, v \times \log 2$$

∴ For sinusoidal input

$$\left(\frac{S}{N}\right)_0 \text{ in dB} = 1.8 + 6 \, v \text{ dB} \qquad \ldots (2.12)$$

Following table shows various values of L and v with corresponding $(SNR)_0$.

L (Levels)	v (bits/sample)	SNR (dB)
256	8	49.8
128	7	43.8
64	6	37.8
32	5	31.8

For non-sinusoidal signals, such as voice, music etc. the signal to noise ratio is specified in terms peak signal power to average quantization noise power.

The average quantization noise power

$$N_q = \frac{\Delta^2}{12}$$

The peak signal power = A_{max}^2

But, $A_{max} = \frac{\Delta \times L}{2}$

$\therefore \quad A_{max}^2 = \frac{\Delta^2 L^2}{4}$

∴ Peak signal power to average quantization noise power is,

$$\left(\frac{S}{N}\right)_{0\,peak} = \frac{\Delta^2 L^2/4}{\Delta^2/12}$$

$$\left(\frac{S}{N}\right)_{0\,peak} = 3L^2$$

Thus, it can be seen that the signal to quantization noise ratio in PCM depends on L (number of levels).

As $L \to \infty$, signal to noise ratio will be infinite. It means with infinite quantization levels (No quantisation) there will be no quantization noise.

Thus, we have following results.

(i) Average signal power to average quantization noise power ratio is given by:

$$\left(\frac{S}{N}\right)_0 = \frac{P_s}{N_q} = \frac{P_s}{\Delta^2/12} = \frac{3P_s}{A_{max}^2} \times 2^{2V}$$

(ii) Average signal power to average quantization noise power ratio **if signal is sinusoidal** is given by,

$$\left(\frac{S}{N}\right)_0 = \frac{3L^2}{2} = \frac{3}{2} 2^{2V}$$

$$\left(\frac{S}{N}\right)_0 \text{ in dB } = 1.8 + 6v$$

(iii) Peak signal power to average quantization noise power ratio **for non-sinusoidal signal** is given by,

$$\left(\frac{S}{N}\right)_{0\,peak} = 3L^2 = 3 \times 2^{2V}$$

$$\left(\frac{S}{N}\right)_{0\,peak\,in\,dB} = 4.8 + 6V$$

(iv) If P_s is average signal power and A_{max}^2 is peak signal power.

Then peak to average signal power is $\frac{A_{max}^2}{P_s}$

The average signal power to quantization noise power

$$\left(\frac{S}{N}\right)_0 = \frac{3P_s}{A_{max}^2} \times 2^{2v}$$

$$= \frac{3 \times 2^{2v}}{A_{max}^2/P_s}$$

$$= \frac{3L^2}{A_{max}^2/P_s}$$

$$\therefore \left(\frac{S}{N}\right)_0 \text{ in dB} = 4.8 + 6v - \alpha$$

where, $\alpha = \log_{10} \frac{A_{max}^2}{P_s}$ is peak to average signal power ratio

For sinusoidal signal $\alpha = 3$ dB
For voice signal $\alpha = 10$ dB (due to large crest factor)

Note: Analog signals such as voice, music etc. are specified in terms crest factor which is defined as,

$$\text{Crest factor} = \frac{|x(t)|_{max}}{\sigma_x}$$

$\sigma_x^2 << 1$ implies large crest factor.

2.1.3 Multiplexing and Synchronization

One of the advantages PCM has is, number of signals can be simultaneously transmitted over a single channel. This is possible with time division multiplexing of the signals. There is a time available between two samples of same source where we can accommodate samples from other sources. Of course, the signaling rate (bit rate) will increase and bandwidth requirement also. Consider a case of N identical sources having maximum frequency W Hz. If these sources are sampled at rate f_s and then multiplexed then the signaling rate will be,

$$r = N \times v \times f_s \text{ bps}$$

where, v is the number of bits used per sample.

Hence, bandwidth requirement will be,

$$B_T = \frac{1}{2} \times r = \frac{1}{2} N \times v \times f_s \text{ Hz} \quad \quad \ldots (2.13)$$

The minimum bandwidth required will be for

$$f_s = 2W$$

$$\therefore (B_T)_{min} = \frac{1}{2} \times N \times v \times 2 \times W$$

$$= N \times v \times W \text{ Hz} \quad \quad \ldots (2.14)$$

But multiplexing requires timing operations at transmitter and receiver to be synchronized properly.

Hence, we require a local clock at the receiver to keep the same time as that of clock at the transmitter.

Example 2.2:

The bandwidth of TV video plus audio signal is 4.5 MHz. If this signal is converted to PCM bit stream with 1024 quantization levels. Determine number of bits/sec. generated by the PCM system. Assume that the signal is sampled at a rate 20% above Nyquist rate.

Solution: Given:
$$W = 4.5 \text{ MHz}$$
$$L = 1024$$

Now,
$$v = \log_2 L$$
$$\therefore v = \log_2 1024 = 10\text{-bits}$$

$$\text{Nyquist rate} = 2 \times W$$
$$= 2 \times 4.5$$
$$= 9 \text{ MHz}$$

$$\text{Sampling rate} = 9 + 0.2 \times 9$$
$$= 10.8 \text{ MHz}$$

$$\therefore \text{Bit rate} = v \times f_s$$
$$= 10 \times 10.8 \times 10^6 \text{ bit/sec.}$$
$$= 108 \times 10^6 \text{ bits/sec.} = 108 \text{ Mbps}$$

Example 2.3:

The output signal-to-noise ratio of 10-bit PCM was found to be 40 dB. The desired SNR is 42 dB. It was decided to increase SNR to desired level by increasing number of quantization levels. Find fractional increase in transmission bandwidth required for this increase in SNR.

Solution: Given:
$$\left(\frac{S}{N}\right)_{01} = 40 \text{ dB}$$
$$v_1 = 10$$

$$\therefore \left(\frac{S}{N}\right)_{01} = 10000$$

$$\left(\frac{S}{N}\right)_{02} = 42 \text{ dB} = 15{,}849$$

$$\left(\frac{S}{N}\right)_{01} = \frac{3 P_s}{A_{max}^2} \times 2^{2v_1}$$

$$\left(\frac{S}{N}\right)_{02} = \frac{3 P_s}{A_{max}^2} \times 2^{2v_2}$$

$$\therefore \quad \frac{10{,}000}{15{,}849} = \frac{2^{2v_1}}{2^{2v_2}}$$

$$0.63095 = \frac{2^{2v_1}}{2^{2v_2}}$$

$$0.63095 \times 2^{2v_2} = 2^{2v_1}$$

$$\log_2 0.63095 + 2v_2 = 2v_1$$

$$-0.6644 + 2v_2 = 20$$

$$v_2 = 10.33322$$

$$\therefore \quad v_2 \simeq 11$$

$$\text{Bandwidth required for first case} = \frac{10\,f_s}{2}$$

$$\text{Bandwidth required for second case} = \frac{11\,f_s}{2}$$

$$\therefore \quad \text{Fractional increase in BW} = \frac{11-10}{10}$$

$$= 0.1$$

$$\therefore \quad \text{Fractional increase in BW} = 10\%$$

2.2 PCM with Noise

The analog signal received at the receiver end of PCM system is corrupted by noise. Two types of noises are present in it.

(i) Quantization noise caused by quantizer at the transmitter. The detailed analysis of which is covered earlier.

(ii) Bit errors in recovered PCM signal. The bit errors are caused by channel noise and improper channel filtering.

In addition to this, there can be aliasing noise caused by filtering at transmitter end done purposely when the signal is not strictly bandlimited. Another distortion like aperture effect might occur due to flat-top sampling.

2.2.1 Decoding Noise

Due to channel noise an erroneous bit can occur in the codeword which will result in decoding of wrong quantization level. This error is termed as **decoding noise.**
Let us analyse this noise for PCM with uniform quantization.

Let P_e be bit error probability $\ll 1$.

v be number of bits in a codeword.

The probability of one error in a word will be vP_e, when $P_e \ll 1$. Probability of two or more errors can be negligibly small. Consider a received codeword $b_0, b_1, b_2, ..., b_{v-1}$. An error in the mth bit shifts the decoded level by an amount $= \frac{2}{L} \times 2^m$. Hence, the mean square error over the v bit positions will be,

$$\overline{e_m^2} = \frac{1}{v} \sum_{m=0}^{v-1} \left(\frac{2}{L} \times 2^m\right)^2 \qquad \ldots (2.15)$$

$$= \frac{4}{vL^2} \cdot \sum_{m=0}^{v-1} 4^m$$

$$= \frac{4}{vL^2} \times (4^v - 1)/3$$

$$= \frac{4}{3v} \times \frac{L^2 - 1}{L^2} \qquad (\because 4^v = 2^{2v} = L^2)$$

$$\simeq \frac{4}{3v} \qquad \ldots (2.16)$$

The decoding noise power will be,

$$\sigma_d^2 = vP_e \times \overline{e_m^2}$$

$$\simeq v \times P_e \times \frac{4}{3v} \qquad \ldots (2.17)$$

$$\simeq \frac{4}{3} P_e$$

The quantization noise power

$$\sigma_q^2 = \frac{1}{3L^2} \qquad \ldots (2.18)$$

Total destination noise power

$$\therefore \quad N_0 = \sigma_q^2 + \sigma_d^2 = \frac{1}{3L^2} + \frac{4}{3} P_e$$

$$= \frac{1 + 4L^2 P_e}{3L^2}$$

If P_s is signal power.

$$\therefore \left(\frac{S}{N}\right)_0 = \frac{3L^2}{1 + 4L^2 P_e} P_s \qquad \text{... (2.19)}$$

If $P_e << \frac{1}{4L^2}$

$$\left(\frac{S}{N}\right)_0 = 3L^2 P_s \qquad \text{... (2.20)}$$

and $P_e >> \frac{1}{4L^2}$

$$\left(\frac{S}{N}\right)_0 = \frac{3}{4P_e} P_s \qquad \text{... (2.21)}$$

Hence for small P_e quantization noise is more significant whereas for large P_e decoding noise dominates.

The error probability P_e is determined from received signal-to-noise ratio $\left(\frac{S}{N}\right)_R$ i.e. $P_e = Q\left[\sqrt{\left(\frac{S}{N}\right)_R}\right]$. (We will see this in Chapter 9).

As $\left(\frac{S}{N}\right)_R$ falls below a particular threshold value, there is sharp decline in detected output signal-to-noise ratio $\left(\frac{S}{N}\right)_D$. This is called threshold effect. It is caused by increasing errors. Below the error threshold $P_e >> \frac{1}{4L^2}$, the errors occur frequently causing totally wrong reconstruction of waveforms.

2.2.2 Error Threshold

The PCM error threshold level is the point where decoding noise $\left(\frac{S}{N}\right)_D$ falls by 1 dB. But it is not possible to analyse error threshold from this definition. Hence, we will assume that decoding errors are negligible if $P_e << 10^{-5}$. Then we can obtain condition on $\left(\frac{S}{N}\right)_R$ for polar M-ary signaling as,

$$P_e = 2\left(1 - \frac{1}{M}\right) Q\left[\sqrt{\frac{3}{M^2 - 1} \times \left(\frac{S}{N}\right)_R}\right] \leq 10^{-5}$$

Solving for minimum value of $\left(\dfrac{S}{N}\right)_R$,

$$\left(\dfrac{S}{N}\right)_{R_{th}} = 6(M^2 - 1)$$

This equation says if $\left(\dfrac{S}{N}\right)_R < 6(M^2 - 1)$ then PCM output cannot be reconstructed satisfactorily due to decoding noise.

We also have analog transmission parameter.

$$v = \dfrac{S_R}{N_0 W}$$

$$= \left(\dfrac{B_T}{W}\right) \times \left(\dfrac{S}{N}\right)_R$$

For PCM, $\quad B_T >> \dfrac{r}{2} \geq v\,W$

$\therefore \quad\quad v_{th} = \left(\dfrac{B_T}{W}\right)\left(\dfrac{S}{N}\right)_{R_{th}}$

$$\cong 6 \times \dfrac{B_T}{W} \times (M^2 - 1)$$

$\therefore \quad\quad v_{th} = 6\,v\,(M^2 - 1)$

Hence, given v and M we can find v needed for PCM above threshold. This will help in comparing PCM with other methods.

2.3 Multiplexers

Multiplexing is a technique of accommodating signals from number of sources for transmitting them on a single channel. Multiplexing helps in considerable reduction of cost of the communication system. The device that takes output from a number of terminals and combines the various data streams into one composite output signal is called as multiplexer.

A similar device will be required at the receiver end to separate these signals. This device is called demultiplexer. Digital communication as has been seen earlier has the advantage of multiplexing signals from different types of sources such as voice, data, video, etc. It is possible because digital signals are transmitted as a sequence of symbols. These symbols from different sources can be interleaved easily using time-division multiplexing.

2.3.1 Time-Division Multiplexing (TDM)

It is a method of time interleaving of digital symbols from several sources so that the information from the sources can be transmitted serially over a single channel. TDM interleaves bits or characters from each source and transmits them at a higher speed over a wideband channel.

Each source is assigned unique time slot that contains a predefined number of characters or bits. The allocation of time slot depends on bit rates of the sources to be multiplexed. Let us consider the two possible cases :

Case 1: Bit rates of all sources are identical. We can either interleave bits or words from these sources. Fig. 2.10 (a) shows bit-by-bit interleaving whereas Fig. 2.10 (b) shows word-by-word interleaving.

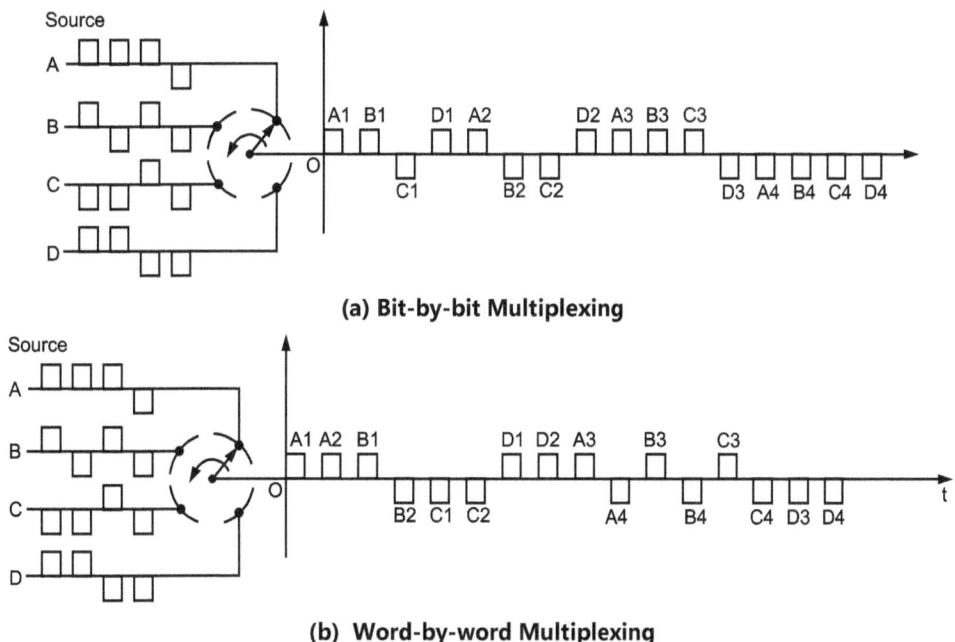

(a) Bit-by-bit Multiplexing

(b) Word-by-word Multiplexing

Fig. 2.10

Case 2: Bit rates of sources are not identical. In this case, the source with high bit rate is allocated more time slots. Fig. 2.11 (a) and (b) shows the two schemes for interleaving sources A, B, C and D, where, A, B has bit rate r and C, D has bit rate r/2. The minimum length of multiplexed frame is multiple of lowest common multiple of incoming source bit rates.

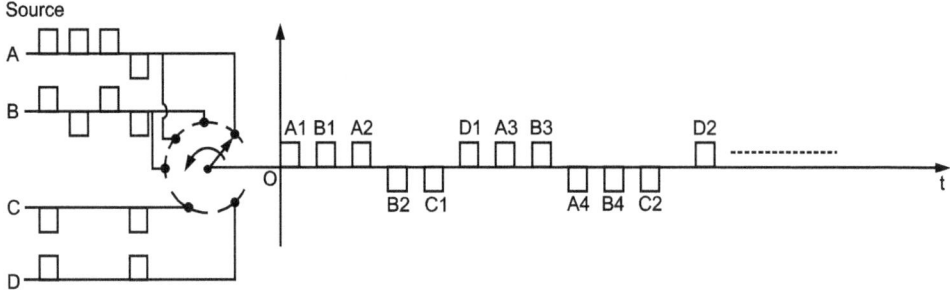

(a) Multiplexing with Different Bit Rate (Scheme 1)

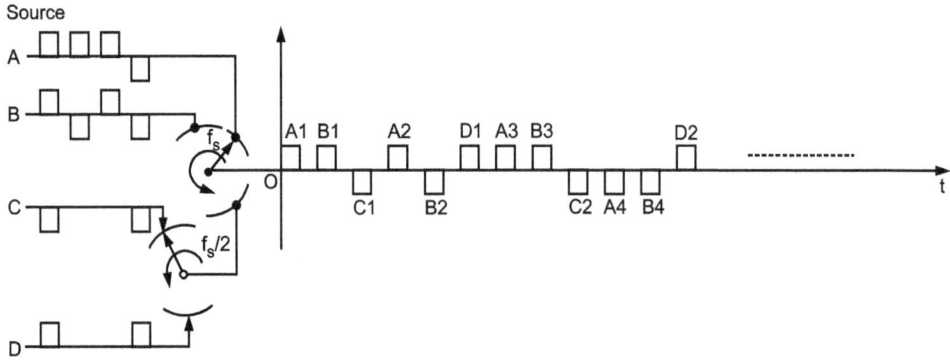

(b) Multiplexing with Different Bit Rate (Scheme 2)

Fig. 2.11

At the receiving end, the incoming stream of bits/words must be divided and distributed to appropriate destinations.

Apart from identifying the bit interval the frame interval also has to be known for this : framing and synchronization bits are added to data bits to identify the bit time and frame time.

2.3.2 Multiplexer Design Issues

The design of multiplexer depends on following factors:

1. Multiplexers must assign unique bit slots to each input in a frame.
2. There should be atleast one bit from each input in the frame.
3. It should insert additional bits for frame identification.
4. It should take care of variations in input bit rates.

Bit rate variations is a major problem in the design of multiplexers as seen earlier. Accordingly, multiplexers are categorised as below.

(i) Synchronous Multiplexers:

There is a master clock which governs all sources. These systems have highest efficiency. But they require master-clock to be distributed to all levels. Each bit of data is clocked in synchronism with master clock. The synchronization signal is provided by separate clocking line. In addition to this, a higher level of synchronization is required to identify beginning and end of frame. A synchronous multiplexer is shown in Fig. 2.12 (a).

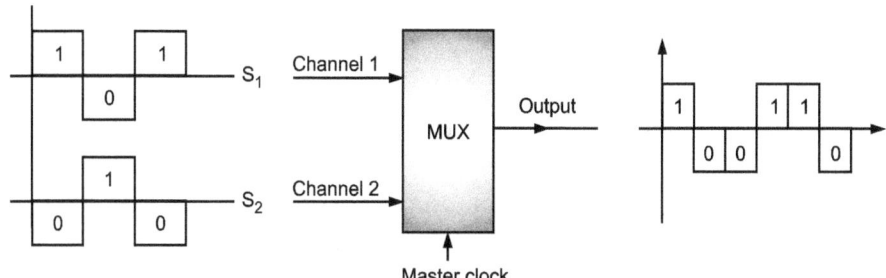

Fig. 2.12 : (a) Synchronous Multiplexer

(ii) Asynchronous Multiplexers :

These are used where the traffic is bursty. The start and end of transmissions are marked by start and stop bits. This is called start-stop signaling. The receiver clock is started aperiodically and no synchronisation is required with master-clock. Keyboard terminals is an example of source which generates bursty traffic. Hence, A 7-bit character generated by these terminals is to be allotted with 1 start bit, 1 stop bit and 1 parity bit. It is shown in Fig. 2.12 (b).

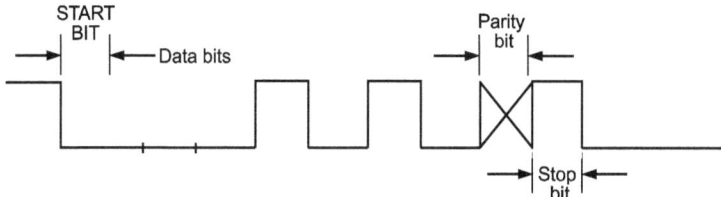

Fig. 2.12: (b) Asynchronous Transmission of a Word

Buffering and character interleaving can be used to multiplex these sources using synchronous multiplexing.

(iii) Quasi-Synchronous Multiplexers:

They are used when the sources to be multiplexed are not synchronised in frequency i.e. there is slight variation in bit rates of these sources. In some applications, the input bit rates are not related with each other by a rational number. In such situations, to accommodate these asynchronous inputs, output clock rate has to be increased above nominal value. Some dummy bits are to be added called stuff bits when input is not available from input sources. This is illustrated in Fig. 2.12 (c).

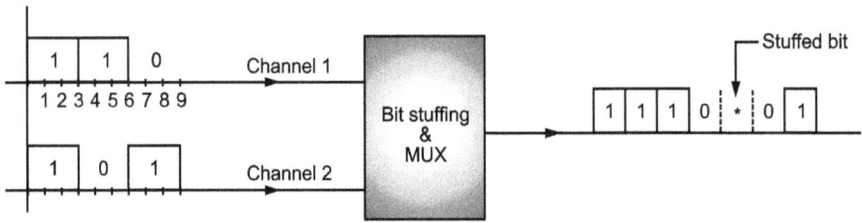

Fig. 2.12: (c) Quasi Synchronous Multiplexer

Example 2.4:

Design an efficient TDM telemetry system, which accepts five data channels with minimum sampling rates of 3000, 700, 600, 300 and 200 Hz. Use 8 : 1 multiplexer with sampling frequency f_s = 750 Hz one input of multiplexer is reserved for marker of the frame and remaining inputs are used to accommodate the data channels. Draw complete system block diagram. Find total output signaling rate and bandwidth.

Explain the operation of the system.

Solution: Given: f_s = 750 Hz

Channel	Minimum Sampling Rate	Actual f_s
1	3000 Hz	4 × 750 Hz
2	700 Hz	750 Hz
3	600 Hz	750 Hz
4	300 Hz	375 Hz
5	200 Hz	375 Hz

Hence, following inputs will be given to multiplexer.
1 Input from marker.
4 Inputs from channel 1.
1 Input from channel 3.
1 Inputs from channel 4 and 5 combined at previous stage with 2 : 1 MUX (f_s = 375 Hz).

This scheme is shown in Fig. 2.13.

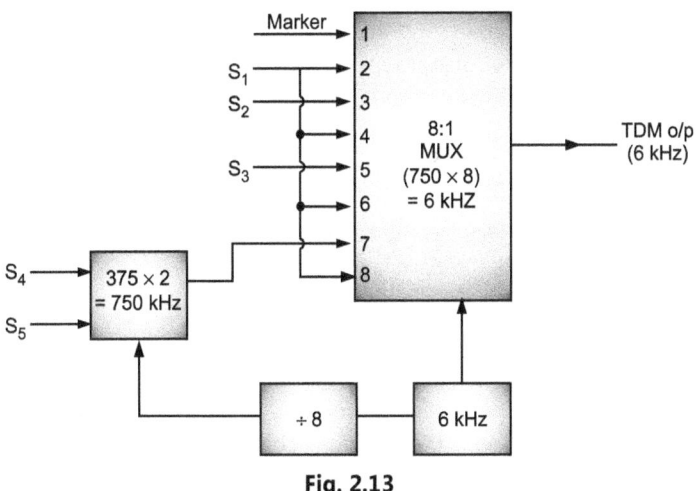

Fig. 2.13

2.3.3 Multiplexing Hierarchies

There are two types of digital multiplexers.

(i) **Low Speed Multiplexers:**
- These are used with digital computer systems to merge digital signals from several sources.
- The output rates of these multiplexers are standardized to 1.2, 2.4, 3.6, 4.8, 7.2, 7.6 and 19.2 kbps. The output is designated as digital signal level 0 (DS0).

(ii) **High Speed Multiplexers:**
- They are used in commercial data transmission systems.
- Two different multiplexing standards have been adopted for digital communication.
- The AT & T hierarchy in North America and Japan and CCITT hierarchy in Europe and rest of world. Both hierarchies are based on 64 kbps voice PCM unit.
- Their structural layout is shown in Fig. 2.14.

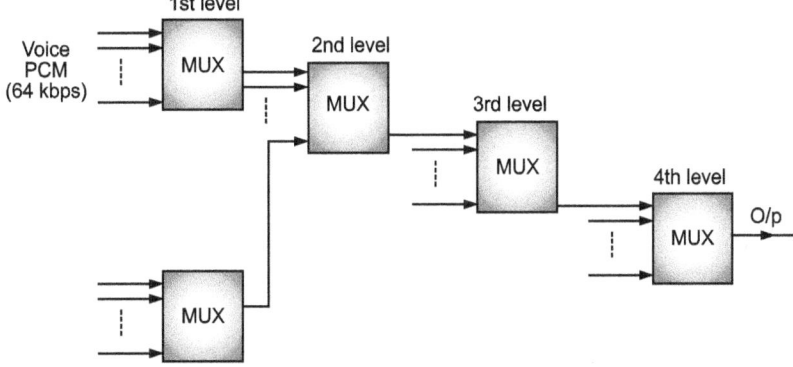

Fig. 2.14: Structural Layout of Standard Multiplexing Schemes

The telephone industry has standardised the bit rates to 1.544 Mbps, 6.312 Mbps, etc. and designates them as DS-1 (Digital Signal type 1) DS-2, etc. Thus, higher the DS level higher will be data rate. Different transmission medium is used for different DS levels.

For example for higher DS - levels, fibre optic cables, microwave links are used. A single DS-1 signal is usually transmitted over a pair of twisted pair cables. This type of DS-1 transmission over a twisted pair medium is called T1-Carrier Systems. Similarly, the higher DS levels transmission are known as T2, T3, T4, carrier systems.

2.3.3.1 T1 Carrier System

Fig. 2.15 (a) shows basic T1 carrier system which is used to transmit 24 voice signals over a single DS-1 line. Two lines, one for transmission and another for reception are used in the system. Repeaters will be required if the T1 line is connecting telephone equipments over a large distance after every 2 km.

1. Sampling rate used, for each voice signal is 8 kHz.
2. Hence, frame length will be $\frac{1}{8000}$ = 125 μ-sec.
3. 8-bit PCM is used, hence frame length will be 24 × 8 = 192 bits.
4. 1-bit is added at the beginning of each frame for frame synchronisation. Hence, total bits in one frame = 193 bits.

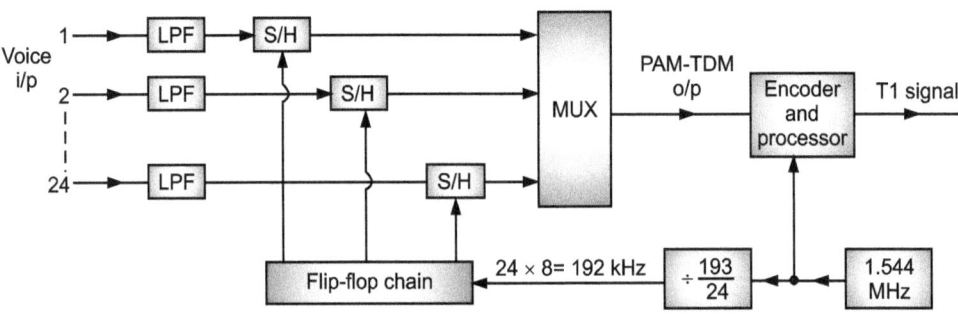

Fig. 2.15 (a): T1 Carrier System

5. Hence, the T1 data rate (r_b) = (193 bits/frame) × 8000 frames/sec.

   = 1.544 Mbps

   Hence, bit duration will be 0.6488 μsec (1/r_b)

6. A telephone system must transmit speech as well as other signals related to call setup, termination etc. This is called signaling. After every 6 frames the 8th bit in every 24 channel is used for signaling purpose. Hence, the signaling data rate for each of 24 input channel is = (1 bit/6 frames) × 8000 frames/sec. = 1.333 kbps and a total equivalent signaling rate for 24 channels = 1.33 × 24 = 32 kbps.

7. T1 signals can be combined at an higher level multiplexer or transmitted directly over short distance links (upto 80 km).
8. It uses bipolar signal format.
9. The T1 transmission line is twisted pair cable.
10. Frame format for T1 system is shown in Fig. 2.15 (b).

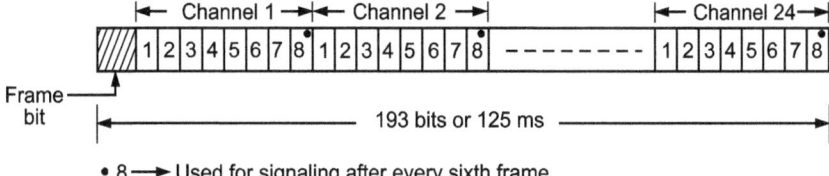

- 8 ⟶ Used for signaling after every sixth frame

Fig. 2.15 (b): Frame Format for T1 System

2.3.3.2 AT & T Hierarchy

Fig. 2.16 shows the AT&T multiplex hierarchy used in North America and Japan. It shows transmission of voice, data from computer visual telephone and colour TV signals on a single T4 line.

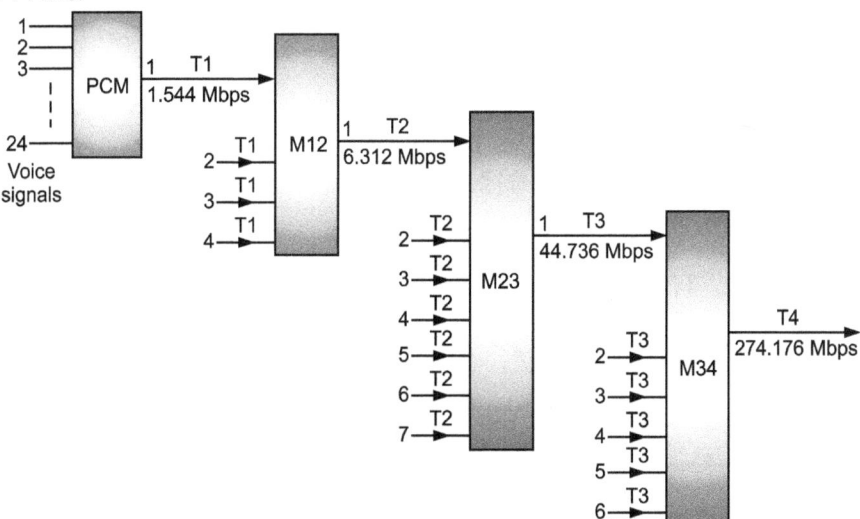

Fig. 2.16: AT & T Hierarchy

1. T1 carrier line carries PCM voice or multiplexed digital data at a speed of 1.544 Mbps.
2. Four such T1 lines (referred as DS_1) are multiplexed by an M12 multiplexer generating T2 line.
3. M12 multiplexer adds 17 bits/frame synchronization and bits stuffing. Hence, number of bits/frame = 193 × 4 + 17 = 789 bits/frame.

Hence, bit rate of T2 line = 789 bits/frame × 8000 frames/sec.
= 6.312 Mbps

4. Seven T2 signals (Referred as DS-2) are multiplexed along with visual telephone signals using M23 multiplexer to generate T3 line.

5. M23 multiplexer adds 69 bits for synchronization and bits stuffing. Hence, number of bits/frame for a T3 line = 789 × 7 + 69 = 5592 bits/frame and signaling rate = 5592 × 8000 = 44.736 Mbps.

6. Six T3 lines (Referred as DS-3) are multiplexed by M34 multiplexer to generate T4 line. PCM encoded TV signals require a data rate of 90 Mbps. Hence, two T3 lines are allocated for this signal.

7. M34 multiplexer adds 720 bits for synchronization of bits stuffing. Hence, number of bits/frame for T4 line = 5592 × 6 + 720 = 34,272 bits/frame.

And bit rate = 34,272 × 8000
= 274.176 Mbps

8. The higher level multiplexors (M12, M23, M34) are quasisynchronous.

2.3.3.3 CCITT Hierarchy

- In Europe and rest of the world, CCITT (Consultative Committee on International Telephony and Telegraphy) hierarchy is adopted.
- This hierarchy is shown in Fig. 2.17.
- It has data rate of 2.048 mbps/(30 channel) at first level.

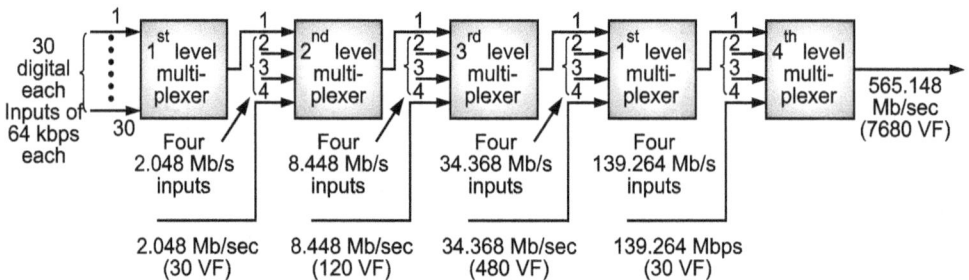

Fig. 2.17: CCITT Digital TDM Hierarchy

Rest of the specifications are as below:

1. 30 voice frequency channels of 64 kbps are multiplexed at first level to generate 2.048 Mbps line.

2. Four 2.048 Mbps lines are multiplexed to generate 8.448 Mbps output rate at second level.

3. Four 8.448 Mbps line are multiplexed to generate 34.368 Mbps output line at 3rd level.

4. Four 34.368 lines are multiplexed to generate 139.264 Mbps output line at 4th level.
5. Four 139.264 Mbps lines are multiplexed to generate 565.148 Mbps output line at 5th level.

2.4 Delta Modulation (DM)

It is a system in which corresponding to each sample we will have single encoded bit as opposed to n-bits in PCM. Delta modulator transmits binary output pulses whose polarity depends on difference between the modulating signal and feedback signal constituted from history of the signals previously sent.

It has simple hardware and is less costly than PCM system. It is also more tolerant to transmission errors and does not need synchronization like PCM. But then all this comes with increased signaling rate (or sampling) and hence increased bandwidth requirements and possibility of slope-overload distortion.

The DM transmitter is shown in Fig. 2.18 below.

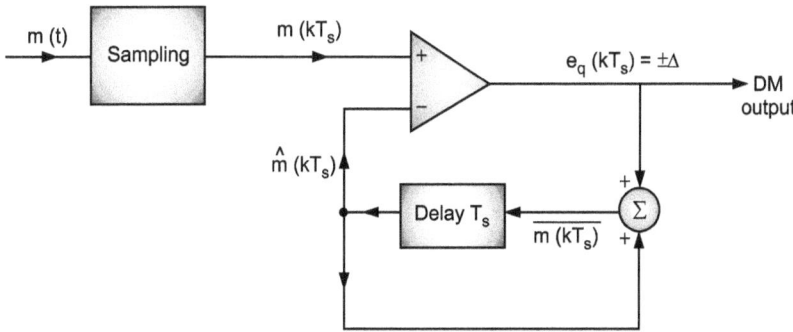

Fig. 2.18: DM Transmitter

1. m(t) is the analog information signal.
2. $m(kT_s)$ is sampled version of m(t) at time kT_s, where k = 0, 1, 2, ……
3. $e_q(kT_s)$ is the difference between current sample and predicted version of previous sample. $e_q(kT_s)$ is going to be either $+\Delta$ or $-\Delta$.
4. Here $\hat{m}(kT_s) = \overline{m(k-1)T_s}$ i.e. $\overline{m(kT_s)}$ delayed by one sampling time.

5. The waveforms are shown in Fig. 2.19 below.

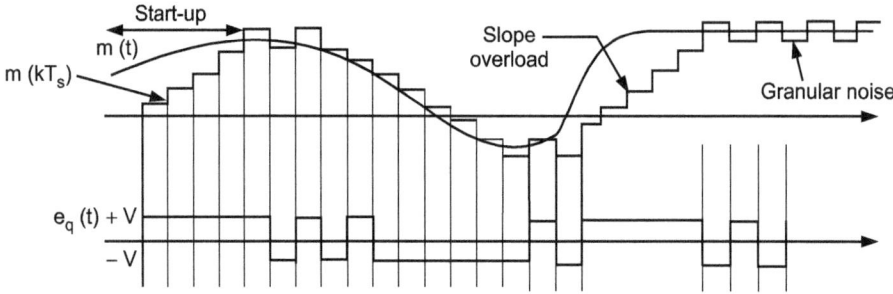

Fig. 2.19: DM Waveforms

6. It can be seen from the waveforms that whenever signal level m(t) is above $\hat{m}(kT_s)$, the output of DM is $+\Delta$ (bit 1) and if m(t) is below $\hat{m}(kT_s)$ output is $-\Delta$ (bit 0).

i.e. if $m(t) > \hat{m}(kT_s)$ output = $+\Delta$

$m(t) < \hat{m}(kT_s)$ output = $-\Delta$

When information signal m(t) is changing rapidly $\hat{m}(kT_s)$ cannot follow m(t) it is called slope overload effect. The error generated due this is called slope overload noise. It is shown in waveforms of Fig. 2.19.

To avoid slope overload we can –

(i) Increase step size Δ.

(ii) Increase sampling frequency. i.e. reduce T_s.

Increasing Δ will increase quantization noise, also called granular noise and increase in f_s will require more transmission bandwidth. Thus, there are two types of quantization errors in DM :

(i) Slope overload noise.

(ii) Granular noise.

Slope overload occurs when the step size is too small to follow fast rate changing part of waveform. Granularity occurs when the staircase function $m(kT_s)$ hunts around a relatively slow varying part of waveform with large step size. Thus, a small value of Δ will give rise to slope overload and large value of Δ will increase granularity.

The bit rate of DM is

$$r_b = \text{No. of samples/sec} \times \text{No. of bits/sample}$$

Since DM has 1-bit per sample,
$$r_b = f_s$$
∴ Bandwidth requirement for DM is
$$\boxed{BW = \frac{r_b}{2} = \frac{f_s}{2}}$$

The DM receiver is shown in Fig. 2.20 below.

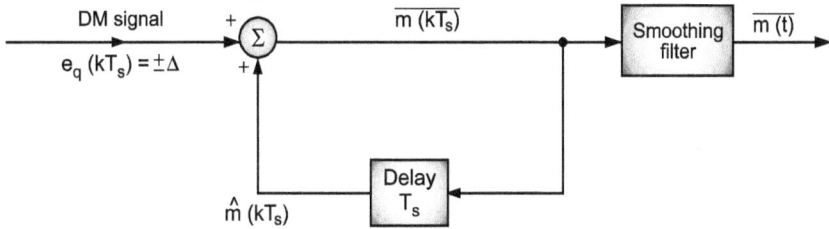

Fig. 2.20: DM Receiver

1. The accumulator will keep on accumulating the pulse ($\pm \Delta$) transmitted.
2. Hence $\overline{m}(kT_s)$ will be addition of received DM signal and delayed version of previous sample i.e. $\hat{m}(kT_s)$.
3. If the information signal m(t) remains constant for a long time or changing very slowly, $\overline{mkT_s}$ will hunt (fluctuate) and the resulting quantization noise becomes square wave with a period twice that of sampling period.
4. This is also called Idling noise or granular noise. This noise will be removed by smoothing filter (LPF) shown in DM receiver.

In practice, we can use a circuit shown in Fig. 2.21 to generate and reconstruct Delta modulator and demodulator. The first order predictor can be replaced by a low-cost (accumulator) integrator as shown in Fig. 2.21 (a).

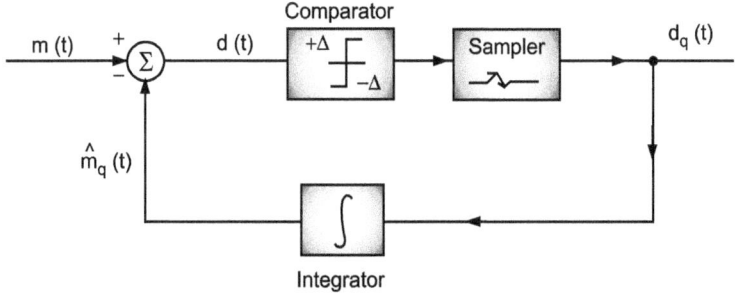

(a) Delta Modulator

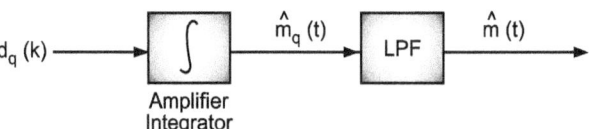

(b) Delta Demodulator

Fig. 2.21

2.4.1 Performance of Delta Modulator

Delta modulator can work well if the step size and T_s are sufficiently small. When m(t) increases or decreases too rapidly (as seen in the later part of waveform in Fig. 2.20) $\hat{m}_q(t)$ cannot catch up with m(t). This phenomenon is called slope overload. It gives rise to slope overload noise. This noise is basic limiting factor in the performance of delta modulator.

Slope overload can be avoided by decreasing the step size and increasing f_s. But then this gives rise to another problem called granular noise. This effect is also shown in Fig. 2.20. When the signal varies too slowly, then there are alternate positive and negative pulses. This effect is more prominent if step size is small. Hence, we have to select optimum value for the step size. If the step size Δ and sampling time is T_s, then to avoid slope overload,

$$\max\left(\frac{dm}{dt}\right) \leq \frac{\Delta}{T_s} \leq \Delta \times f_s \qquad \ldots (2.22)$$

Let,
$$m(t) = A_m \cos(2\pi f_m t) \qquad \ldots (2.23)$$

$\therefore$
$$\frac{dm}{dt} = -2\pi f_m A_m \sin(2\pi f_m t) \qquad \ldots (2.24)$$

$$\max\left(\frac{dm}{dt}\right) = 2\pi f_m A_m \qquad \ldots (2.25)$$

From equation (2.22), we can write,
$$2\pi f_m A_m \leq \Delta \times f_s$$
$$f_s \geq \frac{2\pi f_m A_m}{\Delta}$$

Hence to avoid slope overload,

$\therefore$
$$\boxed{f_s \geq \frac{2\pi f_m A_m}{\Delta}} \qquad \ldots (2.26)$$

Also,
$$\boxed{\frac{A_m}{\Delta} \leq \frac{1}{2\pi}\left(\frac{f_s}{f_m}\right)}$$

The step size Δ should be very small compared to peak-to-peak signal amplitude 2A_m.

i.e. $\Delta \ll 2A_m$

∴ $f_s \geq \pi \times W \left(\dfrac{2A_m}{\Delta} \right)$

∴ $f_s \gg W$

The performance of DM thus depends on –

(i) Slope overload.

(ii) Granular noise.

(iii) Regeneration errors.

Out of the three parameters granular noise is major parameter to be considered. It is nothing but quantization error and is defined as,

$$e(t) = \hat{m}_q(t) - m(t)$$

The step size is Δ and hence the quantization error can be either $+\Delta$ or $-\Delta$. (**Note:** that this error in case of PCM was $-\dfrac{\Delta}{2}$ to $\dfrac{\Delta}{2}$. Hence, e(t) has uniform distribution over $-\Delta$ to $+\Delta$ as plotted in Fig. 2.22.

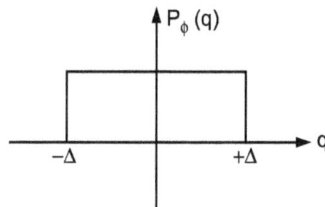

Fig. 2.22: PDF of Quantization Error Signal in DM

Hence, the quantization noise or granular noise can be given by,

$$\sigma_q^2 = \int_{-\Delta}^{\Delta} q^2 \, P_\phi(q) \, dq$$

$$= \int_{-\Delta}^{\Delta} q^2 \times \dfrac{1}{2\Delta} \, dq$$

$$= \frac{1}{2\Delta}\left[\frac{q^3}{3}\right]_{-\Delta}^{\Delta}$$

$$= \frac{\Delta^2}{3}$$

$$\therefore \quad \boxed{\sigma_q^2 = \frac{\Delta^2}{3}} \qquad \ldots (2.27)$$

$\left(\text{In case of PCM this noise was } \frac{\Delta^2}{12}\right)$.

Let us now find the signal-to-noise ratio for DM.

To find the noise power at the output of a low pass filter, we need the noise power spectral density.

Experimentally, it is found that the power spectrum of granular noise is flat over a range extending beyond f_s, i.e.

$$S_{qn}(f) = \frac{\sigma_q^2}{2f_s} = \frac{\Delta^2}{3} \times \frac{1}{2f_s}, \text{ for } |f| \leq f_s \qquad \ldots (2.28)$$

Since σ_q^2 is mean square value (Average Power).

But then this noise is filtered by LPF with cut-off frequency W Hz at the receiver. Hence, the noise power at the output of the filter will be,

$$N_q = \int_{-W}^{W} S_{qn}(f)\, df$$

$$= \int_{-W}^{W} \frac{\Delta^2}{3} \times \frac{1}{2f_s}\, df$$

$$= \frac{\Delta^2}{3} \times \frac{1}{2f_s} \times 2W$$

$$= \frac{\Delta^2}{3} \times \frac{W}{f_s}$$

$$\therefore \quad \boxed{N_q = \frac{\Delta^2}{3} \times \frac{W}{f_s}}$$

Since granular noise is the most significant of the three noise types. Neglecting other two we can write the signal-to-noise ratio as,

$$\left(\frac{S}{N}\right)_o = \frac{P_s}{N_q}$$

$$\therefore \left(\frac{S}{N}\right) = \frac{P_s}{\frac{\Delta^2}{3} \times \frac{W}{f_s}} = \frac{3f_s}{\Delta^2 W} \times P_s \qquad \ldots (2.29)$$

$$\therefore \left(\frac{S}{N}\right)_0 = \frac{3f_s}{\Delta^2 W} \times P_s$$

where, P_s is Average signal power $\overline{m^2(t)}$.

(Note that for PCM this expression was $3 L^2 P_s$).

Example 2.5:

If input to linear delta modulator is $A_m \cos(2\pi f_m t)$, find the signal to quantization noise ratio if sampling frequency and stepsize is such that it is minimum value required to avoid slope overload.

Solution:

We know from equation (2.) that to avoid slope overload in case of sinusoidal signal $A_m \cos(2\pi f_m t)$,

$$\frac{A_m}{\Delta} \leq \frac{1}{2\pi}\left(\frac{f_s}{f_m}\right)$$

Also from equation (2.),

$$\left(\frac{S}{N}\right)_0 = \frac{3f_s}{\Delta^2 W} \times P_s$$

For sinusoidal signal,

$$P_s = \frac{A_m^2}{2}$$

$$\left(\frac{S}{N}\right)_0 = \frac{3f_s}{\Delta^2 W} \times \frac{A_m^2}{2}$$

$$= \left(\frac{A_m}{\Delta}\right)^2 \times \frac{3f_s}{2W}$$

$$\therefore \left(\frac{S}{N}\right)_0 \leq \left(\frac{1}{2\pi} \times \frac{f_s}{f_m}\right)^2 \times \frac{3f_s}{2W}$$

$$\left(\frac{S}{N}\right)_0 \leq \frac{3}{8\pi^2} \times \frac{f_s^3}{f_m^2 \times W}$$

If $f_m = W$

$$\left(\frac{S}{N}\right)_0 = \frac{3}{8\pi^2}\left(\frac{f_s}{f_m}\right)^3$$

SNR in terms of Transmission Bandwidth B_T:

Let us now consider the signal-to-noise ratio for voice signal.

Let A_{max} be peak amplitude of voice signal m(t). This value for A_{max} is calculated by using equation,

$$[A_{max}]_{voice} = \frac{\Delta \times f_s}{W_r}$$

where,
$$W_r = 2\pi \times 800$$

$$\therefore \left(\frac{S}{N}\right)_0 = \frac{3 \times f_s}{\Delta^2 \times W} \times P_s$$

$$= \frac{3 \times f_s}{\left(\frac{A_{max} \times W_r}{f_s}\right)^2 \times W} \times P_s$$

$$= \frac{3 \times f_s^3}{A_{max}^2 \times W_r^2 \times W} \times P_s$$

For voice signal,
$$W = 4 \times 10^3 \text{ Hz}$$
$$W_r = 2\pi \times 800$$

The transmission bandwidth is $B_T = \frac{f_s}{2}$

$$\therefore \left(\frac{S}{N}\right)_0 = \frac{150}{\pi^2} \times \left(\frac{B_T}{W}\right)^3 \times \frac{P_s}{A_{max}^2}$$

For Double Integration DM,

$$\left(\frac{S}{N}\right)_0 = 5.34 \left(\frac{B_T}{W}\right)^3 \times \frac{P_s}{A_{max}^2}$$

Advantages of DM:
(i) Because one sample is represented by one bit hence no need to have word level synchronization at the input of demodulator and hardware is simple.
(ii) Less costly.
(iii) It is more tolerant to transmission errors. Because in DM each digit is separate whereas in PCM detection error depends on bit location.

Disadvantages of DM:
(i) Signaling rate is higher than PCM to take care of slope overload.
(ii) Slope overload distortion.
(iii) Granular noise.
(iv) Multiplexing of DM signal requires separate coder and decoder whereas in case of PCM single coder and decoder is shared by all channels.

Example 2.6:

In a single integrator DM scheme, the voice signal is sampled at a rate of 64 kHz. The maximum signal amplitude is 1 volt, voice signal bandwidth is 3.5 kHz.

(i) Determine minimum value of step size to avoid slope overload.
(ii) Determine granular noise power N_q.
(iii) Assuming signal to be sinusoidal calculate signal power S_0 and Signal-to-Noise ratio.
(iv) Assuming that voice signal amplitude is uniformly distributed in the range $(-1, 1)$ determine signal power and signal to noise ratio.

Solution: Given:
$$f_s = 64 \text{ kHz}$$
$$f_m = W = 3.5 \text{ kHz}$$
$$A_{max} = 1 \text{ v}$$

(i) We know to avoid slope overload

$$f_s \geq \frac{A_{max} \times \omega_r}{\Delta}$$

$\therefore$ Step-size $\Delta \geq \dfrac{A_{max} \times 2\pi \times 800}{f_s}$

$\therefore \quad \Delta \geq \dfrac{1 \times 2\pi \times 800}{64 \times 10^3}$

$\therefore \quad \Delta \geq 0.0786$

(ii) Granular noise power is given by,

$$N_q = \frac{\Delta^2}{3} \times \frac{f_m}{f_s}$$
$$= \frac{(0.34375)^2}{3} \times \frac{3.5 \times 10^3}{64 \times 10^3}$$
$$= 2.154 \times 10^{-3} \text{ W}$$
$$= 2.154 \text{ mW}$$

(iii) If signal is sinusoidal, signal power is given by,

$$P_s = \frac{A_{max}^2}{2}$$
$$= \frac{(1)^2}{2}$$
$$= 0.5 \text{ W}$$

$\therefore \quad \left(\dfrac{S}{N}\right)_0 = \dfrac{P_s}{N_q}$

$$= \frac{0.5}{2.154 \times 10^{-3}}$$
$$= 232.126$$

(iv) Given that voice signal is uniformly distributed over $(-1, 1)$. Hence, signal power can be calculated by mean square value.

$$\sigma_x^2 = \int_{-1}^{1} x^2 \, p_X(x) \, dx$$

$$= \int_{-1}^{1} x^2 \times \frac{1}{2} \cdot dx$$

$$= \frac{1}{2} \times \left[\frac{x^3}{3}\right]_{-1}^{1}$$

$$= \frac{1}{3}$$

$$= 0.3333 \text{ watt}$$

$$\therefore \quad P_S = 0.3333 \text{ watt}$$

Also, $A_{max} = 1$

Now, signal-to-noise ratio is,

$$\therefore \quad \left(\frac{S}{N}\right)_o = \frac{150}{\pi^2} \left(\frac{B_T}{W}\right)^3 \frac{P_S}{A_{max}^2}$$

$$B_T = \frac{f_s}{2} = 32 \text{ kHz}$$

$$W = 4 \text{ kHz}$$

$$\left(\frac{S}{N}\right)_o = \frac{150}{\pi^2} \times \left(\frac{32}{4}\right)^3 \times \frac{0.3333}{1}$$

$$= 2590.56$$

2.5 Digital PAM Signals

Digital symbols can amplitude modulate some carrier to generate amplitude modulated pulse train. Such signal may be represented as,

$$x(t) = \sum_n a_n \, p(t - nD) \qquad \ldots (2.30)$$

Here a_n is the modulating amplitude. It is the nth symbol in the message sequence. $p(t)$ is the carrier signal. It's pulses are modulated by a_n. D is the maximum duration (time period) allowed for the carrier pulse. The unmodulated pulse $p(t)$ is the rectangular pulse and it can take variable duty cycle. It can be represented as,

$$p(t) = 1 \qquad \text{for } t = 0$$
$$= 0 \qquad \text{for } t = \pm D, \pm 2D \qquad \ldots (2.31)$$

$x(t)$ is the baseband signal and continuous in time. To recover the original digital signal, we have to sample $x(t)$ at some fixed intervals and check the signal in these intervals. This checking is the detection of the transmitted symbols. From equation (2.30) we see that when $p(t)$ is zero, $x(t)$ is zero. Therefore, it is preferable to sample $x(t)$ when $p(t)$ is zero. That is at this time [P(t) = 0] no digital information is present/transmitted in the baseband signal. Therefore, x(t) can be sampled periodically at t = nD where n = 0. ± 1, ± 2, ... etc. p(t) is the rectangular pulse and can be written as,

$$P(t) = rect\left(\frac{t}{\tau}\right) \qquad \ldots (2.32)$$

Since the pulse to pulse interval is 'D', the width of the pulse τ should be less than or equal to D,

i.e. $\tau < D$

The signaling rate will be given as,

$$r = \frac{1}{D} \qquad \ldots (2.33)$$

If 'D' represents the duration of one bit, then $D = T_b$ and signaling rate will be,

$$r = \frac{1}{T_b} \qquad \ldots 2.34)$$

Various PAM formats are shown in Fig. 2.23. All the formats are shown for a binary message 10110100.

2.5.1 Unipolar RZ and NRZ

In Unipolar Format the waveform does have a single polarity. The waveform can have +5 or +12 volts when high. The waveform is simple on-off. In the unipolar RZ form, the waveform has zero value when symbol '0' is transmitted and waveform has 'A' volts when '1' is transmitted. In RZ form, the 'A' volts is present for $T_b/2$ period if symbol '1' is transmitted and for remaining $T_b/2$ waveform returns to zero value, i.e. for unipolar RZ form,

If symbol '1' is transmitted,

$$x(t) = A \text{ for } 0 \leq t < T_b/2 \text{ (Half interval)}$$
$$= 0 \text{ for } T_b/2 \leq t < T_b \text{ (Half interval)}$$

and if symbol '0' is transmitted,

$$x(t) = 0 \text{ for } 0 \leq t < T_b \text{ (complete interval)}$$

Thus, in Unipolar RZ format every pulse returns to a zero value. Fig. 2.23 (a) shows this signal format. A unipolar NRZ (not return to zero) format is shown in Fig. 2.23 (b). When symbol '1' is to be transmitted, the signal has 'A' volts for full duration. When symbol '0' is to be transmitted, the signal has zero volts (no signal) for complete symbol duration. i.e. for unipolar NRZ form.

If symbol '1' is transmitted,

$$x(t) = A \text{ for } 0 \leq t < T_b \quad \text{(complete interval)}$$

If symbol '0' is transmitted,

$$x(t) = 0 \text{ for } 0 \leq t < T_b \quad \text{(complete interval)}$$

For NRZ format we can see that, the pulse does not return to zero on its own. If symbol '0' is to be transmitted, then pulse becomes zero. Internal computer waveforms are usually of unipolar NRZ type.

Since there is no separation between the pulses, the receiver needs synchronization to detect unipolar NRZ pulses. As compared to RZ format, NRZ pulse width (pulse to pulse interval is same) is more. Hence energy of the pulse is more. Unipolar format has some average DC value. This DC value does not carry any information.

2.5.2 Polar RZ and NRZ

In the polar RZ format, symbol '1' is represented by positive voltage polarity and symbol '0' is represented by negative voltage polarity. Since this is RZ format, the pulse is transmitted only for half duration. That is for polar RZ,

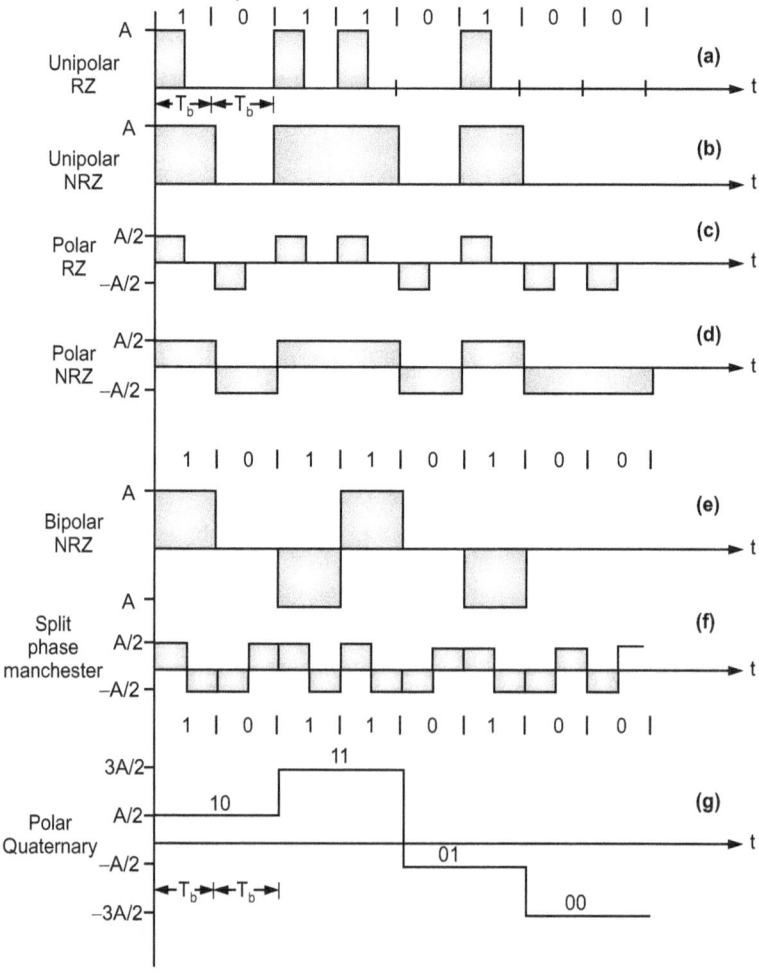

Fig. 2.23: Various digital PAM signals formats
(a) Unipolar RZ, (b) Unipolar NRZ, (c) Polar RZ, (d) Polar NRZ, (e) Bipolar NRZ, (f) Split phase Manchester, (g) Polar quaternary NRZ

If symbol '1' is transmitted,

$$x(t) = +\frac{A}{2} \quad \text{for } 0 \le t < T_b/2$$

$$= 0 \quad \text{for } \frac{T_b}{2} \le t < T_b$$

and if symbol '0' is transmitted,

$$x(t) = -\frac{A}{2} \quad \text{for } 0 \le t < \frac{T_b}{2}$$

$$= 0 \quad \text{for } \frac{T_b}{2} \le t < T_b$$

Polar RZ waveform is shown in Fig. 2.23 (c). The polar NRZ format is shown in 2.23 (d). In polar NRZ format, symbol '1' is represented by positive polarity and symbol '0' is represented by negative polarity. These polarities are maintained over the complete pulse duration i.e. for polar NRZ,

if symbol '1' is transmitted,

$$x(t) = +\frac{A}{2} \quad \text{for } 0 \le t < T_b$$

and if symbol '0' is transmitted,

$$x(t) = -\frac{A}{2} \quad \text{for } 0 \le t < T_b$$

Since polar RZ and NRZ formats are bipolar, the average DC value is minimum in these Waveforms. If probabilities of occurrence of symbols '1' and '0' are same, then average DC components of the waveform will be zero.

2.5.3 Bipolar NRZ [Pseudo-trinary or Alternate Mark Inversion (AMI)]

In this format successive '1's are represented by pulses with alternate polarity and 0's are represented by no pulses. Fig. 2.23 (e) shows the Bipolar NRZ or AMI waveform. If there are even number of 1's, the DC component of the waveform will be zero. The advantage of this format is that the ambiguities due to transmission sign inversion are eliminated.

2.5.4 Split Phase Manchester

This type of waveform is shown in Fig. 2.23 (f). Here if symbol '1' is to be transmitted, then a positive half interval pulse is followed by a negative half interval pulse. If symbol '0' is to be transmitted, then a negative half interval pulse is followed by a positive half interval pulse. Thus for any symbol the pulse takes positive as well as negative value i.e.,

If symbol 1 is to be transmitted,

$$x(t) = \frac{A}{2} \quad \text{for } 0 \leq t < \frac{T_b}{2}$$

$$= -\frac{A}{2} \quad \text{for } \frac{T_b}{2} \leq t < T_b$$

and if symbol '0' is to be transmitted,

$$x(t) = -\frac{A}{2} \quad \text{for } 0 \leq t < \frac{T_b}{2}$$

$$= \frac{A}{2} \quad \text{for } \frac{T_b}{2} \leq t < T_b$$

The main advantage of this format is that irrespective of the probability of occurrence of symbols '1' and '0', the waveform has zero average value. Therefore by this mode, the power saving is more.

The drawback of this format is that it needs absolute sense of polarity at the receiver.

2.5.5 Polar Quaternary NRZ

Fig. 2.23 (g) shows the waveform of this format. This format is derived to reduce the signaling rate r. The message bits are grouped in the blocks of two. Therefore, there are four possible combinations 00, 01, 10 and 11 to these four combinations, four amplitude levels are assigned. The table 2.1 shows how this is done.

Table 2.1: Polar quaternary NRZ : combinations of bits

Message combination	$x(t) = a_n$
00	$-\frac{3A}{2}$
01	$-\frac{A}{2}$
10	$\frac{A}{2}$
11	$\frac{3A}{2}$

In the waveform of Fig. 2.23 (g), the first combination of two bits is 10. Therefore from table 2.1 we can see that the level should be $\frac{A}{2}$. The second combination in Fig. 2.23 (g) is 11, hence from table 2.1, the level taken is $\frac{3A}{2}$. Similarly other levels are selected. Thus for two

message bits only one pulse is transmitted with duration $2T_b$, i.e.
$$D = 2T_b$$
and signaling rate is given as,
$$r = \frac{r_b}{2} = \frac{1}{2T_b} \qquad \ldots (2.35)$$

2.5.6 M-ary Coding

In polar quaternary NRZ type of coding we combine two successive bits. In M-ary coding, we combine V successive message bits. Hence we get $M = 2^k$ distinct symbols or levels. Therefore, this type of coding is called M-ary coding. For example consider that the given message string of Fig. 2.23 i.e. 10110100.

Let k = 3.

Then we have $M = 2^3 = 8$ distinct levels or symbols. Thus this coding will be 8-ary coding. The duration of each symbol will equal to 3 bits, $3T_b$. Thus, the signaling rate is reduced.

Let us represent the signaling rate of 2 level coding (i.e. RZ and NRZ) be r_b. Then the signaling rate of M-ary coding is given as,

$$r = \frac{r_b}{k} \qquad \ldots (2.36)$$

Here k is the message bits in M-ary coding.

and $\qquad M = 2^k$

$\therefore \qquad k = \log_2 M \qquad \ldots (2.37)$

Hence equation (2.36) becomes,

$$r = \frac{r_b}{\log_2 M}$$

Complexing increases in M-ary coding.

2.5.7 High Density Bipolar (HDB) Signaling

Observe the bipolar NRZ signal of Fig. 2.23 (e). It shows that there is no signal transmitted during the period when linary '0' is presents. This creates a problem in synchronization when a long sequence of '0's is present. This problem is eliminated by adding 'pulses' when number of consecutive '0's exceeds n. This type of coding is called High Density Bipolar (HDB) coding and it is denoted as HDBN. Here N takes values like 1, 2, 3, ... when N = 3, the code becomes HDB3, which is most widely used format.

In the message sequence, when the mn and N + 1 zeros occurs, this group of zeros is replaced by special N + 1 binary digit sequences. These sequences contain some binary 1's so that they can be detected at the receiver. For HDB3 coding, those special sequences used are 000V and B00V.

2.6 Power Spectra of Discrete PAM Signals

The PAM signals have different amplitudes and shapes. Therefore, spectral properties of these signals are also different. Fig. 2.24 shows the power spectra of different PAM signals. These power spectra are normalized.

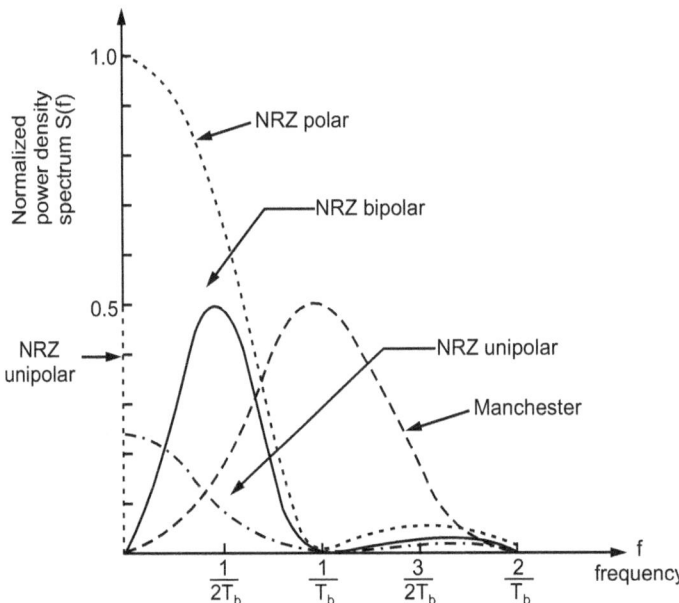

Fig. 2.24: Power spectra of various PAM signals

2.6.1 NRZ Unipolar Format

In this format, the signal is unipolar. Its amplitude can be +A or zero. Hence the signal has some DC component. Hence most of the power lies between DC and bit rate $\left(\frac{1}{T_b}\right)$ of the input signal. Observe that the power spectra is sinc shaped and its main lobe extends from DC to $\frac{1}{T_b}$. Power contained in frequencies above bit rate is very small.

2.6.2 NRZ Polar Format

In this format, the waveform takes positive as well as negative amplitudes. If occurrence of binary '1' or '0' is not equal, then waveform has some DC value. The power spectra is shown in Fig. 2.24. It is sinc pulse and contains most of the power from DC to bit rate $\left(\frac{1}{T_b}\right)$. The main lobe of sinc pulse is from DC to bit rate frequency. The power contained in frequencies above bit rate is very small.

2.6.3 NRZ Bipolar Format

In this format, the successive 1's are assigned pulses of alternating amplitudes. Hence, waveform does not contain any DC component. This is reflected in the power spectra also. The spectra is a pulse having peak power near $\frac{1}{2T_b}$ i.e. half bit rate and $2T_b$ negligible power at DC and bit rate. Thus power lies inside the bandwidth equal to bit rate $\left(\frac{1}{T_b}\right)$. The power content in frequencies above bit rate is very small.

2.6.4 Manchester Format

In manchester format, every symbol is transmitted with positive as well as negative amplitude. Hence there is no possibility of DC component in the signal. Fig. 2.24 shows the power spectra of manchester format. Most of the power lies in the bandwidth of twice of bit rate $\left(\frac{2}{T_b}\right)$. Negligible power is contained at DC and $\left(\frac{2}{T_b}\right)$. Peak of the spectra occur somewhere near bit rate. Observe that the width of the main pulse is twice of other formats.

2.7 Intersymbol Interference (ISI)

The bandwidth of flat top pulses is infinity. There are various filters in transmitter, channel and receiver of the communication systems. If these pulses are filtered improperly as they pass through a communication system, they will spread in time and the pulse for each symbol may be smeared into adjacent time slots and cause intersymbol interference as shown in Fig. 2.25.

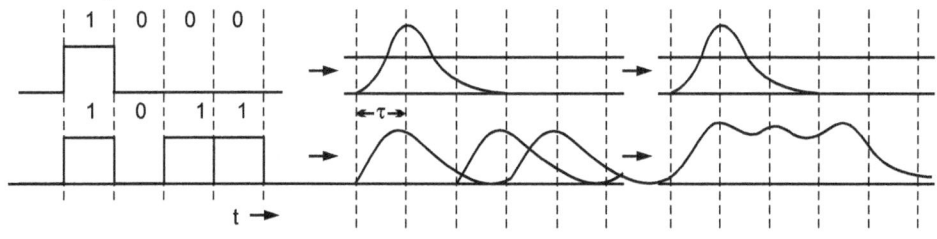

Fig. 2.25

The question is : How we can restrict bandwidth and still not introduce ISI ? With restricted bandwidth the pulses would have rounded tops.

Thus our aim is to –

(1) Study ISI problem.

(2) Use baseband pulse shaping as solution to the problem.

2.7.1 Baseband Transmission of Binary Data

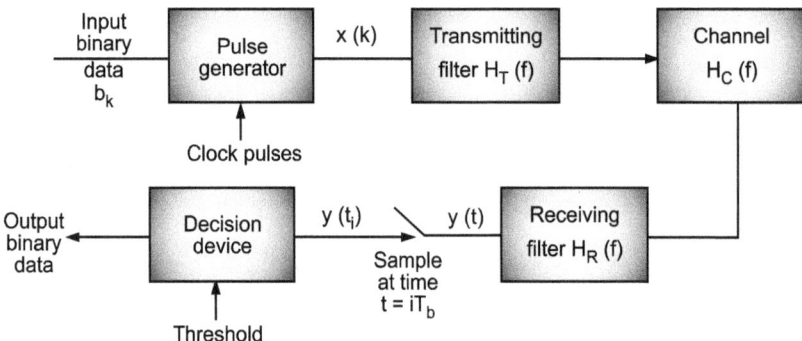

Fig. 2.26

For the baseband transmission of digital data, use of the discrete pulse amplitude modulation (PAM) provides the most efficient form of discrete pulse modulation in terms of power and bandwidth. The basic elements of binary PAM systems are shown in Fig. 2.26. The signal applied is the baseband binary data sequence $\{b_k\}$ with bit duration T_b seconds. b_k is in the form of 1 and 0. This signal is applied to the pulse generator producing waveform.

$$x(t) = \sum_{k=-\infty}^{\infty} A_k\, g(t - kT_b) \quad \ldots (2.38)$$

g(t) – pulse shaping waveform.

where, $g(0) = 1$

and
$$A_k = \begin{cases} + a & \text{if input bit is 1} \\ - a & \text{if input bit is 0} \end{cases}$$

The PAM signal x(t) passes through transmitting filter with transfer function $H_T(f)$.

The resulting filter output defines transmitted signal, which is modified as a result of transmission through channel of transfer f^n $H_C(f)$.

The signal at the receiver input is passed through a receiving filter of transfer function $H_R(f)$. This filter output is sampled synchronously with the transmitter and then these samples are used to reconstruct the original data sequence by means of a decision device.

2.7.2 The ISI Problem

We assume the channel is noiseless. The receiving filter output may be written as,

$$y(t) = \mu \sum_{k=-\infty}^{\infty} A_k \, p(t - kT_b) \quad \ldots (2.39)$$

μ – Scaling factor
$p(0) = 1$ (pulse $p(t)$ is normalised).
$\mu A_k \, p(t)$ – Response of cascade of $H_T(f)$, $H_R(f)$ and $H_C(f)$ produced by the pulse $A_k \, g(t)$.

∴ We may relate $p(t)$ to $g(t)$ as,

$$\mu \, p(f) = G(f) \, H_T(f) \, H_C(f) \, H_R(f) \quad \ldots (2.40)$$

The receiving filter output $y(t)$ is sampled at time $t_i = iT_b$ (with i taking an integer values) yielding

$$y(t_i) = \mu \sum_{k=-\infty}^{\infty} A_k \, p[(i-k)T_b] \quad \ldots (2.41)$$

∴
$$y(t_i) = \mu A_i + \mu \sum_{\substack{k=-\infty \\ k \neq u}}^{\infty} A_k \, p[(i-k)T_b] \quad \ldots (2.42)$$

In above equation first term μA_i represents the contribution of the ith transmitted bits.

The second term represents the residual effects of all other transmitted bits on the secondary of ith received bit, this residual effect is called **intersymbol interference (ISI)**.

In absence of ISI, we observe that,

$$y(t_i) = \mu A_i$$

which shows that, under these ideal conditions the ith transmitted bit can be decoded correctly.

The unavoidable presence of ISI in the system, however introduces errors in decision device at the receiver output. Therefore, in designing transmitting and receiving filters, the objective is to minimise the effect of ISI.

Typically, the channel transfer function $H_C(f)$ and pulse spectrum $G(f)$ are specified, and the problem is to determine $H_T(f)$ and $H_R(f)$, so as to enable the receiver to correctly decode the receiving sequence of sample values $y(t_i)$.

2.8 Nyquist Criterion for Distortion Less Baseband Binary Transmission

2.8.1 Ideal Solution

Control of ISI is achieved by controlling the function p(t), or in the frequency domain by controlling p(f).

One signal waveform that produces zero intersymbol interference is defined by sinc function.

$$p(t) = \frac{\sin(2\pi B_0 t)}{2\pi B_0 t} = \text{sinc}(2B_0 t) \qquad \ldots (2.43)$$

where, $B_0 = \dfrac{1}{2T_b}$ (Analogous with sampling theorem)

The parameter B_0 is called Nyquist BW, it is minimum transmission BW for zero ISI equal to half the bit rate.

$$P(f) = \begin{cases} \dfrac{1}{2B_0} & 0 \leq |f| \leq B_0 \\ 0 & |f| \geq B_0 \end{cases} \qquad \ldots (2.44)$$

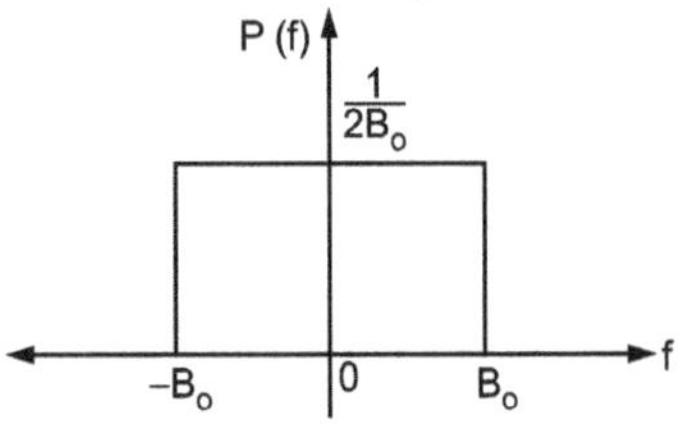

Fig. 2.27

Thus, function p(t) is impulse response of ideal LPF with amplitude response $\dfrac{1}{2B_0}$ in the passband and BW = B_0. The function p(t) has its peak value at its origin and goes to zero at every integer multiplies of bit duration T_b.

If y(t) is sampled at t = 0, ± T_b, ± $2T_b$ ... then the pulses defined by $A_i\, p(t - iT_b)$ will not interfere with each other.

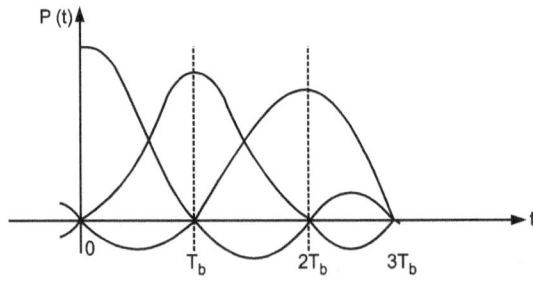

Fig. 2.28

Although ideal choice of pulse shape solved ISI problem there are two difficulties that make its design impractical.

(i) It requires that frequency response P(f) be flat from $-B_0$ to B_0 and resolution elsewhere. This is physically unrealizable and very difficult to approximate in practice.

(ii) The time function p (t) decreases as $1/|t|$ for large $|t|$ resulting in slow rate of decay. This is caused by discontinuity of P(f) at $\pm B_0$. Accordingly, there is practically no margin of error in sampling times in the receiver. i.e. P(t) decays only as $1/|t|$ and is zero in adjacent time slots only when t is at exactly at correct sampling time. Thus, inaccurate synchronisation will cause ISI.

To evaluate the effect of timing error, consider the sample y (t) at $t = \Delta t$. where, Δt is the timing error.

To simplify the analysis we put the correct sampling time $t_i = 0$. We obtain,

$$y(\Delta t) = \mu \sum_k A_k \, p(\Delta t - kT_b)$$

$$= \mu \sum_k A_k \, \text{sinc}[2B_0(\Delta t - kT_b)] \qquad \ldots (2.45)$$

Since $2B_0 T_b = 1$.

$$y(\Delta t) = \mu \sum_k A_k \, \text{sinc}(2B_0 \Delta t - k)$$

$$= \mu A_0 \, \text{sinc}(2B_0 t) + \mu \, \frac{\text{sinc}(2\pi B_0 \Delta t)}{\pi} \times \sum_{k \neq 0} \frac{(-1)^k A_k}{2B_0 \Delta t - k}$$

1st term – derived symbol.

Rest – ISI caused by timing error Δt in sampling y(t).

The practical difficulties of ideal solution can be overcome by extending bandwidth from B_0 to an adjustable value between B_0 and $2B_0$.

The solution is called Raised cosine spectrum.

2.8.2 Raised Cosine Waveform

In Raised cosine spectrum, the overall frequency response P(f) decreases towards zero gradually rather than abruptly.

$$P(f) = \begin{cases} \dfrac{1}{2B_0} & ; \ 0 \leq |f| < f_1 \\ \dfrac{1}{4B_0}\left[1 + \cos\left(\dfrac{\pi f}{2B_0}\right)\right] & ; \ f_1 \leq |f| \leq 2B_0 - f_1 \\ 0 & ; \ |f| \geq 2B_0 - f_1 \end{cases} \qquad \ldots (2.46)$$

The frequency f_1 and Nyquists BW B_0 are related by roll-off factor.

$$\alpha = 1 - \frac{f_1}{B_0}$$

For $\alpha = 0$, $f_1 = B_0$

The normalised plot is shown in Fig. 2.29 as follows.

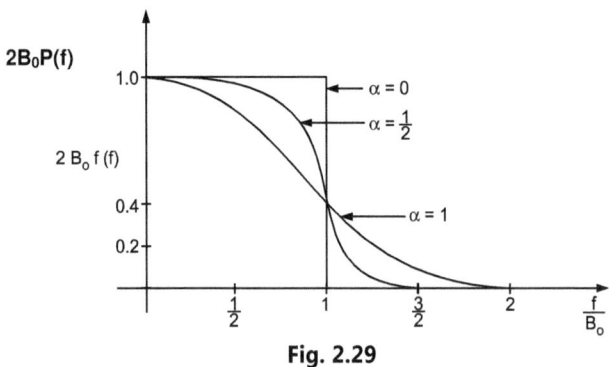

Fig. 2.29

The time response p(t) i.e. inverse Fourier transform of P(f) is,

$$p(t) = \text{sinc}(2B_0 t) \frac{\cos(2\pi\alpha B_0 t)}{1 - 16\alpha^2 B_0^2 t^2} \quad \ldots (2.47)$$

The time response p(t) has two parts :

(i) The first part sinc $(2B_0 t)$ is ideal Nyquist solution which ensures zero crossings at $t = iT_b$.

(ii) The second part decreases as $\frac{1}{|t|^2}$ for large t, which reduces the tails of pulse rapidly.

For special case $\alpha = 1$.

$$p(t) = \frac{\text{sinc}(2B_0 t)}{1 - 16 B_0^2 + t^2}$$

This time response has two interesting properties.

(i) At $t = \pm T_b/2 = \pm 1/4B_0$ we have p(t) = 0.5 i.e., the pulse width measured at half amplitude is = bit duration T_b.

(ii) There are two zero crossings at $t = \pm 3T_b/2, \pm 5T_b/2$ in addition to normal zero crossings at $t = \pm T_b, \pm 2T_b$.

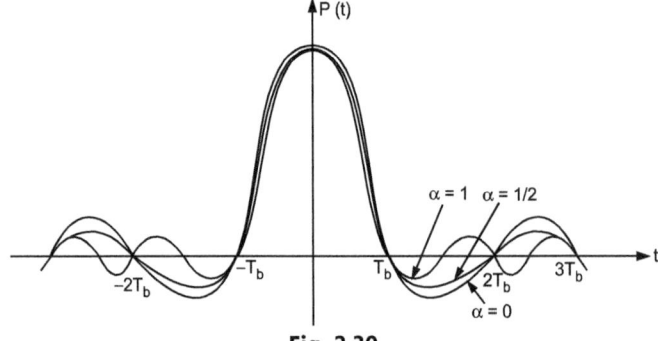

Fig. 2.30

Note that a value of α = 1, the response goes to zero, not only at zeros of $\frac{\sin(2\pi B_0 t)}{2\pi B_0 t}$. But also at midpoints between these samples.

It is therefore possible to sample at the same rate as for ideal channel; with no resulting ISI. We note in the next section that the price paid for this is increased bandwidth which is $2B_0$ in case of α = 1.

2.9 Eye Pattern

One way to study intersymbol interference in a PCM or data transmission system experimentally is to apply received wave to vertical deflection plates of an oscilloscope and a sawtooth wave at transmitted symbol rate 1/T to horizontal deflection plates.

The successive symbol intervals are thereby translated into one interval on oscilloscope display.

The effect of channel filtering and channel noise can be seen by observing the pattern.
The resulting display is called eye pattern because of its resemblance with human eye.
The Fig. 2.31 shows eye pattern for the three cases.

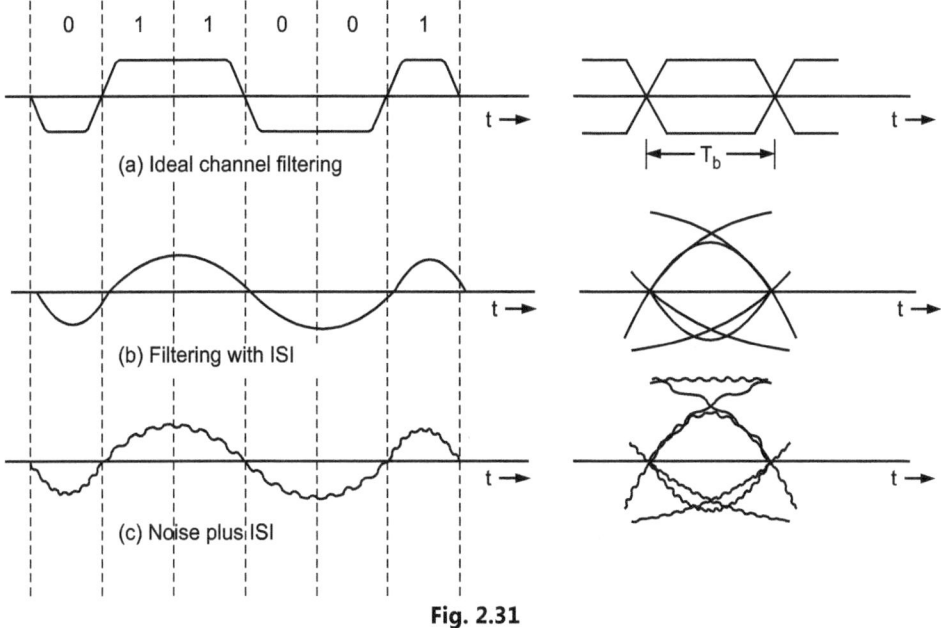

Fig. 2.31

Eye pattern gives information about –
1. The width of eye opening defines the time interval over which received wave can be sampled without error from ISI.
   Time for sampling – time at which is eye is open widest.

2. The sensitivity of the system to timing error is determined by rate of chosen of eye. [Slope of the open eye (evaluated near zero crossing point)].

3. Height of eye opening at specified sampling time, defines noise, margin.

4. Maximum distortion is given by the vertical width of the upper (or lower) portion of the eye at sampling time.

5. The range of amplitude differences (D_A) is a measure of distortion caused due to ISI.

6. The range of timing differences of zero crossings (J_T) is a measure of the timing jitter.

7. Measure of noise merging is M_N.

8. Sensitivity of timing error is S_T as shown in Fig. 2.32.

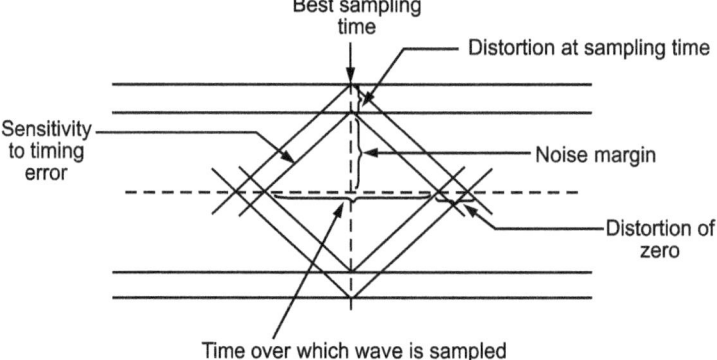

Fig. 2.32

For severe ISI upper portion of eye pattern cross the lower portion resulting in closure of eye.

EXERCISE

1. What is quantization noise. Derive the expression for signal-to-quantization noise power in PCM.

2. What is non-uniform quantizer ? Explain the process of companding in PCM.

3. Explain A-law and µ-law companding.

4. What is decoding noise in PCM. Derive the expression for decoding noise power in PCM.

5. Explain with suitable graph the performance of PCM with and without companding.

Unit III

DIGITAL MODULATION TECHNIQUES

3.1 Introduction

We have seen transmission of digital signal directly without any modulation (or frequency shift). This is called **baseband communication.**

Following points are worth notable related to baseband signals.

1. These signals have significant power spectrum at low frequency hence, they can be transmitted over twisted pair cables, coaxial cables and fibre optic cables.

2. They cannot be transmitted over a radio link or satellites because this would require large sized antennas to take care of low frequency spectrum.

3. They can be used only over a short distance.

Hence, for transmission of digital signals over long distance would require the spectrum of the signal to be shifted in high frequency region. This is called *bandpass modulation*. Thus, we have to modulate a carrier of frequency f_c using baseband digital signal. The amplitude, phase or frequency of the carrier can be varied in accordance with the baseband signal. The resulting signal is bandpass signal and this type of transmission is called **bandpass transmission.**

The bandpass modulation can also be used to separate different signals over single channel. When the amplitude of carrier is varied in accordance with baseband signal, it is called On-Off keying (OOK) or Amplitude Shift Keying (ASK) Fig. 3.1 (b). When the phase of carrier is varied in accordance with baseband signal, it is called Phase Shift Keying (PSK) Fig. 3.1 (c). When the frequency of carrier is varied in accordance with baseband signal, it is called Frequency Shift Keying (FSK) Fig. 3.1 (d).

In addition to these basic modulation schemes there are some modulation schemes that employ combination of amplitude and phase modulation. The details of these schemes are also discussed in this chapter.

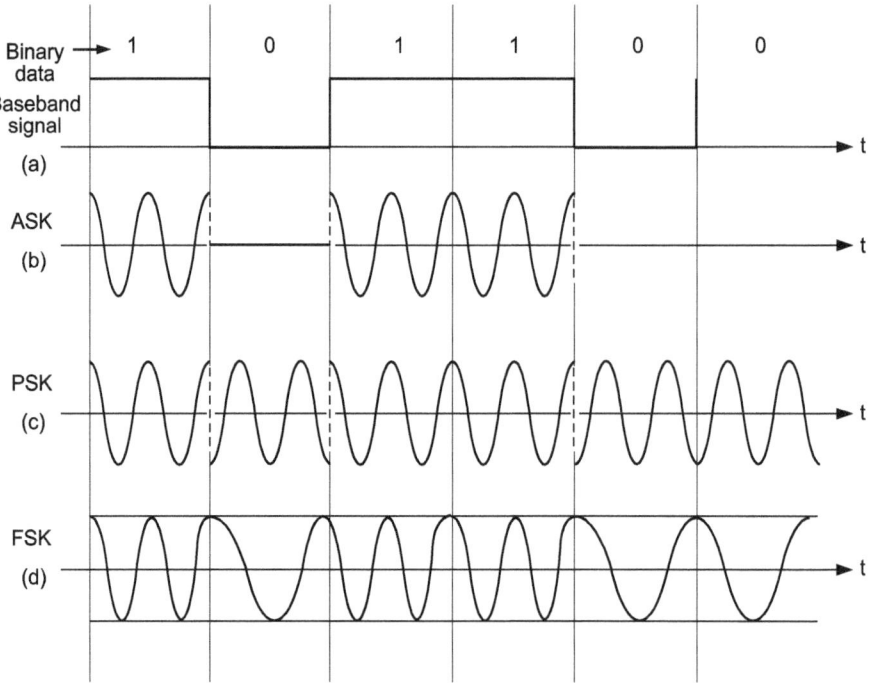

Fig. 3.1: Basic Digital Modulation Techniques ASK, PSK, FSK

In each of these modulation schemes we require a modulator at the transmitter and a demodulator at the receiver to recover the baseband signal. Hence, for full-duplex transmission we need modulator and demodulator at both ends. This combination of modulator and demodulator is called **MODEM.**

Ideally, PSK and FSK signals have a constant envelope as can be seen in Fig. 3.1. Due to this amplitude, non-linearities encountered in microwave and satellite links do not cause detection problems. Whereas, ASK performance is poor in such applications. Hence, ASK is not used much in practice.

The demodulation at the receiver can be done using two different methods.

1. Coherent detection.
2. Non-coherent detection.

In coherent detection, the local carrier generated at the receiver is in synchronization with the carrier at the transmitter. Thus, carrier at the receiver end is phase locked with the transmitter. Coherent detection is performed by correlating the received signal with locally generated carrier. This is also called **synchronous detection.** The modulation technique which employs coherent detection at the receiver is called coherent modulation technique.

In non-coherent detection, knowledge of carrier wave's phase is not required or receiver need not be phase locked with transmitter. Since we do not require the carrier to be recovered or correlated with received signal, the system becomes very simple. But the detection has poor quality i.e. error performance of the system degrades. This method is also called **envelope detection.** The modulation technique employing non-coherent detection is called non-coherent modulation.

A modulation scheme is classified as either a narrowband modulation or wideband modulation. For linear time invariant channel model with additive white Gaussian noise, if the transmission bandwidth of the carrier-modulated signal is small (< 10%) compared to carrier frequency, then it is called a narrowband modulation. For wideband modulation the bandwidth may be of the order of carrier frequency.

Modulation schemes for digital transmission system are also categorized as:
(i) Bandwidth efficient
(ii) Power efficient.

Bandwidth efficient schemes are able to accommodate more information (bits/sec.) per unit transmission bandwidth (Hz). Bandwidth efficient schemes are preferred in digital terrestrial microwave radios, satellite communication and cellular telephony. Power efficient schemes are able to transmit information reliably at low energy per information bit. Power efficient schemes are preferred in some cellular telephony systems and some spread spectrum systems (FHSS).

From the number of digital modulation schemes available for data transmission over a band-pass channel, which one to select ? The choice is made taking into account following design parameters.
(i) Minimum use of channel bandwidth.
(ii) High data rate should be supported between the end users.
(iii) Minimum error probability.
(iv) Minimum transmission power should be used.
(v) Maximum resistant to interfering signal and it should not cause interference beyond a limit.
(vi) Minimum circuit complexity and cost competitive.

Some of these requirements are conflicting. Hence, some trade offs are to be made by the designer.

3.2 Coherent Binary Modulation Techniques

These are modulation techniques which use coherent detection method. Let us see different techniques under this scheme.

3.2.1 Amplitude Shift Keying (ASK)

Amplitude shift keying is a simplest form of digital modulation in which amplitude of a carrier sinusoid is modified in a discrete manner depending on the value of modulating symbol.

In binary ASK the pair of signals used to represent 1 and 0 are defined as

$$S_1(t) = A_m \cos(2\pi f_c t) = \sqrt{2P_s} \cos(2\pi f_c t)$$

$$S_2(t) = \frac{A_m}{k} \cos(2\pi f_c t) = \frac{\sqrt{2P_s}}{k} \cos(2\pi f_c t)$$

where, k is a constant greater than 0.

We can also have the signals

$$S_1(t) = A_m \cos(2\pi f_c t) \quad \text{for binary 1}$$
$$S_2(t) = 0 \quad \text{for binary 0}$$

It is called on-off keying.

The signal constellation consists of two points in a straight lines located near to each other. Hence, the scheme is not immune to noise.

Bandwidth of ASK signal will be same as baseband signal. The baseband signal is long and random sequence of pulses and discrete values. Hence, ASK modulation is not bandwidth efficient.

It is implemented in practice when simplicity and low cost are principal requirements.

An OOK modulator can be implemented as a simple switch or double balanced modulator as shown in Fig. 3.2 below.

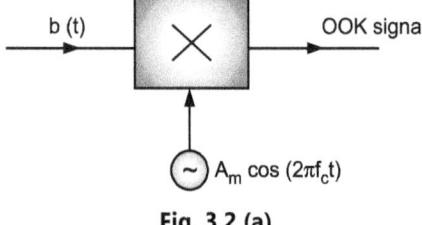

Fig. 3.2 (a)

The modulated signal has PSD as shown in Fig. 3.2 (b) below.

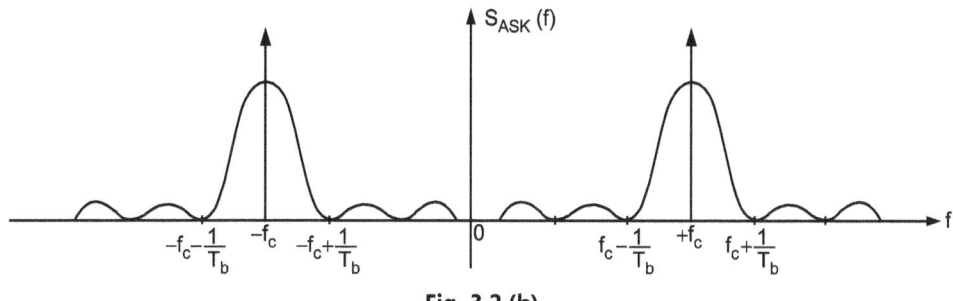

Fig. 3.2 (b)

The receiver of OOK system is shown in Fig. 3.2 (c) below.

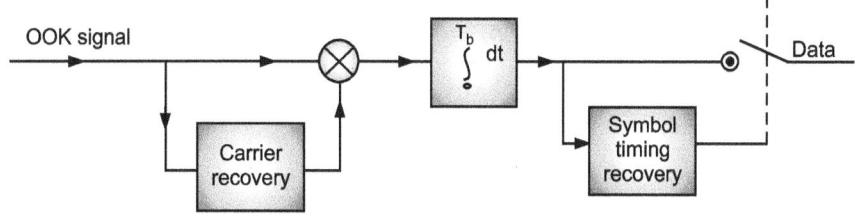

Fig. 3.2 (c)

3.2.2 Coherent Binary PSK (BPSK)

In Binary Phase Shift Keying System, the pair of time limited signals, $S_1(t)$ and $S_2(t)$ are used to represent 1 and 0. These signals are defined as,

$$S_1(t) = \sqrt{2P_s} \cos(2\pi f_c t) \qquad \ldots (3.1)$$

$$S_2(t) = \sqrt{2P_s} \cos(2\pi f_c t + \pi) \qquad \ldots (3.2)$$

where, P_s is signal power given by,

$$P_s = \frac{A^2}{2} \qquad \text{(A being amplitude of signal i.e. } A = \sqrt{2P_s})$$

Thus, when data is 1, the signal will have a fixed phase and when data is 0, it will have phase difference of 180° w.r.t. first signal.

Air narrowband transmission, $f_c >> \frac{1}{T_b}$. That is there will be multiple cycles of carrier sinusoid within one bit duration (T_b).

Generation of BPSK:

We have to generate two signals $S_1(t)$ and $S_2(t)$ given in equations (3.1) and (3.2) corresponding to 1 and 0.

Now,
$$S_1(t) = \sqrt{2P_s} \cos(2\pi f_c t) \quad \ldots (3.3)$$
$$S_2(t) = \sqrt{2P_s} \cos(2\pi f_c t + \pi)$$
$$= -\sqrt{2P_s} \cos(2 f_c t) \quad \ldots (3.4)$$

Now, we can write $S_1(t)$ and $S_2(t)$ as,
$$S(t) = b(t) \times \sqrt{2P_s} \cos(2\pi f_c t) \quad \ldots (3.5)$$

where, $b(t) = +1$ when binary 1 is transmitted
$= -1$ when binary 0 is transmitted

Above equation suggests that BPSK signal can be generated by applying baseband signal in NRZ polar format and carrier signal to a balanced modulator (Product Modulator). Fig. 3.3 (a) shows the block diagram of BPSK generator.

A commonly available balanced modulator (IC 1496) may be used as product modulator to actually generate modulated signal.

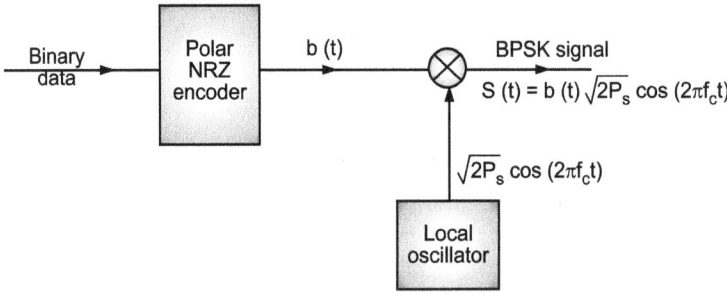

Fig. 3.3: (a) BPSK Generation

Reception of BPSK:

The BPSK signal is given by,
$$S(t) = b(t) \sqrt{2P_s} \cos(2\pi f_c t)$$

The BPSK signal when transmitted through a channel, undergoes a phase change depending on propagation delay between transmitter and receiver. Hence, the received signal, without considering effect of noise can be written as,
$$r(t) = b(t) \sqrt{2P_s} \cos(2\pi f_c t + \phi) \quad \ldots (3.6)$$

where, ϕ is fixed phase shift corresponding to propagation delay $\phi/2\pi f_c$.

Since, we are using coherent detection, we have to generate carrier from the received signal. The demodulator for recovering the baseband signal is shown in Fig. 3.3 (b).

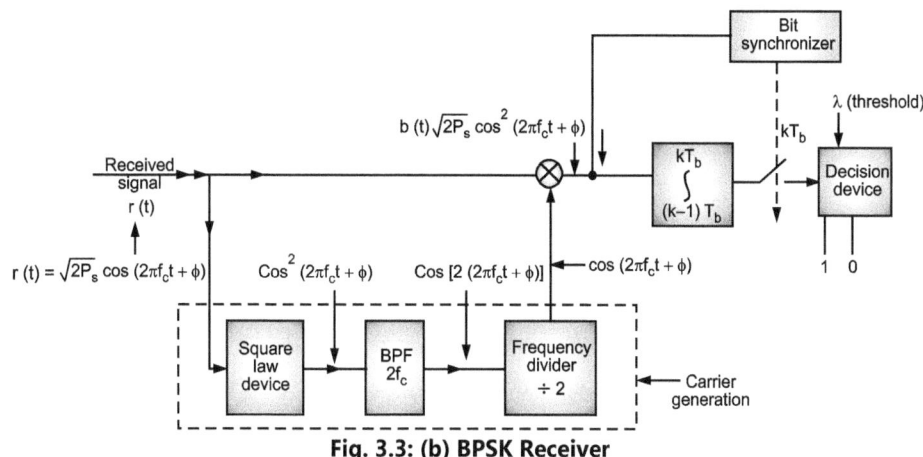

Fig. 3.3: (b) BPSK Receiver

The carrier generator part consists of square law device whose output will be,

$$\cos^2(2\pi f_c t + \phi) = \frac{1}{2} + \frac{1}{2}\cos[2(2\pi f_c t + \phi)]$$

This is passed through a bandpass filter which eliminates the dc component $+\frac{1}{2}$. Hence, we get at the output of BPF,

$$\cos[2(2\pi f_c t + \phi)]$$

This signal is given to frequency divider hence the output will be,

$$\cos(2\pi f_c t + \phi)$$

which is nothing but carrier shifted by phase ϕ.

The synchronous demodulator (multiplier shown in diagram) multiplies carrier signal with received signal r(t). The output of multiplier will be,

$$\begin{aligned}
r(t) &= b(t)\sqrt{2P_s}\cos(2\pi f_c t + \phi) \times \cos(2\pi f_c t + \phi) \\
&= b(t)\sqrt{2P_s}\cos^2(2\pi f_c t + \phi) \\
&= b(t)\sqrt{2P_s} \times \frac{1}{2}[1 + \cos[2(2\pi f_c t + \phi)]] \\
&= b(t)\sqrt{\frac{P_s}{2}}[1 + \cos[2(2\pi f_c t + \phi)]]
\end{aligned}$$

This signal is applied to an integrator and bit synchronizer. The integrator integrates the signal over one bit period. The timing (one bit period) is provided by bit synchronizer. At the end of one bit period output of integrator is sampled. e.g. in k^{th} bit interval the output of integrator will be,

$$S_0(kT_b) = b(kT_b)\sqrt{\frac{P_s}{2}} \int_{(k-1)T_b}^{kT_b} [1 + \cos[2(2\pi f_c t + \phi)]]\, dt$$

$$= b(kT_b)\sqrt{\frac{P_s}{2}} \int_{(k-1)T_b}^{kT_b} 1\, dt + \int_{(k-1)T_b}^{kT_b} \cos[2(2\pi f_c t + \phi)]\, dt$$

$$= b(kT_b)\sqrt{\frac{P_s}{2}} [t]_{(k-1)T_b}^{kT_b} + 0$$

$$= b(kT_b)\sqrt{\frac{P_s}{2}} \times T_b$$

$$= \sqrt{\frac{P_s}{2}} \times T_b \times b(kT_b) \qquad \ldots (3.7)$$

Thus, sampled output of integrator is proportional to $b(kT_b)$.

This signal is given to a decision device to decide whether one was transmitted or zero, by comparing it with some threshold value.

e.g. if 1 is transmitted the detector output will be $\sqrt{\frac{P_s}{2}} T_b$ and if 0 is transmitted detector output will be $-\sqrt{\frac{P_s}{2}} T_b$. Hence by setting threshold at 0, we can detect correctly transmitted bit.

Spectrum of BPSK:

The BPSK signal is given by,

$$S(t) = b(t)\sqrt{2P_s} \cos(2\pi f_c t)$$
$$= \sqrt{P_s}\, b(t) \times \sqrt{2} \cos(2\pi f_c t)$$

Here, $\sqrt{P_s}\, b(t)$ is NRZ polar waveform whose amplitude varies from $+\sqrt{P_s}$ to $-\sqrt{P_s}$. Hence, PSD of this signal is given by,

$$S_b(f) = P_s T_b \sin c^2(fT_b)$$

Since NRZ waveform is multiplied by $\sqrt{2} \cos(2\pi f_c t)$, using the frequency shifting property, i.e. $g(t) e^{j2\pi f_c t} \rightleftharpoons G(f - f_c)$ we can write PSD of BPSK waveform as,

$$S_{BPSK}(f) = \frac{P_s T_b}{2} \left[\text{sinc}^2[(f - f_c)T_b] + \text{sinc}^2[(f + f_c)T_b] \right] \qquad \ldots (3.8)$$

This PSD is plotted in Fig. 3.4 (a).

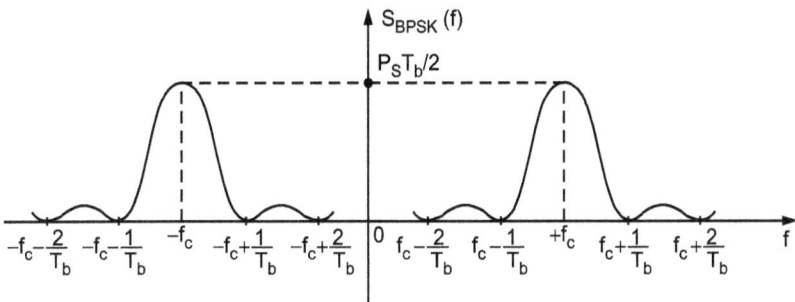

Fig. 3.4: (a) PSD of BPSK Signal

It is seen from the spectrum that it extends over wide frequency band. If we multiplex BPSK signals using different carrier frequencies, there would be overlap in spectra. This overlapping causes interchannel interference. To avoid this, we can keep the side lobes below specified levels. One way of doing this is to pass the NRZ baseband signal through a LPF to supress all side lobes. But then this spreads the signal in time giving rise to Intersymbol Interference (ISI). Equalizers are required to reduce ISI.

Geometrical Representation of BPSK:

The BPSK signal is given by,
$$S(t) = b(t)\sqrt{2P_s} \cos(2\pi f_c t)$$

We have two signals,
$$S_1(t) = +\sqrt{2P_s} \cos(2\pi f_c t)$$
$$= +\sqrt{P_s T_b} \times \sqrt{\frac{2}{T_b}} \cos(2\pi f_c t) \qquad \ldots (3.9)$$

$$S_2(t) = -\sqrt{2P_s} \cos(2\pi f_c t)$$
$$= -\sqrt{P_s T_b} \times \sqrt{\frac{2}{T_b}} \cos(2\pi f_c t) \qquad \ldots (3.10)$$

From equations (3.9) and (3.10), we can select a function
$$\phi_1(t) = \sqrt{\frac{2}{T_b}} \cos(2\pi f_c t) \qquad \ldots (3.11)$$

as basis function.

Hence,
$$S_1(t) = \sqrt{P_s T_b}\, \phi_1(t) \qquad 0 \le t \le T_b \qquad \ldots (3.12)$$
$$S_2(t) = -\sqrt{P_s T_b}\, \phi_1(t) \qquad 0 \le t \le T_b \qquad \ldots (3.13)$$

Here, $P_s \times T_b = E_b$, the energy per bit duration.

The two associated scalars are

$$S_{11}(t) = \int_0^{T_b} S_1(t)\,\phi_1(t)\,dt = +\sqrt{P_s T_b} = +\sqrt{E_b}$$

$$S_{21}(t) = \int_0^{T_b} S_2(t)\,\phi_2(t)\,dt = -\sqrt{P_s T_b} = -\sqrt{E_b}$$

Hence, the signal space of BPSK is one dimensional and with two message points plotted as shown in Fig. 3.4 (b).

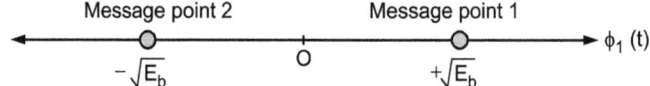

Fig. 3.4: (b) Signal Space Diagram for BPSK

The two points are equidistant from origin, signifying that the two signals carry same energy.

Bandwidth of BPSK:

From the power spectrum of BPSK plotted in Fig. 3.3, it can be seen that the null-to-null bandwidth of BPSK is,

$$\begin{aligned}
BW &= \left(f_c + \frac{1}{T_b}\right) - \left(f_c - \frac{1}{T_b}\right) \\
&= f_c + \frac{1}{T_b} - f_c + \frac{1}{T_b} \\
&= \frac{2}{T_b} \\
&= 2f_b
\end{aligned}$$

Thus, bandwidth of BPSK is twice the bit rate.

Disadvantages of BPSK:

1. Coherent detection of BPSK requires both phase and timing synchronization. Hence, the design of receiver becomes complicated.
2. We cannot use non-coherent detection for BPSK because envelope of PSK is same for both 1 and 0. The solution to this is Differential Phase Shift Keying Method which will be discussed in Section 3.3.2.

3.2.3 Coherent Binary FSK

Frequency shift keying is used in a low-cost applications for transmitting data at moderate or low rate over wired as well as wireless channels. In this modulation technique frequency of carrier is changed according to the baseband signal b(t). Since, there are two symbols to be transmitted, two different frequency sinusoidal signals are used as follows.

- **For Binary 1:**
$$S_H(t) = \sqrt{2P_s} \cos[2\pi (f_c + f_1) t] \quad \ldots (3.14)$$

- **For Binary 0:**
$$S_L(t) = \sqrt{2P_s} \cos[2\pi (f_c - f_1) t] \quad \ldots (3.15)$$

In general, we can write the FSK signal as,
$$S(t) = \sqrt{2P_s} \cos[2\pi (f_c + b(t) f_1) t] \quad \ldots (3.16)$$

where, $\quad b(t) = +1 \quad$ for Binary 1
$\quad\quad\quad\ b(t) = -1 \quad$ for Binary 0

Thus, we have two carrier frequencies transmitted for the two symbols as,

$f_H = f_c + f_1 \quad$ for Binary 1
$f_L = f_c - f_1 \quad$ for Binary 0

where, f_H is called mark frequency and f_L is called space frequency.

The two frequencies are selected such that they are integer multiples of bit rate $1/T_b$.

Generation of BFSK:

We need to generate two signals as,
$$S_H(t) = \sqrt{2P_s} \cos(2\pi f_H t) \quad \ldots (3.17)$$
$$= \sqrt{P_s T_b} \times \sqrt{\frac{2}{T_b}} \cos(2\pi f_H t)$$
$$S_L(t) = \sqrt{2P_s} \cos(2\pi f_L t) \quad \ldots (3.18)$$
$$= \sqrt{P_s T_b} \times \sqrt{\frac{2}{T_b}} \cos(2\pi f_L t)$$

Above equations suggest we need two carriers of frequency $f_H = f_c + f_1$ and $f_c - f_1$ to be generated. The block diagram of FSK receiver is shown in Fig. 3.5 (a).

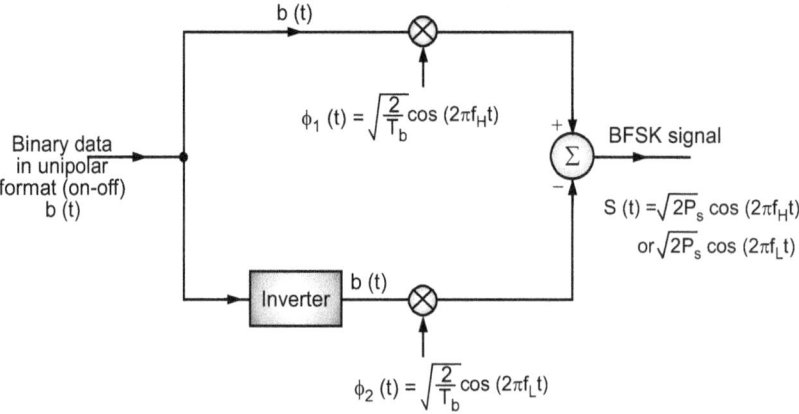

Fig. 3.5: (a) Generation of BFSK Coherent

The binary signal to be modulated has unipolar format and has amplitude $+\sqrt{P_s T_b}$ volt, for symbol 1 and zero volt for symbol 0.

When Binary 1 is transmitted the signal in upper branch will be,

$$\sqrt{P_s T_b} \times \sqrt{\frac{2}{T_b}} \cos(2\pi f_H t)$$

Signal in lower branch will be,

$$0 \times \sqrt{\frac{2}{T_b}} \cos(2\pi f_L t) = 0$$

Hence, the output BFSK signal will be,

$$S_H(t) = \sqrt{2P_s} \cos 2\pi f_H t$$

When Binary 0 is transmitted the signal in upper branch will be,

$$0 \times \sqrt{\frac{2}{T_b}} \cos 2\pi f_H t$$

Signal in lower branch will be,

$$\sqrt{P_s \times T_b} \times \sqrt{\frac{2}{T_b}} \cos(2\pi f_L t)$$

Hence, output BFSK signal will be,

$$S_H(t) = \sqrt{2P_s} \cos(2\pi f_L t)$$

Reception of BFSK:

The block diagram of BFSK receiver is shown in Fig. 3.5 (b).

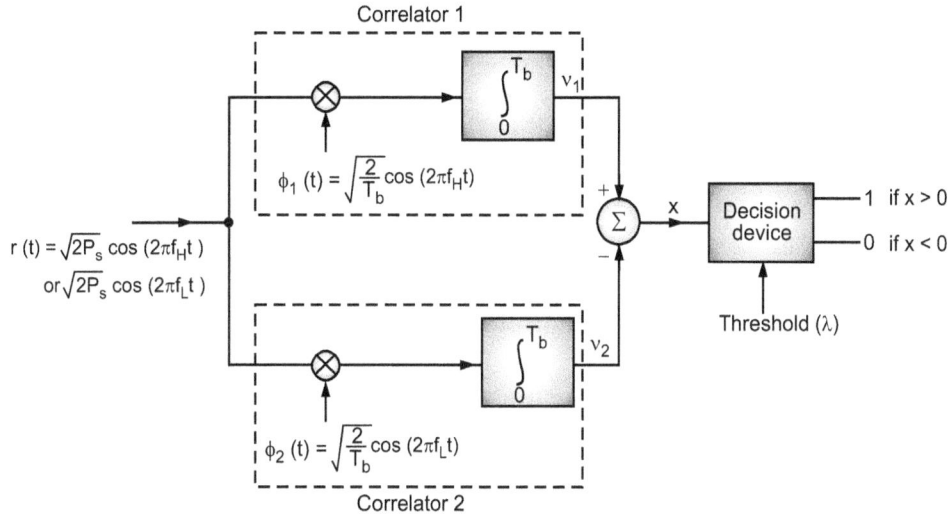

Fig. 3.5: (b) Reception of Coherent BFSK

It consists of two multipliers and integerators (correlators) which are supplied with common received input and locally generated coherent reference signals $\phi_1(t) = \sqrt{\frac{2}{T_b}} \cos(2\pi f_H t)$ and $\phi_2(t) = \sqrt{\frac{2}{T_b}} \cos(2\pi f_L t)$. The output of two correlators are subtracted and the difference is compared with same preset threshold by decision device to decide in favour of 1 or 0.

When signal $S_H(t) = \sqrt{2P_s} \cos(2\pi f_H t)$ is received (corresponding to binary 1) it will have maximum correlation with $\phi_1(t)$. Hence, output v_1 will be more than v_2 making the difference positive and decision device will make decision in favour of 1. When signal $S_L(t) = \sqrt{2P_s} \cos(2\pi f_L t)$ is received (corresponding to binary 0) it will have maximum correlation with $\phi_2(t)$. Hence, output v_2 will be more than v_1, making the difference negative and decision device will make decision in favour of 0.

Spectrum of BFSK:

The BFSK signal consists of two signals.

$$S_H(t) = \sqrt{2P_s} \cos(2\pi f_H t) \quad \text{for Binary 1}$$
$$S_L(t) = \sqrt{2P_s} \cos(2\pi f_L t) \quad \text{for Binary 0}$$

Hence, combined BFSK signal can be written as,

$$S(t) = \sqrt{2P_s} \times b_H(t) \cos(2\pi f_H t) + \sqrt{2P_s}\, b_L(t) \cos(2\pi f_L t)$$

Hence, when 1 is transmitted,
$$b_H(t) = 1,\ b_L(t) = 0$$
When 0 is transmitted,
$$b_H(t) = 0,\ b_L(t) = 1$$

Let us convert these coefficients $b_H(t)$ and $b_L(t)$ in polar format.

Hence, $\quad b_H(t) = \dfrac{1}{2} + \dfrac{1}{2} b_H'(t) \quad$ where, $\quad b_H'(t) = +1/-1$

$\quad b_L(t) = \dfrac{1}{2} + \dfrac{1}{2} b_L'(t) \quad$ where, $\quad b_L'(t) = -1/+1$

$\therefore \quad S(t) = \sqrt{2P_s}\left[\dfrac{1}{2} + \dfrac{1}{2} b_H'(t)\right] \cos(2\pi f_H t) \qquad \ldots (3.19)$

$\qquad + \sqrt{2P_s}\left[\dfrac{1}{2} + \dfrac{1}{2} b_L'(t)\right] \cos(2\pi f_L t) \qquad \ldots (3.20)$

$\therefore \quad S(t) = \sqrt{\dfrac{P_s}{2}} \cos(2\pi f_H t) + \sqrt{\dfrac{P_s}{2}} \cos(2\pi f_L t)$

$\qquad + \sqrt{\dfrac{P_s}{2}}\, b_H'(t) \cos 2\pi f_H(t) + \sqrt{\dfrac{P_s}{2}}\, b_L'(t) \cos(2\pi f_L t) \qquad \ldots (3.21)$

In above equation, first term and second term represent impulses at f_H and f_L respectively. The last two terms resemble with BPSK equation ($b(t) \sqrt{2P_s} \cos 2\pi f_c t$). Hence, spectrum of BFSK signal will be,

$$S_{BFSK}(f) = \sqrt{\dfrac{P_s}{2}}\{\delta(f - f_H) + \delta(f + f_L) + T_b\, \text{sinc}^2[(f - f_H) T_b] + T_b\, \text{sinc}^2[(f - f_L) T_b]\}$$

This PSD is plotted as shown in Fig. 3.6.

Assuming $\qquad f_H - f_L = \dfrac{2}{T_b} = 2 f_b$

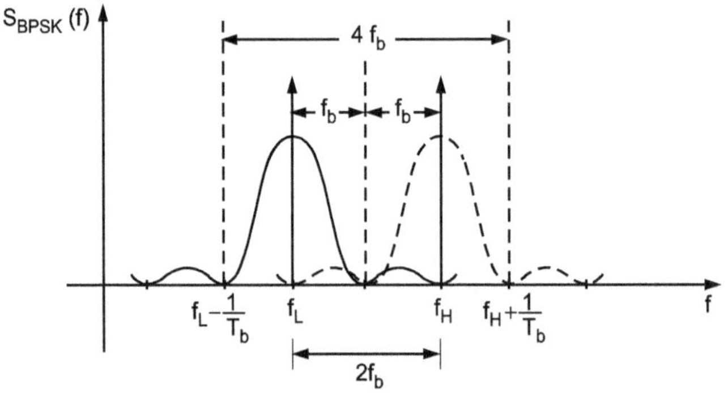

Fig. 3.6: Power Spectrum of BFSK

Bandwidth of BFSK:

As seen from the spectrum the total bandwidth is given by,

$$BW = \left(f_H + \frac{1}{T_b}\right) - \left(f_L - \frac{1}{T_b}\right)$$

$$BW = (f_H - f_L) + \frac{2}{T_b} = f_H - f_L + 2f_b \quad \ldots (3.22)$$

For the case, $\quad f_H - f_L = 2f_b$

See that this is the minimum separation we should have between f_H and f_L

$$BW = 2f_b + 2f_b$$
$$= 4f_b$$

Thus, bandwidth of BFSK is twice the BPSK.

Geometrical Representation of BFSK:

We have two sinusoidal waves representing BFSK as,

$$S_H(t) = \sqrt{2P_s} \cos(2\pi f_H t) \quad 0 \leq t < T_b$$
$$S_L(t) = \sqrt{2P_s} \cos(2\pi f_L t) \quad 0 \leq t \leq T_b$$

where, f_H and f_L are selected such that they are integer multiples of $f_b = \frac{1}{T_b}$. i.e. there are integer number of cycles in one bit duration in both cases.

Hence, they are orthogonal functions.

Hence, these functions can be selected as basis functions for representing these signals geometrically. We need to make them orthonormal i.e. having unit energy.

Hence, the two basis functions are –

$$\phi_1(t) = \sqrt{\frac{2}{T_b}} \cos(2\pi f_H t) \quad 0 \leq t \leq T_b$$

$$\phi_2(t) = \sqrt{\frac{2}{T_b}} \cos(2\pi f_L t) \quad 0 \leq t \leq T_b \quad \ldots (3.23)$$

$$\therefore \quad S_H(t) = \sqrt{P_s T_b} \, \phi_1(t)$$
$$\text{and} \quad S_L(t) = \sqrt{P_s T_b} \, \phi_2(t) \quad \ldots (3.24)$$

- The signal space representation of these signals is given in Fig. 3.7 (a).

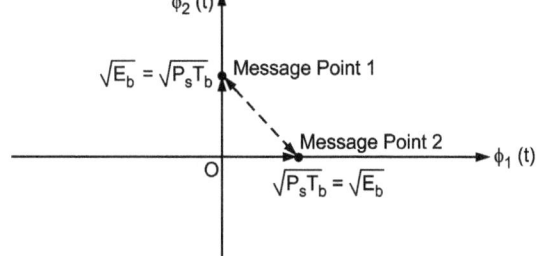

Fig. 3.7 (a): Signal Space Diagram for BFSK

When $\phi_1(t)$ and $\phi_2(t)$ are non-orthogonal, then the signal points $S_H(t)$ and $S_L(t)$ would not lie on the same axes $\phi_1(t)$ and $\phi_2(t)$. The representation for this case is shown in Fig. 3.7 (b).

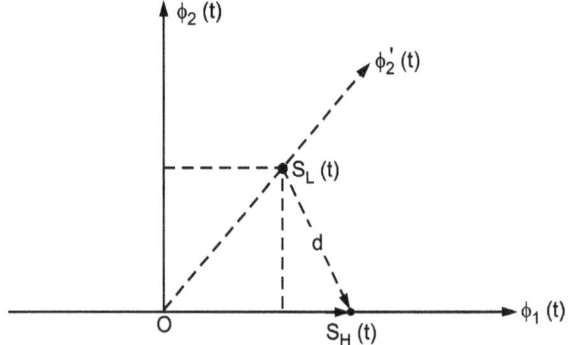

Fig. 3.7: (b) Signal Space for BFSK for Non-orthogonal Basis Function

3.3 Coherent Binary Modulation Techniques

3.3.1 Quadrature Phase Shift Keying

- This modulation scheme is expanded version of BPSK.
- It is a bandwidth conserving modulation scheme for transmission of digital data.
- It is an example of quadrature-carrier multiplexing system.
- The information carried by the signal is contained in phase.
- The phase of carrier is changed in four ways.
- Two successive bits are combined to form four distinct levels or symbols.
- When the level is changed, the phase of carrier is changed by $\pi/4$ radians (45°). Thus, the QPSK signal can be represented as,

$$S_i(t) = \begin{cases} \sqrt{2P} \cos\left[2\pi f_c t + (2i-1)\dfrac{\pi}{4}\right] & ; \quad 0 \le t \le T \\ 0 & ; \quad \text{otherwise} \end{cases} \quad \ldots (3.25)$$

where,   i = 1, 2, 3, 4
and   T is symbol duration = $2T_b$
       P is average power of symbol.

$$f_c = n \times \dfrac{1}{T} = n\dfrac{1}{2T_b} \text{ is carrier frequency}$$

- Thus, the four waveforms are –

$$S_1(t) = \sqrt{2P} \cos\left(2\pi f_c t + \dfrac{\pi}{4}\right)$$

$$S_2(t) = \sqrt{2P} \cos\left(2\pi f_c t + \dfrac{3\pi}{4}\right)$$

$$S_3(t) = \sqrt{2P} \cos\left(2\pi f_c t + \frac{5\pi}{4}\right)$$

$$S_4(t) = \sqrt{2P} \cos\left(2\pi f_c t + \frac{7\pi}{4}\right) \quad \ldots (3.26)$$

Equation (3.25) can also be written as,

$$S_i(t) = \sqrt{2P} \cos(2i-1)\frac{\pi}{4} \cos(2\pi f_c t)$$

$$\quad - \sqrt{2P} \sin(2i-1)\frac{\pi}{4} \sin(2\pi f_c t) \qquad 0 \le t \le T$$

$$= 0 \qquad \text{otherwise} \quad \ldots (3.27)$$

Thus,
$$S_1(t) = +\sqrt{2P} \cos(2\pi f_c t) - \sqrt{2P} \sin(2\pi f_c t)$$
$$S_2(t) = -\sqrt{2P} \cos(2\pi f_c t) - \sqrt{2P} \sin(2\pi f_c t)$$
$$S_3(t) = -\sqrt{2P} \cos(2\pi f_c t) + \sqrt{2P} \sin(2\pi f_c t)$$
$$S_4(t) = +\sqrt{2P} \cos(2\pi f_c t) + \sqrt{2P} \sin(2\pi f_c t) \quad \ldots (3.28)$$

Generation of QPSK:

Above equation (3.28) suggest the scheme of generation of QPSK signals.

We can use two carriers which will be multiplied with input bits converted into polar formats. The block diagram is shown in Fig. 3.8 (a).

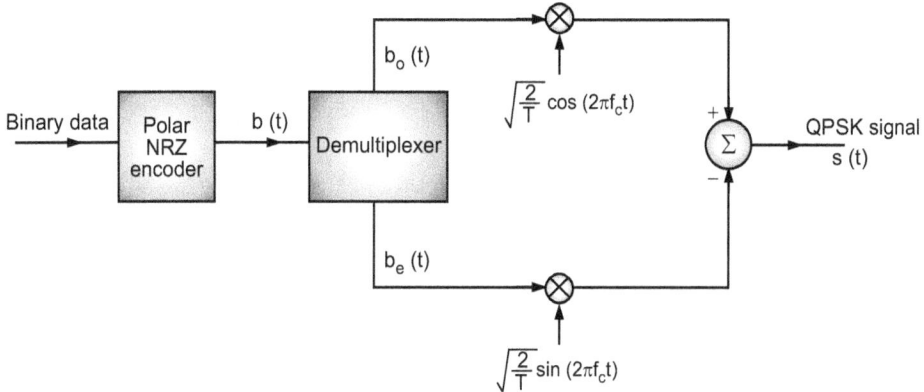

Fig. 3.8: (a) Generation of QPSK

The incoming binary wave in polar format is divided into two separate binary waves consisting of odd numbered and even numbered bits by means of a demultiplexer.

Let us call these binary waves as $b_o(t)$ and $b_e(t)$.

Thus, $b_o(t)$ and $b_e(t)$ can be $+\sqrt{\frac{P \times T}{2}}$ or $-\sqrt{\frac{P \times T}{2}}$ depending on input bit stream.

e.g. if first two input bits are 1 and 0,

$$b_o(t) = +\sqrt{\frac{PT}{2}} \quad \text{and} \quad b_e(t) = -\sqrt{\frac{PT}{2}}$$

$$= +\sqrt{\frac{E}{2}} \quad\quad\quad\quad = -\sqrt{\frac{E}{2}}$$

where, E is energy per symbol duration (T).

Following table shows all four combinations of $b_o(t)$ and $b_e(t)$.

Signal $S_i(t)$	Inputs Bits		Phase of QPSK	$b_o(t)$	$b_e(t)$
$S_1(t)$	1	0	$\pi/4$	$+\sqrt{\frac{PT}{2}}$	$-\sqrt{\frac{PT}{2}}$
$S_2(t)$	0	0	$3\pi/4$	$-\sqrt{\frac{PT}{2}}$	$-\sqrt{\frac{PT}{2}}$
$S_3(t)$	0	1	$5\pi/4$	$-\sqrt{\frac{PT}{2}}$	$+\sqrt{\frac{PT}{2}}$
$S_4(t)$	1	1	$7\pi/4$	$+\sqrt{\frac{PT}{2}}$	$+\sqrt{\frac{PT}{2}}$

The odd numbered waveform is multiplied with carrier $\sqrt{\frac{2}{T}} \cos(2\pi f_c t)$ and even number carrier is multiplied with $\sqrt{\frac{2}{T}} \sin(2\pi f_c t)$.

These two are then added to generate QPSK waveform.

e.g. if input bits are 1 and 0, the waveform generated will be –

$$S_o(t) = +\sqrt{\frac{PT}{2}} \times \sqrt{\frac{2}{T}} \cos(2\pi f_c t) - \sqrt{\frac{PT}{2}} \times \sqrt{\frac{2}{T}} \sin(2\pi f_c t)$$

$$= \sqrt{PT} \cos(2\pi f_c t) - \sqrt{PT} \sin(2\pi f_c t)$$

This is same as $S_1(t)$. Similarly, other signals $S_2(t)$, $S_3(t)$ and $S_4(t)$ are generated.

The BPSK waveforms are shown in figure for an input bit pattern 10011100 in Fig. 3.8 (b).

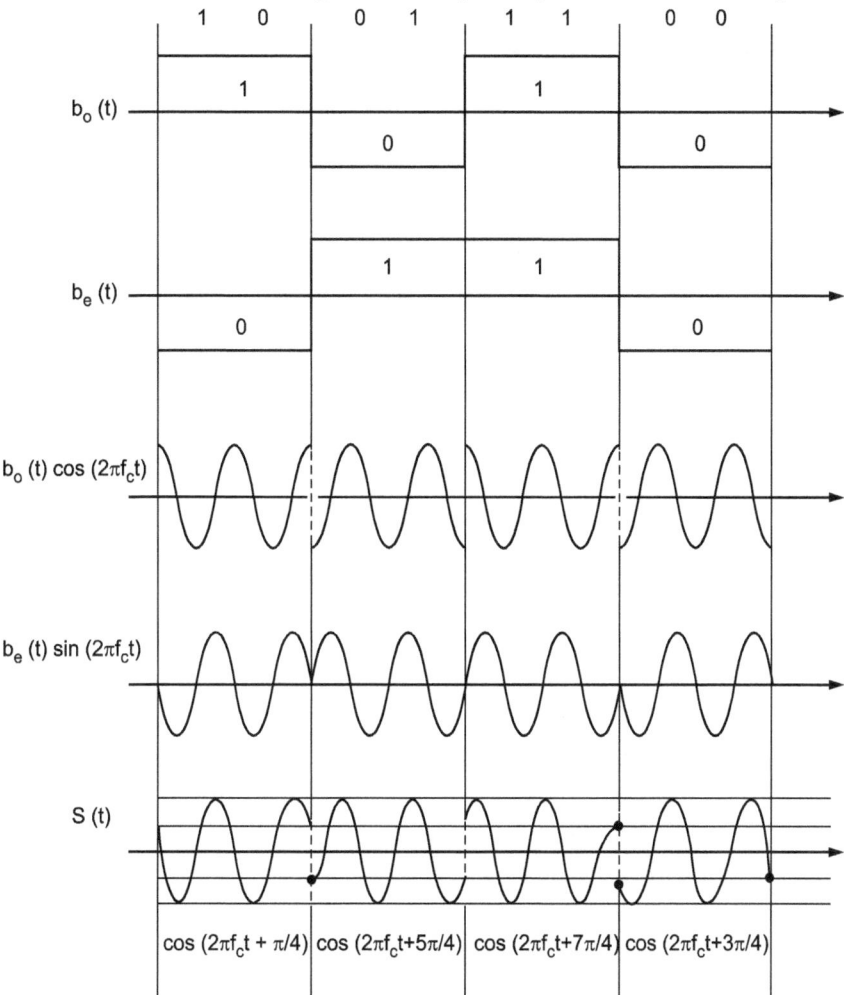

Fig. 3.8: (b) QPSK Waveforms

Reception of QPSK:

The QPSK receiver is shown in Fig. 3.8 (c).

It consists of a pair of correlators with a common input r(t) and locally generated carriers $\sqrt{\frac{2}{T}} \cos(2\pi f_c t)$ and $\sqrt{\frac{2}{T}} \sin(2\pi f_c t)$.

The output of correlators (multiplier and integrator) v_1 and v_2 are compared with a threshold voltage (zero volt).

If the output is positive, decision is made in favour of 1 and if output is negative, decision is made in favour of 0. These two bits from the two correlators are combined in a multiplexer to reproduce original binary sequence.

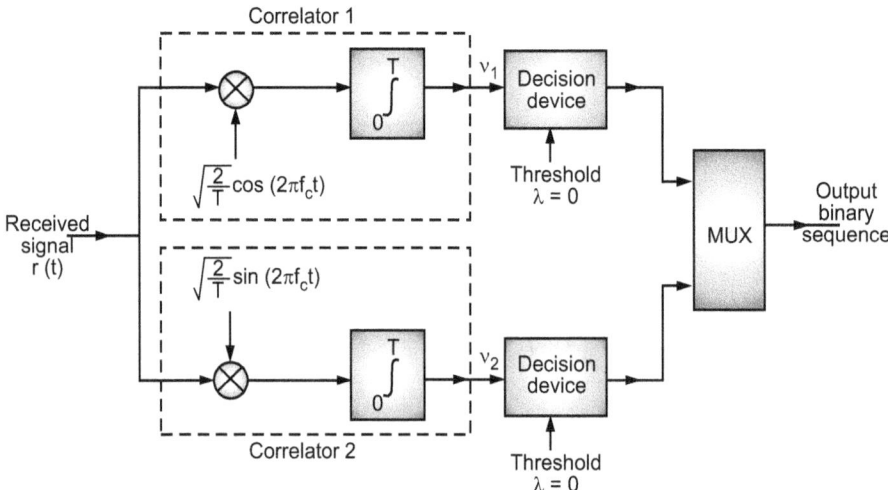

Fig. 3.8: (c) QPSK Receiver

Spectrum of QPSK:

The QPSK signal is represented as,

$$S_i(t) = \sqrt{2P} \cos(2\pi f_c t + \phi_i) \quad ; \quad 0 \leq t \leq T$$
$$= 0 \quad ; \quad \text{otherwise}$$

where, $\quad \phi_i = (2i - 1) \times \dfrac{\pi}{4}$

and $\quad i = 1, 2, 3, 4$

$$S_i(t) = \left(\sqrt{2P} \cos \phi_i\right) \cdot \cos 2\pi f_c t$$
$$\quad - \left(\sqrt{2P} \sin \phi_i\right) \sin 2\pi f_c t \quad ; \quad 0 \leq t \leq T$$
$$= 0 \quad ; \quad \text{otherwise}$$
$$= \sqrt{2P} \cos \phi_i \, \text{rect}\left(\dfrac{t}{T}\right) \cos(2\pi f_c t) \quad \ldots (3.29)$$
$$\quad - \sqrt{2P} \sin \phi_i \, \text{rect}\left(\dfrac{t}{T}\right) \sin(2\pi f_c t) \quad \ldots (3.30)$$

Hence, PSD of above signal will be obtained by finding PSD of,

$$g_1(t) = \sqrt{2P} \cos \phi_i \, \text{rect}\left(\dfrac{t}{T}\right)$$

$$g_2(t) = \sqrt{2P} \sin \phi_i \, \text{rect}\left(\frac{t}{T}\right) \qquad \ldots (3.31)$$

But $\cos \phi$ and $\sin \phi$ are random processes assuming any four possible values.

$$S_{g_1}(f) = \text{PSD of } g_1(t) = \frac{\overline{|G_1(f)|^2}}{T}$$

$$= 2PT \, \overline{\cos^2 \phi_i} \, \text{sinc}^2(fT) \qquad \ldots (3.32)$$

$$S_{g_2}(f) = \text{PSD of } g_2(t) = \frac{\overline{|G_2(f)|^2}}{T}$$

$$= 2PT \, \overline{\sin^2 \phi_i} \, \text{sinc}^2(fT) \qquad \ldots (3.33)$$

But $\quad \overline{\sin^2 \phi_i} = \overline{\cos^2 \phi_i} = \dfrac{1}{2}$

$$\therefore \quad S_{g_1}(f) = S_{g_2}(f) = PT \, \text{sinc}^2(fT) \qquad \ldots (3.34\,a)$$

These spectra will be shifted by f_c due to multiplication of $\cos(2\pi f_c t)$ and $\sin(2\pi f_c t)$.

$$\therefore \quad S_{QPSK}(f) = PT \, \text{sinc}^2[T(f - f_c)] + PT \, \text{sinc}^2[T(f + f_c)] \qquad \ldots (3.34\,b)$$

Hence, the spectrum of QPSK signal will be centred around f_c as shown in Fig. 3.9.

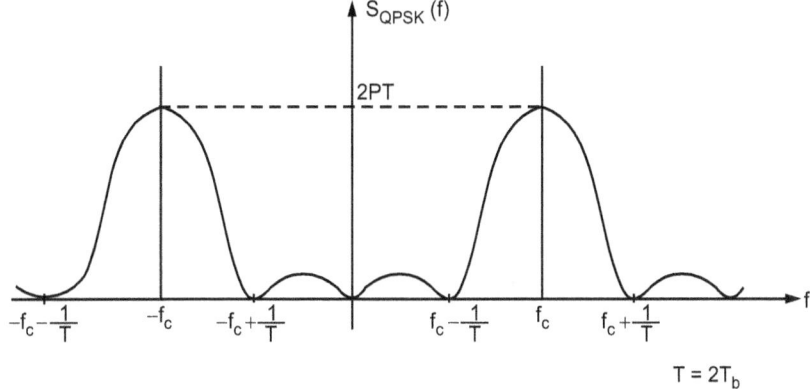

Fig. 3.9: Spectrum of QPSK

Bandwidth of QPSK:

As seen from the spectrum of QPSK (Fig. 3.9), the bandwidth will be,

$$BW = \left(f_c + \frac{1}{T}\right) - \left(f_c - \frac{1}{T}\right)$$

$$= \frac{2}{T}$$

Since $T = 2T_b$

Bandwidth of QPSK is,

$$BW = \frac{2}{2T_b}$$

$$\boxed{BW = f_b} \qquad \ldots (3.35)$$

Thus, the bandwidth of QPSK is half of PSK.

Geometrical Representation of QPSK:

The QPSK signals are given in equation (3.28). These equations can be rearranged as below.

$$S_1(t) = \left(\sqrt{\frac{PT}{2}}\right) \times \sqrt{\frac{2}{T}} \cos(2\pi f_c t) + \left(-\sqrt{\frac{PT}{2}}\right) \times \sqrt{\frac{2}{T}} \sin(2\pi f_c t)$$

$$S_2(t) = \left(-\sqrt{\frac{PT}{2}}\right) \times \sqrt{\frac{2}{T}} \cos(2\pi f_c t) + \left(-\sqrt{\frac{PT}{2}}\right) \times \sqrt{\frac{2}{T}} \sin(2\pi f_c t)$$

$$S_3(t) = \left(-\sqrt{\frac{PT}{2}}\right) \times \sqrt{\frac{2}{T}} \cos(2\pi f_c t) + \left(\sqrt{\frac{PT}{2}}\right) \times \sqrt{\frac{2}{T}} \sin(2\pi f_c t)$$

$$S_4(t) = \left(-\sqrt{\frac{PT}{2}}\right) \times \sqrt{\frac{2}{T}} \cos(2\pi f_c t) + \left(\sqrt{\frac{PT}{2}}\right) \times \sqrt{\frac{2}{T}} \sin(2\pi f_c t) \qquad \ldots (3.36)$$

We can have two basis functions,

$$\phi_1(t) = \sqrt{\frac{2}{T}} \cos(2\pi f_c t)$$

$$\phi_2(t) = \sqrt{\frac{2}{T}} \sin(2\pi f_c t)$$

$$\therefore \quad S_1(t) = \sqrt{\frac{PT}{2}} \phi_1(t) + \left(-\sqrt{\frac{PT}{2}}\right) \phi_2(t)$$

$$S_2(t) = \left(-\sqrt{\frac{PT}{2}}\right) \phi_1(t) + \left(-\sqrt{\frac{PT}{2}}\right) \phi_2(t)$$

$$S_3(t) = \left(-\sqrt{\frac{PT}{2}}\right) \phi_1(t) + \left(+\sqrt{\frac{PT}{2}}\right) \phi_2(t)$$

$$S_4(t) = \left(-\sqrt{\frac{PT}{2}}\right) \phi_1(t) + \left(+\sqrt{\frac{PT}{2}}\right) \phi_2(t) \qquad \ldots (3.37)$$

These four signals can be plotted as shown in Fig. 3.10.

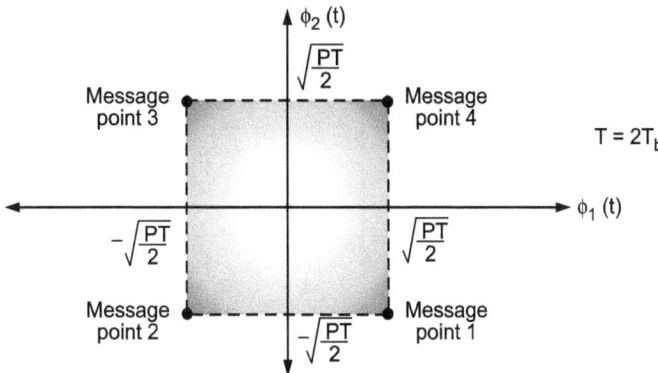

Fig. 3.10: QPSK Signal Space Diagram

Advantages of QPSK:
(i) Bandwidth required for QPSK is half that of BPSK.
(ii) From the signal space diagram, it can be seen that the distance between two message points is $2\sqrt{\frac{PT}{2}} = \sqrt{2PT} = \sqrt{4PT_b} = 2\sqrt{PT_b}$ which is same as BPSK hence noise immunity of two systems are same.

3.3.2 Quadrature Amplitude Shift Keying (QASK) or Quadrature Amplitude Modulation (QAM)

In the last section, we have seen that amplitude of signal remains constant in case of BPSK, QPSK and M-ary PSK whereas phase varies. The constrained envelope (sample amplitude) of signal gives rise to a circular constellation for message points. Since these points are very near to each other, it gives rise to poor noise immunity. Hence, we can remove the amplitude constraint and make the amplitude also variable alongwith phase.

Such a system is called Quadrature Amplitude Shift Keying (QASK) or Quadrature Amplitude Modulation (QAM). Let us consider a particular QAM system where we want to transmit a symbol every 4-bit. Hence, there will be 16 possible symbols for which we require separate signals. The signal space diagram for these signals is shown in Fig. 3.11. It can be seen from the diagram that the 4 bits which are used to generate a particular signal can be divided into 2 bits each to contribute to inphase and quadrature phase components of the signal.

The general form of QAM signal is given as,

$$S_i(t) = \sqrt{2P_0} \times a_i \cos(2\pi f_c t) + \sqrt{2P_0} \times b_i \sin(2\pi f_c t) \quad \ldots (3.38)$$

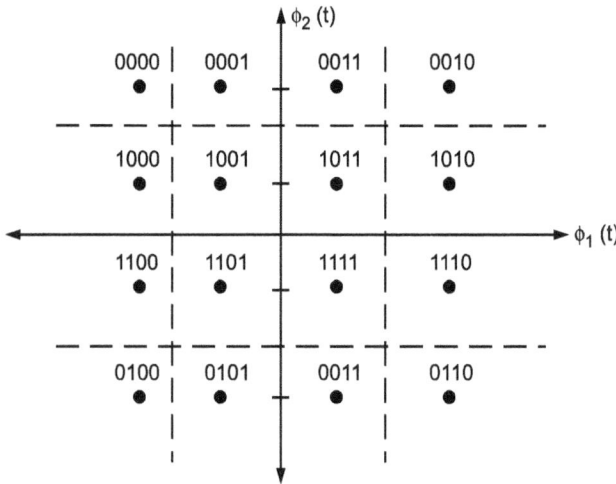

Fig. 3.11: Signal Space Representation of QAM (M = 16)

where, P_0 is signal power of lowest amplitude signal. a_i and b_i decide the location of message points.

Transmitter and Receiver for QAM:

The transmitter for QAM is shown in Fig. 3.12 (a).

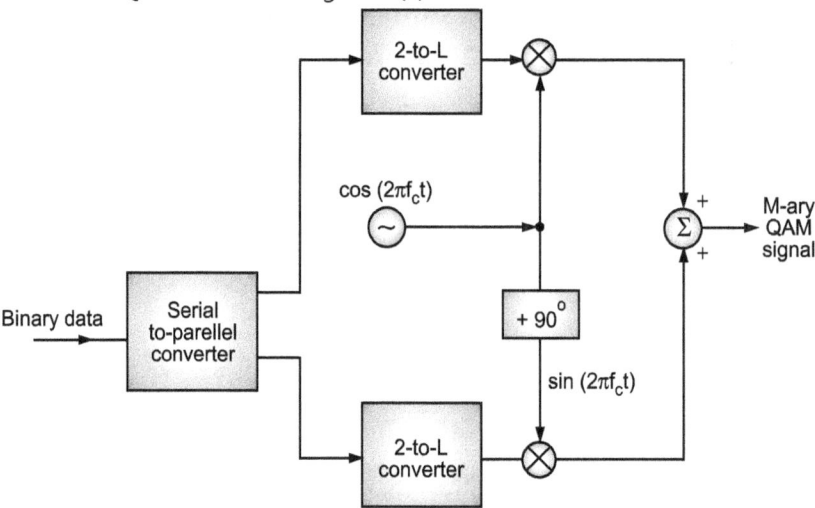

Fig. 3.12: (a) QAM Transmitter

It consists of a serial to parallel converter which converts N bit input data into 2 parallel binary sequences. (e.g. if 4-bit sequence 1001 is input, it is converted into 1 0 and 0 1). These binary sequences are given to 2 to L level converter.

This converter converts these sequences into corresponding level. This output is multiplied with inphase and quadrature phase carrier which are combined by the adder to generate desired QAM signal. The receiver for QAM is shown in Fig. 3.12 (b).

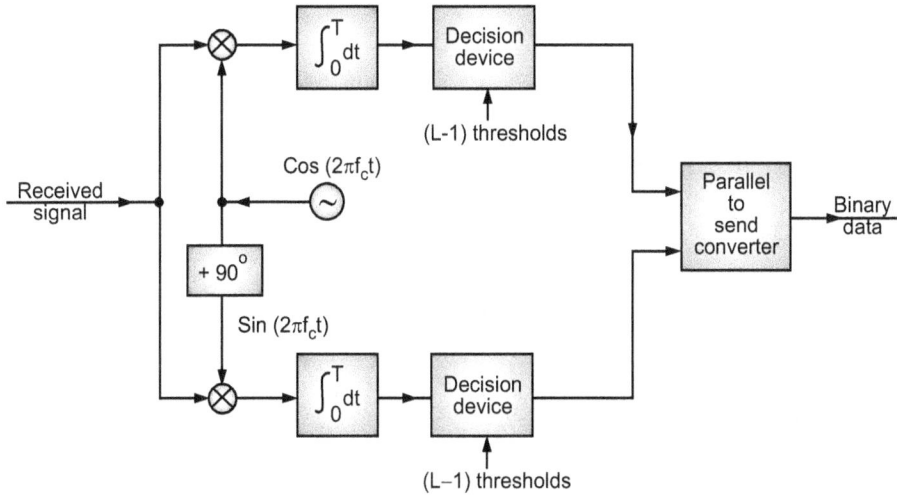

Fig. 3.12: (b) QAM Receiver

The received signal r(t) is given to two correlators (multiplier and integrator). The output of correlators is given to decision devices which is designed to compare the L level signals against L – 1 decision threshold. The decision devices give out two binary sequences based on the comparison. These sequences are combined by a parallel-to-serial converter to get back the original transmitted binary sequence.

Bandwidth of QAM Signal:

The QAM/QASK signal is given by,

$$S_i(t) = \sqrt{2P_0} \times a_i \cos(2\pi f_c t) + \sqrt{2P_0} \times b_i \sin(2\pi f_c t)$$

This equation is similar to M-ary PSK. Hence proceeding on the same line that of M-ary PSK we can write PSD of QAM as,

$$S_{QAM}(f) = \frac{PT}{2} \operatorname{sinc}^2[(f - f_c)T] + \frac{PT}{2} \operatorname{sinc}^2[(f + f_c)T] \qquad \ldots (3.39)$$

where, T is symbol duration given by $T = NT_b$

Hence, the plot of PSD of QAM is shown in Fig. 3.13.

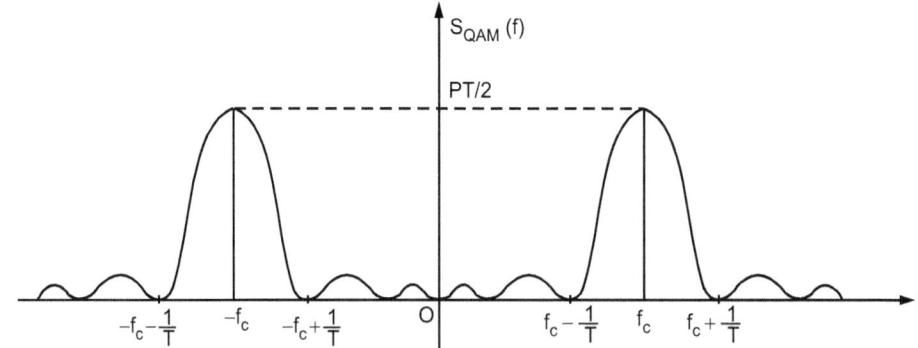

Fig. 3.13: PSD of QAM

From the plot, it can be seen that the bandwidth of QAM is given by,

$$BW = \left(f_c + \frac{1}{T}\right) - \left(f_c - \frac{1}{T}\right)$$

$$= \frac{2}{T}$$

$$= \frac{2}{NT_b}$$

$$= \frac{2f_b}{N} = \frac{2f_b}{\log_2 M} \qquad \ldots (3.40)$$

Hence, bandwidth of QASK/QAM and M-ary PSK is same.

Thus, QASK/QAM system has an advantage of better noise immunity than M-ary PSK retaining the low bandwidth requirement.

3.3.3 Minimum Shift Keying (MSK)

Linear modulation schemes such as QPSK, FSK etc. exhibit phase discontinuity in the modulated waveform. There is one more variant of QPSK called offset QPSK (OQPSK). In OQPSK odd and even bit streams do not change simultaneously as in case of QPSK. It results into a phase change of 90° instead of 180°. Hence, it eliminates the effect of abrupt phase change to some extent.

The phase transitions cause problems for band limited and power efficient transmission especially in interference limited environment. The sharp phase changes in the modulated signal result into more power inside lobes of spectrum compared to the main lobe. In a cellular communication system, these side lobes should be as small as possible. In power limited environment, a non-linear power amplifier alongwith a bandpass filter in the transmitter front-end results in phase distortion for the modulated signal waveform with sharp phase transitions.

The abrupt phase transitions generate frequency components that have significant amplitudes. Thus, the resultant power in sidelobes cause co-channels and inter-channel interference. We can use high power amplifiers or non-linear amplifiers with extensive distortion compensation. However, high power amplifiers are to be operated in non-linear region. This results in power inefficiency. Continuous phase modulations, in which there is smooth phase change are preferred to counter these problems. Minimum Phase Shift Keying (MSK) is free from many of these problems mentioned above.

MSK has following advantages:
(i) Eliminates the abrupt phase changes.
(ii) It makes main lobe wider making side lobes insignificant.

The waveforms of MSK are shown in Fig. 3.14. Let us understand the scheme through these waveforms.

1. Input waveform b(t) is divided into two waveforms $b_o(t)$ representing odd numbered bits and $b_e(t)$ representing even numbered bits. The duration of each bit $b_o(t)$ and $b_e(t)$ is $2T_b$. Fig. 3.14 (b) and (c).
2. There is staggering in $b_o(t)$ and $b_e(t)$ just like OQPSK of duration T_b.
3. Two waveforms $\sin[2\pi(t/4T_b)]$ and $\cos[2\pi(t/4T_b)]$ are generated at the MSK transmitter as shown in Fig. 3.14 (d).

   Note that these waveforms are such that $\sin[2\pi(t/4T_b)]$ crosses zero at the end of the symbol time $b_e(t)$ and $\cos 2\pi(t/4T_b)$ crosses zero at the end of symbol time $b_o(t)$.
4. $b_o(t)$ and $b_e(t)$ are multiplied with the waveform $\sin[2\pi(t/4T_b)]$ and $\cos[2\pi(t/4T_b)]$ respectively to produce waveforms in Fig. 3.14 (e) and (f).
5. The original baseband waveform is converted into smoother waveforms (e) and (f) which are modulated using in-phase and quadrature phase carrier and the resultant MSK signal will be,

$$S(t) = \sqrt{2P}\left[b_e(t)\sin\left(\frac{2\pi t}{4T_b}\right)\right]\cos(2\pi f_c t)$$
$$+ \sqrt{2P}\left[b_o(t)\cos\left(\frac{2\pi t}{4T_b}\right)\right]\sin(2\pi f_c t) \quad \ldots (3.41)$$

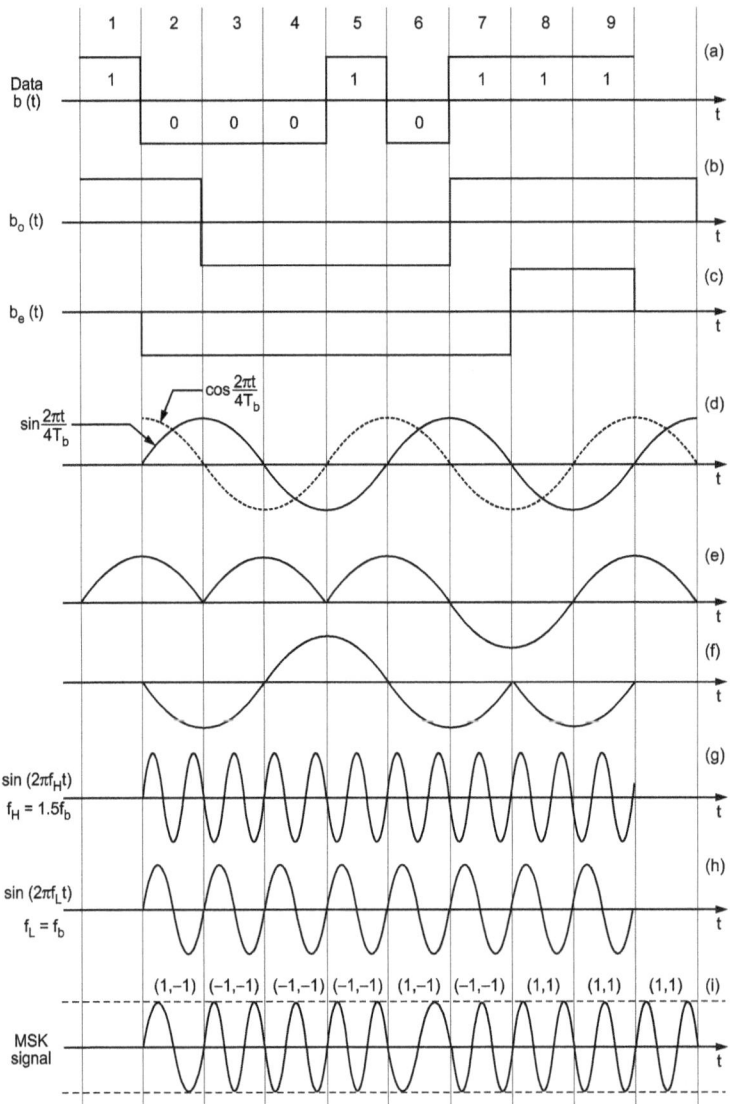

Fig. 3.14: MSK Waveforms

$$S(t) = \sqrt{2P}\left[\frac{b_o(t) + b_e(t)}{2}\right]\sin\left(2\pi f_c t + \frac{2\pi t}{4T_b}\right)$$

$$+ \sqrt{2P}\left[\frac{b_o(t) - b_e(t)}{2}\right]\sin\left(2\pi f_c t - \frac{2\pi t}{4T_b}\right) \quad \ldots (3.42)$$

$$\therefore \quad S(t) = \sqrt{2P} \cdot B_H(t)\sin(2\pi f_H t)$$

$$+ \sqrt{2P}\, B_L(t)\sin(2\pi f_L t) \quad \ldots (3.43)$$

where,
$$B_H(t) = \frac{b_o(t) + b_e(t)}{2}$$
$$B_L(t) = \frac{b_o(t) - b_e(t)}{2}$$
$$f_H = f_c + \frac{f_b}{4}$$
$$f_L = f_c - \frac{f_b}{4}$$

6. When $b_o(t) = b_e(t)$
$$B_H(t) = \pm 1$$
$$B_L(t) = 0$$
∴
$$S(t) = \sqrt{2P}\, B_H(t) \sin(2\pi f_H t) \qquad \ldots (3.44)$$

When $b_o(t) = -b_e(t)$
$$B_H(t) = 0$$
$$B_L(t) = \pm 1$$
∴
$$S(t) = \sqrt{2P}\, B_L(t) \sin(2\pi f_L t) \qquad \ldots (3.45)$$

7. f_H and f_L are selected such that
$$2\pi(f_H + f_L) T_b = m\pi \qquad \text{m is an integer}$$
$$2\pi(f_H - f_L) T_b = n\pi \qquad \text{n is an integer}$$

Hence, the two signals $\cos(2\pi f_H t)$ and $\sin(2\pi f_H t)$ are orthogonal i.e.

$$\int_0^{T_b} \sin 2\pi f_H t \, \sin 2\pi f_L t \, dt = 0$$

∴
$$2\pi\left(f_c + \frac{f_b}{4} + f_c - \frac{f_b}{4}\right) \times T_b = m\pi$$

∴
$$f_c = \frac{m f_b}{4}$$

and
$$2\pi \times \left[\left(f_c + \frac{f_b}{4}\right) - \left(f_c - \frac{f_b}{4}\right)\right] \times T_b = n\pi$$

∴
$$2 \times \frac{f_b}{2} \times T_b = n$$

∴
$$n = 1$$
∴
$$2\pi(f_H - f_L) T_b = 1 \times \pi$$

∴
$$f_H - f_L = \frac{1}{2T_b}$$

∴
$$f_H - f_L = \frac{1}{2} f_b$$

The name minimum shift keying has come from the fact that $f_H - f_L$ is minimum since $n = 1$. It is the minimum difference between f_H and f_L for which the signals are orthogonal.

8. The carrier frequency selected should be integer multiple of $f_b/4$.

i.e. $$f_c = \frac{mf_b}{4}$$

$$\therefore \quad f_H = f_c + \frac{f_b}{4} = \frac{mf_b}{4} + \frac{f_b}{4} = (m+1)\frac{f_b}{4}$$

$$f_L = f_c - \frac{f_b}{4} = (m-1)\frac{f_b}{4}$$

Signal Space Representation of MSK:

The MSK signal given by equation (3.43) can be rewritten as,

$$S(t) = \sqrt{PT} \times B_H(t) \sqrt{\frac{2}{T}} \sin(2\pi f_H t)$$

$$+ \sqrt{PT} \times B_L(t) \sqrt{\frac{2}{T}} \sin(2\pi f_L t) \quad \ldots (3.46)$$

Hence, the two basis functions are,

$$\phi_1(t) = \sqrt{\frac{2}{T}} \sin(2\pi f_H t)$$

$$\phi_2(t) = \sqrt{\frac{2}{T}} \sin(2\pi f_L t) \quad \ldots (3.47)$$

$$\therefore \quad S(t) = B_H(t) \cdot \sqrt{PT}\, \phi_1(t) + B_L(t) \sqrt{PT}\, \phi_2(t) \quad \ldots (3.48)$$

Depending on $B_H(t)$ and $B_L(t)$ there will be four signal points as plotted in Fig. 3.15.

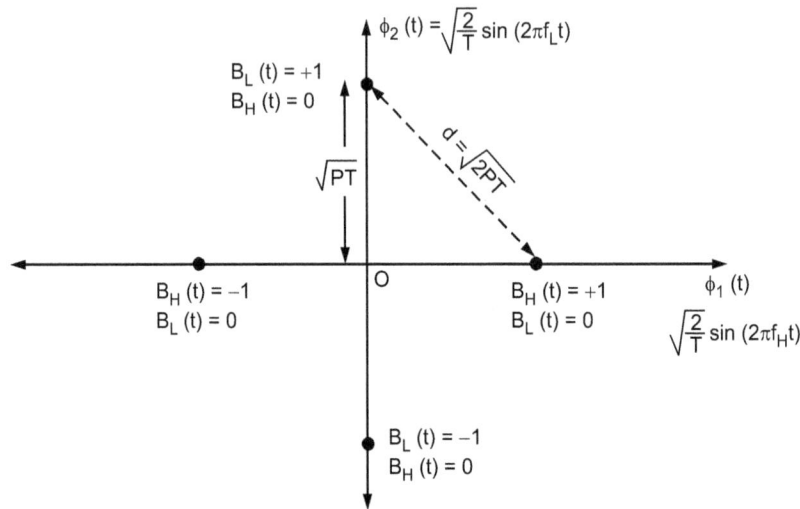

Fig. 3.15: Signal Space Diagram for MSK

The distance between two nearest point will be,

$$d^2 = (\sqrt{PT})^2 + (\sqrt{PT})^2$$
$$\therefore d = \sqrt{2PT}$$

Power Spectral Density:

The MSK waveform is given by,

$$S(t) = \sqrt{2P}\, b_e(t) \sin\left(\frac{2\pi t}{4T_b}\right) \cos(2\pi f_c t)$$
$$+ \sqrt{2P}\, b_o(t) \cos\left(\frac{2\pi t}{4T_b}\right) \cdot \sin(2\pi f_c t) \quad \ldots (3.49\,a)$$

Consider the waveform,

$$g(t) = \sqrt{2P}\, b_o(t) \cos\left(\frac{2\pi t}{4T_b}\right) \qquad -T_b \le t \le T_b$$

The PSD of above signal is,

$$S_g(f) = \frac{32\, E_b}{\pi^2} \left[\frac{\cos 2\pi f T_b}{1 - (4fT_b)^2}\right]^2 \quad \ldots (3.49\,b)$$

where, $E_b = \dfrac{PT}{2}$ (Energy per bit duration)

Hence, PSD of MSK will be,

$$S_{MSK}(f) = \frac{8}{\pi^2} E_b \left[\left\{\frac{\cos 2\pi (f - f_c) T_b}{1 - [4(f - f_c) T_b]^2}\right\}^2 + \left\{\frac{\cos 2\pi (f + f_c) T_b}{1 - [4(f - f_c) T_b]^2}\right\}^2\right]$$
$$\ldots (3.50)$$

This PSD is plotted in Fig. 3.16 for normalised power along with QPSK for comparison.

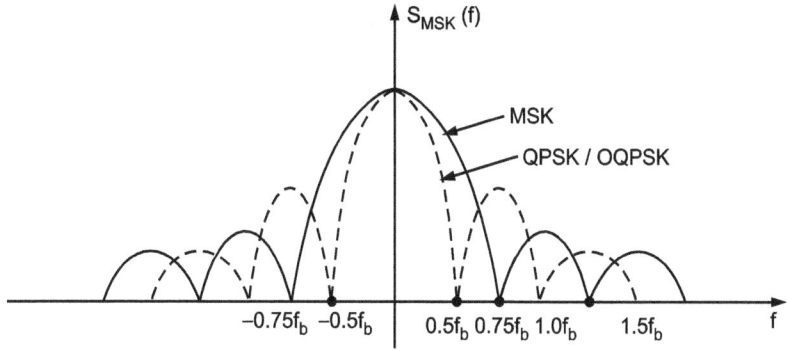

Fig. 3.16: PSD of MSK Alongwith PSD of QPSK

Bandwidth of MSK:

It can be seen from Fig. 3.16 that the bandwidth of MSK is,

$$BW = \frac{3}{4}f_b - \left(-\frac{3}{4}f_b\right)$$

$$= 1.5\, f_b$$

It can be seen that the main lobe width of MSK is larger than QPSK and has higher bandwidth.

Generation of MSK:

The MSK transmitter block diagram is shown in Fig. 3.17 (a).

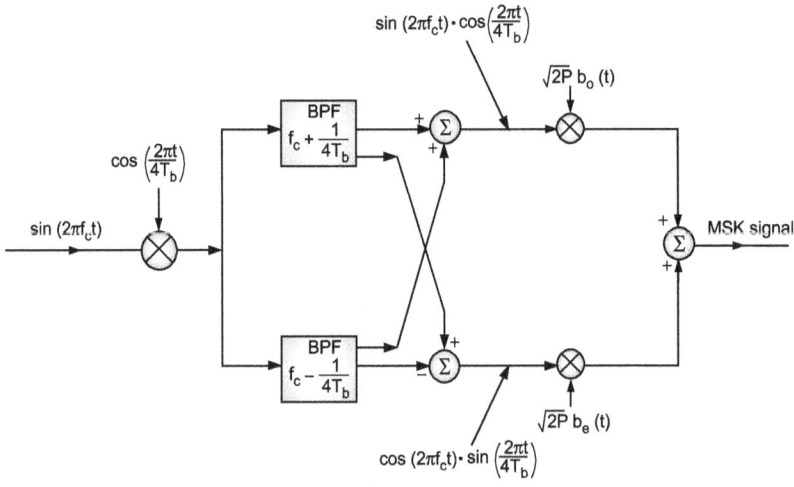

Fig. 3.17: (a) Generation of MSK Signal

The MSK signal is given by,

$$S(t) = \sqrt{2P}\, b_e(t) \sin\left(\frac{2\pi t}{4T_b}\right) \cdot \cos(2\pi f_c t)$$

$$+ \sqrt{2P}\, b_o(t) \cos\left(\frac{2\pi t}{4T_b}\right) \cdot \sin(2\pi f_c t) \quad \ldots (3.51)$$

First we generate $\sin(2\pi f_c t)$ and $\sin\left(\frac{2\pi t}{4T_b}\right)$ and use 90° phase shifter to get $\cos(2\pi f_c t)$ $\cos\left(\frac{2\pi t}{4T_b}\right)$.

Then we use multiplier to get the terms $\sin\left(\frac{2\pi t}{4T_b}\right) \cdot \cos(2\pi f_c t)$ and $\cos\left(\frac{2\pi t}{4T_b}\right) \sin(2\pi f_c t)$.

Another set of multiplier will generate $\sqrt{2P}\, b_e(t) \sin\left(\frac{2\pi t}{4T_b}\right) \cdot \cos(2\pi f_c t)$ and $\sqrt{2P}\, b_o(t) \cos\left(\frac{2\pi t}{4T_b}\right) \cdot \sin(2\pi f_c t)$. Then an adder adds these two terms to get the signal represented in equation (3.51).

Reception of MSK:

The detection is performed by correlating received signal with two waveforms.

$$\phi_1(t) = \cos\left(\frac{2\pi t}{4T_b}\right) \sin(2\pi f_c t)$$

$$\phi_2(t) = \sin\left(\frac{2\pi t}{4T_b}\right) \cos(2\pi f_c t)$$

The received signal r(t) is multiplied and integrated by the two separate correlators whose another input is $\phi_1(t)$ and $\phi_2(t)$. In both the cases integration interval is $2T_b$ seconds and the integration in quadrature channel is delayed by T_b w.r.t. in-phase channel. The resulting in-phase and quadrature phase channel outputs v_1 and v_2 are stored and then the integrator output is dumped. The block diagram is shown in Fig. 3.17 (b).

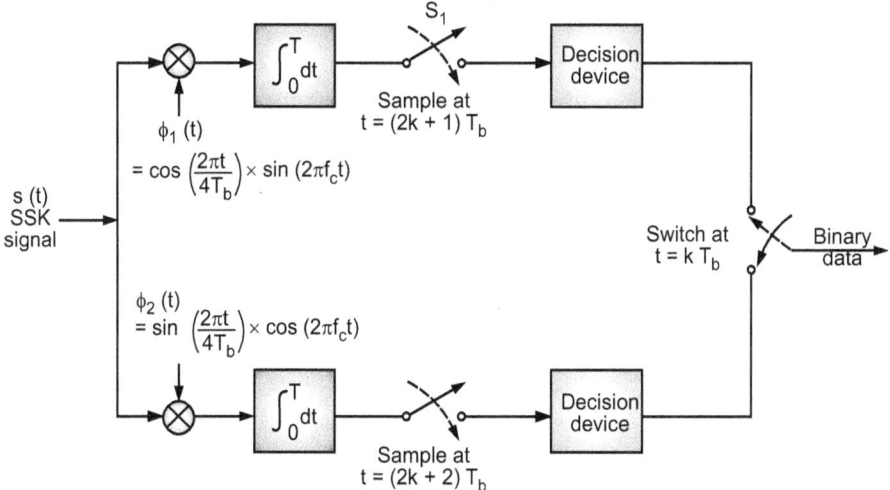

Fig. 3.17: (b) MSK Receiver Block Diagram

Phase Continuity in MSK:

The MSK signal is given by,

$$S(t) = \sqrt{2P}\left[\frac{b_o(t) + b_e(t)}{2}\right] \sin[2\pi(f_c + f_1)t]$$

$$+ \sqrt{2P}\left[\frac{b_o(t) - b_e(t)}{2}\right] \sin[2\pi(f_c - f_1)t]$$

This equation can be rewritten as,

$$S(t) = b_o(t)\sqrt{2P} \sin[2\pi(f_c + b_o(t) \cdot b_e(t) f_1)t]$$

Now, following table gives the MSK signal for various combinations of $b_o(t)$ and $b_e(t)$.

$b_o(t)$	$b_e(t)$	$S(t)$
+1	+1	$\sqrt{2P} \sin[2\pi(f_c + f_1)t]$ $= \sqrt{2P} \sin(2\pi f_H t)$
+1	-1	$-\sqrt{2P} \sin[2\pi(f_c - f_1)t]$ $= -\sqrt{2P} \sin(2\pi f_L t)$
-1	+1	$\sqrt{2P} \sin[2\pi(f_c - f_1)t]$ $= \sqrt{2P} \sin(2\pi f_L t)$
-1	-1	$\sin[2\pi(f_c + f_1)t]$ $= \sin(2\pi f_H t)$

Accordingly the MSK waveforms for f_H and f_L are drawn in Fig. 3.14 (g) and (h) from the MSK waveforms drawn and referring above table we can observe the following things.

1. $b_o(t)$ and $b_e(t)$ do not change at the same time.
2. The product $b_o(t) \cdot b_e(t)$ will cause a change of phase $k\pi$ (where, k is integer) whenever it changes from +1 to −1 or −1 to +1.
3. $b_o(t)$ changes only at odd bit intervals i.e. $T_b, 3T_b$, etc.
   $b_e(t)$ can change only at even bit intervals i.e. $2T_b, 4T_b$, etc.
4. Change in $b_e(t)$ will change the phase by multiple of 2π. It is equivalent to no change of phase.
5. Change in $b_o(t)$ will cause a phase change of $k\pi$ since it changes at odd bit intervals. But $b_o(t)$ will further cause a phase change of π since it multiplies $\sqrt{2P} \sin[2\pi(f_c + b_o(t) \cdot b_e(t) f_1)]$. Hence, this will also result in phase change of multiple of 2π.
6. From (4) and (5) we can conclude that there is phase continuity in MSK signal.

Comparison of MSK and QPSK:

MSK	QPSK
1. It has continuous phase change in transmitted waveforms.	1. It has abrupt phase change in transmitted waveforms.
2. When filtered there is no amplitude variation.	2. When filtered they gives rise to amplitude variations.
3. Interchannel interference is very small due to small side lobes.	3. Interchannel interference is large due to large side lobes.
4. Main lobe is wider and has more than 95% energy in it.	4. Main lobe is narrow and has around 90% energy in it.
5. Bandwidth of MSK is 1.5 f_b.	5. Bandwidth of QPSK is f_b.
6. Generation and detection circuit is more complex.	6. Generation and detection circuit is less complex.
7. Receiver uses a coherent phase decoding process over two successive bits to recover original bit stream.	7. Receiver uses coherent phase decoding process over two successive bits to recover original bit stream.
8. While generating signal the baseband is modified first to make it smoother.	8. While generating QPSK signal original baseband signal is not modified.
9. The bit pattern is divided into odd and even pattern and there is offset of T_b in these patterns.	9. The bit pattern is divided into odd and even patterns but there may not be offset of T_b in these patterns.

3.4 Non-coherent Binary Modulation Techniques

Coherent detection techniques seen in last section use carrier wave's phase reference. When it is not possible to have carrier recovered at the receiver's end we use non-coherent detection. In this section, we will study these non-coherent detection techniques. viz. FSK, DPSK. Note that we cannot have non-coherent detection of PSK. Hence, we have DPSK technique used for non-coherent detection.

3.4.1 Non-coherent BFSK

BFSK signal is represented as,

$$S_H(t) = \sqrt{2P_s} \cos(2\pi f_H t) \qquad \text{... (3.52)}$$

and

$$S_L(t) = \sqrt{2P_s} \cos(2\pi f_L t) \qquad \text{... (3.53)}$$

where, $f_H = f_c + f_1$

and $f_L = f_c - f_1$

Even though they have same amplitude (envelope) the different carrier frequencies make non-coherent detection possible in BFSK. The receiver for non-coherent detection of BFSK is shown in Fig. 3.18. The received signal is applied to two bandpass filters with centre frequencies f_H and f_L.

As we have seen f_H and f_L are selected such that $f_H - f_L = 2f_b$. Hence, the filter frequency ranges do not overlap the main lobe, can be filtered by each filter which will pass nearly all energy. The output of filters is given to envelope detector. Suppose that we have transmitted 1. Hence, the waveform received at the input of receiver will be,

$$r(t) = \sqrt{2P_s} \cos(2\pi f_H t)$$

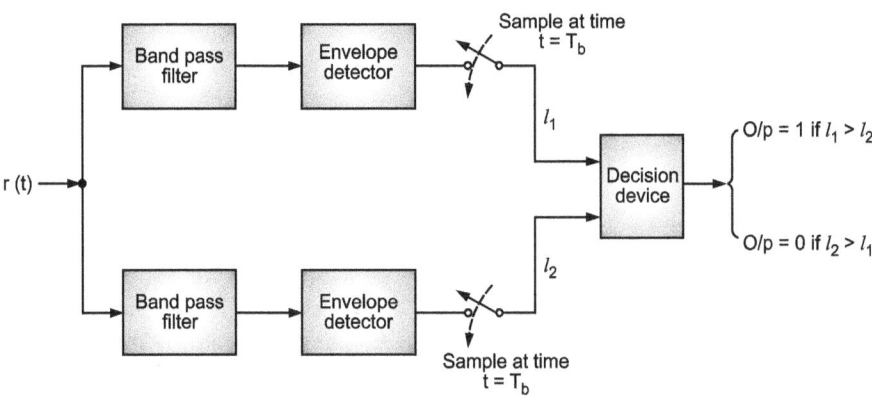

Fig. 3.18: Non-coherent BFSK

It is given to two bandpass filters. The output of upper bandpass filter will be $\sqrt{2P_s} \cos(2\pi f_H t)$ whereas lower bandpass filter will be zero. (This is assuming that there is no noise or distortion in the received waveform). The envelope detector output in the upper branch will be more than that of lower. Hence, the decision device which compares the two sampled outputs will be making decision in favour of 1. Similarly, when 0 is transmitted, lower branch is going to have higher specified output than upper. In presence of noise, the performance of the receiver is going to be affected depending on the signal energy and noise power.

3.4.2 Differential Phase Shift Keying (DPSK)

It is non-coherent version of PSK i.e. this modulation technique eliminates the synchronous carrier recovery at the receiver end simplifying the receiver circuit. There is one more problem associated with coherent PSK detection. We recover the carrier from received signal by squaring it. But then changing the sign of input signal will not alter the carrier. Hence, there is phase ambiguity of 180° in PSK detection. The DPSK technique eliminates this phase ambiguity.

At the transmitter, it uses two basic operations:
    (i)   Differential encoding of input binary wave.
    (ii)   Phase Shift Keying.

The block diagram of DPSK transmitter is shown in Fig. 3.19 (a). The data stream d(t) to be transmitted is applied to an EX-OR logic along with delayed version of output of EX-OR gate (feedback). Thus, the output of EX-OR gate can be expressed as,

$$b(t) = d(t) + b(t - T_b) \qquad \ldots (3.54)$$

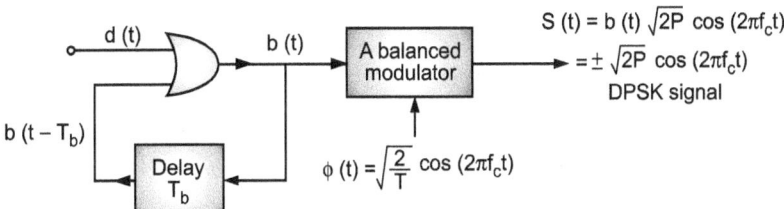

Fig. 3.19: (a) Block Diagram for Generation of DPSK

The waveforms corresponding to input bit stream 0 0 1 0 1 1 1 0 0 1 is shown in Fig. 3.19 (b).

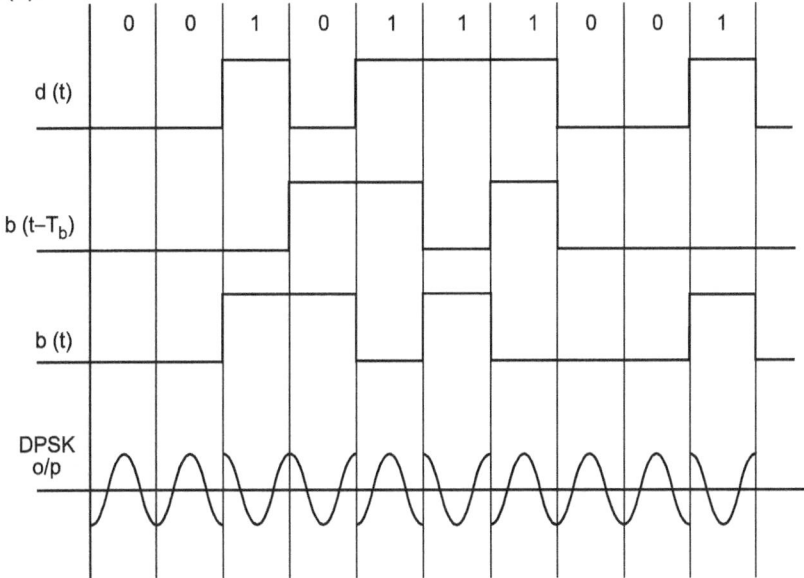

Fig. 3.19: (b) DPSK Waveforms

While drawing these waveforms the initial bit of b(t) is assumed to be 0. It can be seen from the waveforms that b(t) changes its level whenever the input bit d(t) = 1 and it remains same as previous whenever d(t) = 0. The output of EX-OR gate b(t) is applied to a balanced modulator (multiplier) which is applied with carrier $\cos 2\pi f_c t$ as other input. The output of balanced modulator will be,

$$S(t) = b(t)\sqrt{2P_s} \cos(2\pi f_c t) \qquad \ldots (3.55)$$
$$= \pm\sqrt{2P_s} \cos(2\pi f_c t)$$

Since b(t) varies whenever input 1 phase of carrier also changes when input is 1 by 180°. The receiver for DPSK as mentioned earlier is simple and is shown in Fig. 3.19 (c).

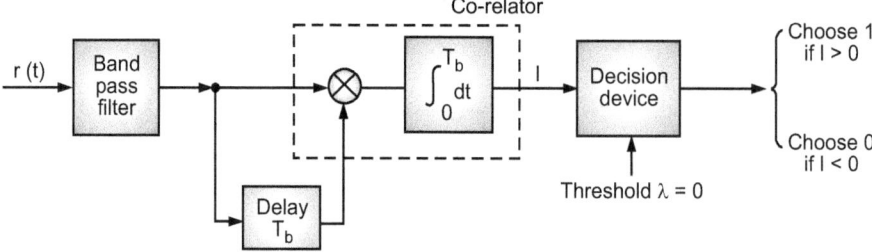

Fig. 3.19: (c) DPSK Receiver

Here, the received signal $r(t) = b(t)\sqrt{2P_s} \cos 2\pi f_c t$ is multiplied with its delayed version. Hence, the output of multiplier will be,

$$b(t)\, b(t - T_b) \cdot 2 P_s \cos(2\pi f_c t + \theta) \cdot \cos[2\pi f_c (t - T_b) + \theta]$$

$$= P_s\, b(t)\, b(t - T_b) \left\{ \cos 2\pi f_c T_b + \cos\left[4\pi f_c \left(t - \frac{T_b}{2}\right) + 2\theta\right] \right\} \qquad \ldots (3.56)$$

This output is given to an integrator. As seen in case of BPSK, the integrator will suppress the second terms and if we select $2\pi f_c \times T_b = 2n\pi$ (or f_c is integral multiple of $1/T_b$), then the output of integrator will be $b(t) \cdot b(t - T_b)$. The transmitted data can be recovered from this product $b(t)\, b(t - T_b)$ easily.

When transmitted data,

$$d(t) = 0, \quad b(t)\, b(t - T_b) = +1$$

and

$$d(t) = 1, \quad b(t)\, b(t - T_b) = -1$$

Hence, if the product $b(t)\, b(t - T_b)$ is positive, decision can be made in favour of 0 and if it is negative decision is made in favour of 1.

Comparison of PSK and DPSK:

PSK	DPSK
1. It is coherent modulation technique.	1. It is non-coherent modulation technique.
2. Local carrier needs to be generated at receiver which makes receiver circuit complex.	2. No carrier generated at receiver hence circuit is simple.

PSK	DPSK
3. Transmitter does not require differential encoding of input binary stream.	3. Transmitter requires differential encoding to be done.
4. Noise in one bit can cause only single error.	4. Noise in one bit can cause errors in two successive bits.
5. Error rate is less compared to DPSK due to coherent detection.	5. Error rate is more due to non-coherent detection.

3.5 M-ary Modulation Techniques

3.5.1 M-ary PSK

This is a family of two dimensional phase shift keying modulation schemes. Several bandwidth efficient schemes of this family are important for practical wireless applications. In this technique, the phase of carrier takes on one of M possible values. Hence, the M-ary PSK signal can be expressed as,

$$S_i(t) = \sqrt{2P} \cos(2\pi f_c t + \phi_i) \quad \ldots (3.57)$$

where,
$$\phi_i = (2i - 1)\frac{\pi}{M}$$

$$i = 1, 2, 3, \ldots, M$$

(Note that QPSK is M-ary PSK with M = 4).

The M possible signals are generated using M different phase values.

Generation of M-ary PSK :

Fig. 3.20 shows transmitter of M-ary PSK.

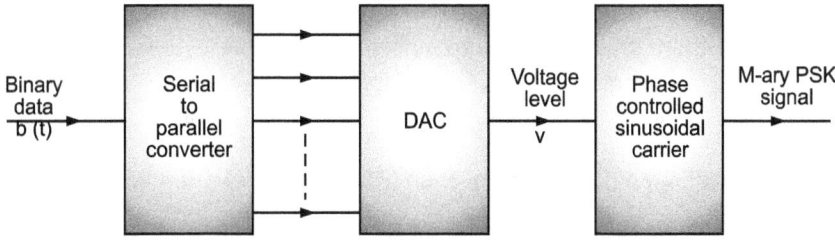

Fig. 3.20: M-ary PSK transmitter

It consists of a serial to parallel converter which takes N bits serially and presents it parallely to a Digital to Analog Converter (DAC). The DAC output will assume $2^N = M$ levels corresponding to N bit input. The DAC output v is used to determine the phase of sinusoidal signal to be transmitted. Thus, the N-bit symbol corresponds to particular phase of sinusoidal.

Reception of M-ary PSK :

The optimum receiver for M-ary PSK is shown in Fig. 3.21.

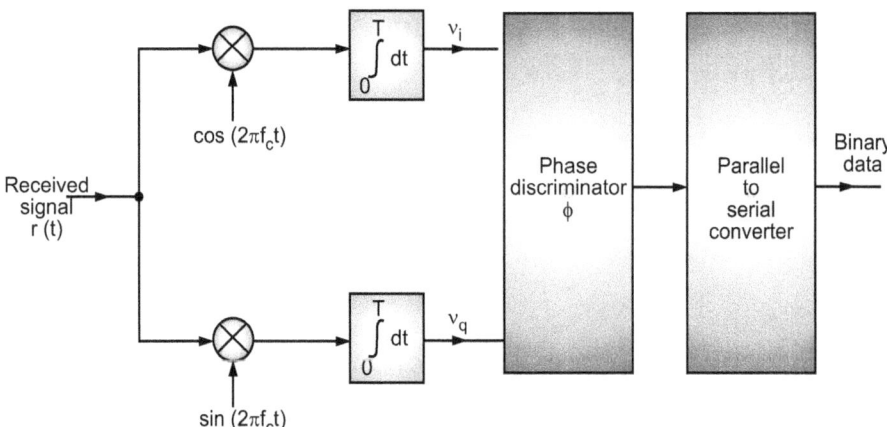

Fig. 3.21: M-ary PSK Receiver

It has a pair of correlators (Multiplier and Integrator) which are fed with received signal r(t) and carrier signals. The two correlators output v_i and v_q are given to a phase descriminator which estimates the phase.

$$\hat{\phi} = \tan^{-1}\left(\frac{v_q}{v_i}\right)$$

Depending on this value, it selects one of the M possible N-bit bit patterns corresponding to the phase. The N bits are the converted into serial format by parallel to serial converter.

Spectrum of M-ary PSK:

The M-ary PSK signal is represented in equation (3.58) can be rewritten as,

$$S_i(t) = \left(\sqrt{2P} \cos \phi_i\right) \cos(2\pi f_c t)$$
$$- \left(\sqrt{2P} \sin \phi_i\right) \sin(2\pi f_c t) \quad \ldots (3.58)$$

This signal representation is same as QPSK waveform. Except that here, we have $T = NT_b$ (whereas in case of QPSK we had $T = 2T_b$).

Hence the power spectrum of M-ary PSK signal will be –

$$S_{M\text{-ary PSK}}(f) = P \times T \, \text{sinc}^2[(f - f_c)T] + P \times T \, \text{sinc}^2[(f + f_c)T] \quad \ldots (3.59)$$

$$= P \times NT_b \, \text{sinc}^2[(f - f_c)NT_b] + PNT_b \, \text{sinc}^2[(f + f_c)NT_b]$$

where, $T = NT_b$

The spectrum is plotted in Fig. 3.22.

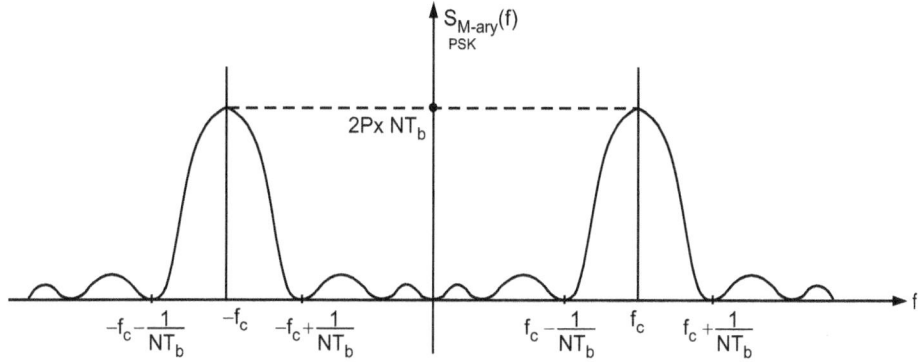

Fig. 3.22: PSD of M-ary PSK

Geometrical Representation of M-ary PSK:

The M-ary PSK signal given in equation (3.58) suggests that we have two basic functions (having unit energy)

$$\phi_1(t) = \sqrt{\frac{2}{T}} \cos 2\pi f_c t \quad ; \quad 0 \leq t \leq T$$

$$\phi_2(t) = \sqrt{\frac{2}{T}} \sin 2\pi f_c t \quad ; \quad 0 \leq t \leq T$$

The signal space diagram (signal constellation) is two dimensional with M message points given by $\sqrt{PT} \cos \phi_i$ and $\sqrt{PT} \sin \phi_i$. Fig. 3.23 shows M-ary PSK signal space diagram for $M = 8$.

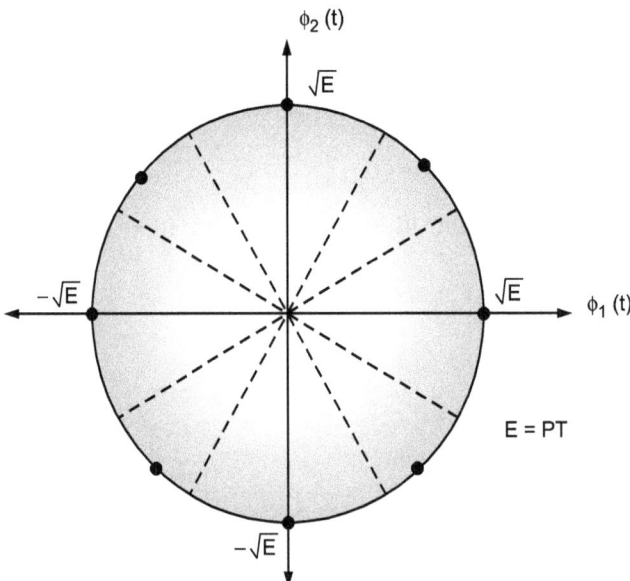

Fig. 3.23: Signal Space Representation for M-ary QPSK (M = 8)

Bandwidth of M-ary PSK:

From the spectrum plotted in Fig. 3.22 shows that the null-to-null bandwidth can be given by,

$$BW = \left(f_c + \frac{1}{T}\right) - \left(f_c - \frac{1}{T}\right)$$

$$= \frac{2}{T}$$

Since, $T = NT_b$

$$BW = \frac{2}{NT_b} = \frac{2f_b}{N} = \frac{2f_b}{\log_2 M} \quad \ldots (3.60)$$

Hence, for M = 8,

$$BW = \frac{2f_b}{\log_2 8} = \frac{2f_b}{3}$$

Merits and Demerits of M-ary PSK :

(i) The bandwidth requirement of M-ary PSK is small. Hence, data rate is high.

(ii) M-ary PSK (and BPSK, QPSK) systems transmit information through phase. The amplitude remains constant. Hence, these systems are useful where transmission medium causes variations in amplitude (fading channels).

(iii) Coherent M-ary PSK requires knowledge of carrier and phase of receiver to accurately synchronise transmitter. Hence, they are not suitable when carrier recovery at receiver is difficult.

(iv) As seen from the signal space diagram, the message points of M-ary PSK lie on circumference of a circle. These signal points are close together hence degrade the noise immunity.

3.5.2 M-ary FSK

It is an extension of BFSK. M-ary FSK is a power efficient modulation scheme and used in spread spectrum communications and other wireless applications. The input bit stream to be transmitted is grouped into N number of bits and one of M carrier frequency signal is transmitted; where $M = 2^N$.

The transmitter of M-ary FSK system is shown in Fig. 3.24 (a).

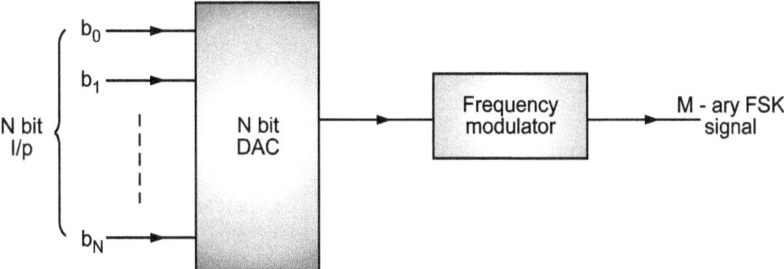

Fig. 3.24: (a) M-FSK Transmitter

An N-bit symbol of duration $T = NT_b$ is converted into an analog voltage level by an N-bit Digital to Analog Converter (DAC). The output of DAC is given to a frequency modulator which generates a carrier waveform depending on the DAC output. A signal of frequency f_1 or f_2, ..., or f_m is transmitted for symbol duration NT_b.

The receiver of M-ary FSK system is shown in Fig. 3.23 (b). The received signal is applied to a bank of parallel bandpass filters each one is followed by an envelope detector. (This arrangement is similar to BFSK). The bandpass filters have centre frequencies $f_1, f_2, ..., f_m$. The output of bandpass filter whose centre frequency matches with received signal will be higher i.e. envelope of the signal from this bandpass filter will be higher than other bandpass filters.

Hence the envelope detector following the matched bandpass filter will have highest output (provided noise/distortions are minimum) compared to other envelope detectors. Hence, decision will be made in favour of the bit pattern corresponding to the bandpass filter frequency i.e. the output of decision device will be the largest value from envelope detectors which is given to an N-bit analog to digital converter. The frequencies $f_1, f_2, f_3, ..., f_m$ are selected such that the signals are mutually orthogonal.

One commonly used selection is carrier frequencies of successive harmonics of symbol frequency i.e. $f_s = \frac{1}{T_s} = \frac{1}{NT_b}$. Thus, if lowest frequency $f_1 = nf_s$ then $f_2 = (n+2) f_s$ $f_3 = (n+4) f_s$, etc. In such case, the PSD of M-ary FSK signal is shown in Fig. 3.24 (c). It can be seen from the PSD that the bandwidth required to transmit M-ary FSK signal will be,

$$BW = 2 Mf_s$$

$$= 2 \times 2^N \times \frac{1}{NT_b}$$

$$= 2^{N+1} \times \frac{f_b}{N} = \frac{2^{N+1} f_b}{\log_2 M} \qquad \ldots (3.61)$$

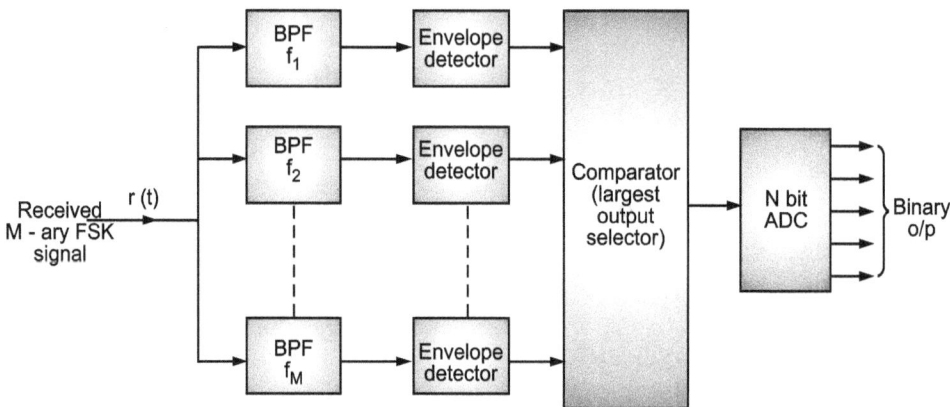

Fig. 3.24: (b) M-ary FSK Receiver

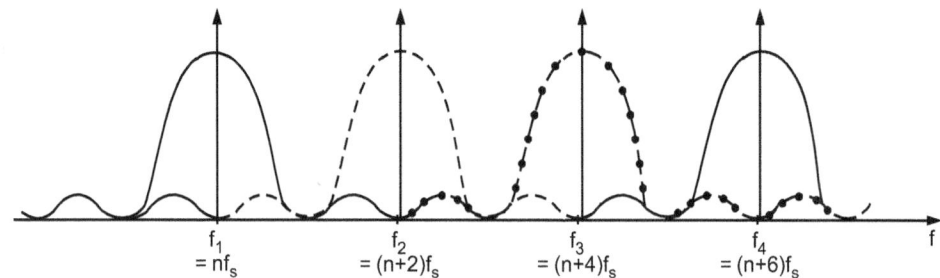

Fig. 3.24: (c) PSD of M-ary FSK

Thus, M-ary FSK requires larger bandwidth than the corresponding M-ary FSK. Whereas error probability of M-ary FSK decreases as M is increased and in case of M-ary PSK error probability increases as M increases.

Signal space representation of M-ary FSK:

The M-ary FSK signal is represented as,

$$S_i(t) = \sqrt{2P} \cos(2\pi f_i t) \quad \ldots (3.62)$$

where, $i = 1, 2, 3, \ldots, M$ and $f_i = [n + (2i - 2)] f_s$.

n is the integer.

f_i's are selected such that they are mutually orthogonal. Hence, there will be M basis vectors corresponding to the M carriers given by,

$$\phi_i(t) = \sqrt{\frac{2}{T}} \cos(2\pi f_i t) \quad \ldots (3.63)$$

$$\therefore \quad S_i(t) = \sqrt{PT} \times \sqrt{\frac{2}{T}} \cos(2\pi f_i t) \quad \ldots (3.64)$$

$$= \sqrt{PT}\, \phi_i(t) \quad \ldots (3.65)$$

We require M co-ordinate axes for reproducing the signal space of M-ary FSK. Fig. 3.24 (d) shows signal space representation of M-ary FSK for M = 3.

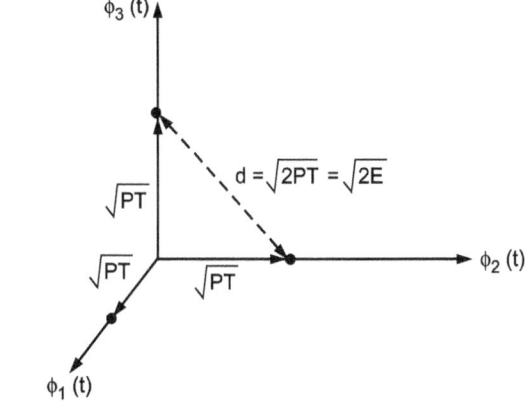

Fig. 3.24: (d) Signal Space Diagram for M-ary PSK (M = 3)

3.5.3 Comparison of Digital Modulation Technique

Table 3.1 shows the comparison of various digital modulation techniques.
Following Table 3.1 gives a few digital modulation schemes and their applications.

Table 3.1

Sr. No.	Modulation Scheme	Applications
1.	BPSK	Telemetry and Telecommand
2.	QPSK	Satellite, Cellular Telephony, Digital Video Broadcasting.
3.	8-PSK	Satellite communication.
4.	16-QAM	Digital Video Broadcasting, Microwave Digital Radio Links.

Sr. No.	Modulation Scheme	Applications
5.	64-QAM	Digital Video Broadcasting, Multimedia Data Services, Set Top Boxes.
6.	FSK	Cordless Telephony, Paging.
7.	MSK	Cellular Telephony.

Following table gives bandwidth efficiency limits of the modulation schemes.

Table 3.2

Sr. No.	Modulation Scheme	Bandwidth Efficiency Bit/s/Hz
1.	BPSK	1
2.	QPSK	2
3.	8-PSK	3
4.	16-QAM	4
5.	32-QAM	5
6.	256-QAM	8
7.	MSK	1

3.6 Bit Vs. Symbol Error Probability

3.6.1 Bit Error Rate (BER) and Symbol Error Rate (SER)

The performance of a digital communication is measured in terms of Bit Error Rate. It is defined as 'the ratio of total number of bits received in error and total number of bits received over a fairly large number of transmitted bits. Bit error rate is system-level performance. It is an indication of how good a digital communication system has been designed to perform. It also indicates the quality of service the users of a communication system should expect.

It is not possible to have zero BER, but a system can ensure a BER below an 'acceptable' level. For example, a BER of 10^{-5} is acceptable for voice signal but not acceptable for a data service, where BER should be less than 10^{-7}. Symbol Error Rate (SER) is also used to describe performance of digital communication system. It is ratio of total number of the total symbols detected erroneously to the total number of symbols received. The performance of a digital communication system is also measured in terms of E_b/N_0 which is defined as,

$$\frac{E_b}{N_0} = \frac{\text{Energy received per bit of information}}{\text{One sides PSD of in-band noise}}$$

$\frac{E_b}{N_0}$ is dimensionless and is also expressed in dB. We can express the bit error rate in terms of P_e called as error probability. For detection of a signal we can either use matched filter of correlator. We have seen that the performance of matched filter and correlator as same and can be expressed in terms of error probability. The knowledge of signal space is essential for calculation of error probability. We will discuss various digital modulation schemes and their performance.

3.6.2 Error Probability of BPSK (Using Signal Space)

The signal space can be partitioned into two regions Z_1 and Z_2. The decision boundary is mid-point of joining these two points. The decision rule is to decide that $s_1(t)$ i.e. binary 1 was transmitted if the received signals falls in region Z_1 and decide that signal $s_2(t)$ i.e. binary 0 was transmitted if the received signal falls in region Z_2.

Two kinds of errors can occur :
1. Signal $s_1(t)$ is transmitted but the noise is such that the received signal falls into region z_1 and receiver decides in favour of $s_1(t)$.
2. Signal $s_2(t)$ is transmitted but the noise is such that the received signal falls into region z_2 and receiver decides in favour of $s_2(t)$.

Let us consider case 1 to calculate the probability of making error of the first kind. Let us call it as p_{e_0}.

The observation scalar or response generated by receiver is given by,

$$x_1 = \int_0^{T_b} r(t) \phi_1(t) \, dt \qquad \ldots (3.66)$$

where, r(t) is received signal given by
$$r(t) = s_2(t) + w(t)$$

x_1 is value of random variable X_1 generated from response to signal $s_2(t)$. The conditional probability density function of random variable X_1 given that symbol 0 i.e. signal $s_2(t)$ was transmitted is given as,

$$p_{X_1}(x_1/0) = \frac{1}{\sqrt{2\pi\sigma_{n_0}^2}} e^{-(x_1 - m_{X_1})^2/\sigma_{X_1}^2} \qquad \ldots (3.67)$$

But,
$$m_{X_1} = E[X_1] = s_{21} = \int_0^{T_b} s_2(t) \phi_1(t) \, dt$$
$$= -\sqrt{E_b} \qquad \ldots (3.68)$$

and $$\sigma_{x_1}^2 = \frac{N_0}{2} \qquad \ldots (3.69)$$

$$\therefore \quad p_{x_1}(x_1/0) = \frac{1}{\sqrt{2\pi \times \frac{N_0}{2}}} \times e^{-(x_1 + \sqrt{E_b})^2/2 \times \frac{N_0}{2}}$$

$$= \frac{1}{\sqrt{\pi N_0}} e^{-(x_1 + \sqrt{E_b})^2/N_0} \qquad \ldots 3.70)$$

Now probability that the decision will be made in favour of 1 will be probability that x_1 lies in region 1.

$$\therefore \quad P_{eo} = \int_0^\infty p_{x_1}(x_1/0) \, dx_1$$

$$= \frac{1}{\sqrt{\pi N_0}} \int_0^\infty e^{-(x_1 + \sqrt{E_b})^2/N_0} \qquad \ldots (3.71)$$

Put $$z = \frac{x_1 + \sqrt{E_b}}{\sqrt{N_0}}$$

$\therefore$ When $x_1 = 0$, $z = \sqrt{E_b}$ and $x_1 = \infty$, $z = \infty$

$$dz = \frac{1}{\sqrt{N_0}} dx_1$$

$$\therefore \quad P_{eo} = \frac{1}{\sqrt{\pi}} e^{-z^2} dz$$

$$P_{eo} = \frac{1}{2} \text{erfc}\left(\sqrt{\frac{E_b}{N_0}}\right) \qquad \ldots (3.72)$$

or $$P_{eo} = Q\left(\sqrt{\frac{2E_b}{N_0}}\right) \qquad \ldots (3.73)$$

Similarly, the probability of making second kind of error (let w) call it as p_{e_1} will be,

$$P_{e_1} = \frac{1}{2} \text{erfc}\left(\sqrt{\frac{E_b}{N_0}}\right) \qquad \ldots (3.74)$$

or $$P_{e_1} = Q\left(\sqrt{\frac{2E_b}{N_0}}\right) \qquad \ldots (3.75)$$

The average error probability will be,

$$P_e = p(0) \times p(1/0) + p(1) \times p(0/1)$$
$$= p_0 \times p_{e0} + p_1 \times p_{e1}$$

$$\therefore P_e = \frac{1}{2} \times \frac{1}{2} \text{erfc}\left(\sqrt{\frac{E_b}{N_0}}\right) + \frac{1}{2} \times \frac{1}{2} \text{erfc}\left(\sqrt{\frac{E_b}{N_0}}\right)$$

$$\boxed{\therefore P_e = \frac{1}{2} \text{erfc}\left(\sqrt{\frac{E_b}{N_0}}\right)} \quad \ldots (3.76)$$

$$\boxed{P_e = Q\left(\sqrt{\frac{2E_b}{N_0}}\right)} \quad \ldots (3.77)$$

Thus, error probability depends on E_b and N_0. For specified N_0, when E_b is increased the message points corresponding to symbols 1 and 0 move further apart, and average probability of error p_e is reduced according to above equation.

3.6.3 Error Probability of QPSK

The received signal r(t) is defined as,

$$r(t) = s_i(t) + w(t) \qquad [0 \leq t \leq T; i = 1, 2, 3, 4]$$
$$\ldots (3.78)$$

where w(t) is sample function of white guassian noise process.
The observation vector r has two elements r_1 and r_2 given by,

$$r_1 = \int_0^T r(t)\, \phi_1(t)\, dt$$
$$= \sqrt{E} \cos\left[(2i-1)\frac{\pi}{4}\right] + w_1$$
$$= \pm\sqrt{\frac{E}{2}} + w_1 \quad \ldots (3.79)$$

and

$$r_2 = \int_0^T r(t)\, \phi_2(t)\, dt$$
$$= -\sqrt{E} \sin\left[(2i-1)\frac{\pi}{4}\right] + w_2 \quad \ldots (3.80)$$
$$= \mp\sqrt{E} + w_2$$

Thus, r_1 and r_2 are sample values of independent Guassian random variables with mean $\pm \sqrt{\dfrac{E}{2}}$ and $\mp \sqrt{\dfrac{E}{2}}$ and variance $\dfrac{N_0}{2}$.

The decision rule is
  (i) $s_1(t)$ is transmitted if received signal point associated with observation vector s falls in region z_1.
  (ii) $s_2(t)$ is transmitted if received signal point associated with observation vector s falls in region z_2.
  (iii) $s_3(t)$ is transmitted if received signal point associated with observation vector s falls in region z_3.
  (iv) $s_4(t)$ is transmitted if received signal point associated with observation vector s falls in region z_4.

- To calculate the symbol error probability, we can consider QPSK system equivalent to two coherent binary PSK systems working in parallel and using two carriers that are in quadrature phase as shown in Fig. 3.25.

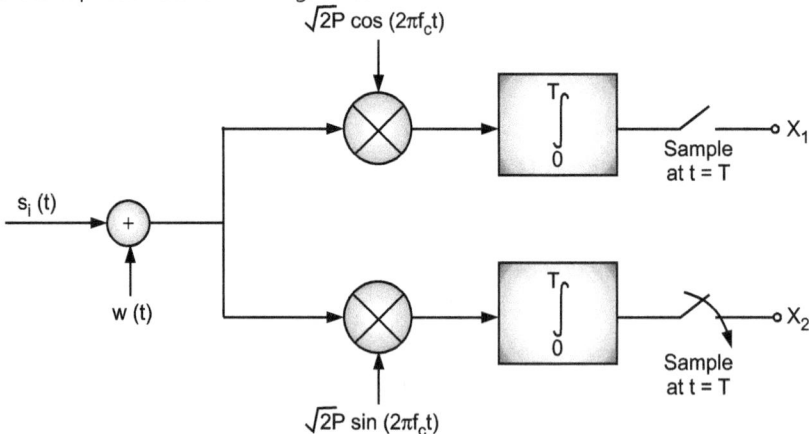

Fig. 3.25: QPSK Receiver

There are two outputs corresponding to one symbol. The in-phase output x_1 and quadrature channel output x_2 may be viewed as individual of two coherent BPSK. The energy per bit will be $E/2$ and noise PSD $N_0/2$. The error probability of each channel of QPSK is,

$$P_{e_1} = P_{e_2} = \dfrac{1}{2} \text{erfc}\left(\sqrt{\dfrac{E/2}{N_0}}\right)$$

$$= \dfrac{1}{2} \text{erfc}\left(\sqrt{\dfrac{E}{2N_0}}\right) \quad \ldots (3.81)$$

The decision will be correct corresponding to a symbol if both bits are correct. The probability that both bits in symbol are correct will be,

$$P_c = (1 - P_{e_1})(1 - P_{e_2})$$

$$= \left[1 - \frac{1}{2}\text{erfc}\left(\sqrt{\frac{E}{2N_0}}\right)\right]^2$$

$$= 1 - \text{erfc}\left(\sqrt{\frac{E}{2N_0}}\right) + \frac{1}{4}\text{erfc}^2\left(\sqrt{\frac{E}{2N_0}}\right) \quad \ldots (3.82)$$

Hence, average probability of symbol error.

$$p_e = (1 - p_c)$$

$$= \text{erfc}\left(\sqrt{\frac{E}{2N_0}}\right) - \frac{1}{4}\text{erfc}^2\left(\sqrt{\frac{E}{2N_0}}\right)$$

$$\simeq \text{erfc}\left(\sqrt{\frac{E}{2N_0}}\right) \quad \ldots (3.83)$$

where, E is energy for symbol duration T.

i.e. $\quad E = \frac{A^2 T}{2}$

The symbol error probability of QPSK is,

$$\boxed{p_e = \text{erfc}\left(\sqrt{\frac{E}{2N_0}}\right)} \quad \ldots (3.84)$$

or

$$\boxed{p_e = 2Q\left(\sqrt{\frac{E}{N_0}}\right)} \quad \ldots (3.85)$$

Now since $E = 2E_b$, the average probability of symbol error in terms of E_b/N_0 ratio can be written as,

$$p_e = \text{erfc}\left(\sqrt{\frac{E_b}{N_0}}\right) \quad \ldots (3.86)$$

where, E_b is energy per bit duration.

i.e. $\quad E_b = \frac{A^2 T_b}{2}$

Thus, bit error rate in each channel of QPSK can be given by,

$$p_{e_1} = p_{e_2} = \frac{1}{2}\text{erfc}\left(\sqrt{\frac{E_b}{2N_0}}\right) \quad \ldots (3.87)$$

$$= Q\left(\sqrt{\frac{E_b}{N_0}}\right) \quad \ldots (3.88)$$

The above result is same as BPSK. Thus, QPSK has same performance as BPSK but uses half bandwidth. In other words, QPSK system transmits information at twice the bit rate of coherent BPSK for same bandwidth and same E_b/N_0 with same BER.

3.6.4 Error Probability of M-PSK

The error probability in terms of Euclidean distance for circularly symmetric signal constellation is given by,

$$p_e \leq \frac{1}{2} \sum_{\substack{k=1 \\ k \neq i}}^{M} \text{erfc}\left(\frac{d_{ik}}{2\sqrt{N_0}}\right) \qquad \ldots (3.89)$$

$$\therefore \quad p_e \simeq \frac{1}{2} \text{erfc}\left(\frac{d_{12}}{2\sqrt{N_0}}\right) + \frac{1}{2} \text{erfc}\left(\frac{d_{18}}{2\sqrt{N_0}}\right)$$

$$\simeq \text{erfc}\left(\frac{d_{12}}{2\sqrt{N_0}}\right)$$

$$\simeq \text{erfc}\left(\frac{2\sqrt{E}\sin\left(\frac{\pi}{8}\right)}{2\sqrt{N_0}}\right)$$

$$\boxed{p_e \simeq \text{erfc}\left(\sqrt{\frac{E}{N_0}} \cdot \sin\left(\frac{\pi}{8}\right)\right)} \qquad \ldots (3.90)$$

In general for M-ary PSK,

$$p_e = \text{erfc}\left(\sqrt{\frac{E}{N_0}} \sin\left(\frac{\pi}{M}\right)\right) \qquad \ldots (3.91)$$

Hence, the symbol error probability,

For M = 4 i.e. QPSK

$$p_e = \text{erfc}\left(\sqrt{\frac{E}{2N_0}}\right) = 2Q\left(\sqrt{\frac{E}{N_0}}\right) \qquad \ldots (3.92)$$

For M = 8

$$p_e = \text{erfc}\left(\sqrt{\frac{E}{N_0}} \sin\left(\frac{\pi}{8}\right)\right) = 2Q\left(\sqrt{\frac{2E}{N_0}} \sin\left(\frac{\pi}{8}\right)\right) \qquad \ldots (3.93)$$

For M = 16

$$p_e = \text{erfc}\left(\sqrt{\frac{E}{N_0}} \sin\left(\frac{\pi}{16}\right)\right) \qquad \ldots (3.94)$$

For large value of M we can approximate the above formula as below.

The Euclidean distance between the two adjacent points for large M is given as,

$$d = \frac{2\pi \times \sqrt{E}}{M} \qquad \ldots (3.95)$$

(Note that $\sqrt{E}$ is radius of circular constellation hence $2\pi \times \sqrt{E}$ is circumference of the circle).

$$\therefore \quad d^2 = \frac{4\pi^2 \times E}{M^2}$$

$$= \frac{4\pi^2 \times P \times T}{M^2}$$

$$= \frac{4\pi^2 \times P \times N \times T_b}{M^2} \qquad \ldots (3.96)$$

$$= \frac{4\pi^2 \times NE_b}{M^2}$$

$$\therefore \quad d = 2\pi \sqrt{\frac{NE_b}{M^2}}$$

$$= 2\sqrt{\frac{\pi^2 NE_b}{M^2}}$$

Taking into account only two nearest signal points to S_1 and using equation (3.89), we get,

$$p(e/S_1) = p_e \leq 2 \times \frac{1}{2} \text{erfc}\left(\sqrt{\frac{\pi^2 NE_b}{M^2 N_0}}\right) \qquad \ldots (3.97)$$

where, $\quad M = 2^N$

Thus, $\quad p_e = \text{erfc}\left(\sqrt{\frac{\pi^2 NE_b}{M^2 N_0}}\right) \qquad \ldots (3.98)$

or $\quad p_e = 2Q\left(\sqrt{\frac{\pi^2 NE_b}{M^2 N_0}}\right) \qquad \ldots (3.99)$

To keep p_e constant as number of bits per symbol N changes, we can have,

$$\frac{\pi^2 NE_b}{M^2 \times N_0} = \text{Constant} = K$$

$$\therefore \quad \frac{E_b}{N_0} = \frac{K}{\pi^2} \times \frac{M^2}{N} = \frac{K}{\pi^2} \times \frac{2^{2N}}{N}$$

Thus, signal energy-to-noise ratio increases nominally in exponential manner with N for constant p_e in M-ary PSK. The error probabilities of M-ary PSK are plotted in Fig. 3.26 for M = 2, 4, 8, 16, 32, 64.

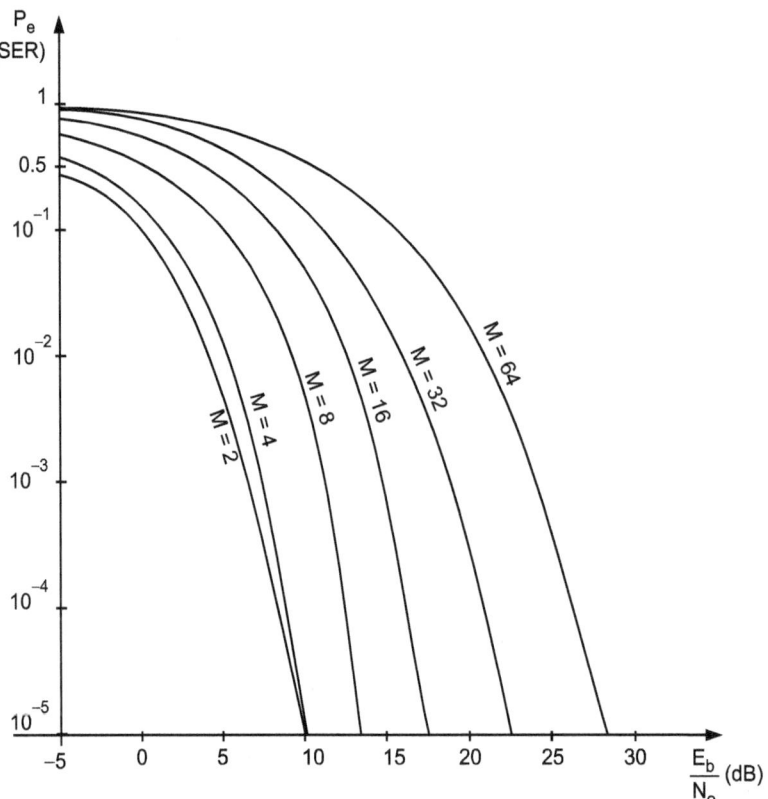

Fig. 3.26: Symbol Error Probability for Coherent M-ary PSK

It can be seen from above plot that, for constant N_0, to achieve same error performance we have to put in more energy per symbol as M increases.

3.7 Synchronization

The timing operation at the receiver should closely follow the corresponding operation at the receiver. This is called synchronization between transmitter and receiver. For synchronization we require a clock signal at the receiver that should have a precise frequency and phase relationship with the received signal. Of course, some allowance has to be made to take into account propagation delay between transmitter and receiver.

Digital communication needs three types of synchronizing signals.
1. Bit synchronization.
2. Frame synchronization
3. Carrier synchronization

Bit synchronization is required to identify the bit interval. Frame synchronization identifies a group of bits belonging to a time slot. Carrier synchronization extracts carrier signals timing with coherent detection.

Fig. 3.27 shows synchronization in binary receiver.

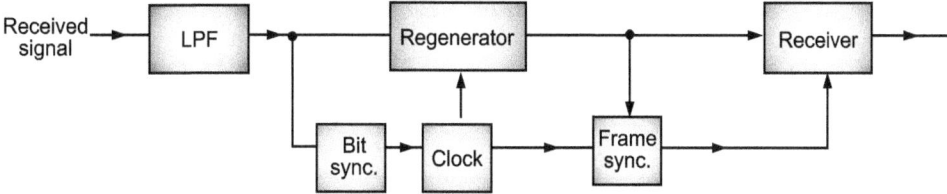

Fig. 3.27: Frame and Bit Synchronization

3.7.1 Bit Synchronization

In order to detect a binary signal at the receiver, we have to sample received signal at a precise instant. This will require clock signal at the receiver in synchronization with receiver. The method of extracting bit duration is called bit synchronization.

There are three methods of bit synchronization.
1. Derivation of clock signal from master timing source both at transmitter and receiver.
2. Transmitting the clock from transmitter to receiver.
3. Extracting clock signal from the signal itself called self-synchronization.

The first method is used for large volume of data and high-speed communication. Its cost is high. The second method uses channel capacity for transmission of clock. Hence, there should be spare capacity available. The third method is more efficient and used very often. Let us look into the method of self-synchronization. If we have unipolar or on-off signaling format, it contains a discrete component of clock frequency. We apply this received signal to a resonant circuit (BPF) tuned to clock frequency. The output of resonant circuit will be a sinusoid cos $(2\pi f_b t + \phi)$, where, f_b is clock frequency. Hence, the output is required clock signal. For polar format, the signal is passed through a square law device. The resulting signal will be unipolar waveforms. It is shown in Fig. 3.28.

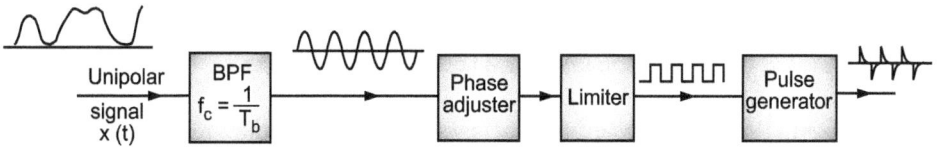

Fig. 3.28: (a) Bit Synchronizor for Unipolar Signal

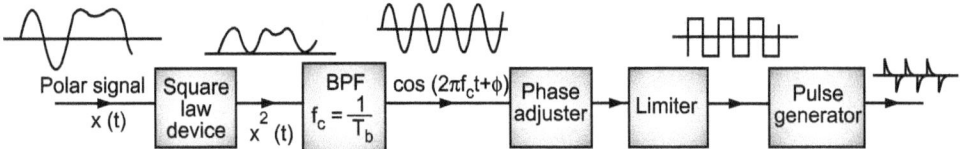

Fig. 3.28: (b) Bit Synchronizor for Polar Signal

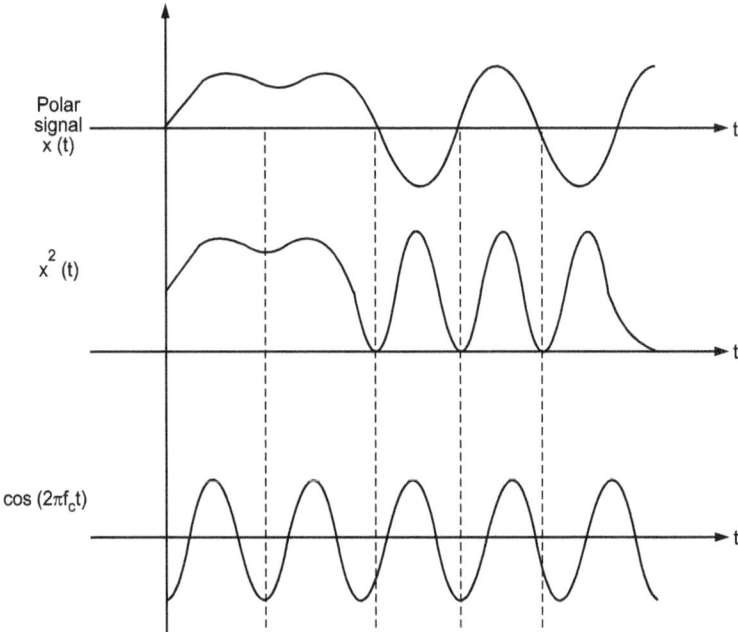

Fig. 3.28: (c) Synchronization Waveforms

The output of square law device is passed through band pass filter and phase adjuster to produce sinusoid of frequency f_b. This is amplified and passed through a limiter to produce clock signal. A closed loop bit synchronizer as shown in Fig. 3.29 (a) can be used to extract synchronization signal from unipolar RZ waveform.

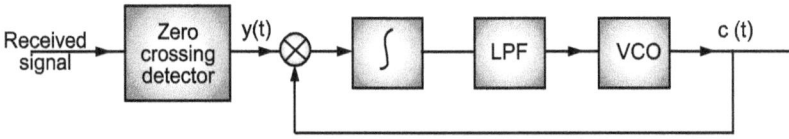

Fig. 3.29: (a) Closed Loop Bit Synchronizer

A zero crossing detector gives out a rectangular pulse of duration $T_b/2$ at each zero crossing. (Refer Fig. 3.29 (b)). The pulse train is then multiplied with a clock signal generated by Voltage Controlled Oscillator (VCO). If there is difference in half duration of clock and $T_b/2$ the multiplication will yield two pulses of unequal duration. These pulses are integrated and filtered to generate VCO control voltage. This control voltage will speed up or slow down the clock accordingly. If the pulses are of equal duration ($T_b/4$), the control voltage will remain same keeping clock frequency constant at $1/T_b$.

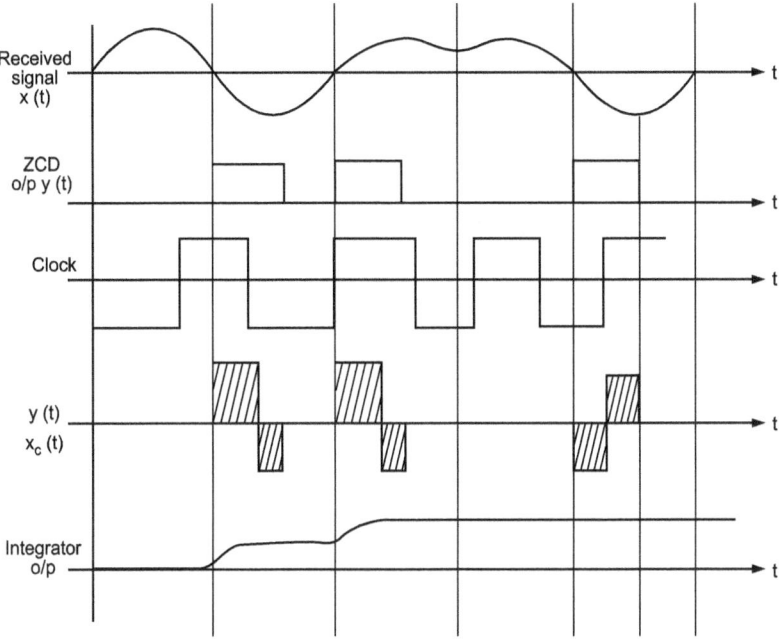

Fig. 3.29: (b) Waveforms of Closed Loop Bit Synchroniser

The above techniques work well if the zero crossings of received signal are spaced by integer multiple of T_b. Small random deviations in this will result (known as timing jitter) into loss of synchronization. Another problem with above techniques is long stream of 1's and 0's will not have zero crossings. Hence, another technique which uses the fact that a filtered signal has peaks at optimum sampling time and is symmetric on either side as shown in Fig. 3.30 (a).

$$|y(nT_b - \Delta)| > |y(nT_b + \Delta)|$$

If $t = nT_b$ is the sampling time and $\Delta < \dfrac{T_b}{2}$ and there is proper synchronization at $t = nT_b$ then,

$$|y(nT_b - \Delta)| \simeq |y(nT_b - \Delta)| < y(nT_b)$$

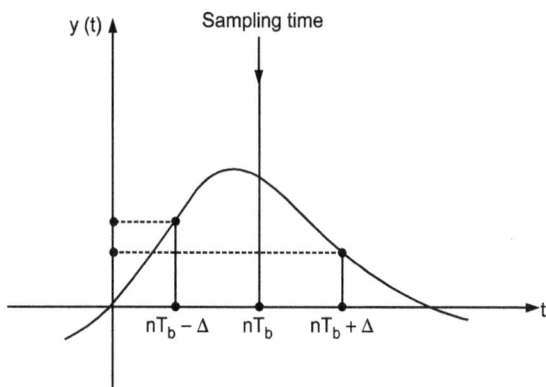

Fig. 3.30: (a) Late Synchronization Signal

If $|y(nT_b - \Delta)| > |y(nT_b + \Delta)|$ meaning the synchronization signal is late and if $|y(nT_b - \Delta)| < |y(nT_b + \Delta)|$ means the synchronization signal is early. Use of this difference in outputs can be made to achieve synchronization. The technique is called as Early-late synchronization. As shown in Fig. 3.30 (b), a late synchronization (sampling beyond peak) will result into increase in control voltage of VCO which will speed up the clock. An early synchronization (sampling before peak) will cause control voltage to reduce resulting into slowing down of clock. A perfect synchronization (sampling at peak) will keep control voltage constant in turn the clock frequency.

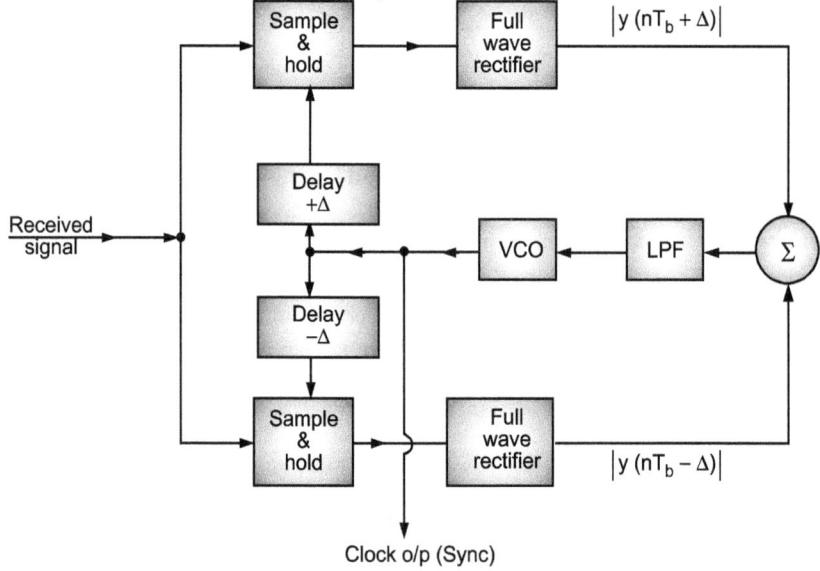

Fig. 3.30: (b) Early Late Synchronizer

3.7.2 Scrambling

The synchronization technique based on zero crossing detectors suffers from loss of synchronization due to long stream of 1's and 0's. Scrambling technique is a solution to this problem. A long stream 1's or 0's is converted into random 1's and 0's. This apart from helping synchronization will also eliminate dc components in the power spectrum and avoid dc wandering. This requires a descrambling operation at the receiver end to get back the original sequence.

A simple shift register and modulo-2 (EX-OR) adder arrangement as shown in Fig. 3.30 (a) can be used for scrambling and descrambling. The scrambler and descrambler circuits are shown in Fig. 3.31 (b) and (c).

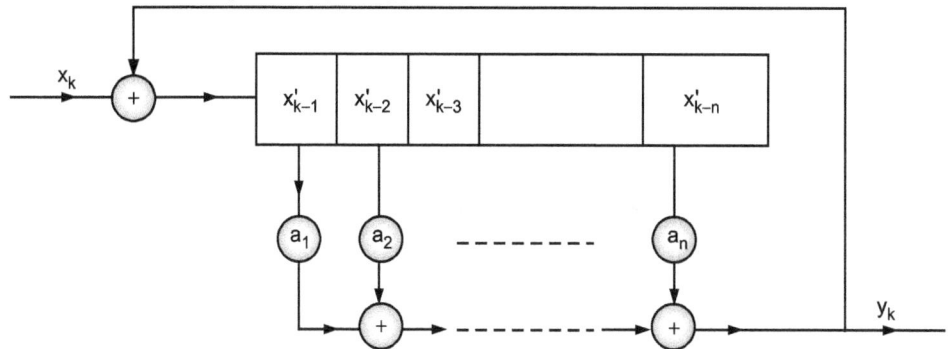

(a) Scrambler Using Tapped Shift Register

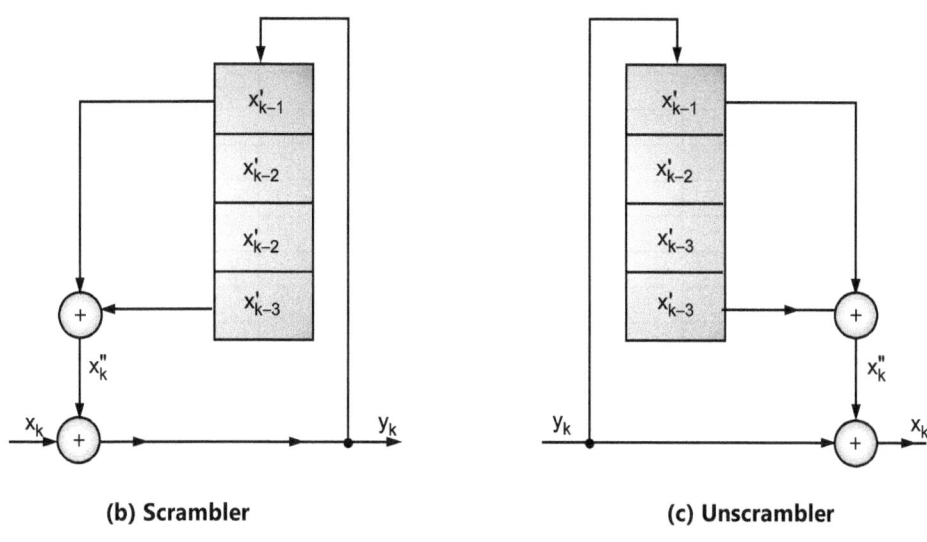

(b) Scrambler   (c) Unscrambler

Fig. 3.31

COMMUNICATION SYSTEM - II   DIGITAL MODULATION TECHNIQUES

If Y is the output of the scrambler and X is the input sequence, then we can write,

$$y_k = a_1 x'_{k-1} + a_2 x'_{k-2} + \ldots + a_n x'_{k-n}$$

A scrambler with 4 shift registers is shown in Fig. 3.31 (b). Hence, we can write,

$$y_k = x_k + x''_k$$

$$= x_k + x'_{k-1} + x'_{k-3}$$

The unscrambler shown in Fig. 3.31 (c) has reverse structure.

Let us see how it reproduces original message. The unscrambled output can be written as,

$$x''_k + y_k = x''_k + (x_k + x''_k) \qquad \text{(Substituting } y_k = x_k + x''_k\text{)}$$

$$= x''_k + x''_k + x_k$$

$$= x_k$$

which is sequence.

Let us now consider an example.

Let 101010100000111 be the input sequence. Following table shows the output sequence obtained. Initially the register contents are assumed to be zeros.

Input (x_k)	x'_{k-1}	x'_{k-2}	x'_{k-3}	x'_{k-4}	x''_k	Output (y_k)
1	0	0	0	0	0	1
0	1	0	0	0	1	1
1	1	1	0	0	1	0
0	0	1	1	0	0	0
1	0	0	1	1	1	0
0	0	0	0	1	1	1
1	1	0	0	0	1	0
0	0	1	0	0	0	0
0	0	0	1	0	0	0
0	0	0	0	1	1	1
0	1	0	0	0	1	1
0	1	1	0	0	1	1
1	1	1	1	0	1	0
1	0	1	1	1	1	0
1	0	0	1	1	1	0

Thus, the output sequence has eliminated the long streams of zeros and also the initial periodic nature of the data stream. The disadvantage of this method is that if there is error in the transmitted bit y_k it is going to cause several errors at the receiver end i.e. error propagation occurs.

3.7.3 Frame Synchronization

The receiver should know when the transmission begins and when it ends. Otherwise when there is no transmission, noise signal will produce random bits. In case of time division multiplexing messages from various sources form a part of the frame. Thus, entire message has many subdivisions. These subdivisions are to be identified at the receiver end in order to distribute them at proper destinations.

Hence, at the beginning of each transmission or each frame a particular bit pattern is used, which can be identified at the receiver end as start of transmission or start of frame. This is called frame synchronization. A typical frame structure is shown in Fig. 3.32 (a).

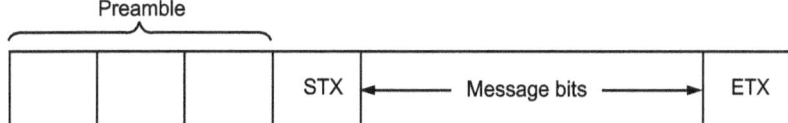

Fig. 3.32: (a) A Typical Frame Structure

At the beginning of transmission several repetitions of a synchronization word are transmitted to acquire bit synchronization. Then start of message word is transmitted which tells the receiver that the message is following. When the transmission is over, end of message word is sent to inform receiver that there is no more data available for transmission. In case of identification of frame, a synchronization word is attached at the beginning of each frame.

A frame synchroniser circuit is shown in Fig. 3.32 (b).

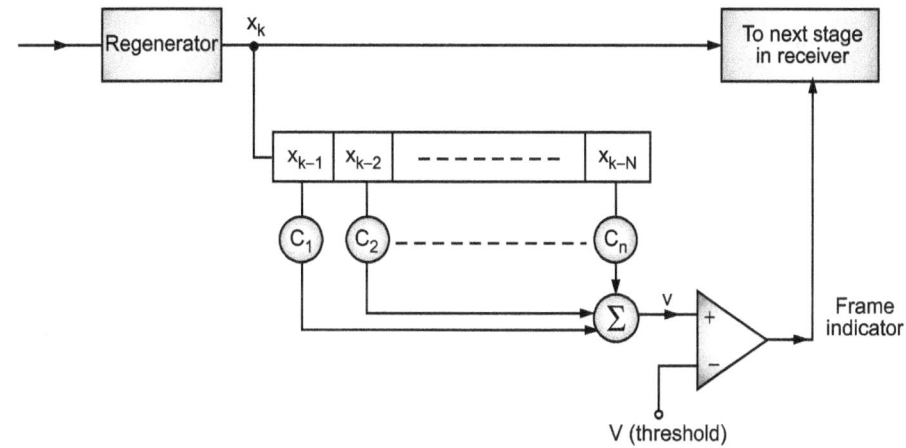

Fig. 3.32: (b) Frame Synchronizer

The output of regenerator is reconstructed message sequence. It is stored in N-stage shift register. Where, N is number of bits in the synchronization word to be identified. The bits are in polar format (± 1). The tap gains of the shift register are adjusted depending on the synchronization word. Let the synchronization word be $(S_1, S_2, ..., S_N)$ and the tap gains adjusted such that,

i.e.
$$\left. \begin{array}{l} c_i = 2 S_{N+1-i} - 1 \\ c_1 = 2 S_N - 1 \\ c_2 = 2 S_{N-1} - 1 \\ \vdots \\ c_N = 2 S_1 - 1 \end{array} \right\}$$

These tap gains are multiplied with received voltage collected in shift register and then added. This sum is compared with a preset threshold voltage V. The output of comparator will indicate whether the word in shift register is a valid synchronization word or not. This is because when valid synchronization word is present in the register, the voltage produced by the summer

$$v = \sum_{i=1}^{N} c_i \times x_{k-i}$$

will exceed the threshold voltage V. Otherwise it will remain below V.

When the register word is same as synchronization word. $x_{k-1} = c_i$. Therefore, $c_i \times x_{k-1} = c_i^2$ = 1 and v = N. The threshold voltage V is set slightly below N. When synchronization word does not match with register word let us say it differs by one bit, the output v = N − 2. Hence, threshold should be in between N and N − 2. Now what will happen if there is one bit error in the synchronization word. It will go undetected ! Hence, instead of keeping the threshold between N and N − 2, it can be kept slightly below N − 2. This will take care of single error in synchronization word. There is a problem of false frame synchronization in case the synchronization word is part of message. What is the probability of occurrence of this ? It will be equal to the probability that all N bits match or N − 1 bits match. Let the probability of 1 and 0 be equally likely, then the probability of false frame synchronization is given by,

$$p_{ff} = \underset{\text{all N bits match}}{\left(\frac{1}{2}\right)^N} + \underset{\text{N − 1 bits match}}{\left(\frac{1}{2}\right)^{N-1}}$$

EXERCISE

1. Discuss Minimum Shift Keying Technique of digital CW Modulation with the help of expressions, necessary waveforms, signals space representation, generation/reception techniques etc. What is minimum in this technique ? How is the phase continuity maintained ?

2. With the help of expressions, signal space and spectral representations and necessary waveforms, explain Binary Phase Shift Keying technique of Digital CW modulation. Discuss the method of generate and receive the BPSK signal.

3. Explain Quadrature Phase Shift Keying technique of Digital CW modulation. Elaborate your answer with suitable expressions, signal space and spectral representations and necessary waveform. How is QPSK signal generated and received ? What is the difference between OQPSK and non-offset QPSK ?

4. Discuss Minimum Shift Keying technique of digital CW modulation. Elaborate your answer with necessary waveforms, expressions, signal space representation, spectral diagrams etc. Explain with neat block diagram, the generation and reception of MSK signal.

5. With suitable block diagram, explain generation and reception of FSK signal in digital CW modulation system. Elaborate your answer with necessary waveforms and expressions. What is bandwidth requirement of FSK system ?

6. Sketch the power spectral density of BPSK signal and state the bandwidth occupied by BPSK signal.

7. State the advantages of digital CW modulation over baseband digital transmission.

8. Discuss the different techniques in brief to recover the carrier in coherent digital CW modulation system.

9. What is Differential Phase Shift Keying ? Discuss with block schematic the generation and reception of DPSK signal. State merits and demerits of DPSK system over PSK system.

10. In a QPSK system, the bit rate of NRZ stream is 10 Mbps and carrier frequency is 1 GHz. Find the symbol rate of transmission and bandwidth requirement of the channel. Sketch the power spectral density of the QPSK signal.

11. Explain generation and reception of BFSK signal with suitable block schematic. Sketch necessary waveforms, signal space representation and frequency spectrum of BFSK signal.

12. What is Gaussian MSK ? State area of application for the same.

13. For a BPSK modulator with a carrier frequency of 70 MHz and an input bit rate of 10 Mbps. Draw the spectrum of output signal and determine the minimum Nyquist bandwidth.

14. Write short notes on:
    (i) 16 QAM
    (ii) M-ary FSK
    (iii) Quadrature Amplitude Modulation
    (iv) Gaussian MSK
    (v) Frequency Shift Keying
    (vi) Gaussian MSK
    (vii) M-ary PSK
    (viii) DPSK and DEPSK Modulation

15. Explain working of BFSK transmitter and receiver. Show signal space representation of the orthogonal and non-orthogonal BFSK signals.

Unit IV

INFORMATION AND DETECTION THEORY

4.1 Introduction

Information and Communication Technology (ICT) has become backbone of today's economy. Communication systems transmit the information generated by source to some destination. This information can be voice, electronic mail, computer generated data, video, fax etc. Communication systems, through which this information is passed, are likely to distort this information. There is uncertainty at transmitter, channel and receiver in the communication system. Performance of a communication system must, therefore, be analyzed from the point of view of information transmitted and processed in the system. This will require use of probabilistic techniques because of uncertainty involved.

C. E. Shannon in 1948 published his revolutionary work which laid the foundation of "Information Theory". He stated that we can transmit information through a channel at any rate less than the capacity of channel with arbitrarily small error, whatever may be the disturbances in the channel.

Information theory deals with –
- (i) Mathematical laws governing systems that communicate and process information.
- (ii) Quantitative measures of information and capacity of various systems that transmit, receive or process information.

We have to come out with mathematical models of source which is generating information, channel which is transmitting information and receiver which is receiving information. Measurement of information involved in each stage also needs to be done so that we can design an effective and efficient communication system.

To summarize, information theory is used for mathematical modelling and analysis of communication system, so that we will be able to transmit minimum information and maximize the transmission rate, yet there is reliability in transmission.

4.1.1 Mathematical Model for Information Sources

There are two types of information sources.
- (i) Analog sources such as voice, video etc.
- (ii) Discrete sources such as computer generated data, PCM output etc.

Information produced by any source is random. Consider a discrete information source with m different letters or digits given by {$x_1, x_2, x_3, ... x_m$}. It emits a sequence of letters selected from the set of letters. To construct mathematical model, we assume that each letter has a probability –

$$p(x_j) = p(X = x_j) \quad ; \quad 1 \leq j \leq m$$

where, $\sum_{j=1}^{m} p(x_j) = 1$

Discrete Memoryless Source (DMS): If the current letter produced by a source is statistically independent of all past and future outputs, then such source is called Discrete Memoryless Source (DMS).

Discrete Stationary Source (DSS): If the joint probability of two sequences of length n say ($x_1, x_2, x_3, ... x_n$} and {$x_{1+n}, x_{2+n}, ... x_{m+n}$} are identical for all n ≥ 1 and for all shifts m, then such source is said to be stationary source.

4.2 Uncertainty and Information

The most important feature of any communication system is its uncertainty. Information produced by the source is random in nature. The transmitter, channel and receiver, which carry this information, are also statistical in nature. The performance of communication system can be best described by modelling it statistically.

Let us first understand how information is measured. Consider the following three statements.
1. Today the sun will set in the West.
2. It will rain somewhere in India tomorrow.
3. Man bites dog.

The amount of information contained in each of above three statements is different. The first statement conveys no information at all, or it is certain to happen. The second statement conveys some information, whereas the last statement carries lot of information as the probability of man biting dog is very very small. It means there is an inverse relationship between probability of an event and amount of information carried by it. Thus, information is an inverse function of probability of occurrence of the event. If we denote $I(x_j)$ as information associated with event x_j, we can write,

$$I(x_j) = f\left[\frac{1}{p(x_j)}\right] \quad \quad ... (4.1)$$

1. $p(x_j) = 0$, $I(x_j)$ should be highest, say ∞.
2. $p(x_j) = 1$, $I(x_j)$ should be lowest, say, 0.
3. If $p(x_j) < p(x_k)$ then $I(x_j) > I(x_k)$

4. If x_j and y_k are statistically independent,

then, $I(x_j, y_k) = I(x_j) + I(y_k)$

i.e. $I(x_j, y_k) = f\left[\dfrac{1}{p(x_j) \cdot p(y_k)}\right]$

Logarithmic function can give such results.
Hence,

Definition: $\boxed{I(x_j) = \log\left[\dfrac{1}{p(x_j)}\right] = -\log p(x_j)}$ ... (4.2)

Thus, for discrete source X producing outputs $x_1, x_2, x_3, \ldots x_m$, information of an event x_j is given by equation (4.2). It is also called self-information. Unit of information depends on base of logarithm. If base is 2, unit is bit. If base is 10, unit is decit or Hartley and if base is e, unit is nat. Most of the time we deal with binary information, hence base 2 is often used and it is default base for log that we will be assuming hence forth.

Note that since $0 \leq p(x_j) \leq 1$, then self-information $I(x_j)$ will be non-negative i.e. $I(x_j) \geq 0$.

4.3 Entropy

Till now, we were talking about information of single message generated by the source. What about information generated by the source ? It can be total information or average information generated by the source. But only average information can characterize the source. Average information of a source is information generated per individual message. It is also called entropy of the source.

Definition: *Entropy of a source is average amount of information generated by the source per message.*

Let us consider a source X generating m different messages, $x_1, x_2, x_3, \ldots x_m$ with corresponding probabilities $p(x_1), p(x_2), p(x_3), \ldots p(x_m)$. It means in a long stream of messages generated by source, the probability of generating message x_i will be $p(x_i)$.
(If $p(x_i) = 0.1$, then 10 out of 100 messages generated by the source will be x_i). Suppose, this source generates L number of messages at a particular time, where L >> m.

∴ Number of x_1 messages generated by the source

$$= p(x_1) \times L$$

∴ Total amount of information contained in all x_1's will be

$$= p(x_1) \times L \times \log \dfrac{1}{p(x_1)}$$

Similarly, number of x_2 messages generated by the source

$$= p(x_2) \times L$$

Total amount of information contained by all x_2's will be

$$= p(x_2) \times L \times \log \frac{1}{p(x_2)}$$

and so on.

Therefore, total amount of information contained in all L messages will be

$$I_{total} = p(x_1) \times L \log \frac{1}{p(x_1)} + p(x_2) \times L \log \frac{1}{p(x_2)}$$

$$+ \ldots\ldots + p(x_m) \times L \log \frac{1}{p(x_m)} \quad \ldots (4.3)$$

Therefore, average amount of information generated by the source per message will be $\frac{I_{total}}{L}$.

It is called entropy and is denoted by H.

Therefore, entropy of the source X will be

$$H(X) = \frac{I_{total}}{L} \text{ bits/message}$$

$$= p(x_1) \log \frac{1}{p(x_1)} + p(x_2) \log \frac{1}{p(x_2)} + \ldots\ldots p(x_m) \log \frac{1}{p(x_m)}$$

$$= \sum_{j=1}^{m} p(x_j) \log \frac{1}{p(x_j)} \text{ bits/message}$$

$$= - \sum_{j=1}^{m} p(x_j) \log p(x_j) \quad \ldots (4.4)$$

Note that the unit of entropy is bits/message. It can also be given as **bits/symbol.**

Example 4.1:

Find entropy of a source X generating 4 types of messages with probabilities $\frac{1}{4}, \frac{1}{8}, \frac{1}{8}$ and $\frac{1}{2}$.

Solution:

Let given source be

$$X = \{x_1, x_2, x_3, x_4\}$$

$$\therefore \quad P(X) = \left\{ \frac{1}{4}, \frac{1}{8}, \frac{1}{8}, \frac{1}{2} \right\}$$

Entropy of the source is given by

$$H(X) = \sum_{j=1}^{4} p(x_j) \log_2 \frac{1}{p(x_j)}$$

$$= \frac{1}{4} \log \frac{1}{\left(\frac{1}{4}\right)} + \frac{1}{8} \log \frac{1}{\left(\frac{1}{8}\right)} + \frac{1}{8} \log \frac{1}{\left(\frac{1}{8}\right)} + \frac{1}{2} \log \frac{1}{\left(\frac{1}{2}\right)}$$

$$= \frac{1}{4} \times \log 4 + \frac{1}{8} \log 8 + \frac{1}{8} \log 8 + \frac{1}{2} \log 2$$

$$= \frac{1}{4} \times 2 + \frac{1}{8} \times 3 + \frac{1}{8} \times 3 + \frac{1}{2} \times 1$$

$$= 1.75 \text{ bits/message}$$

∴ Entropy = 1.75 bits/message

If a source is generating only single message i.e. m = 1, $p(x_1)$ = 1. Entropy of this source –

$$H(X) = p(x_1) \log \left[\frac{1}{p(x_1)}\right]$$

$$= 1 \cdot \log \frac{1}{1}$$

$$= 0 \text{ bits/message}$$

Thus, this source is generating no information at all ! It is because there is no uncertainty in generating message. We are certain that the source is going to generate message x_1 only. Now, consider a source which is generating two messages (Binary source) x_1 and x_2. Let the probabilities be $p(x_1)$ and $p(x_2)$ respectively. The entropy of this source is given by

$$H(X) = p(x_1) \log \frac{1}{p(x_1)} + p(x_2) \log p(x_2) \qquad \ldots (4.5)$$

Let $p(x_1) = p$ and $p(x_2) = q = 1 - p$

∴

$$H(X) = p \log \frac{1}{p} + q \log \frac{1}{q} \qquad \ldots (4.6)$$

$$= p \log \frac{1}{p} + (1-p) \log \frac{1}{(1-p)} \qquad \ldots (4.7)$$

If we plot H(X) against p, the graph will be as shown in Fig. 4.1.

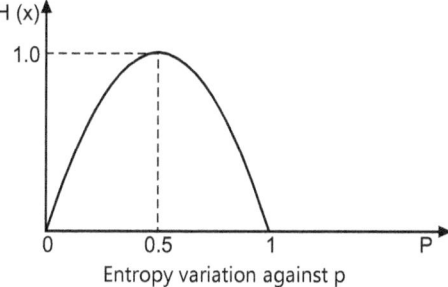

Entropy variation against p

Fig. 4.1: Plot of H(X) for Binary Source

It can be observed from graph that –

(i) H(X) is non-negative.

(ii) H(X) is zero only for p = 0 and p = 1 as there is no uncertainty.

(iii) H(X) is maximum at $p = \frac{1}{2}$.

The value of p, where maximum value of H(X) occurs, can be found by differentiating equation (4.7) w.r.t. p and equating it to zero.

$$H(X) = p \log \frac{1}{p} + (1-p) \log \frac{1}{(1-p)} \quad \ldots (4.8)$$

$$H(X) = p \frac{\log_e \left(\frac{1}{p}\right)}{\log_e (2)} + (1-p) \frac{\log_e \left(\frac{1}{1-p}\right)}{\log_e (2)}$$

$$\therefore \quad H(X) = \frac{1}{\log_e (2)} \left[p \log_e \left(\frac{1}{p}\right) + (1-p) \log_e \frac{1}{(1-p)} \right] \quad \ldots (4.9)$$

$$\therefore \quad \frac{d\,H(X)}{dp} = \frac{1}{\log_e (2)} \left[p \times p \times \left(-\frac{1}{p^2}\right) + \log_e \left(\frac{1}{p}\right) \times 1 + (1-p) \right.$$

$$\left. \times (1-p) \times \frac{-1}{(1-p)^2} \times (-1) + \log_e \left(\frac{1}{1-p}\right) \times (-1) \right]$$

$$= \frac{1}{\log_e (2)} \left[-1 + \log_e \left(\frac{1}{p}\right) + 1 - \log_e \frac{1}{(1-p)} \right]$$

$$= \frac{1}{\log_e (2)} \left[\log_e \left(\frac{1}{p}\right) - \log_e \frac{1}{(1-p)} \right]$$

$$\therefore \quad \frac{1}{\log_e (2)} \left[\log_e \left(\frac{1}{p}\right) - \log_e \frac{1}{(1-p)} \right] = 0$$

$$\therefore \quad \log \frac{1}{p} = \log \frac{1}{1-p}$$

$$\therefore \quad p = 1 - p$$

$$\therefore \quad \boxed{p = \frac{1}{2}}$$

It can also be seen that,

$$\boxed{\frac{d^2 H(X)}{d^2 p} = -\frac{1}{p} - \frac{1}{1-p} < 0} \quad \ldots (4.10)$$

Hence, maxima occurs at $p = \frac{1}{2}$.

and
$$H(X)_{max} = \frac{1}{2} \times \log \frac{1}{\left(\frac{1}{2}\right)} + \frac{1}{2} \times \log \frac{1}{\left(\frac{1}{2}\right)}$$

$$= 1 \text{ bit/message}$$

Above result can be extended for a source generating m messages. The entropy of this source will be maximum when all messages are equally likely or equiprobable. The maximum value of entropy will be

$$H(X)_{max} = \sum_{j=1}^{m} p(x_j) \log \frac{1}{p(x_j)} \quad \ldots (4.11)$$

$$= \sum_{j=1}^{m} \frac{1}{m} \log \frac{1}{\left(\frac{1}{m}\right)} \quad \ldots (4.12)$$

$$= \log m \text{ bits/message} \quad \ldots (4.13)$$

When the messages are equally likely, there is maximum uncertainty. Hence, we have maximum value of entropy. Thus, more is uncertainty, more will be the entropy.

4.3.1 Properties of Entropy

From above discussion on entropy, we can state following two important properties of entropy.

Property 1:
- (i) $H(X) \geq 0$ i.e. entropy is non-negative.
- (ii) $H(X) = 0$ if and only if $p(x_j) = 1$ for some j and all other probabilities are zero.

Proof:
We know that,

$$H(X) = \sum_{j=1}^{m} p(x_j) \log \frac{1}{p(x_j)}$$

In this equation, $p(x_j)$ ranges between zero and unity, hence the quantity $p(x_j) \log \frac{1}{p(x_j)}$ is always non-negative (≥ 0). Hence, sum of all such terms will also be non-negative.

i.e. $H(X) \geq 0$.

We also see that $p(x_j) \log \frac{1}{p(x_j)}$ will be zero if $p(x_j) = 0$ or 1.

Hence, $H(X) = 0$ if and only if $p(x_j) = 1$ for some j and all other probabilities are zero.

Property 2:

   (i) $H(X) \leq \log m$

   (ii) $H(X) = \log m$, if and only if, all probabilities are equal so that $p(x_j) = \frac{1}{m}$ for all j.

Proof:

Consider any two probability distributions $\{p(x_1), p(x_2), p(x_3), \ldots p(x_m)\}$ and $\{p(y_1), p(y_2), p(y_3), \ldots p(y_m)\}$.

We can write,

$$\sum_{i=1}^{m} p(x_j) \log \frac{p(y_j)}{p(x_j)} = \frac{1}{\log_e 2} \sum_{j=1}^{m} p(x_j) \log_e \left[\frac{p(y_j)}{p(x_j)}\right] \quad \ldots (4.14)$$

Now, we know that,

$$\log_e x \leq x - 1 \quad \text{for } x \geq 0$$

Using this result we can write equation (4.9) as

$$\sum_{j=1}^{m} p(x_j) \log_e \left[\frac{p(y_j)}{p(x_j)}\right] \leq \sum_{j=1}^{m} p(x_j) \left[\frac{p(y_j)}{p(x_j)} - 1\right]$$

$$\leq \sum_{j=1}^{m} p(y_j) - \sum_{j=1}^{m} p(x_j)$$

$$\leq 1 - 1$$

$$\leq 0 \quad \ldots (4.15)$$

Let, $\quad p(y_j) = \frac{1}{m}$

$$\therefore \sum_{j=1}^{m} p(x_j) \log \frac{p(y_j)}{p(x_j)} = \sum_{j=1}^{m} p(x_j) \log \frac{1}{m \, p(x_j)}$$

$$= \sum_{j=1}^{m} p(x_j) \log \frac{1}{p(x_j)} - \sum_{j=1}^{m} p(x_j) \log m$$

$$= H(X) - \log m \quad \ldots (4.16)$$

From equations (4.15) and (4.16), we can write,

$$H(X) - \log m \leq 0 \quad \ldots (4.17)$$

$$\therefore \quad H(X) \leq \log m \quad \ldots (4.18)$$

$$\therefore \quad \boxed{H(X)_{max} = \log m} \quad \ldots (4.19)$$

4.3.2 Entropy and Information Rate

If a discrete memoryless source generates messages at a rate r message per second, the average amount of information generated per second by the source, can be given by

$$\text{Rate of Information (R)} = [\text{Number of messages/sec.}] \times \begin{bmatrix} \text{Average information} \\ \text{per message} \end{bmatrix}$$

We know that H(X) is average information per message.

$$\therefore \quad R = r\,H(X) \text{ bits/sec.} \quad \ldots (4.20)$$

This quantity is important as it describes source in the form of rate of information generated by it. Consider two sources X and Y with entropies H(X) and H(Y). If rates of generation of messages by them are r_x and r_y respectively, then,

$$R_X = r_x\,H(X)$$
$$R_Y = r_y\,H(Y)$$

If $r_x < r_y$ and $H(X) = H(Y)$

$$R_X < R_Y \quad \ldots (4.21)$$

Thus, source X transmits less information than source Y.

Hence, source is described by its rate of information and entropy. Sometime rate of information is called as bits/sec. entropy.

Example 4.2:

If source is generating messages of two bits 1 and 0 each and probability of generating 1 is $\frac{2}{5}$, then find the rate of generation of information if 100 messages are generated per second.

Solution:

Since, source is generating four messages, these messages will be 00, 01, 10 and 11 and their probabilities will be as below.

$$p(0, 0) = p(0) \cdot p(0) = \frac{3}{5} \times \frac{3}{5} = \frac{9}{25}$$

$$p(0, 1) = p(0) \cdot p(1) = \frac{3}{5} \times \frac{2}{5} = \frac{6}{25}$$

$$p(1, 0) = p(1) \cdot p(0) = \frac{2}{5} \times \frac{3}{5} = \frac{6}{25}$$

$$p(1, 1) = p(1) \cdot p(1) = \frac{2}{5} \times \frac{2}{5} = \frac{4}{25}$$

Therefore, entropy of the source will be

$$H(X) = \sum_{i=1}^{4} p(x_i) \log \frac{1}{p(x_i)}$$

$$= \frac{9}{25} \log \frac{25}{9} + \frac{6}{25} \log \frac{25}{6} + \frac{6}{25} \log \frac{25}{6} + \frac{4}{25} \log \frac{25}{4}$$

$$= 1.942 \text{ bits/message}$$

Since, r = 100 messages/sec., rate of information is given by

$$R = r H(X)$$
$$= 100 \times 1.942$$
$$= 194.2 \text{ bits/sec.}$$

Example 4.3:

An 8-bit PCM system generates 8,000 samples per second. If the quantized samples produced by the systems are equiprobable, what is the rate of transmission of information?

Solution:

Since, the PCM system has 8-bits per sample, there will be 256 quantization levels. These quantized samples are equiprobable. Hence, probability of each sample = $\frac{1}{256}$.

Therefore, entropy of the PCM transmitter

$$= \log 256$$
$$= 8 \text{ bits}$$

Since, r = 8,000 samples/sec.

$$\text{Rate of Information} = r \times H$$
$$= 8,000 \times 8$$
$$= 64,000 \text{ bits/sec.}$$
$$= 64 \text{ kbps}$$

Example 4.4:

A 3-bit PCM system generates 1,000 samples per second. If the quantized samples produced by the system have probabilities - $\left\{\frac{1}{4}, \frac{1}{4}, \frac{1}{8}, \frac{1}{8}, \frac{1}{16}, \frac{1}{16}, \frac{1}{16}, \frac{1}{16}\right\}$, find the rate of information if the samples are equiprobable. What will be the rate of information?

Solution:

Given: Number of bits used in PCM system = 3 bits

Hence, there will be 8 quantized samples.

(i) Probabilities of samples = $\left\{\dfrac{1}{4}, \dfrac{1}{4}, \dfrac{1}{8}, \dfrac{1}{8}, \dfrac{1}{16}, \dfrac{1}{16}, \dfrac{1}{16}, \dfrac{1}{16}\right\}$

$\therefore$ Entropy H $= \dfrac{1}{4}\log 4 + \dfrac{1}{4}\log 4 + \dfrac{1}{8}\log 8 + \dfrac{1}{8}\log 8 + \dfrac{1}{16}\log 16$
$+ \dfrac{1}{16}\log 16 + \dfrac{1}{16}\log 16 + \dfrac{1}{16}\log 16$

$= \dfrac{1}{2} + \dfrac{1}{2} + \dfrac{3}{8} + \dfrac{3}{8} + \dfrac{4}{16} + \dfrac{4}{16} + \dfrac{4}{16} + \dfrac{4}{16}$

$= 2.75$ bits/sample

Rate of information $= R = rH$

Since, $r = 1{,}000$ samples/sec.

$\therefore \quad R = 2.75 \times 1000 = 2750$ bits/sec.

(ii) If samples are equiprobable,

$H = \log m \quad$ where, $m = 8$
$= 3$ bits/sample

$\therefore$ Rate of information $R = rH$
$= 1{,}000 \times 3$
$= 3{,}000$ bits/sec.

> **Note:** From above example, it can be seen that when all messages are equally likely, $R = r \log m$; whereas, when the probabilities are different, $R < r \log m$.

4.4 Source Coding Theorem (Shannon's First Theorem)

Coding is a technique of transforming symbols or messages generated by a source into another format, so as to improve efficiency of communication system. Coding is a procedure for mapping a given set of messages $[x_1, x_2, x_3, \ldots x_N]$ into a set of encoded messages $[y_1, y_2, y_3, \ldots y_N]$ in such a way that, for each message, there is only one encoded message. Since, we are encoding messages generated by source, this method is called source coding. This helps in improving transmission efficiency.

Following terminologies are used with coding.
1. **Letter or character:** Individual member of alphabet set (message).
2. **Message or word:** Finite sequence of letters.
3. **Length of message:** Number of letters in a word or message.
4. **Encoding or enciphering:** It is a procedure of associating words generated by a source into another language or format in one-to-one manner.
5. **Decoding or Deciphering:** The inverse operation of assigning words of second language corresponding to words in first language.

COMMUNICATION SYSTEM - II   INFORMATION AND DETECTION THEORY

6. **Code word:** Word generated by encoding procedure in second language.
7. **Code or Codebook:** Set of all code words.
8. **Fixed length code:** Code with fixed length of code words.
9. **Variable length code:** Code with variable length of code words.
10. **Irreducible or Prefix condition:** If no code word forms prefix of any other code word, it is called prefix condition or irreducible property.
11. **Uniquely decipherable or decodable:** The decoding operation, in which it is possible to recognize the correspondence between two languages without space mark between the words. Such codes are also called instantaneous codes as there is no decoding delay.

Now, consider that a source generates 4 messages x_1, x_2, x_3, x_4. Then one way of encoding these messages will be as below.

Message Word	Code Word
x_1	0 0
x_2	0 1
x_3	1 0
x_4	1 1

This is called fixed length code, as there are fixed length code words in it. We can encode these messages as below also.

Message Word	Code Word
x_1	0
x_2	10
x_3	110
x_4	111

This is called variable length coding, as code consists of variable length code words. Obvious question that will come is, how we decode it? If you observe the code words, they are found to be uniquely decipherable. Also, they satisfy prefix condition. i.e. if we add 0 or 1 at the end of code word, it does give rise to another code word.

A code which satisfies prefix property, can be decoded easily. Consider that we want to transmit the messages generated by the source using above scheme. The messages generated are $x_1, x_1, x_2, x_3, x_3, x_4, x_4, x_3$. Then we will be transmitting 0 0 1 0 1 1 0 1 1 0 1 1 1 1 1 0. This bit stream can be recognized as below.

```
0   0   1 0   1 1 0   1 1 0   1 1 1   1 1 0
x₁  x₁  x₂   x₃      x₃      x₄      x₃
```

We can decode the code words by observing bit pattern, e.g. if 0 occurs, we can decode it to x_1. If 1 0 occurs, we can decode it as x_2. If 1 1 1 occurs, we can observe third bit and decode it as x_4.

When a code is irreducible, it is also uniquely decipherable. But reverse is not true. If we encode the messages as below, we see that the code is not irreducible, though it is uniquely decipherable.

Message Word	Code Word
x_1	0
x_2	01
x_3	001
x_4	011

In this case, if a source is generating messages x_1, x_1, x_2, x_3, x_4, x_4, x_3, we will be transmitting 0 0 0 1 0 0 1 0 0 1 0 1 1 0 1 1 0 0 1. But it is not possible to decode this code uniquely.

4.4.1 Code Efficiency

From above discussion, it must have been clear to you that the encoding method should give rise to uniquely decodable code, so that original message sequence generated by source can be reconstructed perfectly. Let us now see another aspect of encoding, the efficiency of coding. The source, which is generating messages, may be generating them with different probabilities. The message, which is generated with higher probability, will be generated more number of times than other messages. In such case, instead of using fixed length code, if we use variable length code, we will be improving the efficiency by assigning less number of bits to higher probability message compared to lower probability messages.

For example, if a source generates 4 messages x_1, x_2, x_3, x_4 with probability $\frac{1}{2}, \frac{1}{4}, \frac{1}{8}, \frac{1}{8}$, then we can use following two schemes for coding.

Scheme I: Fixed Length Coding:

Message	Probability	Code
x_1	$\frac{1}{2}$	00
x_2	$\frac{1}{4}$	01
x_3	$\frac{1}{8}$	10
x_4	$\frac{1}{8}$	11

If one hundred messages are generated by one source per second, then 50 of them will be x_1, 25 will be x_2, 12.5 will be x_3 and 12.5 will be x_4.

Number of code bits transmitted per second will be $50 \times 2 + 25 \times 2 + 12.5 \times 2 = 200$ bits/sec.

Scheme II: Variable Length Coding:

Message	Probability	Code
x_1	$\frac{1}{2}$	0
x_2	$\frac{1}{4}$	10
x_3	$\frac{1}{8}$	110
x_4	$\frac{1}{8}$	111

If again one hundred messages are generated by the source per second, the total number of bits transmitted in one second will be

$$= 50 \times 1 + 25 \times 2 + 12.5 \times 3 + 12.5 \times 3$$
$$= 175 \text{ bits/sec.}$$

Thus, in Scheme II, we are transmitting less number of bits per second than Scheme I. Clearly Scheme II is more efficient than Scheme I.

Theorem:

For constructing a binary code, which satisfies prefix condition, we can use Kraft's inequality theorem. It states that it is possible to construct a binary code with code words of lengths $n_1 \leq n_2 \leq \ldots n_m$ that satisfy prefix condition, provided the necessary and sufficient condition –

$$\sum_{j=1}^{m} 2^{-n_j} \leq 1 \text{ is satisfied} \quad \ldots (4.22)$$

where, factor 2 is number of symbols (radix) in binary alphabet.

Now let us formulate an equation for coding efficiency. Let there be m number of messages generated by a source $x_1, x_2, x_3, \ldots x_m$ with probabilities $p(x_1), p(x_2), p(x_3), \ldots p(x_m)$ respectively. Let code words of each message have variable number of bits. If n_j is number of bits in code words corresponding to message x_j, then total number of bits of first message in a bit stream of L messages (where L >> m) is $p(x_j) \times L \times n_j$

∴ Total number of bits in L messages

$$= \sum_{j=1}^{m} p(x_j) \times L \times n_j \quad \ldots (4.23)$$

∴ Number of bits per message

$$= \sum_{j=1}^{m} p(x_j) \times n_j \quad \ldots (4.24)$$

This quantity is called average code word length and is denoted as $\bar{L}$.

$$\therefore \quad \bar{L} = \sum_{j=1}^{m} n_j \times p(x_j) \text{ bits/message} \quad \ldots (4.25)$$

Thus, $\bar{L}$ represents average number of bits per source symbol. For highest coding efficiency, $\bar{L}$ should be minimum. This value of $\bar{L}$ will depend on how you have encoded message. Let $\bar{L}_{min}$ be the minimum possible value of $\bar{L}$. Then coding efficiency is defined as

$$\eta = \frac{\bar{L}_{min}}{\bar{L}} \quad \ldots (4.26)$$

Now, how do we get minimum value of average code word length? The answer to this question lies in the Shannon's source coding theorem, which is called Shannon's First Theorem.

Shannon's Source Coding Theorem:

If X is discrete memoryless source generating symbols $x_1, x_2, \ldots x_m$ with probabilities $p(x_1), p(x_2), \ldots p(x_m)$, then it is possible to construct a code that satisfies prefix condition and has average code word length $\bar{L}$ that satisfies the inequality

$$H(X) \leq \bar{L} < H(X) + 1 \quad \ldots (4.27)$$

Proof:

Consider the quantity $H(X) - \bar{L}$

$$H(X) - \bar{L} = \sum_{j=1}^{m} p(x_j) \log \frac{1}{p(x_j)} - \sum_{j=1}^{m} p(x_j) \cdot n_j \quad \ldots (4.28)$$

$$= \sum_{j=1}^{m} p(x_j) \log_2 \left[\frac{2^{-n_j}}{p(x_j)} \right] \quad \ldots (4.29)$$

Since, $\log_e x \leq x - 1$

we can write,

$$H(X) - \bar{L} \leq \log_2 e \sum_{j=1}^{m} p(x_j) \left[\frac{2^{-n_j}}{p(x_j)} - 1 \right] \quad \ldots (4.30)$$

$$\leq \log_2 e \left[\sum_{j=1}^{m} 2^{-n_j} - \sum_{j=1}^{m} p(x_j) \right] \quad \ldots (4.31)$$

$$\leq 0 \quad \text{[Using Kraft's inequality]} \quad \ldots (4.32)$$

$$\therefore \quad H(X) - \bar{L} \leq 0 \quad \ldots (4.33)$$

$$\therefore \quad H(X) \leq \bar{L} \quad \ldots (4.34)$$

Now, consider code words of lengths n_j such that $2^{-n_j} \leq p(x_j) < 2^{-n_j + 1}$

$$\therefore \quad \sum_{j=1}^{m} 2^{-n_j} \leq \sum_{j=1}^{m} p(x_j) \quad \ldots (4.35)$$

$$\leq 1 \quad \ldots (4.36)$$

and $\quad p(x_j) < 2^{-n_j + 1} \quad \ldots (4.37)$

$$\therefore \quad \log p(x_j) < -n_j + 1 \quad \ldots (4.38)$$

$$\therefore \quad n_j < 1 - \log p(x_j) \quad \ldots (4.39)$$

$$\therefore \quad n_j p(x_j) < p(x_j) - p(x_j) \log p(x_j) \quad \ldots (4.40)$$

$$\therefore \quad \sum_{j=1}^{m} n_j p(x_j) < \sum_{j=1}^{m} p(x_j) + \left(-\sum p(x_j) \log p(x_j)\right) \quad \ldots (4.41)$$

$$\therefore \quad \bar{L} < 1 + H(X) \quad \ldots (4.42)$$

Thus, from equations (4.34) and (4.42), we can write,

$$\boxed{H(X) \leq \bar{L} < H(X) + 1}$$

The above theorem tells us that for a prefix code, the minimum number of average bits per symbol ($\bar{L}_{min}$) should be at least equal to entropy of the source.

It can also be seen that, higher the value of entropy of source (more uncertainty), one requires more number of bits to represent the source symbols.

Hence, $\bar{L}_{min} = H(X)$ and coding efficiency is given by

$$\eta = \frac{\bar{L}_{min}}{\bar{L}}$$

$$\boxed{\eta = \frac{H(X)}{\bar{L}}} \quad \ldots (4.43)$$

Above formula is valid for binary code only. For m-ary code,

$$\bar{L}_{min} = \frac{H(X)}{\log m} \cdot \frac{\text{bits/message}}{\text{bits/letter}}$$

$$\therefore \quad \eta = \frac{H(X)}{\bar{L} \log m} \quad \ldots (4.44)$$

Redundancy is defined as $1 - \eta$.

$$\therefore \quad \boxed{\text{Redundancy (R)} = 1 - \eta} \quad \ldots (4.45)$$

Example 4.5:

Find coding efficiency of a source encoder generating messages with probabilities $\frac{1}{2}, \frac{1}{4}, \frac{1}{8}, \frac{1}{8}$ using binary encoding scheme as follows.

Message	Code
x_1	00
x_2	01
x_3	10
x_4	11

Solution:

Given: $\quad p(X) = \left\{ \frac{1}{2}, \frac{1}{4}, \frac{1}{8}, \frac{1}{8} \right\}$

Entropy, $\quad H(X) = \sum_{i=1}^{4} p(x_i) \log \frac{1}{p(x_i)}$

$$= \frac{1}{2} \times \log 2 + \frac{1}{4} \log 4 + \frac{1}{8} \log 8 + \frac{1}{8} \log 8$$

$$= \frac{1}{2} + \frac{1}{2} + \frac{3}{8} + \frac{3}{8}$$

$$= 1.75 \text{ bits/message}$$

Average length, $\quad \bar{L} = \sum_{i=1}^{4} n_i \times p(x_i)$

$n_1 = n_2 = n_3 = n_4 = 2$

$$\therefore \quad \bar{L} = 2 \times \frac{1}{2} + 2 \times \frac{1}{4} + 2 \times \frac{1}{8} + 2 \times \frac{1}{8}$$

$$= 2 \text{ bits/message}$$

$$\eta = \frac{H(X)}{\bar{L} \log m} \times 100$$

Here, m = 2, as binary encoding is used.

∴ log m = 1

∴ $\eta = \frac{1.75}{2 \times 1} \times 100$

= 87.5%

4.4.2 Shannon-Fano Coding

From above discussion, we have seen that the coding efficiency increases if we assign less number of bits for more probable messages. More probable messages are going to occur more number of times compared to less probable messages. Hence, if we assign less bits to such messages while encoding, coding efficiency will naturally improve. Shannon-Fano coding and Huffman coding methods use this principle.

Shannon-Fano coding method is used to encode messages generated by a Discrete Memoryless Source (DMS) with reasonable efficiency. Let [X] be ensemble of messages $x_1, x_2, x_3, \ldots x_m$ and [p(X)] denote the corresponding probabilities of generating these messages $p(x_1), p(x_2), \ldots p(x_m)$. If we use binary encoding, then let c_k denote the sequence of binary digits of length n_k associated with message x_k.

c_k should satisfy the following two conditions:
  (i) Prefix condition i.e. it should not give rise to another code word by adding 1 or 0.
  (ii) Number of 1's and 0's appear with almost equal probability.
  The procedure for Shannon-Fano coding is as below:
  (i) Write message [X] in non-increasing order of probabilities [p(x)].
  (ii) Partition message set [X] into two equally probable subsets $[X_1]$ and $[X_2]$ i.e. sum of probabilities in $[X_1]$ and $[X_2]$ should be approximately same.
  (iii) Assign 0 to each message contained in $[X_1]$ and 1 to each message in $[X_2]$.
  (iv) Repeat (ii) and (iii) for $[X_1]$ and $[X_2]$ till single message is left out in the sets.

Note: You can also assign 1 to messages $[X_1]$ and 0 to messages $[X_2]$. But the same should be followed throughout.

Example 4.6:

Apply Shannon-Fano coding for following source encoder.

$$[X] = [x_1\ x_2\ x_3\ x_4]$$

$$[p] = \left[\frac{1}{4}\ \frac{1}{8}\ \frac{1}{2}\ \frac{1}{8}\right]$$

Also find coding efficiency.

Solution:

Let us write given messages in non-increasing order of probability.

Message	Probability
x_3	$\frac{1}{2}$
x_1	$\frac{1}{4}$
x_2	$\frac{1}{8}$
x_4	$\frac{1}{8}$

Sum of probabilities = 1

Therefore, messages to be divided such that sum of probability = $\frac{1}{2}$

Above messages can be divided into parts as $[x_3]$ and $[x_1, x_2, x_4]$ and assign 0 and 1 to them as below.

Message	Probability	Code	
x_3	$\frac{1}{2}$	0	} Assign 0
x_1	$\frac{1}{4}$	1	} Assign 1
x_2	$\frac{1}{8}$	1	
x_4	$\frac{1}{8}$	1	

Now, $[x_1, x_2, x_4]$ can be split as $[x_1]$ and $[x_2, x_4]$ as sum of probabilities in these two sets are equal to $\frac{1}{4}$.

Message	Probability	Code	
x_3	$\frac{1}{2}$	0	
x_1	$\frac{1}{4}$	1 0	} Assign 0
x_2	$\frac{1}{8}$	1 1	} Assign 1
x_4	$\frac{1}{8}$	1 1	

Now, the two messages x_2, x_4 have equal probabilities. Hence, they can be split as below and assigned bits are 0 and 1.

Message	Probability	Code		Number of Bits
x_3	$\frac{1}{2}$	0		1
x_1	$\frac{1}{4}$	1 0		2
x_2	$\frac{1}{8}$	1 1 0	$\}$ Assign 0	3
x_4	$\frac{1}{8}$	1 1 1	$\}$ Assign 1	3

To find coding efficiency:

$$\eta = \frac{H(X)}{\bar{L} \times \log m} \times 100$$

$$m = 2$$

$$H(X) = \sum_{j=1}^{4} p(x_j) \log \frac{1}{p(x_j)}$$

$$= \frac{1}{2} \log 2 + \frac{1}{4} \log 4 + \frac{1}{8} \log 8 + \frac{1}{8} \log 8$$

$$= \frac{1}{2} + \frac{1}{4} \times 2 + \frac{1}{8} \times 3 + \frac{1}{8} \times 3$$

$$= 1.75 \text{ bits/message}$$

$$\bar{L} = \sum_{j=1}^{4} x_i \, p(x_j)$$

$$= 1 \times \frac{1}{2} + 2 \times \frac{1}{4} + 3 \times \frac{1}{8} + 3 \times \frac{1}{8}$$

$$= 1.75 \text{ bits/message}$$

$$\eta = \frac{1.75}{1.75} \times 100\%$$

$$= 100\%$$

Example 4.7:

Apply Shannon-Fano code for following message ensemble and find coding efficiency.

$$[X] = [x_1 \ x_2 \ x_3 \ x_4 \ x_5 \ x_6 \ x_7 \ x_8]$$

$$[p] = \left[\frac{1}{4} \ \frac{1}{8} \ \frac{1}{16} \ \frac{1}{16} \ \frac{1}{16} \ \frac{1}{4} \ \frac{1}{16} \ \frac{1}{8} \right]$$

COMMUNICATION SYSTEM - II   INFORMATION AND DETECTION THEORY

Solution:

Given:

Message	Probability	Step I	Step II	Step III	Step IV	Number of Bits
x_1	$\frac{1}{4}$	0	0			2
x_6	$\frac{1}{4}$	0	1			2
x_2	$\frac{1}{8}$	1	0	0		3
x_8	$\frac{1}{8}$	1	0	1		3
x_3	$\frac{1}{16}$	1	1	0	0	3
x_4	$\frac{1}{16}$	1	1	0	1	3
x_5	$\frac{1}{16}$	1	1	1	0	4
x_7	$\frac{1}{16}$	1	1	1	1	4

To find coding efficiency:

$$H(X) = \sum_{j=1}^{8} p(x_j) \log \frac{1}{p(x_j)}$$

$$= \frac{1}{4} \log 4 + \frac{1}{8} \log 8 + \frac{1}{16} \log 16 + \frac{1}{16} \log 16 + \frac{1}{16} \log 16$$

$$+ \frac{1}{4} \log 4 + \frac{1}{16} \log 16 + \frac{1}{8} \log 8$$

$$= \frac{2}{4} + \frac{3}{8} + \frac{4}{16} + \frac{4}{16} + \frac{4}{16} + \frac{2}{4} + \frac{4}{16} + \frac{3}{8}$$

$$= 2.75 \text{ bits/message}$$

$$\bar{L} = \sum_{j=1}^{8} n_j \, p(x_j)$$

$$= 2 \times \frac{1}{4} + 3 \times \frac{1}{8} + 4 \times \frac{1}{16} + 4 \times \frac{1}{16} + 4 \times \frac{1}{16} + 2 \times \frac{1}{4} + 4 \times \frac{1}{4} + \frac{1}{8} \times 3$$

$$= 2.75 \text{ bits/message}$$

$m = 2$ $\therefore \log m = 1$

$$\therefore \quad \eta = \frac{H(X)}{\bar{L} \log m} \times 100$$

$$= \frac{2.75}{2.75} \times 100\%$$

$$= 100\%$$

4.4.3 Huffman Coding

We have seen that, Shannon-Fano Source Coding may not always give optimum solution. Huffman has suggested a simple method for constructing source code with minimum redundancy. It leads to design of an optimum code i.e. average code word length ($\bar{L}$) approaches the fundamental limit set by entropy of a discrete memoryless source i.e. H(x).

For optimum encoding, following conditions must be satisfied.

(i) Longer code word should correspond to a message with lower probability.

i.e. if $p(x_1) \geq p(x_2) \geq p(x_3) \geq \ldots \geq p(x_m)$

then $n_1 > n_2 \geq n_3 \ldots n_m$

where, $p(x_i)$ is probability of ith message and n_i is length of that code word.

(ii) Assign each message a sequence of bits roughly equal in length to the amount of information conveyed by the message.

The procedure for Huffman coding is as below.

(i) Arrange the messages generated by the source in order of decreasing probability.

(ii) Assign 0 and 1 to the two source symbols of lowest probability. (Splitting stage).

(iii) The two source symbols are combined into a new source symbol with probability equal to sum of their probabilities. The resulting m – 1 symbols are reordered as per their probabilities. This is called reduction.

(iv) Above procedure is repeated until we have two messages left out, for which a 0 and a 1 is assigned.

(v) The code for each message is found by going backward from last reduction, till the message such that we trace the sequence of 1s and 0s leading to the message.

Example 4.8:

Apply Huffman coding for following message ensemble using binary digits. Find coding efficiency.

$$[X] = [x_1 \; x_2 \; x_3 \; x_4]$$

$$[p] = \left\{\frac{1}{2}, \frac{1}{8}, \frac{1}{4}, \frac{1}{8}\right\}$$

Solution:

We write the messages in decreasing order of probability as shown in Fig. 4.2 below. The figure also shows the coding procedure.

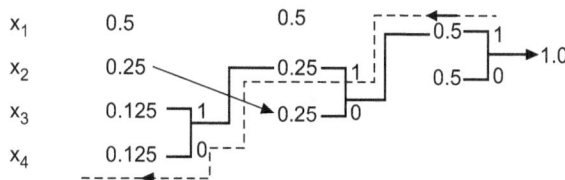

Fig. 4.2: Huffman Code

The codes are shown as below.

x_1 0
x_3 1 0
x_2 1 1 1
x_4 1 1 0

Tracing of code for x_4 is shown in Fig. 4.2.

We could have another method of generating the code as below.

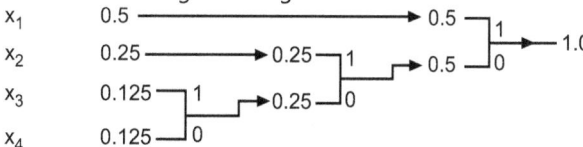

Fig. 4.3: Huffman Code

Observe that the combined symbol is placed as low as possible; whereas in previous case, we had placed it as high as possible. The resulting code will be

x_1 1
x_3 0 1
x_2 0 0 1
x_4 0 0 0

There can be another code resulting from assignment of 0 to first message and 1 to second message in each reduction stage. Thus, Huffman encoding process is not unique.

It is found that when combined symbol is moved as high as possible, the variance of average code word length $\bar{L}$ over the ensemble of source symbols comes out to be minimum. This variance is defined as

$$\sigma^2 = \sum_{i=1}^{m} p(x_i)(n_i - \bar{L})^2 \qquad \ldots (4.46)$$

One more thing about this coding is that it becomes difficult to trace the code of given message when there are large number of messages. The process of tracing can be done by constructing a binary tree from above diagrams. The binary tree is constructed by tracing the reductions backwards. The binary trees for above two cases are shown in Fig. 4.4.

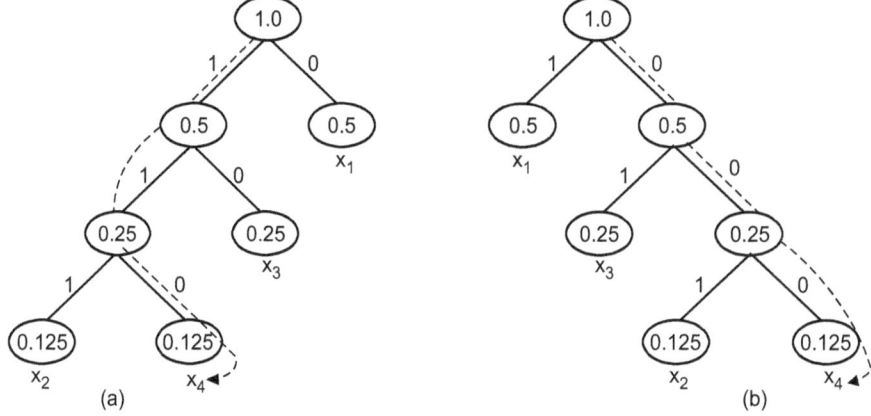

Fig. 4.4: Huffman Coding Tree

The code for each message can be traced from root to leaf node at which the message is designated. Note that the leaf nodes of the tree are messages, whereas non-terminals in the tree are sums at each reduction stage. The left tree has always 1 assigned to it and right tree has 0 assigned to it.

To find coding efficiency:

$$H(X) = \sum_{j=1}^{n} p(x_j) \log \frac{1}{p(x_j)}$$

$$= \frac{1}{2} \log 2 + \frac{1}{4} \log 4 + \frac{1}{8} \log 8 + \frac{1}{8} \log 8$$

$$= \frac{1}{2} + \frac{1}{4} \times 2 + \frac{1}{8} \times 3 + \frac{1}{8} \times 3$$

$$= 1.75 \text{ bits/message}$$

$$\bar{L} = \sum_{j=1}^{n} n_j \times p(x_j)$$

$$= 1 \times \frac{1}{2} + 2 \times \frac{1}{4} + 3 \times \frac{1}{8} + 3 \times \frac{1}{8}$$

$$= 1.75 \text{ bits/message}$$

$$\therefore \text{Efficiency} = \frac{H(X)}{\bar{L}} \times 100$$

$$= \frac{1.75}{1.75} \times 100$$

$$= 100\%$$

In the above examples, encoding is done symbol by symbol. We can increase the efficiency of coding further by encoding blocks of B symbols at a time. For example, if we have two messages with probabilities $\frac{1}{16}$ and $\frac{15}{16}$, following are the ways in which we can encode these messages.

Case 1:

Messages	Probability	Code
x_1	$\frac{1}{16}$	0
x_2	$\frac{15}{16}$	1

$$H(X) = \frac{1}{16} \log 16 + \frac{15}{16} \log \frac{16}{15}$$

$$= \frac{5.2}{16} \text{ bits/message}$$

$$\bar{L} = \frac{1}{15} \times 1 + \frac{15}{16} \times 1$$

$$= 1 \text{ bit/message}$$

$$\therefore \quad \eta = \frac{5.2/16}{1} \times 100$$

$$= 32\%$$

Case 2: Paired Coding

Messages	Probability	Code
$x_1 x_1$	$\frac{1}{16} \times \frac{1}{16} = \frac{1}{256}$	1 1 1
$x_1 x_2$	$\frac{1}{16} \times \frac{15}{16} = \frac{15}{256}$	1 1 0
$x_2 x_1$	$\frac{15}{16} \times \frac{1}{16} = \frac{15}{256}$	1 0
$x_2 x_2$	$\frac{15}{16} \times \frac{15}{16} = \frac{225}{256}$	0

$$\bar{L} = \frac{225}{256} \times 1 + \frac{15}{256} \times 2 + \frac{15}{256} \times 3 + 3 \times \frac{1}{256}$$

$$= \frac{303}{256} \text{ bits/message pair}$$

$$\bar{L} = \frac{303}{512} \text{ bits/message}$$

Since, two symbols are used at a time,

$$2H(x) = \frac{225}{256}\log\frac{256}{225} + \frac{15}{256}\log\frac{256}{15} + \frac{15}{256}\log\frac{256}{15}$$

$$+ \frac{1}{256}\log 256$$

$$= 10.4 \text{ bits/message}$$

∴ $$H(x) = \frac{5.2}{16} \text{ bits/message}$$

∴ $$\eta = \frac{H(X)}{\bar{L}} = \frac{5.2}{16} \times \frac{512}{303} \times 100\%$$

$$= 54.91\%$$

What above encoding means is that, if a source generates messages $x_1\ x_1\ x_2\ x_2\ x_1\ x_2\ x_2\ x_2$, they will be paired and encoded as

Messages $x_1\ x_1$ $x_2\ x_1$ $x_1\ x_2$ $x_2\ x_2$
Code   1 1 1   1 0   1 1 0   0

Thus, paired coding has improved efficiency. You can verify that the efficiency improves further if you combine 3 messages and encode.

Example 4.9:

Apply Huffman's encoding procedure to following message ensemble and determine the average length of encoded messages. Find coding efficiency.

$$[X] = [x_1\ \ x_2\ \ x_3\ \ x_4\ \ x_5\ \ x_6]$$
$$[p(X)] = [0.3\ \ 0.2\ \ 0.2\ \ 0.15\ \ 0.10\ \ 0.05]$$

Use encoding alphabet {0, 1, 2}.

Solution:

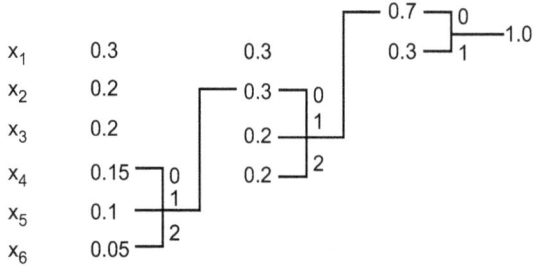

Fig. 4.5

Message		Code
x_1	→	1
x_2	→	0 1
x_3	→	0 2
x_4	→	0 0 0
x_5	→	0 0 1
x_6	→	0 0 2

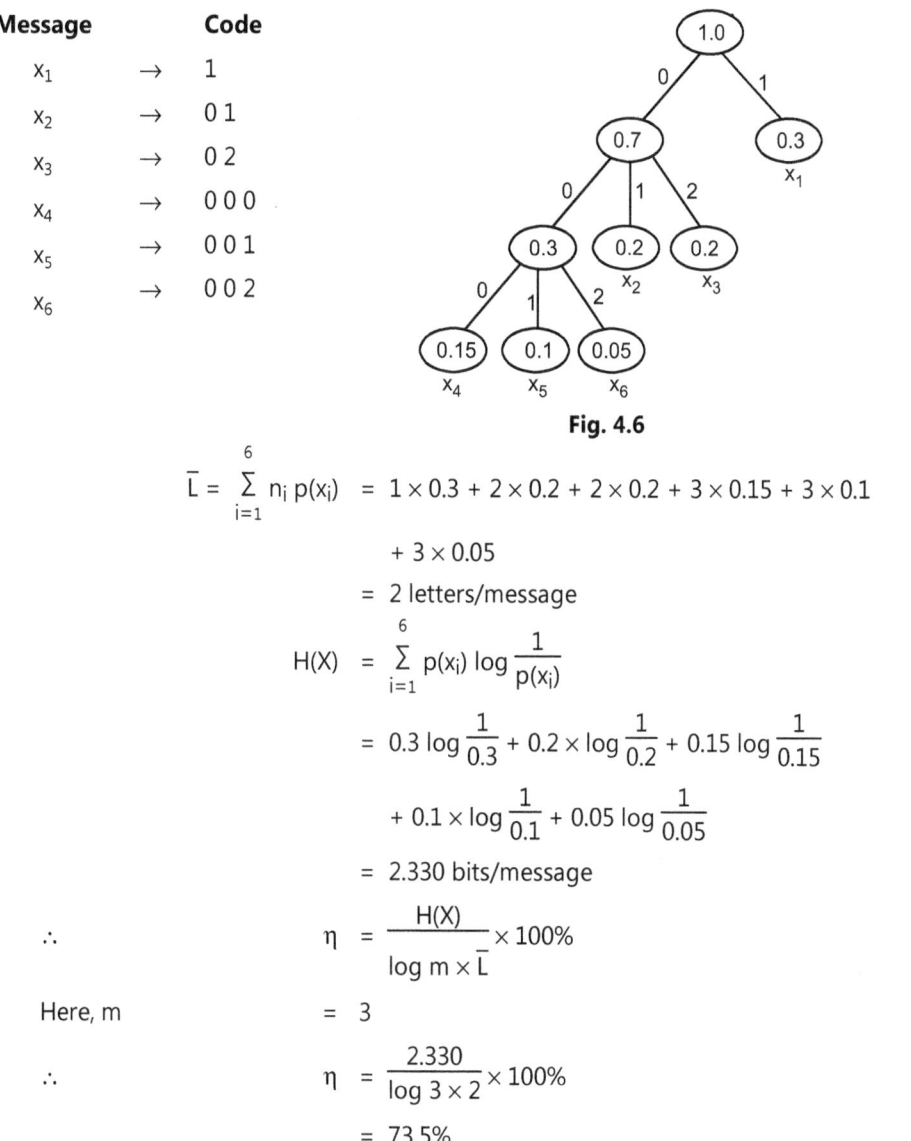

Fig. 4.6

$$\bar{L} = \sum_{i=1}^{6} n_i \, p(x_i) = 1 \times 0.3 + 2 \times 0.2 + 2 \times 0.2 + 3 \times 0.15 + 3 \times 0.1$$

$$+ 3 \times 0.05$$

$$= 2 \text{ letters/message}$$

$$H(X) = \sum_{i=1}^{6} p(x_i) \log \frac{1}{p(x_i)}$$

$$= 0.3 \log \frac{1}{0.3} + 0.2 \times \log \frac{1}{0.2} + 0.15 \log \frac{1}{0.15}$$

$$+ 0.1 \times \log \frac{1}{0.1} + 0.05 \log \frac{1}{0.05}$$

$$= 2.330 \text{ bits/message}$$

∴ $$\eta = \frac{H(X)}{\log m \times \bar{L}} \times 100\%$$

Here, m = 3

∴ $$\eta = \frac{2.330}{\log 3 \times 2} \times 100\%$$

$$= 73.5\%$$

4.4.4 Run Length Encoding (RLE)

Most of the times, streams have repeated strings called runs. We can encode the data using number of repetitions.

For example, if we are given a data stream

    0 0 0 0 0 0 0 1 1 1 1 0 0 0 0 0 1 1 1 1 1 1

then, we can encode it as,

seven 0's, 4 1's, 5 0's, 6 1's

i.e. as

111 0 100 1 101 0 110 1

RLE is used in encoding FAX images. RLE is supported by most bitmap file formats such as TIFF, BMP and PCX.

PCX Format:

It uses run length encoding for compression of images in the PCX format. If pixels in an image are identical in colour, we encode them as special flag byte. The code consists of number of pixels followed by the flag value. If pixel is not repeated, it is encoded as the byte itself. If there are 256 colours, we might have to use one byte for string colour and one byte for storing count. Thus, two bytes may be required for every coded pixel making the code less efficient. Above problem can be solved by using 192 colour values instead of 256, as many drawings are unlikely to have 256 colours. This scheme works as below.

- If colour of pixel is 0 to 191, check whether there is run.
- If there is run of length n < 63, encode it as

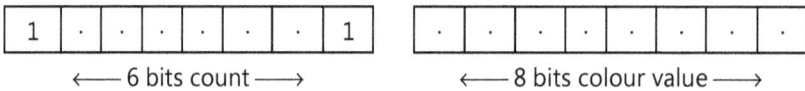

Fig. 4.7

- If the run is more than 63, split the run so that each run will have maximum 63 bits and follow above technique.
- If there is single occurrence (no run), encode the pixel as it is using single byte.
- If colour of pixel is above 191, use two byte code as above. First byte will have count of run and second byte the colour value.

4.4.5 Dictionary Techniques for Data Compaction (LZW Data Compaction)

This is another technique used for data compression. When a source generates recurring patterns, we can keep dictionary of the frequently occurring patterns. When a pattern in the dictionary occurs, it is encoded with a reference to the dictionary. There are two approaches to build dictionary.

(i) Static Dictionary

(ii) Adaptive Dictionary.

If we have prior knowledge of probability of frequently occurring patterns we can use static dictionary approach otherwise we have to use Adaptive Dictionary approach. Most of the practical applications require Adaptive Dictionary approach. Jacob Ziv and Abraham Limpel suggested these techniques and hence known as Limpel Ziv (LZ) techniques. There are number of versions of LZ techniques. We will discuss the following three approaches

    (i)   LZ 77 (also called LZ1)

    (ii)   LZ 78 (also called LZ2)

    (iii)   LZW.

4.4.5.1 Limpel-Ziv-Welch (LZW) Algorithm

Terry Welch modified the LZ78 algorithm which is known as LZW algorithm. Welch proposed a technique which eliminated encoding of second element of the double < index, code >. Only index to the dictionary will be set. All the letters of source alphabet are put into dictionary first. We keep on accumulating input till the pattern p formed is there in the dictionary. The moment a new pattern is formed, index of the p is transmitted and the new pattern is added in the dictionary. Then we start with new pattern starting with recently added letter.

The following example illustrates this process.

Example 4.10:

Encode the sequence using LZW method a b c d e f g a b c r d e f a b c

Also decode the sequence.

Solution:

Let us assume the source alphabet as {a, b, c, d, e, f, g, r}.

These letters will be added to the dictionary as below.

Index	Entry
1	a
2	b
3	c
4	d
5	e
6	f
7	g
8	r

Now, we take first letter, it is there at location 1. Combine this with next letter 'b' and add a b to dictionary and transmit 1 (index of a).

Then, we take next letter b, it is at location 2. Combine this with next letter 'c' and add b c to dictionary and transmit 2 (index of b). Like this, we continue. Following table shows the process.

Input	Index	Entry	Output
a	9	a b	1
b	10	b c	2
c	11	c d	3
d	12	d e	4
e	13	e f	5
f	14	f g	6
g	15	g a	7
a b	16	a b c	9
c	17	c r	3
r	18	r d	8
d e	19	d e f	12
f	20	f a	6
a b c	-	-	16

Thus, encoded output is 1 2 3 4 5 6 7 9 3 8 12 6 16.

The decoding process will be as below. The initial dictionary entries will be same as encoder dictionary which had 8 entries.

The first output is 1 hence we decode the entry as 'a'. Next output is 2. Hence, we decode it as 'b' and combined 'a b' will be entered in dictionary at location 9 like this we continue. The process is shown in following table.

Input	Decoded	Dictionary	
		Index	Entry
1	a	-	-
2	b	9	a b
3	c	10	b c
4	d	11	c d
5	e	12	d e
6	f	13	e f
7	g	14	f g
9	a b	15	g a
3	c	16	a b c
8	r	17	c r
12	d e	18	r d
6	f	19	d e f
16	a b c	20	f a

Thus, decoded sequence is a b c d e f g a b c r d e f a b c.

Example 4.11:

Encode the string 1 0 1 1 0 0 1 0 0 1 0 1 1 1 0 1 using L-Z algorithm.

Solution:

1. Given string is
   1 0 1 1 0 0 1 0 0 1 0 1 1 1 0 1
2. Take first bit (1). Put it in dictionary at position 1.
   1, 0 1 1 0 0 1 0 0 1 0 1 1 1 0 1
3. Take second bit (0). It is not in dictionary. Put it in the dictionary at position 2.
   1, 0, 1 1 0 0 1 0 0 1 0 1 1 1 0 1
4. Take third bit (1). It is already in dictionary, hence take fourth bit (1). Put 1 1 in dictionary at position 3.
   1, 0, 1 1, 0 0 1 0 0 1 0 1 1 1 0 1
5. Take fifth bit (0). It is already in dictionary, hence take sixth bit (0). Put 0 0 in dictionary at position 4.
   1, 0, 1 1, 0 0, 1 0 0 1 0 1 1 1 0 1
   Like this, if we continue, following will be grouping of bits.
   1, 0, 1 1, 0 0, 1 0, 0 1, 0 1 1, 1 0 1

The dictionary will be as below.

Dictionary Location	Content
0 0 1	1
0 1 0	0
0 1 1	1 1
1 0 0	0 0
1 0 1	1 0
1 1 0	0 1
1 1 1	0 1 1
–	1 0 1

Using above dictionary, the code for given string can be constructed as follows. The code consists of location of prefix in dictionary and innovation bit.

Phrase	Code	
	Prefix Location	Innovation Bit
1	0 0 0	1
0	0 0 0	0
1 1	0 0 1	1
0 0	0 1 0	0
1 0	0 0 1	0
0 1	0 1 0	1
0 1 1	1 1 0	1
1 0 1	1 0 1	1

Hence, the code is
0 0 0 1, 0 0 0 0, 0 0 1 1, 0 1 0 0, 0 0 1 0, 0 1 0 1, 1 1 0 1, 1 0 1 1

Note that for phrases 0 and 1, there is no prefix. Hence, prefix location is put as 0 0 0.

L-Z algorithm is actually used for compression. But if we see above example, it has expanded the given string ! We have done above coding for smaller string. For larger strings we get desired compression, as large prefixes are represented using smaller location numbers.

Another point to consider is size of dictionary. It should be large enough to take care of all the phrases to be stored in the dictionary. We can increase the efficiency by updating the dictionary by replacing less frequently used phrases with more frequently used ones.

The decoder for Limpel-Ziv method uses the location number to find the prefix and then appends innovation bit to it.

The decoding of above code will be as below.

Code	Decoded Phrase	Dictionary	
		Location	Phrase
0 0 0 1	1	0 0 1	1
0 0 0 0	0	0 1 0	0
0 0 1 1	1 1	0 1 1	1 1
0 1 0 0	0 0	1 0 0	0 0
0 0 1 0	1 0	1 0 1	1 0
0 1 0 1	0 1	1 1 0	0 1
1 1 0 1	0 1 1	1 1 1	0 1 1
1 0 1 1	1 0 1	–	1 0 1

It can be seen that –
- Lempel-Ziv coding technique uses fixed length codes which makes them suitable for synchronous transmission. In contrast, Huffman codes use variable length.
- In practice, fixed blocks of 12 bits are used. It means there will be 4096 codes (2^{12}).
- Lempel-Ziv algorithm is now the standard algorithm for file compression. It achieves compression of 55%, whereas Huffman code achieves 43% for English text. Hence, L-Z algorithm has taken over almost completely from Huffman.
- L-Z algorithm takes advantage of intercharacter redundancies, whereas Huffman algorithm does not. Hence, L-Z algorithm is superior to Huffman algorithm.

4.5 Discrete Memoryless Channel

We have seen that, entropy of a source gives average amount of information generated by it per message or alphabet. Entropy can also be associated with receiver in the form of average information received by it. The transmitter and receiver can be characterized by their entropies. In order to characterize the communication system as a whole, we have to consider the interdependence of transmitter, channel and receiver. This will require the concept of two dimensional probability scheme.

Just like discrete memoryless source, let us consider a discrete memoryless channel. Let X be the input to the channel and Y be the output, where, Y is noisy version of X. X and Y are random variables. Let $x_1, x_2, x_3, \ldots x_m$ be the messages belonging to input alphabet X and let $y_1, y_2, y_3, \ldots y_n$ be the messages belonging to output alphabet Y.

Let $p(x_j)$ denote the probability of message x_j, where $j = 1, 2, 3, \ldots m$.

Let $p(y_k)$ denote the probability of message y_k, where $k = 1, 2, 3, \ldots n$.

Since, X and Y are interdependent, there will be another set of probabilities given by $p(y_k/x_j)$ for all j and k. These are called transition probabilities. These probabilities can be written in the form of a matrix as below.

$$p(Y/X) = \begin{bmatrix} p(y_1/x_1) & p(y_2/x_1) & \cdots & p(y_n/x_1) \\ p(y_1/x_2) & p(y_2/x_2) & \cdots & p(y_n/x_2) \\ \vdots & \vdots & & \vdots \\ p(y_1/x_m) & p(y_2/x_m) & \cdots & p(y_n/x_m) \end{bmatrix} \quad \ldots(4.47)$$

Since, above matrix characterises a discrete memoryless channel, it is called **channel matrix.** We can also have joint probability distribution of random variables X and Y represented by the following matrix.

$$p(X, Y) = \begin{bmatrix} p(x_1, y_1) & p(x_1, y_2) & \cdots & p(x_1, y_n) \\ p(x_2, y_1) & p(x_2, y_2) & \cdots & p(x_2, y_n) \\ \vdots & \vdots & & \vdots \\ p(x_m, y_1) & p(x_m, y_2) & \cdots & p(x_m, y_n) \end{bmatrix} \quad \ldots(4.48)$$

Above matrix can be obtained from the channel matrix using relation –

$$p(x_j, y_k) = p(y_k/x_j) \cdot p(x_j) \quad \ldots(4.49)$$

The probability distribution of output random variable Y can be obtained by

$$p(y_k) = \sum_{j=1}^{n} p(y_k, x_j) \quad \ldots(4.50)$$

i.e. $\quad p(y_k) = p(x_1, y_k) + p(x_2, y_k) + \ldots + p(x_m, y_k)$

i.e. probability of y_k is probability that y_k and x_1 occurs or y_k and x_2 occurs or y_k and x_3 occurs and so on upto y_k and x_m occurs.

Since, $\quad p(x_j, y_k) = p(y_k/x_j) \cdot p(x_j) \quad \ldots(4.51)$

$p(y_k)$ can also be written as

$$p(y_k) = \sum_{j=1}^{m} p(y_k/x_j) \cdot p(x_j) \qquad \ldots (4.52)$$

Thus, we have the following sets of probability schemes:

(i) Probability of transmitted symbols, called marginal probability of input variable or Priori Probability.

$$P(X) = [p(x_j)]$$

(ii) Probability of received symbols, called marginal probability of output random variable or Posteriori Probability.

$$P(Y) = [p(y_k)] \qquad \ldots (4.53)$$

(iii) Probability that symbol x_j is transmitted and y_k is received i.e. $p(x_j/y_k)$, called Joint Probability.

$$P(XY) = \{p(x_j, y_k)\} \qquad \ldots (4.54)$$

(iv) Probability that symbol y_k is received given x_j is transmitted, called Conditional Probability, also called Transition Probability.

$$P(Y/X) = \{p(y_k/x_j)\} \qquad \ldots (4.55)$$

(v) We can also have another scheme representing probability that x_j is transmitted, given y_k is received.

$$P(X/Y) = \{p(x_j/y_k)\} \qquad \ldots (4.56)$$

Note: A probability scheme is said to be complete if the sum of all the probabilities in that scheme is equal to 1.

4.5.1 Joint and Conditional Entropies

$p(X)$, $p(Y)$ and $p(X, Y)$ are complete probability schemes. Hence, we can associate entropy with these schemes as below.

1. Marginal entropy of source or input [X] is given by

$$H(X) = - \sum_{j=1}^{m} p(x_j) \cdot \log p(x_j) \qquad \ldots (4.57)$$

2. Marginal entropy of destination or output [Y] is given by

$$H(Y) = - \sum_{k=1}^{n} p(y_k) \log p(y_k) \qquad \ldots (4.58)$$

3. Joint entropy of input [X] and output [Y] is given by

$$H(X, Y) = - \sum_{j=1}^{m} \sum_{k=1}^{n} p(x_j, y_k) \log p(x_j, y_k) \qquad \ldots (4.59)$$

COMMUNICATION SYSTEM - II INFORMATION AND DETECTION THEORY

Let us now consider another scheme which can be obtained from conditional probabilities. Let y_k occur in conjunction with $x_1, x_2, x_3, \ldots x_m$. Thus, we have the set of events defined by

$$[X/y_k] = [x_1/y_k, x_2/y_k, x_3/y_k, \ldots x_m/y_k] \qquad \ldots (4.60)$$

The probability scheme associated with this set will be

$$p(X/Y) = [p(x_1/y_k), p(x_2/y_k), \ldots, p(x_m/y_k)]$$

Since,

$$p(x_j/y_k) = \frac{p(x_j, y_k)}{p(y_k)}$$

$$p(X/y_k) = \left[\frac{p(x_1, y_k)}{p(y_k)}, \frac{p(x_2, y_k)}{p(y_k)}, \ldots, \frac{p(x_m, y_k)}{p(y_k)}\right] \qquad \ldots (4.61)$$

$$p(x_1, y_k) + p(x_2, y_k) + p(x_3, y_k) + \ldots + p(x_m, y_k) = p(y_k)$$

Hence, sum of probabilities of $p(X/y_k)$ is 1.

The scheme is complete scheme and entropy can be associated with it. Thus, we have

$$H(X/y_k) = -\sum_{j=1}^{m} \frac{p(x_j, y_k)}{p(y_k)} \log \frac{p(x_j, y_k)}{p(y_k)} \qquad \ldots (4.62)$$

$$= -\sum_{j=1}^{m} p(x_j/y_k) \log p(x_j/y_k) \qquad \ldots (4.63)$$

Above entropy represents the event that one of x_j is transmitted with given probability and y_k is received. Now, if we consider all such entropies for different y_k's, and take average, we get another quantity called average conditional entropy. It is given by

$$H(X/Y) = \overline{H(X/y_k)} = \sum_{k=1}^{n} p(y_k) H(X/y_k)$$

$$= \sum_{k=1}^{n} p(y_k) \times (-1) \sum_{j=1}^{m} p(x_j/y_k) \log p(x_j/y_k)$$

$$= -\sum_{j=1}^{m} \sum_{k=1}^{n} p(y_k) \cdot p(x_j/y_k) \cdot p(x_j/y_k)$$

$$= -\sum_{j=1}^{m} \sum_{k=1}^{n} p(x_j, y_k) \log p(x_j/y_k) \qquad \ldots (4.64)$$

Similarly, we can have another average conditional entropy given by

$$H(Y/X) = -\sum_{j=1}^{m} \sum_{k=1}^{n} p(x_j, y_k) \log p(y_k/x_j) \qquad \ldots (4.65)$$

where,

$$H(Y/X) = \overline{H(x_j/Y)} \qquad \ldots (4.66)$$

where, $H(x_j/Y)$ represents entropy of the event that x_j is transmitted given one of y_k is received with given probability. Thus, we have in all five entropies associated with two dimensional probability scheme of two random variables X and Y. If X represents source or transmitter and Y represents destination or receiver, then we interpret different entropies as given below.

Sr. No.	Entropy	Interpretation
1.	H(X)	Average information per message at transmitter or entropy of transmitter.
2.	H(Y)	Average information per message at the receiver or entropy of receiver.
3.	H(X/Y)	One of x_j is transmitted with given probability and specific y_k is received. It is entropy associated with this scheme when y_k covers all symbols i.e. $\overline{H(x/y_k)}$. It is measure of information about transmitter when it is known that Y is received.
4.	H(Y/X)	A specific x_j is transmitted and one of y_k is received with given probability. The entropy associated with this scheme when x_j covers all symbols i.e. $\overline{H(y/x_j)}$. It is measure of information about the receiver where, it is known that X is transmitted.
5.	H(X, Y)	Average information per pair of transmitted and received messages or average uncertainty of the communication system as a whole.

4.5.2 Relationship between Different Entropies

The joint entropy is given by

$$H(X, Y) = -\sum_{j=1}^{m}\sum_{k=1}^{n} (x_j, y_k) \log p(x_j, y_k)$$

$$= -\sum_{j=1}^{m}\sum_{k=1}^{n} p(x_j, y_k) \log [p(x_j/y_k) \cdot p(y_k)]$$

$$= -\sum_{j=1}^{m}\sum_{k=1}^{n} p(x_j, y_k) \log p(x_j/y_k) + p(x_j, y_k) \log p(y_k)$$

$$= H(X/Y) + \left\{ -\sum_{j=1}^{m}\sum_{k=1}^{n} p(x_j, y_k) \log p(y_k) \right\}$$

$$= H(X/Y) + \left\{ -\sum_{k=1}^{n} \left[\sum_{j=1}^{m} p(x_j, y_k) \right] \log p(y_k) \right\}$$

$$= H(X/Y) + \left\{ -\sum_{k=1}^{n} p(y_k) \log p(y_k) \right\} \qquad \ldots (4.67)$$

$$= H(X/Y) + H(Y) \qquad \ldots (4.68)$$

Similarly, $H(X, Y) = H(Y/X) + H(X)$ ... (4.69)
Thus, $H(X, Y) = H(X/Y) + H(Y)$
and $H(X, Y) = H(Y/X) + H(X)$

4.6 Mutual Information

In a communication system, information is transferred from source (X) or transmitter to destination (Y) or receiver through a channel. We have seen that H(X) gives average information of transmitter. It is a measure of prior uncertainty about X. In order to find information transferred from X to Y, we consider conditional entropy.

The state of knowledge at the receiver about a transmitted symbol x_j will be $p(x_j)$ before reception of the symbol. This is known as priori probability. After reception of the symbol y_k, the state of knowledge about x_j will be $p(x_j|y_k)$ i.e. probability that x_j is transmitted, given y_k is received. This is called posteriori probability. Hence, initial uncertainty before y_k is received about x_j will be $-\log p(x_j)$. When y_k is received, this uncertainty will be equal to $-\log p(y_k/x_j)$. Information gained about x_j by reception of y_k is not reduction in its uncertainty. It is known as **Mutual information** $I(x_j; y_k)$.

$$\text{Thus,} \quad I(x_j; y_k) = \text{Initial uncertainty} - \text{Final uncertainty}$$
$$= -\log p(x_j) - [-\log(p(x_j/y_k))]$$
$$= \log \frac{p(x_j/y_k)}{p(x_j)} \quad \text{... (4.70)}$$

The average mutual information i.e. the entropy corresponding to mutual information is given by average value of $I(x_j; y_k)$.

i.e. $I(X; Y) = \overline{I(x_j; y_k)}$ ... (4.71)

$I(x_j, y_k)$ is mutual information when x_j is transmitted and y_k is received. If we have $p(x_j, y_k)$ i.e. number of times the pair (x_j, y_k) occurs out of total number of times (say N) x_j's and y_k's are observed. Hence, the mutual information contributed by the pair (x_j, y_k) will be $p(x_j; y_k) \times I(x_j, y_k) \times N$. The average value will be sum of all such terms with $j = 1$ to m and $k = 1$ to n, divided by N. The average mutual information is

$$I(X; Y) = \sum_{j=1}^{m} \sum_{k=1}^{n} p(x_j, y_k) I(x_j; y_k) \quad \text{... (4.72)}$$

$$= \sum_{j=1}^{m} \sum_{k=1}^{n} p(x_j, y_k) \log \frac{p(x_j/y_k)}{p(x_j)} \quad \text{... (4.73)}$$

$$= \sum_{j=1}^{m} \sum_{k=1}^{n} p(x_j, y_k) [\log p(x_j/y_k) - \log p(x_j)]$$

$$= -\sum_{j=1}^{m}\sum_{k=1}^{n} p(x_j, y_k) \log p(x_j) - \left[-\sum_{j=1}^{m}\sum_{k=1}^{n} p(x_j, y_k) \log p(x_j/y_k)\right]$$

$$= -\sum_{j=1}^{m} \log p(x_j) \sum_{k=1}^{n} p(x_j, y_k) - H(X/Y)$$

$$= -\sum_{j=1}^{m} p(x_j) \times \log p(x_j) - H(X/Y)$$

$$= H(X) - H(X/Y) \qquad \ldots (4.74)$$

$$\therefore \quad \boxed{I(X; Y) = H(X) - H(X/Y)}$$

We know that,

$$H(X/Y) = H(XY) - H(Y)$$

$$\therefore \quad I(X; Y) = H(X) - [H(XY) - H(Y)] \qquad \ldots (4.75)$$

$$= H(X) - H(XY) + H(Y)$$

$$= H(X) + H(Y) - H(XY)$$

$$\therefore \quad \boxed{I(X; Y) = H(X) + H(Y) - H(XY)} \qquad \ldots (4.76)$$

Also substituting $H(Y/X) = H(X) - H(XY)$, we have,

$$\boxed{I(X; Y) = H(Y) - H(Y/X)} \qquad \ldots (4.77)$$

From above results, we have some interesting interpretations.

- I(X; Y) does not depend on individual symbols x_j and y_k, but it is a property of communication system as a whole.
- I(X; Y) is a measure of information transferred through channel, hence it is also known as transferred information or transinformation.
- I(X; Y) = H(X) − H(X/Y) suggests that average mutual information I(X; Y) will be average information generated by transmitter H(X) minus average amount of information lost in the channel i.e. H(X/Y) gives information lost in the channel.
- I(X; Y) = H(Y) − H(Y/X) suggests that average mutual information is information received by receiver minus that part of receiver entropy which is not the information about the source. In other words, information received [H(Y) = I(X; Y) + H(Y/X)] is information transferred from source to receiver and noise added in the channel [H(Y/X)]. Thus, H(Y/X) signifies noise or entropy added in the channel.
- H(X/Y) also indicates how well one can recover the transmitted symbol from received symbol i.e. it is a measure of equivocation.
- H(Y/X) indicates how well one can recover received symbol from transmitted symbols.

Example 4.12:

A discrete source transmits messages x_1 and x_2 with probabilities $\frac{3}{4}$ and $\frac{1}{4}$. The source is connected to the channel given below. Calculate all entropies and mutual information.

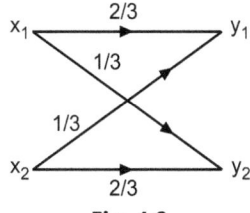

Fig. 4.8

Solution:
Given:

$$X = [x_1 \quad x_2]$$

$$P(X) = \begin{bmatrix} \frac{3}{4} & \frac{1}{4} \end{bmatrix}$$

The channel characteristics are given as conditional probability matrix.

$$P(Y/X) = \begin{array}{c} \\ x_1 \\ x_2 \end{array} \begin{array}{cc} y_1 & y_2 \\ \begin{bmatrix} 2/3 & 1/3 \\ 1/3 & 2/3 \end{bmatrix} \end{array}$$

We can find joint probability matrix by using p(X) and p(Y/X).

Since, $\quad p(x_j, y_k) = p(x_j) \cdot p(y_k/x_j)$

$\therefore \quad p(x_1, y_1) = p(x_1) \cdot p(y_1/x_1) = \frac{3}{4} \times \frac{2}{3}$

$$= \frac{1}{2}$$

Similarly, $\quad p(x_1, y_2) = p(x_1) \cdot p(y_2/x_1) = \frac{3}{4} \times \frac{1}{3}$

$$= \frac{1}{4}$$

$$p(x_2, y_1) = p(x_2) \cdot p(y_1/x_2) = \frac{1}{4} \times \frac{1}{3}$$

$$= \frac{1}{12}$$

and $\quad p(x_2, y_2) = p(x_2) \cdot p(y_2/x_2) = \frac{1}{4} \times \frac{2}{3}$

$$= \frac{1}{6}$$

∴ $$P(X,Y) = \begin{array}{c} \\ x_1 \\ x_2 \end{array} \begin{array}{c} y_1 \quad y_2 \\ \left[\begin{array}{cc} \frac{1}{2} & \frac{1}{4} \\ \frac{1}{12} & \frac{1}{6} \end{array} \right] \end{array}$$

From above matrix we can find p(y) as

$$p(y_k) = \sum_{j=1}^{m} p(x_j, y_k)$$

i.e. sum of columns will give p(y).

∴ $p(y_1) = p(x_1, y_1) + p(x_2, y_1)$

$= \frac{1}{2} + \frac{1}{12}$

$= \frac{7}{12}$

$p(y_2) = p(x_1, y_2) + p(x_2, y_2)$

$= \frac{1}{4} + \frac{1}{6}$

$= \frac{5}{12}$

∴ $y = [y_1 \; y_2]$

and $P(Y) = \left[\frac{7}{12}, \frac{5}{12} \right]$

Now, $H(X) = \sum_{j=1}^{m} p(x_j) \cdot \log \frac{1}{p(x_j)}$

$= \frac{3}{4} \log \frac{4}{3} + \frac{1}{4} \log 4$

$= 0.81$ bits/message

$H(Y) = \sum_{k=1}^{n} p(y_k) \log \frac{1}{p(y_k)}$

$= \frac{7}{12} \times \log \frac{12}{7} + \frac{5}{12} \log \frac{12}{5}$

$= 0.98$ bits/message

$H(XY) = \sum_{j=1}^{m} \sum_{k=1}^{n} p(x_j, y_k) \log \frac{1}{p(x_j, y_k)}$

$= \frac{1}{2} \log 2 + \frac{1}{4} \log 4 + \frac{1}{12} \log 12 + \frac{1}{6} \log 6$

COMMUNICATION SYSTEM - II   INFORMATION AND DETECTION THEORY

$$
\begin{aligned}
&= 1.73 \text{ bits/message} \\
H(X/Y) &= H(XY) - H(Y) \\
&= 1.73 - 0.98 \\
&= 0.75 \text{ bits/messages} \\
H(Y/X) &= H(XY) - H(X) \\
&= 1.73 - 0.81 \\
&= 0.92 \text{ bits/message} \\
I(X; Y) &= H(X) - H(X/Y) \\
&= 0.81 - 0.75 \\
&= 0.06 \text{ bits/message}
\end{aligned}
$$

Example 4.13:

The joint probability matrix representing transmitter and receiver is given as below. Find all entropies and mutual information of communication system.

$$
P(X, Y) = \begin{array}{c} \\ x_1 \\ x_2 \\ x_3 \\ x_4 \end{array} \begin{array}{c} y_1 \quad y_2 \quad y_3 \\ \left[\begin{array}{ccc} 0.3 & 0.05 & 0 \\ 0 & 0.25 & 0 \\ 0 & 0.15 & 0.05 \\ 0 & 0.05 & 0.15 \end{array} \right] \end{array}
$$

Solution:

From given joint probability matrix we can find p(X) and p(Y).

Sum of rows will give P(X).

Sum of columns will give P(Y).

∴ P(X) = [0.35 0.25 0.2 0.2]

   P(X) = [0.3   0.5   0.20]

∴ $H(X) = \sum_{j=1}^{m} p(x_j) \log \frac{1}{p(x_j)}$

$= 0.35 \log \frac{1}{0.35} + 0.25 \log \frac{1}{0.25} + 0.2 \log \frac{1}{0.2} + 0.2 \log \frac{1}{0.2}$

$= 1.96$ bits/message

$H(Y) = \sum_{k=1}^{n} p(y_k) \log \frac{1}{p(y_k)}$

$= 0.3 \log \frac{1}{0.3} + 0.5 \log \frac{1}{0.5} + 0.2 \log \frac{1}{0.2}$

$= 1.49$ bits/message

$$H(X, Y) = \sum_{j=1}^{m} \sum_{k=1}^{n} p(x_j, y_k) \log \frac{1}{(x_j, y_k)}$$

$$= 0.3 \log \frac{1}{0.3} + 0.05 \log \frac{1}{0.05} + 0.25 \log \frac{1}{0.25}$$

$$+ 0.15 \log \frac{1}{0.15} + 0.05 \log \frac{1}{0.05} + 0.05 \log \frac{1}{0.05} + 0.15 \log \frac{1}{0.15}$$

$$= 2.49 \text{ bits/message}$$

Now,
$$H(X/Y) = H(XY) - H(Y)$$
$$= 2.49 - 1.49$$
$$= 1 \text{ bit/message}$$

$$H(Y/X) = H(XY) - H(X)$$
$$= 2.49 - 1.96$$
$$= 0.53 \text{ bits/message}$$

$$I(X; Y) = H(X) - H(X/Y)$$
$$= 1.96 - 1.0$$
$$= 0.96 \text{ bits/message}$$

4.6.1 Properties of Mutual Information

Property 1: Mutual information of a channel is symmetric.

i.e. $\quad I(X; Y) = I(Y; X)$

We know that,

$$I(x_j; y_k) = \log \frac{p(x_j/y_k)}{p(x_j)} \qquad \ldots (4.78)$$

But,
$$p(x_j/y_k) = \frac{p(x_j, y_k)}{p(y_k)}$$

$$\therefore \quad I(x_j; y_k) = \log \frac{p(x_j, y_k)}{p(x_j) \, p(y_k)}$$

But
$$\frac{p(x_j, y_k)}{p(x_j)} = p(y_k/x_j)$$

$$\therefore \quad I(x_j; y_k) = \log \frac{p(y_k/x_j)}{p(y_k)} \qquad \ldots (4.79)$$

$$= I(y_k; x_j) \qquad \ldots (4.80)$$

COMMUNICATION SYSTEM - II INFORMATION AND DETECTION THEORY

Thus, $\quad I(x_j; y_k) = I(y_k; x_j)$ ... (4.81)

$\therefore \quad I(X; Y) = I(Y; X)$ ... (4.82)

Hence, mutual information is symmetric.

It can also be shown that,

$$I(Y; X) = H(Y) - H(Y/X)$$ ... (4.83)

- $I(X; Y)$ is a measure of uncertainty about the channel input that is resolved by observing channel output.
- $I(Y; X)$ is a measure of uncertainty about the channel output that is resolved by sending the channel input.

Property 2: The mutual information is always non-negative.

i.e. $\quad I(X; Y) \geq 0$ ... (4.84)

We know that,

$$I(X; Y) = \sum_{j=1}^{m} \sum_{k=1}^{n} p(x_j, y_k) \log \frac{p(x_j/y_k)}{p(x_j)}$$

But $\quad p(x_j/y_k) = \dfrac{p(x_j, y_k)}{p(y_k)}$

$\therefore \quad I(X; Y) = \sum_{j=1}^{m} \sum_{k=1}^{n} p(x_j, y_k) \log \dfrac{p(x_j, y_k)}{p(x_j) p(y_k)}$

$\quad = -\sum_{j=1}^{m} \sum_{k=1}^{n} p(x_j, y_k) \log \dfrac{p(x_j) \cdot p(y_k)}{p(x_j, y_k)}$

But, we know that,

$$\sum_{j=1}^{n} p(x_j) \log \frac{p(x_j)}{p(y_j)} \leq 0$$

and equality holds when $p(x_j) = p(y_j)$

$\therefore \quad I(X; Y) \geq 0$

Equality holds when

$\quad p(x_j, y_k) = p(x_j) \cdot p(y_k)$ for all j and k.

Above property states that, on an average, information is not lost by observing channel output and that the mutual information is zero if and only if input and output symbols of channels are statistically independent.

Property 3:

The mutual information of a channel is related to the joint entropy of the channel input and channel output by

$$I(X; Y) = H(X) + H(Y) - H(X, Y) \quad \ldots (4.85)$$

We have, $\quad I(X; Y) = H(X) - H(X/Y)$

But $\quad H(X/Y) = H(XY) - H(Y)$

$\therefore \quad I(X; Y) = H(X) + H(Y) - H(XY)$

4.7 Channel Capacity

Consider the Example 4.12, where we had been given a source and channel as below.

$$X = [x_1 \quad x_2]$$

$$P(X) = \begin{bmatrix} \frac{3}{4} & \frac{1}{4} \end{bmatrix}$$

$$P(Y/X) = \begin{bmatrix} \frac{2}{3} & \frac{1}{3} \\ \frac{1}{3} & \frac{2}{3} \end{bmatrix}$$

The value of I(X; Y) we got was 0.06 bits/message. The information processed by a channel depends on input distribution P(X). If we vary P(X), the mutual information will vary. If we vary this distribution P(X) in such a way that mutual information becomes maximum, this is called capacity of channel i.e. there will be some maximum value of information that can be transferred from source to destination. In above example, it can be verified that when P(X) = $\begin{bmatrix} \frac{1}{2}, \frac{1}{2} \end{bmatrix}$, the mutual information is maximum.

The average mutual information is given by

$$I(X; Y) = \sum_{j=1}^{m} \sum_{k=1}^{n} p(x_j, y_k) \log \frac{p(y_k/x_j)}{p(y_k)}$$

$$= \sum_{j=1}^{m} \sum_{k=1}^{n} p(x_j) p(y_k/x_j) \log \frac{p(y_k/x_j)}{p(y_k)} \quad \ldots (4.86)$$

Above formula suggests that $p(y_k/x_j)$ i.e. the channel transition probabilities are fixed for a particular channel. Hence, I(X; Y) can be maximized over $p(x_j)$ i.e. input symbol probabilities.

$$\therefore \quad C = \underset{p(x_j)}{\text{Max}} \, I(X; Y) \quad \ldots (4.87)$$

$$= \underset{p(x_j)}{\text{Max}} \sum_{j=1}^{m} \sum_{k=1}^{n} p(x_j) p(y_k/x_j) \log \frac{p(y_k/x_j)}{p(y_k)} \quad \ldots (4.88)$$

The maximization is performed under following constraints.

$$p(x_j) \geq 0$$

and
$$\sum_{j=1}^{m} p(x_j) = 1$$

Thus, channel capacity is an upper bound of the rate of transmission for a given channel. Efficiency of transmission can be established by comparing actual rate of transmission and the upper bound.

Channel capacity can also be expressed in the form of entropies.

We know
$$I(X; Y) = H(X) - H(X/Y) \qquad \ldots (4.89)$$

Channel capacity,
$$C = \max [I(X; Y)] \qquad \ldots (4.90)$$
$$= \max [H(X) - H(X/Y)] \qquad \ldots (4.91)$$

The unit of capacity is bits per channel use and capacity in bits per second = Capacity in bits per channel use × Rate of channel use.

(This is similar to R = r × H).

In the discussions ahead, we will be considering Capacity in bits per channel use.

The transmission efficiency of channel is defined as

$$\eta = \frac{\text{Actual information}}{\text{Maximum information}} \qquad \ldots (4.92)$$

$$= \frac{I(X; Y)}{\max [I(X; Y)]} \qquad \ldots (4.93)$$

$$= \frac{I(X; Y)}{C} \qquad \ldots (4.94)$$

The redundancy of the channel is defined as

$$R = 1 - \eta \qquad \ldots (4.95)$$

$$= \frac{C - I(X; Y)}{C} \qquad \ldots (4.96)$$

4.7.1 Examples of Various Types of Channel and Their Capacities

Let us now consider different types of channels and evaluate their capacities.

1. Noise-free or Noiseless channel:

In this case, there is one to one correspondence between input and output i.e. each input symbol is received as one and only one output symbol. Also n = m. The channel is shown in Fig. 4.9.

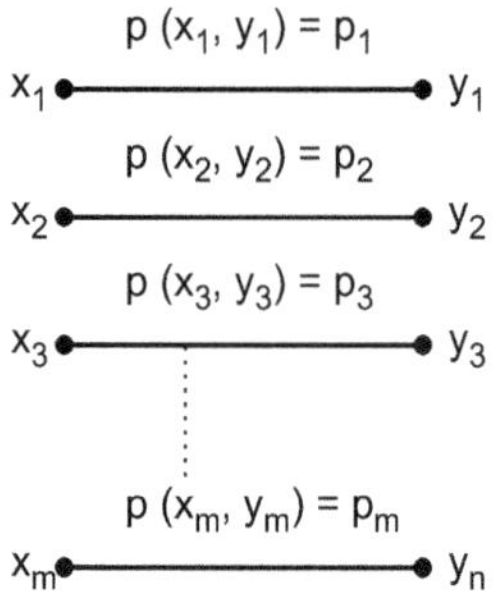

```
                p(x₁, y₁) = p₁
        x₁ •─────────────────• y₁
                p(x₂, y₂) = p₂
        x₂ •─────────────────• y₂
                p(x₃, y₃) = p₃
        x₃ •─────────────────• y₃
                     ⋮
                p(xₘ, yₘ) = pₘ
        xₘ •─────────────────• yₙ
```

Fig. 4.9

The joint probability matrix is given by

$$P(X, Y) = \begin{bmatrix} p_1 & 0 & 0 & \cdots & 0 \\ 0 & p_2 & 0 & \cdots & 0 \\ 0 & 0 & p_3 & \cdots & 0 \\ \vdots & \vdots & & & \vdots \\ 0 & 0 & & & p_m \end{bmatrix}$$

$$P(X) = [p_1 \; p_2 \; p_3 \cdots p_m]$$

$$P(Y) = [p_1 \; p_2 \; p_3 \cdots p_m]$$

It can be seen from above matrices that,

$$H(X, Y) = H(X) = H(Y)$$

∴ $H(X/Y) = H(XY) - H(Y) = 0$

∴ $I(X; Y) = H(X) - H(X/Y)$

$$= H(X) - 0$$

$$= H(X)$$

∴ $I(X; Y) = H(X) = H(Y) = H(X, Y)$

Capacity of channel,

$$C = \max [I(X; Y)]$$

$$= \max [H(X)]$$

We know that $H(X)$ is maximum when the messages are equiprobable and the maximum value is $\log m$, where, m is number of messages.

Hence, capacity of noise-free channel is

∴ $\boxed{C = \log m \text{ bits/channel use}}$ ... (4.97)

where, m is the number of messages generated by source X or transmitter X.

2. Lossless channel:

A channel is loseless if $H(X/Y) = 0$ for all input distributions. In this channel, input is determined by output, hence no errors occur. The channel is as given in figure below.

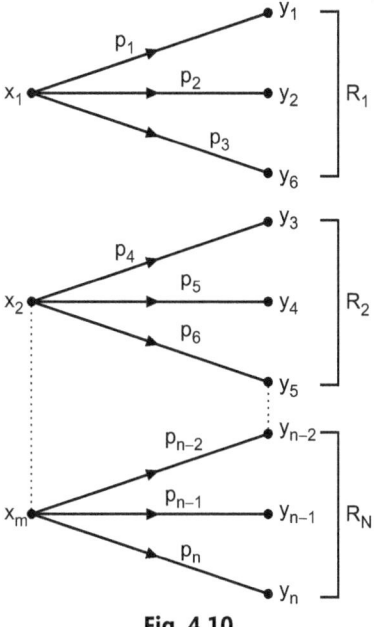

Fig. 4.10

Thus, Y is partitioned into disjoint sets $R_1, R_2, \ldots R_n$, so that $p(Y \in R_i/X = x_i) = 1$.
The channel will be represented as

$$P(X, Y) = \begin{array}{c} \\ x_1 \\ x_2 \\ \vdots \\ \vdots \\ x_m \end{array} \begin{array}{|cccccccccc|} y_1 & y_2 & y_3 & y_4 & y_5 & y_6 & \cdots & y_{n-3} & y_{n-2} & y_{n-1} & y_n \\ p_1 & p_2 & 0 & 0 & 0 & p_3 & \cdots & 0 & 0 & 0 & 0 \\ 0 & 0 & p_4 & p_5 & p_6 & 0 & - & 0 & 0 & 0 & 0 \\ \vdots & \vdots & \vdots & \vdots & \vdots & \vdots & & \vdots & & & \\ \vdots & \vdots & \vdots & \vdots & \vdots & \vdots & & \vdots & & & \\ 0 & 0 & 0 & 0 & 0 & 0 & & 0 & p_{n-2} & p_{n-1} & p_n \end{array}$$

Note that in each column there is only one non-zero element.

$$P(Y) = [p_1 \; p_2 \; p_3 \; p_4 \; p_5 \; p_6 \cdots p_{n-2} \; p_{n-1} \; p_n]$$
$$P(X) = [p_1 + p_2 + p_3 + p_4 + p_5 + p_6 \cdots p_{n-2} + p_{n-1} + p_n]$$

∴ $\quad H(XY) = H(Y)$
∴ $\quad H(X/Y) = H(XY) - H(Y) = 0$
Also, $\quad H(XY) \neq H(X)$
$\quad I(X; Y) = H(X) + H(Y) - H(X, Y)$
∴ $\quad I(X; Y) = H(X)$
∴ $\quad$ Capacity, $(C) = \max[I(X; Y)]$

$$= \max[(H(X)]$$
$$= \log m \text{ bits/channel use}$$

Note: The noiseless channel is lossless, but converse may not be true because, in noiseless channel,

$$H(XY) = H(X) = H(Y)$$
∴ $H(Y/X) = 0$
and $H(X/Y) = 0$

In lossless channel,

$$H(XY) \neq H(Y) \qquad \therefore H(Y/X) \neq 0$$
$$H(XY) = H(X) \qquad H(X/Y) = 0$$

3. Useless channel or Channel with independent input-outputs:

Case I: In this type of channel, there is no correlation between input and output symbols. Consider channel diagram given below indicating joint probability matrix.

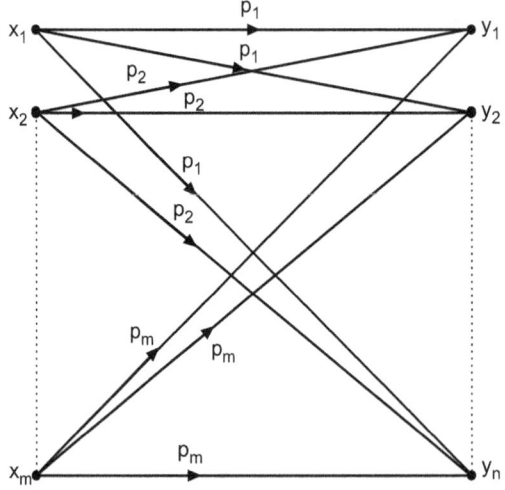

Fig. 4.11

∴ The joint probability matrix is given by

$$P(X, Y) = \begin{array}{c} \\ x_1 \\ x_2 \\ \vdots \\ \vdots \\ x_m \end{array} \begin{array}{c} y_1 \quad y_2 \quad y_3 \qquad y_n \\ \left[\begin{array}{cccc} p_1 & p_1 & p_1 & \cdots & p_1 \\ p_2 & p_2 & p_2 & & p_2 \\ \vdots & \vdots & \vdots & & \vdots \\ \vdots & \vdots & \vdots & & \vdots \\ p_m & p_m & p_m & \cdots & p_m \end{array} \right] \end{array}$$

$$\quad x_1 \quad x_2 \quad x_m$$

$$\therefore \quad P(X) = [np_1 \; np_2 \; \ldots \; np_m]$$

$$P(Y) = \left[\sum_{j=1}^{m} p_j \quad \sum_{j=1}^{m} p_j \quad \ldots \quad \sum_{j=1}^{m} p_j \right]$$

But $\quad np_1 + np_2 + \ldots np_m = 1$

$$\therefore \quad p_1 + p_2 + \ldots p_m = \frac{1}{n}$$

$$\therefore \quad \sum_{j=1}^{m} p_j = \frac{1}{n}$$

$$\therefore \quad P(y) = \begin{bmatrix} y_1 & y_2 & y_3 & & y_n \\ \frac{1}{n} & \frac{1}{n} & \frac{1}{n} & \ldots & \frac{1}{n} \end{bmatrix}$$

Thus, if we compare P(X), P(Y) and P(X, Y) we see that,

$$p(x_j, y_k) = p(x_j) \cdot p(y_k)$$

Thus, x_j and y_k are independent of each other.

i.e. $\quad p(x_j/y_k) = p(x_j)$

and $\quad p(y_k/x_j) = p(y_k)$

$$\therefore \quad H(Y/X) = -\sum_{j=1}^{m} \sum_{k=1}^{n} p(x_j, y_k) \log p(y_k/x_j)$$

$$= -\sum_{j=1}^{m} \sum_{k=1}^{n} p(x_j) \, p(y_k) \log p(y_k)$$

$$= -\sum_{k=1}^{n} p(y_k) \log p(y_k) \sum_{j=1}^{m} p(x_j)$$

$$= -\sum_{k=1}^{n} p(y_k) \log p(y_k)$$

$$= H(Y)$$

$$\therefore \quad I(X; Y) = H(Y) - H(Y/X)$$
$$= 0$$

which shows that no information is transmitted through the channel. It is useless channel.

$$\therefore \quad \text{Capacity} = \max[I(X; Y)]$$
$$= 0$$

Case II: Consider another channel with channel diagram given as follows.

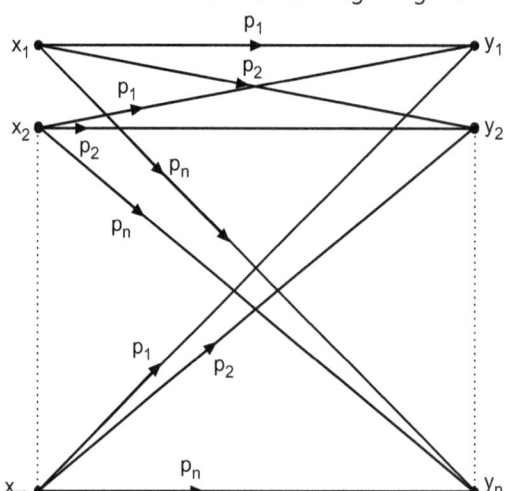

Fig. 4.12

The joint probability matrix for above channel is given by

$$P(X, Y) = \begin{array}{c} \\ x_1 \\ x_2 \\ \vdots \\ \vdots \\ x_m \end{array} \begin{array}{c} y_1 \;\; y_2 \;\; y_3 \; \cdots \; y_n \\ \begin{bmatrix} p_1 & p_2 & p_3 & \cdots & p_n \\ p_1 & p_2 & p_3 & \cdots & p_n \\ \vdots & \vdots & \vdots & & \vdots \\ \vdots & \vdots & \vdots & & \vdots \\ p_1 & p_2 & p_3 & \cdots & p_n \end{bmatrix} \end{array}$$

$$\therefore \quad P(X) = \begin{array}{c} x_1 \qquad x_2 \qquad\quad x_m \\ \left[\sum_{k=1}^{n} p_k \;\; \sum_{k=1}^{n} p_k \cdots \sum_{k=1}^{n} p_k \right] \end{array}$$

$$P(Y) = \begin{array}{c} y_1 \quad\; y_2 \quad\; y_3 \quad\;\; y_n \\ [mp_1 \;\; mp_2 \;\; mp_3 \cdots mp_n] \end{array}$$

Now $mp_1 + mp_2 + mp_3 + \ldots mp_n = 1$

$$\therefore \quad \sum_{k=1}^{n} p_k = \frac{1}{m}$$

$$\therefore \quad P(X) = \begin{array}{c} x_1 \;\; x_2 \;\; x_3 \;\; x_m \\ \left[\dfrac{1}{m} \;\; \dfrac{1}{m} \;\; \dfrac{1}{m} \cdots \dfrac{1}{m} \right] \end{array}$$

From P(X), P(Y) and P(X, Y) values we see that,

$$p(x_j, y_k) = p(x_j) \cdot p(y_k)$$

∴ $p(x_j/y_k) = p(x_j)$

and $p(y_k/x_j) = p(y_k)$

Hence, $H(Y/X) = H(Y)$

and $H(X/Y) = H(X)$

∴ $I(X; Y) = H(X) - H(X/Y)$
$= 0$

Hence, above channel is also useless channel and its capacity is

$$C = \max[I(X; Y)] = 0$$

4. Deterministic Channel:

A channel is deterministic if $p(y_k/x_j) = 1$ or 0 for all i and j i.e. Y is determined by X or $H(Y/X) = 0$ for all input distributions. The deterministic channel is shown in Fig. 4.13.

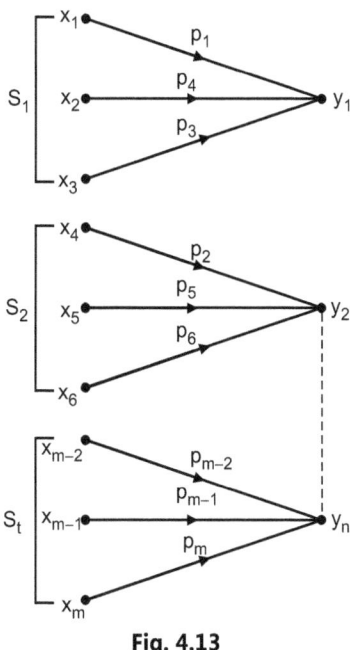

Fig. 4.13

Here, if it is known which of x_j is transmitted, y_k can be determined from it. The joint probability matrix will be of following nature (for some assumed deterministic channel). Note that in a row there is only one non-zero element.

$$P(X, Y) = \begin{array}{c} x_1 \\ x_2 \\ x_3 \\ x_4 \\ x_5 \\ \vdots \\ x_m \end{array} \begin{array}{c} y_1 \;\; y_2 \;\;\;\;\;\;\;\; y_n \end{array} \left[\begin{array}{cccc} p_1 & 0 & \cdots & 0 \\ p_4 & 0 & \cdots & 0 \\ p_3 & 0 & \cdots & 0 \\ 0 & p_2 & \cdots & 0 \\ 0 & p_5 & \cdots & 0 \\ \vdots & \vdots & & 0 \\ 0 & 0 & \cdots & p_m \end{array} \right]$$

∴ $P(X) = [p_1 \; p_4 \; p_3 \; p_2 \cdots p_m]$

$P(Y) = [p_1 + p_4 + p_3 \; p_2 + p_5 \; \cdots\cdots\cdots\cdots \; p_{m-2} + p_{m-1} + p_m]$

Thus, $H(X, Y) = H(X)$

∴ $H(Y/X) = H(XY) - H(X)$

$= 0$

∴ $I(X; Y) = H(X) + H(Y) - H(XY)$

$= H(XY)$

∴ Capacity of deterministic channel,

$C = \max[I(X; Y)]$

$= \max[H(Y)]$

$= \log n$ bits/channel use

where, n is number receiver elements.

We can see that noiseless channel is deterministic, but converse may not be true.

5. **Symmetric Channel:**

A symmetric channel is one for which –

(i) $H(Y/x_j)$ is independent of j.

i.e. entropy of each row of P(Y/X) is same.

(ii) $\sum_{j=1}^{m} p(y_k/x_j)$ is independent of k.

i.e. sum of all columns of P(Y/X) is the same.

Following are examples of symmetric channels.

$$P(Y|X) = \begin{array}{c} \\ x_1 \\ x_2 \end{array} \begin{array}{c} y_1 \quad y_2 \\ \left[\begin{array}{cc} \alpha & 1-\alpha \\ 1-\alpha & \alpha \end{array} \right] \end{array}$$

$$P(Y|X) = \begin{bmatrix} \frac{1}{2} & \frac{1}{4} & \frac{1}{4} \\ \frac{1}{4} & \frac{1}{2} & \frac{1}{4} \\ \frac{1}{4} & \frac{1}{4} & \frac{1}{2} \end{bmatrix}$$

The mutual information for symmetric channel is determined as below.

$$I(X;Y) = H(Y) - H(Y/X)$$

$$= H(Y) - \sum_{j=1}^{m} H(Y/x_j) p(x_j)$$

$$= H(Y) - A \sum_{j=1}^{m} p(x_j)$$

where, $A = H(Y/x_j)$

Since, for symmetric channel $H(Y/x_j)$ is constant,

$$\therefore \quad I(X;Y) = H(Y) - A \qquad \left[\because \sum_{j=1}^{m} p(x_j) = 1 \right]$$

$\therefore$ Capacity of symmetric channel is

$$I(X;Y) = \max[H(Y) - A]$$

$$= \log n - A \qquad \ldots (4.98)$$

Let us consider binary symmetric channel whose channel matrix is

$$P(Y/X) = \begin{bmatrix} p & 1-p \\ 1-p & p \end{bmatrix}$$

As we have seen, the capacity of such channel is given by

$$C = \log n - H(Y/x_j)$$

$$= \log n - \left[-\sum_{j=1}^{m} p(y_k/x_j) \log p(y_k/x_j) \right]$$

Here, n = 2.

$$C = \log 2 + p \log p + (1-p) \log (1-p)$$
$$= 1 + p \log p + (1-p) \log (1-p)$$
$$= 1 - H(p)$$

The capacity of channel varies with transition error probability p. The plot is shown in Fig. 4.14.

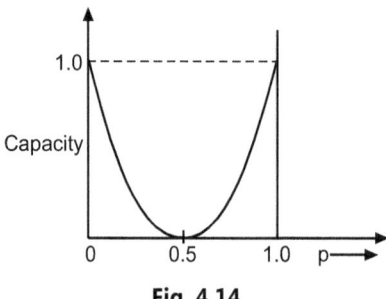

Fig. 4.14

It can be seen that –

(i) When channel is noisefree, p = 0, it has maximum capacity of 1 bit per channel use.

(ii) When error probability = $\frac{1}{2}$, the channel capacity is minimum = 0. The channel is said to be useless.

Example 4.14:

Find capacity of following channel whose channel matrix is,

$$P(Y/X) = \begin{bmatrix} p & 1-p \\ 1-p & p \end{bmatrix}$$

(i) Draw channel diagram.
(ii) If sources are equally likely, find probabilities of outputs if p = 0.8.
(iii) Find capacity of the channel for p = 0.8.

Solution:

(i) Channel diagram:

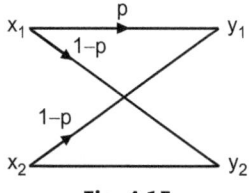

Fig. 4.15

(ii) Given channel matrix with p = 0.8.

$$P(Y/X) = \begin{bmatrix} 0.8 & 0.2 \\ 0.2 & 0.8 \end{bmatrix}$$

$$P(X) = [0.5 \quad 0.5]$$

∴ $$P(X, Y) = \begin{bmatrix} 0.4 & 0.10 \\ 0.10 & 0.4 \end{bmatrix}$$ (Using $p(x_j, y_k) = p(x_j) \cdot p(y_k/x_j)$)

∴ $P(Y) = [0.5 \quad 0.5]$

∴ $P(y_1) = 0.5$

$P(y_2) = 0.5$ (Output probabilities)

(iii) Capacity of binary symmetric channel is

$$C = \log n - H(y/x_j)$$

$$= \log n - \left[-\sum_{j=1}^{m} p(y_k/x_j) \log p(y_k/x_j) \right]$$

Number of outputs, $n = 2$

∴ $C = \log 2 - [-p \log (p) - (1-p) \log (1-p)]$

$C = \log 2 + p \log p + (1-p) \log (1-p)$

$= 1 + p \log p + (1-p) \log (1-p)$

$= 1 + 0.8 \log 0.8 + 0.2 \log 0.2$

$= 0.278$ bits/channel use

4.8 Channel Coding Theorem (Shannon's Second Theorem)

We have seen that we use source coding to improve efficiency of transmission by encoding the source message based on statistics of source. Source coding results into compression of data. If we have to transmit this data through a channel, there will be errors in received data. The error probability may be of the order of 10^{-2}. It means 1 out of 100 bits can go wrong. This is a poor reliability. In order to improve reliability, we use channel coding, so error probability can be 10^{-6} or even lower.

Channel coding is a process of mapping incoming data sequence into another sequence which can be transmitted on the channel. Reverse mapping of received data sequence from channel at the receiver into output data sequence is called channel decoding.

The channel encoder and decoder are shown in Fig. 4.16 below.

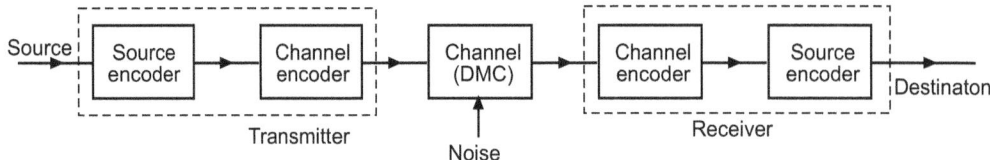

Fig. 4.16: Digital Communication Systems

Thus, in order to increase resistance to channel noise, we introduce redundancy in channel encoder. The channel encoder is designed in such a way that it increases the effectiveness of digital communication system. The channel decoder exploits this redundancy to reconstruct original sequence.

In channel encoding, the bit sequence generated by source or source encoder is divided into k-bit blocks and then encoded into n-bit blocks, where n > k. Thus, n – k bits are added as redundant bits or parity bits. The ratio k/n is called code rate (r_c). Smaller the code rate, more will be redundant bits and more will be reliability.

When we receive the sequence of bits at the receiver, the accuracy of these bits depends on error probability. It should be very small. For achieving small error probability, we need lower code rate. But, it can be seen from Shannon's second theorem that it is possible to devise a channel coding scheme such that the error probability is small, at the same time, code rate need not be too small.

Let X be the source (DMS) with entropy H(X) bits/symbol.

Let rate of generation of symbols, $r = \dfrac{1}{T_s}$.

∴ Average information rate, R = r × H(X) bits/second

$$= \dfrac{H(X)}{T_s} \quad \quad \text{... (4.99)}$$

Let C be the capacity of channel in bits per channel use and the channel is used every T_c seconds by the channel encoder.

Then capacity per unit time = $C \times r = \dfrac{C}{T_c}$ bits/seconds.

The Shannon's Second Theorem (channel coding theorem) is stated as,

(i) Let a DMS with an alphabet X, has entropy H(X) and produce symbols at every T_s seconds and let C be the capacity of DMC and channel is used at every T_c second. Then if,

$$\dfrac{H(X)}{T_s} \leq \dfrac{C}{T_c} \quad \quad \text{... (4.100)}$$

then, there exists a coding scheme for which source output can be transmitted over the noisy channel and be reconstructed with an arbitrarily low probability of error.

(ii) Conversely, if,

$$\frac{H(X)}{T_s} > \frac{C}{T_c} \qquad \ldots (4.101)$$

It is not possible to transmit information over the channel with small probability of error, whatever may be the coding technique used.

Thus, channel capacity decides maximum permissible rate at which error free transmission is possible.

The channel coding theorem is the most important theorem in information theory. Though it does not tell us about good code, it tells us about the condition under which good codes can be designed.

Applications of Channel Coding:

1. Suppose a DMS source with probability of messages p = 0.5 generates messages every T_s seconds.

$$\therefore \quad H(X) = \frac{1}{2}\log 2 + \frac{1}{2}\log 2$$
$$= 1 \text{ bit/message}$$
$$r = \text{Symbol rate}$$
$$= \frac{1}{T_s}$$

∴ Information rate,
$$R = r\,H(X)$$
$$= \frac{1}{T_s} \text{ bits/second}$$

This sequence is applied to channel encoder with code rate = r_c.

The channel encoder uses channel every T_c second to transmit the coded sequence.

For reliable communication, according to channel coding theorem, we have condition that,

if, $$\frac{1}{T_s} \leq \frac{C}{T_c}$$

then, it is possible to devise a suitable code so that error probability will be very small.

Code rate $r_c = \frac{k}{n}$ can be expressed as

$$r_c = \frac{T_c}{T_s} \qquad \ldots (4.102)$$

Hence, the condition for reliable communication can be written as

$$\boxed{r_c \leq C} \qquad \ldots (4.103)$$

Thus, for binary symmetric channel, if code rate is less than or equal to channel capacity, then there can be reliable transmission.

Now, if we have a binary symmetric channel with $p = 10^{-2}$, then,

$$\text{Capacity, } C = 1 + p \log p + (1-p) \log (1-p)$$
$$= 0.919$$

For this channel, code rate should be ≤ 0.919.

2. Repetition Code:

It is a code in which for each message bits we transmit n code bits repeatedly.

e.g. if n = 5 for 0, we transmit 00000 and for 1, we transmit 11111.

$$\text{Code rate, } r_c = \frac{1}{n} \qquad \text{(as k = 1)}$$

Out of n bits, if more than m bits are in error, there will be error in detection where n = 2m + 1. (e.g. n = 5, then if 3 or more bits go wrong). If p is error probability of single bit, the probability that more than m bits will go wrong in a stream of n bits will be

$$P_e = \sum_{i=m+1}^{n} {}^nC_i \, p^i \times (1-p)^{n-i}$$

This will be Average Probability of error.

The code rates required for various error probabilities are given as follows as $p = 10^{-2}$.

Code rate ($r_c = 1/n$)	Error Probability (p_e)
1	10^{-2}
$\frac{1}{2}$	3×10^{-4}
$\frac{1}{5}$	10^{-6}
$\frac{1}{7}$	4×10^{-7}
$\frac{1}{9}$	10^{-8}
$\frac{1}{11}$	5×10^{-10}

Above figures show that we need not have r_c too small for getting reliable communication.

4.9 Differential Entropy and Mutual Information for Continuous Channel

The information theory concepts of discrete channels discussed till now can be extended to continuous channels and continuous sources. This will lead us to another fundamental limit in the information theory.

Let us consider a continuous signal x(t) whose probability density function is p(x). We can view this random variable X as a limiting form of discrete random variable which takes values $x_j = j\Delta x$, where, $j = 0, \pm 1, \pm 2, ...$ and Δx approaches zero. The continuous random variable X takes a value $p(x_j) \Delta x$ in the interval $(x_j, x_j + \Delta x)$. Hence, entropy of this signal x(t) is defined as

$$H(X) = \lim_{\Delta x \to 0} \sum_{j=-\infty}^{\infty} p(x_j) \Delta x \log \left[\frac{1}{p(x_j) \cdot \Delta x}\right] \quad ...(4.104)$$

$$= \lim_{\Delta x \to 0} \sum_{j=-\infty}^{\infty} p(x_j) \log \frac{1}{p(x_j)} \Delta x - \log \Delta x \sum_{j=-\infty}^{\infty} p(x_j) \Delta x \quad ...(4.105)$$

$$= \int_{-\infty}^{\infty} p(x) \log \frac{1}{p(x)} dx - \lim_{\Delta x \to 0} \log \Delta x \int_{-\infty}^{\infty} p(x) dx \quad ...(4.106)$$

Since, $\int_{-\infty}^{\infty} p(x) dx = 1$

$$h(X) = \int_{-\infty}^{\infty} p(x) \log \frac{1}{p(x)} dx - \lim_{\Delta x \to 0} \log \Delta x \quad ...(4.107)$$

But, as $\Delta x \to 0$, $\log \Delta x \to \infty$.

It means entropy of continuous random variable will be infinity. This is obvious as random variable can assume any value between $-\infty$ to $+\infty$. But then this quantity will be of no use to us. Hence, we define another quantity called as differential entropy,

$$h(X) = \int_{-\infty}^{\infty} p(x) \log \frac{1}{p(x)} dx \quad ...(4.108)$$

Using formula for H(X) we can write,

$$h(X) = H(X) \text{ given} \left[-\lim_{\Delta x \to 0} \log \Delta x \right] \quad \ldots (4.109)$$

We can use h(X) for characterizing continuous random variable as $-\log \Delta x$ will be serving as reference.

Now, we consider case of two dimensional random variables used for characterizing source, destinations and channel. The joint probability density function p(x, y) and marginal densities $p_1(x)$ and $p_2(y)$ can be used to define different entropies as

$$h(X) = -\int_{-\infty}^{\infty} p_1(x) \log p_1(x) \, dx$$

$$h(Y) = -\int_{-\infty}^{\infty} p_2(y) \log p_2(y) \, dy$$

$$h(X, Y) = -\int_{-\infty}^{\infty} \int_{-\infty}^{\infty} p(x, y) \log p(x, y) \, dx \, dy \quad \ldots (4.110)$$

$$h(X/Y) = -\int_{-\infty}^{\infty} \int_{-\infty}^{\infty} p(x, y) \log [p(x/y)] \, dx \, dy \quad \ldots (4.111)$$

$$h(Y/X) = -\int_{-\infty}^{\infty} \int_{-\infty}^{\infty} p(x, y) \log [p(y/x)] \, dx \, dy \quad \ldots (4.112)$$

$$\int_{-\infty}^{\infty} p(x) \, dx = 1$$

$$\int_{-\infty}^{\infty} \int_{-\infty}^{\infty} p(x, y) \, dx \, dy = 1$$

Mutual information is defined as

$$I(X;Y) = \int_{-\infty}^{\infty}\int_{-\infty}^{\infty} p(x,y) \log \frac{p(x,y)}{p_1(x)\, p_2(y)}\, dx\, dy \quad \ldots (4.113)$$

The properties of mutual information are

1. $\quad I(X;Y) = I(Y;X)$ ... (4.114)
2. $\quad I(X;Y) \geq 0$ ... (4.115)
3. $\quad I(X;Y) = h(X) - h(X/Y)$ ... (4.116)
   $\qquad\qquad\;\; = h(Y) - h(Y/X)$

EXERCISE

1. State and explain properties of mutual information.
2. What do you mean by extension of discrete memoryless source ? With the help of numerical example, prove that the entropy of nth order extension of DMS is equal to n times entropy of original source.
3. A DMS channel has following alphabet with probability of occurrence as shown below.

Symbol	S_0	S_1	S_2	S_3	S_4	S_5	S_6
Probability	0.125	0.0625	0.25	0.0625	0.125	0.125	0.25

   Generate Huffman code with minimum code variance. Determine code variance and code efficiency. Comment on code efficiency.

4. Prove that mutual information is given by
   $$H(X;Y) = H(X) + H(Y) - H(X,Y)]$$

5. For a discrete memoryless source with k equiprobable symbols, use of fixed length code will provide same efficiency as any other coding technique. Justify. State condition for achieving 100% efficiency in the form of k.

6. The channel matrix is given by
   $$\begin{bmatrix} 0.9 & 0.1 \\ 0.2 & 0.8 \end{bmatrix}$$

   Draw channel diagram and determine the probabilities associated with equiprobable inputs. Also find mutual information.

7. A discrete memoryless source consists of three symbols x_1, x_2, x_3 with probabilities 0.45, 0.35 and 0.2 respectively. Determine minimum variance Huffman codes for the source for following two alternatives:
   (i) Considering symbol by symbol occurrence.
   (ii) Considering second order block extension of the source.
   Determine the code efficiency for two alternatives and comment on efficiency.
8. If 'X' is random variable using values $x_1, x_2, x_3, \ldots x_k$, what should be probability density function of X to get maximum entropy H(X). Determine the value of H(X).
9. Define mutual information, self information and conditional self information.
10. Give the equation for Kraft's inequality and its application.

***

Unit V

CHANNEL CODING

5.1 Introduction

A digital communication system must have higher data rate, minimum signal power, reliable transmission and minimum bandwidth requirement. The channel, over which the transmission takes place, is usually noisy and it will have limited bandwidth. If we have to keep the signal power minimum, the signal-to-noise ratio will be lower. This will lead to increase in error probability (p_e), as it depends on E_b/N_0 ratio. Hence, reliability of the system suffers. Hence, in order to improve reliability for given E_b/N_0 ratio, we can use error control coding techniques.

Error control coding techniques can correct errors, so that messages, which are likely to go wrong in a noisy channel, can be retrieved correctly at the receiver end. This is also known as Forward Error Correction (FEC). For a fixed value of error probability, it is also possible to reduce E_b/N_0 ratio (signal power) using error control coding. Since this technique tries to overcome channel noise, it is also called **channel coding.** The error correcting codes are generated by adding redundancy to original message before transmitting it on a noisy channel. The channel encoder block in the transmitter does this as shown in Fig. 5.1.

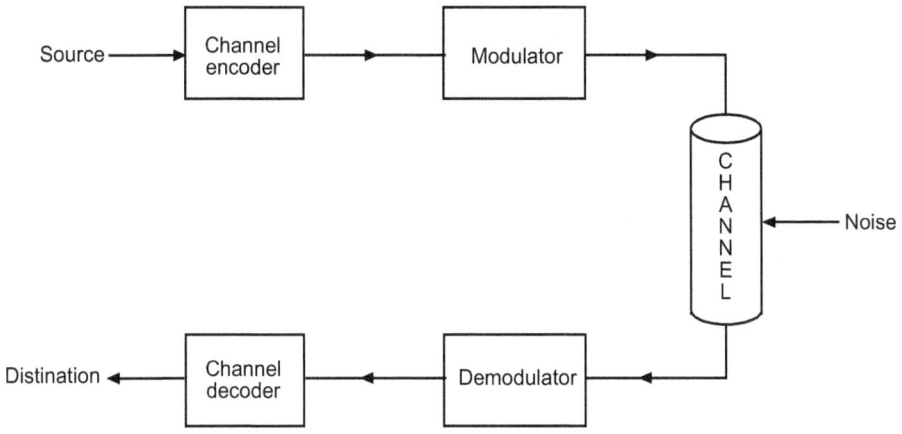

Fig. 5.1: Channel coding in communication system

At the receiver we can recover the original message if the errors are within the limit as per the design of code. The channel decoder block does this recovery.

A good error control coding technique should have –

(i) Better error correcting capability.

(ii) Faster and efficient method of coding and decoding.

(iii) Maximum transfer of information in bits/sec. (or less overheads).

If we try to increase error correcting capability, information rate will reduce and coding and decoding will also be slower. Complexity of design increases in order to achieve better coding technique. The addition of redundancy also increases the bandwidth requirement. Thus, reliability is at the cost of bandwidth and system complexity.

Reliability can be increased by designing error detecting systems. In these systems, we add redundancy at the transmitter end in the message. The code is then transmitted. At the receiver end, we will detect whether the code received is correct or not. If not, we request the transmitter to retransmit the code. The overheads required in this case are lower than that of FEC. This technique is called Automatic Repeat Request (ARQ).

There are number of error correcting codes. They are classified as –

(i) Block codes.

(ii) Convolutional codes.

In block codes, a block of k-bit message is encoded into n bits by adding n – k redundant bits. Convolutional codes are generated using a sliding window, where incoming message slides forward in the window. The window length is usually small and output code consists of encoder output corresponding to the message bits in the window. The memory requirement for linear block code encoder is more than convolutional code.

5.2 Basic Definitions

In digital communication, we use binary symbols (1/0) for transmission of message, Hence, we will be using the word bits instead of symbols in our discussion. But correct and general word should be symbols as a message may generate more than two types of symbols.

Let us first discuss some frequently used terms with coding.

1. **Word:** *It is a sequence of symbols.*

    e.g. Suppose we have a message consisting of 1010, then it is called a **message word.** Similarly, there will be code corresponding to this message, called as **code word.**

2. **Code:** *It is a set of vectors called as code words or code vectors.*
3. **Parity bits:** *The bits, which are added to the message bits, are called parity bits.*
4. **Systematic code:** *Code, in which code words consist of message bits and parity bits separately is called systematic code.*
5. **Block codes:** *These are fixed length code words generated from a block of message words.*
6. **Block code specification:** *The block code is specified in terms of number of code bits and number of message bits. If there are k bits in the message word and n bits are generated to form code word, the block code is called (n, k) block code.*
7. **Code rate:** *For an (n, k) block code, the code rate is defined as the ratio of message bits and code bits (k/n). Code rate is always less than one.*
8. **Parity check codes:** *These are simplest possible block codes. These codes are generated by adding one bit to the message bits. They can be even parity check codes or odd parity check codes. Even parity check codes add 1 to message if number of 1's in message are odd and 0 if number of 1's in message are even.*

   e.g.

Message	Code	Parity bit
100101	100101**1**	
110101	110101**0**	

   Similarly,

   Odd parity check codes:

Message	Code	Parity bit
010011	010011**0**	
010001	010001**1**	

   If single error occurs in these code words, it can be detected at the receiver end.

9. **Weight of a code word:** *The number of non-zero symbols in a code word is called weight of the code word.*

   e.g.

Code word	Weight
10101	3
11110	4

10. **Hamming distance:** *It is a number of symbols in which two code words differ.*

    e.g.
    $$c_1 = 10101$$
    $$c_2 = 11010$$

    Hamming distance between c_1 and c_2 is 4, denoted as $d(c_1, c_2) = 4$.

11. Minimum Hamming distance between any two code words of a code is called minimum Hamming distance of that code. It is denoted as d_{min}.

12. **A linear code:** *It is a code which has the following properties.*
    (i) The sum of any two code words in the code will yield another code word of that code.
    (ii) There is always all-zero code word.
    (iii) The minimum Hamming distance between any two code words is equal to minimum weight of any non-zero code word.

Example 5.1:

Consider the following code.

$$C = \{000, 111\}$$

Solution:

It consists of the two code words.

Weight of 000 is 0.

Weight of 111 is 3.

Hamming distance between the two code words = 3.

Minimum Hamming distance of the code = 3.

It is a linear code since addition of the two code words yield one of the code words 111.

Example 5.2:

Consider a code.

$$C = \{000, 010, 001, 111\}$$

Code word	Weight
000	0
010	1
001	1
111	3

Solution:

Minimum Hamming distance = 1

It is not a linear code as addition of 001 and 010 does not yield valid code word i.e. 011 is not a valid code word of this code.

13. **Minimum Hamming distance (d_{min})** of a linear code is equal to minimum weight of the non-zero code words in that code.

Consider a code $C = \{000, 010, 101, 111\}$

Code word	Weight
000	0
010	1
101	2
111	3

Since, minimum weight of non-zero code is 1,

Minimum Hamming distance, $d_{min} = 1$.

14. **Hard decision decoding:** Consider a communication system using discrete memoryless channel. If binary coding is used, the modulator has only binary 1 and 0 as inputs. The demodulator will also have binary quantized output. Hence, decoder will have binary input. A hard decision is made on demodulator output as to which symbol was actually transmitted. But the use of word decisions prior to decoding causes loss of information which cannot be recovered.

    Two decisions are made when using hard decision decoding. The first decision regarding each bit (whether it is one/zero) and the other is regarding code word as a whole. It is shown in Fig. 5.2 (a).

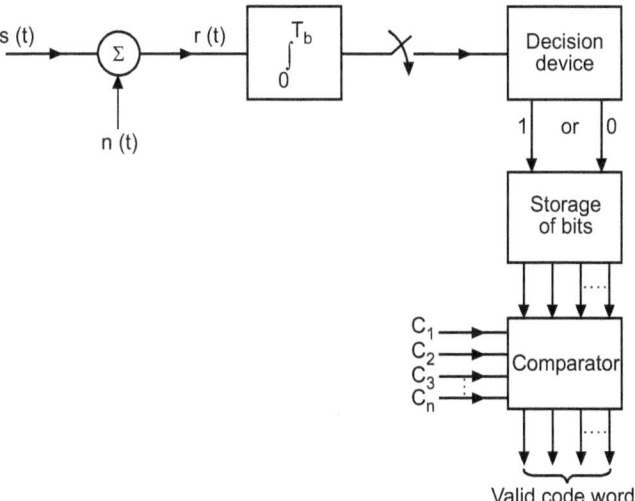

Fig. 5.2 (a): Hard decision decoding

15. **Soft decision decoding:** To avoid the loss of information resulting from hard decision, soft decision decoding is used. The modulator has two input symbols, but the demodulator output has more than two symbols i.e. demodulator is a multilevel quantizer. Thus, soft decision decoder is complex than hard decision decoder, but has improved performance.

Thus, in soft decision decoding, received signal and noise is correlated with all possible signals as shown below in Fig. 5.2 (b).

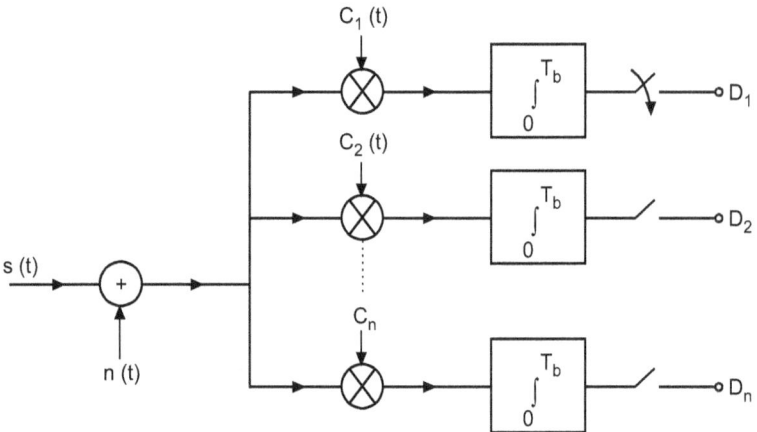

Fig. 5.2 (b): Soft decision decoding

16. **Channel coding theorem:** As discussed in the previous unit, channel coding theorem states that, if a discrete memoryless channel has capacity C which is more than the rate of information generation at source then there exists a coding technique such that the code output can be transmitted at an arbitrarily low probability of symbol error.

    Channel coding theorem tells the condition for existence of good code, but it does not tell how to find them.

5.3 Error Probability with Repetition in the Binary Symmetric Channel

A straightforward idea is to repeat every bit of the message some prearranged number of times, for example, three times, as shown in Table 5.1.

Table 5.1: The repetition code 'R_3'

Source sequence s	Transmitted sequence t
0	000
1	111

Let us imagine what happens if we transmit the source message s = (0 0 1 0 1 1 0) over a binary symmetric channel with noise level f = 0.1 using this repetition code. We can describe the channel as adding a sparse noise vector n to the transmitted vector (in modulo 2 arithmetic, i.e., the binary algebra in which 1 + 1 = 0).

```
s │  0    0    1    0    1    1    0
t │ 000  000  111  000  111  111  000
n │ 000  001  000  000  101  000  000
  ├─────────────────────────────────────
r │ 000  001  111  000  010  111  000
```

If all bits are 0, we decode the triplet as a 0. If, as in the second triplet, there are two 0s and one 1, we decode the triplet as a 0 which in this case corrects the error.

Table 5.2: Decoding algorithm for R_3

Received sequence r	Decoded sequence s
000	0
001	0
010	0
100	0
101	1
110	1
011	1
111	1

Not all errors are corrected, however. If we are unlucky and two errors fall in a single block, as in the fifth triplet, then the decoding rule gets the wrong answer.

```
                     s │  0    0    1    0    1    1    0
                     t │ 000  000  111  000  111  111  000
                     n │ 000  001  000  000  101  000  000
                       ├─────────────────────────────────────
                     r │ 000  001  111  000  010  111  000
                     s │  0    0    1    0    0    1    0
Corrected errors          *                    
Undetected errors                              *
```

Fig. 5.3

Thus, the error probability is reduced by the use of this code. It is easy to compute the error probability. Compute the error probability of R_3 for a binary symmetric channel with noise level f.

Clearly the error probability is dominated by the probability of two bits in a block of three being flipped, which scales as f^2. In the case of our binary symmetric channel f = 0.1, the R_3 code has a probability of error, after decoding of p_b = 0.03 per bit. Fig. 5.3 shows the result of transmitting a binary image over a binary symmetric channel using the repetition code.

The repetition code R_3 has therefore improved our probability of error as desired. At the same time, we have lost something: our rate of information transfer has reduced by a factor of three. So if we use a repetition code to communicate over a telephone line, it will reduce the error rate, but it will also reduce our communication rate. We will have to pay three times as much for each phone call. As for our disc drive, we will need three noisy gigabyte disc drives in order to create a single gigabyte disc drive with $p_b = 0.03$.

Can we push the error probability lower to the sort of values required from a quality disk drive (10^{-5})? Well, we can achieve lower error probabilities by using repetition codes with more repetitions.

Show that it takes a repetition code with rate about 1/60 to get the probability of error down to 10^{-15}. This means that to build a single gigabyte disk drive with the required reliability from noisy gigabyte drives with $f = 0.1$, we would need sixty of the noisy disk drives. The tradeoff between error probability and rate for repetition codes is shown in Fig. 5.4.

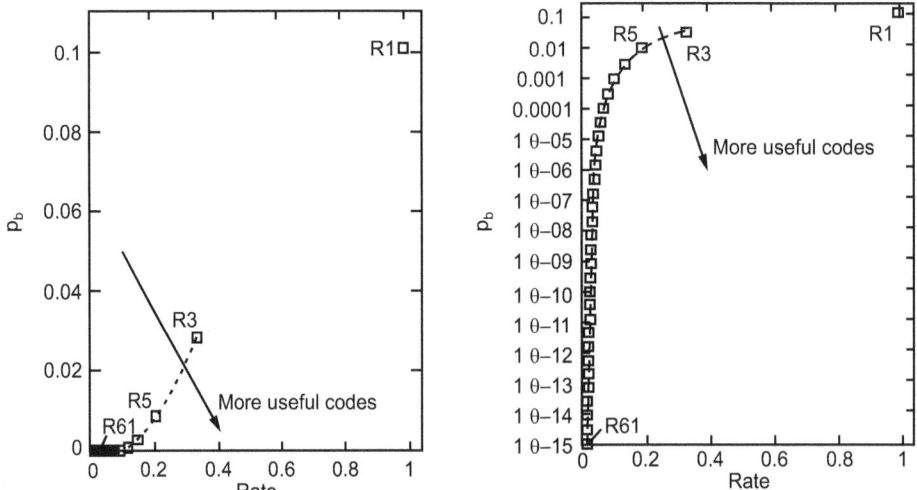

Fig. 5.4: Error probability p_b versus rate for repetition codes over a binary symmetric channel with f = 0.1

Fig. 5.4 (b) shows P on a logarithmic scale. We would like the rate to be large and p_b to be small.

5.4 Linear Block Codes

A linear code: It is a code which has the following properties:
(i) The sum of any two code words in the code will yield another code word of that code.
(ii) There is always all-zero code word.
(iii) The minimum Hamming distance between any two code words is equal to minimum weight of any non-zero code word.

5.4.1 Matrix Description of Linear Block Codes

Consider an (n, k) block code in which there are k message bits (or symbols) and n code bits (or symbols).

Let the code bits be,

$$C = (c_1, c_2, c_3, \ldots c_n) \qquad \ldots (5.1)$$

Let the message bits be,

$$d = (d_1, d_2, d_3, \ldots d_k) \qquad \ldots (5.2)$$

For general case, n bits of code C are generated by linear combinations of k message bits. This is called non-systematic code.

For a special case,

If $c_1 = d_1 \quad c_2 = d_2 \ldots c_k = d_k$

and c_{k+1} to c_n are generated from linear combinations of $d_1, d_2, \ldots d_k$, then the code is called systematic code. First k bits are message bits and (n – k) parity bits added to the message.

As we have seen in earlier section, any code C is a subspace of GF(q^n) and any set of basis vectors S can be used to generate code space C = <S> by linear combinations of basis vectors. Hence, we can put all basis vectors in a matrix which is called generator matrix (G). This matrix is used to generate the code words of C. If we have to generate the code words of length n from k message bits, we will need the generator matrix of the order k × n. Hence, we should have k basis vectors in the generator matrix. The code is generated by,

$$C = d \times G \qquad \ldots (5.3)$$

Now, if we have to generate systematic code, we should have relationship between C and d as below:

$$\begin{aligned}
c_1 &= d_1 \\
c_2 &= d_2 \\
c_3 &= d_3 \\
&\vdots \\
c_k &= d_k \\
c_{k+1} &= p_{11} \cdot d_1 \oplus p_{21} \cdot d_2 \oplus \ldots \oplus p_{k1} \cdot d_k \\
c_{k+2} &= p_{12} \cdot d_1 \oplus p_{22} \cdot d_2 \oplus \ldots \oplus p_{k2} \cdot d_k \\
&\vdots \\
c_n &= p_{1n-k} \cdot d_1 \oplus p_{2n-k} \cdot d_2 \oplus \ldots \oplus p_{kn-k} \, d_k
\end{aligned} \qquad \ldots (5.4)$$

Hence, the generator matrix will be,

$$G = \begin{bmatrix} 1 & 0 & 0 & \cdots & 0 & p_{11} & p_{12} & p_{1n-k} \\ 0 & 1 & 0 & \cdots & 0 & p_{21} & p_{22} & p_{2n-k} \\ \vdots & \vdots & \vdots & & \vdots & & & \\ \vdots & \vdots & \vdots & & \vdots & & & \\ 0 & 0 & 0 & \cdots & 1 & p_{k1} & p_{k2} & p_{kn-k} \end{bmatrix} \quad \ldots (5.5)$$

Thus, generator matrix G consists of two parts: identity matrix I_k and parity matrix P.

Order of I_k is $k \times k$.

Order of P is $k \times n - k$.

i.e. $$G = [I_k | P] \quad \ldots (5.6)$$

The generator matrix provides a concise and efficient way of representing linear block code i.e. a code can be written as,

$$C = dG \quad \ldots (5.7)$$

Thus, we need not store all code words corresponding to all messages, but we can generate them with the help of generator matrix which stores only few code words.

5.4.2 Parity Check Matrix

We have seen that generator matrix is used to generate code words from message words. These code words will be transmitted through a noisy channel. At the receiver end, we have to validate these code words i.e. they are to be checked whether they are correctly received or not. If not, the code words should be corrected with the help of redundant bits that we have added at the transmitter end. For this, consider a matrix H called parity check matrix, which is given by,

$$H = [P^T \; I_{n-k}]_{n-k \times n} \quad \ldots (5.8)$$

i.e. H consists of two parts: transpose of parity matrix whose order will be $n - k \times k$ and identity matrix whose order will be $(n - k) \times (n - k)$.

It can be verified for any code word C.

$$CH^T = 0 \quad \ldots (5.9)$$

i.e. if we multiply any code word with transpose of parity check matrix H, result will be zero-vector.

Thus, the received code word at the receiver is multiplied with H^T and we get zero vector if the code word is correctly received. But if multiplication results into non-zero code word, there will be error in the received code word.

Substitute $C = dG$ in equation (5.9).

∴ $$dGH^T = 0$$

Thus, for equation (5.9) to hold true, we should have,
$$G H^T = 0$$
Now consider, $G = [I_k \ P]$
and $H = [P^T \ I_{n-k}]$

$$G^T = \begin{bmatrix} I_k \\ P^T \end{bmatrix}$$

∴ $H G^T = [P^T \ I_{n-k}] \begin{bmatrix} I_k \\ P^T \end{bmatrix}$

$= P^T \oplus P^T$

$= 0$

∴ $G H^T = 0$

The process of coding and detection is shown in Fig. 5.4.

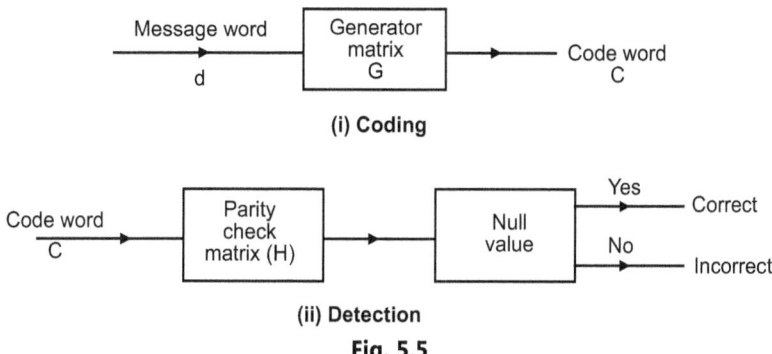

(i) Coding

(ii) Detection

Fig. 5.5

Example 5.3:

Consider a given generator matrix.

$$G = \begin{bmatrix} 1 & 0 & 0 & 0 & 1 & 1 & 0 \\ 0 & 1 & 0 & 0 & 0 & 1 & 1 \\ 0 & 0 & 1 & 0 & 1 & 1 & 1 \\ 0 & 0 & 0 & 1 & 1 & 0 & 1 \end{bmatrix}$$

Find parity check matrix and check whether following code words are valid or not.

(i) 1 0 0 0 1 1 0

(ii) 0 1 0 1 0 1 1.

Solution:

The given generator matrix is of the order 4 × 7.

Hence, $n = 7$

$k = 4$

The parity matrix in the generator is

$$P = \begin{bmatrix} 1 & 1 & 0 \\ 0 & 1 & 1 \\ 1 & 1 & 1 \\ 1 & 0 & 1 \end{bmatrix}$$

Now parity check matrix is given by,

$$H = [P^T \; I_{n-k}]$$

$$= \begin{bmatrix} 1 & 0 & 1 & 1 & 1 & 0 & 0 \\ 1 & 1 & 1 & 0 & 0 & 1 & 0 \\ 0 & 1 & 1 & 1 & 0 & 0 & 1 \end{bmatrix}$$

$$\therefore \quad H^T = \begin{bmatrix} 1 & 1 & 0 \\ 0 & 1 & 1 \\ 1 & 1 & 1 \\ 1 & 0 & 1 \\ 1 & 0 & 0 \\ 0 & 1 & 0 \\ 0 & 0 & 1 \end{bmatrix}$$

To check whether given code words are valid or not, we find CH^T.

(i) Given: $\quad C = [1\,0\,0\,0\,1\,1\,0]$

$$\therefore \quad CH^T = [1\,0\,0\,0\,1\,1\,0] \begin{bmatrix} 1 & 1 & 0 \\ 0 & 1 & 1 \\ 1 & 1 & 1 \\ 1 & 0 & 1 \\ 1 & 0 & 0 \\ 0 & 1 & 0 \\ 0 & 0 & 1 \end{bmatrix}$$

$$= [0\,0\,0]$$

Hence, given code word is valid.

(ii)   C = [0 1 0 1 0 1 1]

$$\therefore \quad CH^T = [0\,1\,0\,1\,0\,1\,1] \begin{bmatrix} 1 & 1 & 0 \\ 0 & 1 & 1 \\ 1 & 1 & 1 \\ 1 & 0 & 1 \\ 1 & 0 & 0 \\ 0 & 1 & 0 \\ 0 & 0 & 1 \end{bmatrix}$$

$$= [1\,0\,1]$$

Hence, given code word is invalid.

5.4.3 Minimum Distance and H^T

Hamming distance between two code words is the number of positions in which their symbols differ. Hamming weight is number of non-zero elements in the code words. The minimum distance d_{min} of a linear block code is the smallest distance between any pair of code vectors in the code. From the closure property of linear block codes, the sum (or difference) of two code words is another code word.

Minimum distance of a linear block code is the smallest hamming weight of the non-zero code word in the code. Parity check matrix H and in turn generator matrix G is also related to minimum distance d_{min} of a code. Since, $CH^T = 0$, the number of 1's in code vector C should be such that, corresponding rows of H^T add to zero i.e. corresponding columns of parity check matrix H must add to zero.

Consider the H^T discussed in earlier example.

$$H^T = \begin{bmatrix} 1 & 1 & 0 \\ 0 & 1 & 1 \\ 1 & 1 & 1 \\ 1 & 0 & 1 \\ 1 & 0 & 0 \\ 0 & 1 & 0 \\ 0 & 0 & 1 \end{bmatrix}$$

Now consider a valid code vector
         C = [1 0 0 0 1 1 0]

There are three non-zero elements at positions 1, 5 and 6 and the sum of 1st, 5th and 6th row of H^T is

$$\begin{bmatrix} 1 \\ 1 \\ 0 \end{bmatrix} + \begin{bmatrix} 1 \\ 0 \\ 0 \end{bmatrix} + \begin{bmatrix} 0 \\ 1 \\ 0 \end{bmatrix} = \begin{bmatrix} 0 \\ 0 \\ 0 \end{bmatrix}$$

The number of non-zero elements in the code is 3. If you check other code words in the (7, 4) code discussed earlier, the minimum number of non-zero elements is 3, which is nothing but minimum weight of that code and it is also minimum Hamming distance.

Hence, the minimum distance of linear block code (d_{min}) is equal to minimum number of rows of H^T (or columns of H) whose sum is equal to zero vector.

5.4.4 Decoding of a Linear Block Code

Decoding is a process of detecting and correcting errors when messages in the form of code words are transmitted on a noisy channel. The important question here is, how many errors can we detect and correct. It will depend on the design of the code. The number of errors, the code can correct or detect is called error correcting or detecting capability of that code.

A code contains certain number of code words which are at some distance from each other, which is specified in terms of Hamming distance.

e.g. Consider the following code.

Message word	Code word
0	0 0 0
1	1 1 1

There are two code words in the code whose Hamming distance is 3.

When one of the code words is transmitted the noise or distortion is likely to change some bits. e.g. when 0 0 0 is transmitted, we might receive 0 0 1. As long as one code word is not transformed into another code words, we can detect whether there was error in transmission or not. Thus, the number of errors, that can be detected, depends on minimum Hamming distance of the code, as it is the minimum distance between any two code words.

i.e. if a code has Hamming distance d_{min}, the number of errors that can be detected is

$$\boxed{t_d \leq d_{min} - 1} \qquad \ldots (5.10)$$

The number of errors, that can be corrected, also depends on minimum Hamming distance. When a code word is received with error, we have to find which code word was actually transmitted. Obviously, the code word nearest to the valid code words will be the answer. But then the received code word might be at same Hamming distance from two or more valid code words. Hence, it is not possible to correct the code with this criteria. Also, if more errors occur, the received code word will go near to another valid code word which was not transmitted.

e.g. If 0 0 0 is transmitted and 0 1 0 is received, we can make decision in favour of 0 0 0 as 0 1 0 is nearer to 0 0 0 than 1 1 1. But if 0 0 0 is transmitted and 0 1 1 is received, we will make decision in favour of 1 1 1 as 0 1 1 is nearer to 1 1 1 than 0 0 0 which is not correct. Hence, this code cannot correct two errors. For error correction capability, any two code words in the code should be separated such that the number of errors (t_c) should result into a received word which is closest to original code word and away from all other code words. The condition for this is

$$t_c \leq \frac{d_{min} - 1}{2} \qquad \ldots (5.11)$$

This can be well understood using pictorial view. We can consider the code words to be placed in spheres separated from each other as shown in Fig. 5.6 (a).

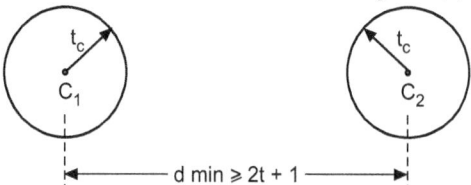

Fig. 5.6 (a): Decoding Spheres

The spheres are of radius t_c, where t_c is number of errors that can be corrected. If t_c errors occur in code c_1/c_2, the new code word will be within their spheres and remain nearer to the valid code word. Hence, the minimum Hamming distance has to be greater than $2t_c + 1$.

If we consider the code C = {0 0 0, 1 1 1}, the code words will be placed from other possible distortions as shown below on the vertices of a cube.

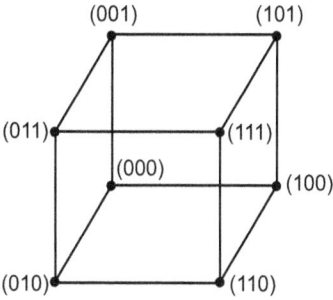

Fig. 5.6 (b): Decoding Cube

If (0 0 0) is transmitted and (0 0 1) is received, we find 0 0 1 is near to 0 0 0 than (1 1 1). Hence, we can make the correction in favour of (0 0 0).

But if (0 0 0) is transmitted and (0 1 1) is received, we find (0 1 1) is nearer to (1 1 1) than (0 0 0). Hence, we cannot correct the two errors here. Thus, this code has error correcting capability of 1 error. This can be verified from the formula also. The code has $d_{min} = 3$.

$$\therefore \quad t_c \leq \frac{d_{min} - 1}{2}$$
$$\leq \frac{3-1}{2}$$
$$\leq 1$$

Note that, if 0 1 1 is received when 0 0 0 was transmitted, decision will be made in favour of 1 1 1, even though it is incorrect. Here, we assume that probability of occurrence of 2 errors is far less than that of 1 error.

Example 5.4:

Find the error correcting capability of code generated in example 5.3.

Solution:

Code word	Hamming weight
0 0 0 0 0 0 0	0
0 0 0 1 1 0 1	3
0 0 1 0 1 1 1	4
0 0 1 1 0 1 0	4
0 1 0 0 0 1 1	3
0 1 0 1 1 1 0	4
0 1 1 0 1 0 0	3
0 1 1 1 0 0 1	4
1 0 0 0 1 1 0	3
1 0 0 1 0 1 1	4
1 0 1 0 0 0 1	3
1 0 1 1 1 0 0	4
1 1 0 0 1 0 1	4
1 1 0 1 0 0 0	3
1 1 1 0 0 1 0	4
1 1 1 1 1 1 1	7

Since, minimum weight of the non-zero code words is 3.

$$d_{min} = 3$$

$\therefore$ Error correcting capability,

$$t_c \leq \frac{d_{min} - 1}{2}$$
$$t_c \leq \frac{3-1}{2}$$
$$t_c \leq 1$$

If the code is such that there is ambiguity in deciding closest code word, then it is called incomplete decoder. A complete decoder can decode every received word, even if there are not more than t_c errors. They will make a good guess about the code word.

There will be limit on maximum distance, on the code which will be

$$d_{max} \leq n - k + 1$$

where, k is number of message bits and n is number of code bits.

This is called **Singleton Bound**.

5.4.5 Syndrome Decoding

Minimum Hamming distance d_{min} of a code decides error correcting capability of a code. Now, let us see how these errors can be corrected.

The generator matrix (G) is used at the transmitter to generate the code corresponding to message. The parity check matrix can be used to decode the received code word.

- Let r be the received code vector.
- This code vector may or may not differ from transmitted code vector C.
- Let there be another vector e which will be called error vector defining the corresponding error pattern.
- Hence, $\quad r = C \oplus e$ ... (5.12)

If there is no error, e will be having all zero symbols. If there are some errors, then there will be that many number of 1's in the corresponding location.

i.e. $\quad e_i = \begin{cases} 1 & \text{If an error has occurred in the } i^{th} \text{ location} \\ 0 & \text{Otherwise} \end{cases}$ ... (5.13)

The received code vector is multiplied with H^T to get what is called syndrome vector. As we see, if received code word is same as transmitted code word, this multiplication will result into 0, as $CH^T = 0$.

Since, the received code vector is $1 \times n$ and H^T is of the order $n \times n - k$, the syndrome vector will have $n - k$ bits.

Thus, $\quad S = r H^T$ ... (5.14)

If r = C, S will have all-zero vectors.

If r ≠ C, $\quad S = r H^T$

$= (C \oplus e) H^T$

$= C \cdot H^T \oplus e H^T$

$= e H^T$ ... (5.15)

Thus, the syndrome depends on error pattern e.

Another property of the syndrome is that, all error patterns, that differ by a code word, have the same syndrome. Let us look into this.

Let there be k message bits.

Hence, there will be 2^k code words $C_1, C_2, C_3, \ldots C_{2^k}$.

Let there be some error pattern e which will also have 2^{k-1} distinct vectors $e_1, e_2, \ldots e_{2^k}$.

$$\therefore \quad e_i = e \oplus C_i \quad \ldots (5.16)$$

Set of vectors $\{e_1, e_2, e_3, \ldots e_{2^k}\}$ is called coset of the code. There will be 2^{n-k} possible cosets of an (n, k) block code.

Now,
$$\begin{aligned} e_i \cdot H^T &= (e \oplus C_i) H^T \\ &= e H^T \oplus C_i H^T \\ &= e H^T = S \end{aligned} \quad \ldots (5.17)$$

Thus, each coset of the code is characterized by unique syndrome.

The vector having minimum weight in the coset is called coset leader.

A standard array is constructed using these coset leaders.

In the first row, all-valid code words are written starting with all-zero code words.

In second row we write vector e_2 which is not in first row as coset leader and then write the cosets $e_2 + c$ below each valid code vector. We continue this till all the cosets are listed.

e.g. $\quad C = \{0\,0\,0, 1\,1\,1\}$

Standard Array:

Syndrome	Coset Leaders	n-tuples	
0 0	0 0 0	1 1 1	← Code vectors
1 1	1 0 0	0 1 1	⎫
1 0	0 1 0	1 0 1	⎬ Single errors
0 1	0 0 1	1 1 0	⎭

The decoding procedure for a linear block code will be as below.

1. Compute $S = r H^T$, where r is received code.
2. Identify the error pattern i.e. coset leader corresponding to the syndrome. Let it be e.
3. Compute code vector.

$$C = r \oplus e$$

Example 5.5:

Decoding procedure for (7, 4) block code whose generator matrix is given in example (5.3).

$$G = \begin{bmatrix} 1 & 0 & 0 & 0 & 1 & 1 & 0 \\ 0 & 1 & 0 & 0 & 0 & 1 & 1 \\ 0 & 0 & 1 & 0 & 1 & 1 & 1 \\ 0 & 0 & 0 & 1 & 1 & 0 & 1 \end{bmatrix}$$

COMMUNICATION SYSTEM - II   CHANNEL CODING

Also find the corrected code words for the following received words.

    (i)   1 0 0 0 1 1 0   (ii) 0 1 0 1 0 1 1   (iii) 0 0 0 1 1 0 0

Solution:

Step I:

The given code has error correcting capability of 1. Hence, there will be $2^{n-k} = 2^3 = 8$ single error patterns.

Step II:

    The parity check matrix is given by,

$$H = [P^T \; I_{n-k}]$$

$$= \begin{bmatrix} 1 & 0 & 1 & 1 & 1 & 0 & 0 \\ 1 & 1 & 1 & 0 & 0 & 1 & 0 \\ 0 & 1 & 1 & 1 & 0 & 0 & 1 \end{bmatrix}$$

$$\therefore \quad H^T = \begin{bmatrix} 1 & 1 & 0 \\ 0 & 1 & 1 \\ 1 & 1 & 1 \\ 1 & 0 & 1 \\ 1 & 0 & 0 \\ 0 & 1 & 0 \\ 0 & 0 & 1 \end{bmatrix}$$

Step III:

    We find syndrome vectors corresponding to each error pattern using

$$S = e \, H^T$$

e.g. for error pattern 0 0 0 0 0 0 1, the syndrome will be

$$S = [0\,0\,0\,0\,0\,0\,1] \begin{bmatrix} 1 & 1 & 0 \\ 0 & 1 & 1 \\ 1 & 1 & 1 \\ 1 & 0 & 1 \\ 1 & 0 & 0 \\ 0 & 1 & 0 \\ 0 & 0 & 1 \end{bmatrix}$$

$$= [0\,0\,1]$$

Following table gives all syndrome vectors with their error patterns.

Error pattern	Syndrome
0 0 0 0 0 0 0	0 0 0
1 0 0 0 0 0 0	1 1 0
0 1 0 0 0 0 0	0 1 1
0 0 1 0 0 0 0	1 1 1
0 0 0 1 0 0 0	1 0 1
0 0 0 0 1 0 0	1 0 0
0 0 0 0 0 1 0	0 1 0
0 0 0 0 0 0 1	0 0 1

Note: If you observe above syndrome vectors they are nothing but matrix H^T itself! Thus, if there is single error in i^{th} bit, the syndrome will be i^{th} row of H^T!.

Step IV:

Once above table is ready, we can now correct the errors in the received code words.

(i) $r = [1\,0\,0\,0\,1\,1\,0]$

∴ $S = r\,H^T$
   $= [0\,0\,0]$

Hence, there is no error.

∴ Corrected code word, $C = r$

(ii) $r = [0\,1\,0\,1\,0\,1\,1]$
   $S = r\,H^T$
   $= [1\,0\,1]$

Corresponding error pattern from above table,
   $e = 0\,0\,0\,1\,0\,0\,0$ [Error in 4th bit]

∴ Corrected code word, $C = r \oplus e$
   $= [0\,1\,0\,1\,0\,1\,1] \oplus [0\,0\,0\,1\,0\,0\,0]$
   $= [0\,1\,0\,0\,0\,1\,1]$

(iii) $r = [0\,0\,0\,1\,1\,0\,0]$
   $S = r\,H^T$
   $= [0\,0\,1]$

∴ Error pattern is $e = [0\,0\,0\,0\,0\,0\,1]$

∴ Corrected code word
   $C = r \oplus e$
   $= [0\,0\,0\,1\,1\,0\,0] + [0\,0\,0\,0\,0\,0\,1]$
   $= [0\,0\,0\,1\,1\,0\,1]$

5.4.6 Dual Code

A linear block code is specified using generator matrix G which is of the order $k \times n$. For this code we have,

$$H \cdot G^T = 0 \qquad \ldots (5.21)$$

where, H is parity check matrix of the order $k \times n - k$.

Taking transpose, we get,
$$GH^T = 0 \qquad ...(5.22)$$

Above equation suggests that H can be used as generator matrix and G will be its parity check matrix. Since, order of H is n – k × n, the code will be (n, n – k) linear block code.

e.g. The dual of (7, 4) LBC will be (7, 3) LBC whose generator matrix will be

$$G = \begin{bmatrix} 1 & 0 & 1 & 1 & 1 & 0 & 0 \\ 1 & 1 & 1 & 0 & 0 & 1 & 0 \\ 0 & 1 & 1 & 1 & 0 & 0 & 1 \end{bmatrix} \qquad ...(5.23)$$

Thus, every Linear Block Code (LBC) will have a dual code.

5.4.7 Circuit Implementation for Linear Block Code

Linear Block Code (LBC) coder and decoder can be implemented using combinational and switching circuits. For this, let us consider a (7, 4) linear block code discussed in example 5.3.

From the generator matrix, we have the parity bits.

$$P_1 = d_1 \oplus d_2 \oplus d_4$$
$$P_2 = d_1 \oplus d_2 \oplus d_3$$
$$P_3 = d_2 \oplus d_3 \oplus d_4$$

Hence, we generate P_1, P_2, P_3 using mod-2 adders, as below (Fig. 5.7).

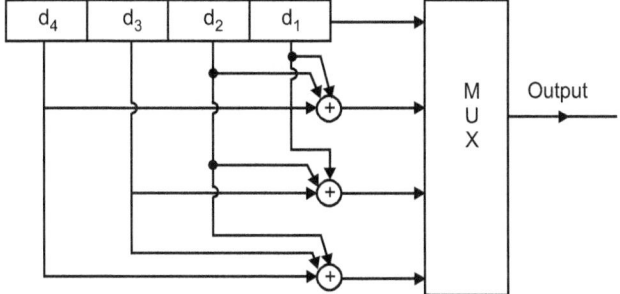

Fig. 5.7 (a) : Coder for (7, 4) LBC

The decoder circuit for the code involves generation of syndrome vectors using the following equations.

$$S_1 = r_1 \oplus r_3 \oplus r_4 \oplus r_5$$
$$S_2 = r_1 \oplus r_2 \oplus r_3 \oplus r_6$$
$$S_3 = r_2 \oplus r_3 \oplus r_4 \oplus r_7$$

From the syndrome, we can generate corresponding error pattern using multiplexer which can be added to received vector to generate corrected code as shown in Fig. 5.8.

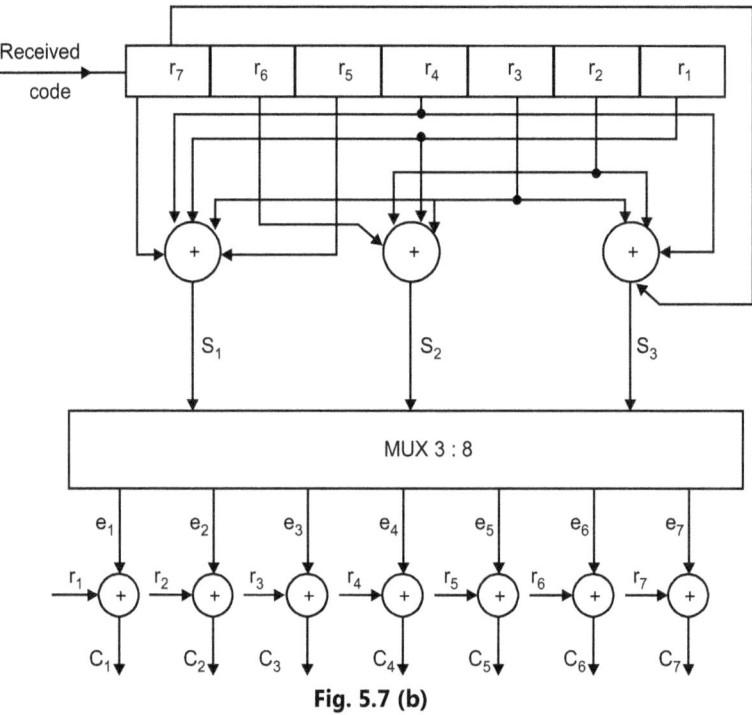

Fig. 5.7 (b)

5.4.8 Optimal Linear Code

It is an (n, k, d_{min}) code, where n is code word length, k is message length and d_{min} is minimum distance of the code such that you will not find a code $(n - 1, k, d_{min})$ or $(n + 1, k + 1, d_{min})$ or $(n + 1, k, d_{min} + 1)$.

Example of an optimal code is the (24, 12, 8) binary code.

$$(n, k, d_{min}) = (24, 12, 8)$$

$$(n - 1, k, d_{min}) = (23, 12, 8) \text{ does not exist}$$

$$(n + 1, k + 1, d_{min}) = (25, 13, 8) \text{ does not exist}$$

$$(n + 1, k, d_{min} + 1) = (25, 12, 9) \text{ does not exist.}$$

Hence, (24, 12, 8) is optimal code.

But $(n - 1, k, d_{min} - 1) = (23, 12, 7)$ exists.

The (23, 12, 7) code is known as **Golay code**.

5.5 Algebraic Codes

Algebraic codes includes:
1. Cyclic codes
2. Convolutional code
3. TCM code
4. BC4
5. RS

5.5.1 Cyclic Codes

Representation of Cyclic Codes Using Polynomials

We have seen that a code word can be represented using polynomial as,

$$c(x) = c_1 x^{n-1} + c_2 x^{n-2} + c_3 x^{n-3} + \ldots + c_{n-1} x + c_n$$

e.g. if you are given a code word C = (1 0 1 1 0), it will be written as,

$$C = (1 \quad 0 \quad 1 \quad 1 \quad 0)$$
$$\downarrow \quad \downarrow \quad \downarrow \quad \downarrow \quad \downarrow$$
$$c(x) = 1 \cdot x^4 + 0 \cdot x^3 + 1 \cdot x^2 + 1 \cdot x + 0 \cdot x$$

$\therefore \quad c(x) = x^4 + x^2 + x$

We have seen that cyclic code satisfies cyclic property. We can verify that if c(x) is a code polynomial corresponding to a code word, then the remainder after dividing $x^i c(x)$ by $x^n + 1$ also represents a valid code word.

e.g. $\quad x^1 \cdot c(x) = c_1 x^n + c_2 x^{n-1} + c_3^{n-2} + \ldots + c_{n-1} x^2 + c_n x \quad \ldots (5.18)$

Divide $x^1 c(x)$ by $x^n + 1$ and find remainder.

$$
\begin{array}{r|l}
 & c_1 \\
\hline
x^n + 1 & c_1 x^n + c_2 x^{n-1} + c_3 x^{n-2} + \ldots + c_{n-1} x^2 + c_n x \\
 & c_1 x^n + c_1 \\
\hline
\text{Remainder} & c_2 x^{n-1} + c_3 x^{n-2} + \ldots + c_{n-1} x^2 + c_n x + c_1 \\
\end{array}
$$

The remainder represents the code word

$$C_1 = (c_2, c_3, \ldots c_{n-1}, c_n, c_1) \quad \ldots (5.19)$$

which is a cyclic shifted version of original code word C. Similarly, you can verify that Remainder after divisor of $x^2 c(x)$ and $x^n + 1$ will give rise to another cyclic shifted code word.

In general,

$$\text{Rem}\left[\frac{x^i \cdot c(x)}{x^n + 1}\right] = c_{i+1} x^{n-1} + c_{i+2} x^{n-2} + \ldots + c_n x^i + c_1 x^{i-1} + \ldots c_i \quad \ldots (5.20)$$

It is denoted as $c^{(i)}(x)$.

i.e. $\quad c^{(i)}(x) = x^i c(x) \bmod (x^n + 1) \quad \ldots (5.21)$

[Mod is a remainder after division operation].

5.5.2 A Method for Generating Cyclic Code

Theorem:

Cyclic code polynomial $c(x)$ can be generated using data polynomial $d(x)$ of degree $k - 1$ and a generator polynomial $g(x)$ of degree $n - k$ as,

$$c(x) = d(x) \cdot g(x) \quad \ldots (5.22)$$

where, $g(x)$ is $(n - k)^{th}$ order factor $x^n + 1$.

Proof:

Let $d(x)$ represent data polynomial of k message bits $d_1, d_2, d_3, \ldots d_k$ as,

$$d(x) = d_1 x^{k-1} + d_2 x^{k-2} + d_3 x^{k-3} + \ldots + d_{k-1} x + d_k \quad \ldots (5.23)$$

Now, consider the polynomial

$$c(x) = d(x) \cdot g(x)$$

$$\therefore \quad c(x) = d_1 x^{k-1} g(x) + d_2 x^{k-2} + \ldots + d_k g(x) \quad \ldots (5.24)$$

Since, $g(x)$ is $(n - k)^{th}$ order polynomial, $c(x)$ will be of degree $n - 1$ or less. i.e. degree of $c(x)$ will be atmost $n - 1$.

Now, we have to prove that this code is cyclic.

Let,

$$c(x) = c_1 x^{n-1} + c_2 x^{n-2} + \ldots + c_n$$

$$x \, c(x) = c_1 x^n + c_2 x^{n-1} + \ldots + c_n x$$

$$= (c_1 x^n + c_1) + (c_2 x^{n-1} + c_3 x^{n-2} + \ldots + c_n x + c_1) \quad \ldots (5.25)$$

Adding $c_1 \oplus c_2$,

$$= c_1(x^n + 1) + (c_2 x^{n-1} + c_3 x^{n-2} + \ldots + c_n x + c_1)$$

$$= c_1(x^n + 1) + c^{(1)}(x) \quad \ldots (5.26)$$

But, $\quad x \, d(x) = x \cdot d(x) \, g(x) \quad \ldots (5.27)$

Thus, from equations (5.26) and (5.27), we get,

$$x\, d(x) \cdot g(x) = c_1(x^n + 1) + c^{(1)}(x) \qquad \ldots (5.28)$$

But $g(x)$ is a factor of $(x^n + 1)$ and if equation (2.28) has to hold good, $c^{(1)}(x)$ also has to be multiple of $(x^n + 1)$. But $c^{(1)}(x)$ is a cyclic shifted version of $c(x)$. Hence, the code $c(x)$ generated by multiplying $d(x)$ and $g(x)$ is cyclic.

Example 5.6:
Find generator polynomial $g(x)$ for a (7, 4) cyclic code and final code words for the following data words.

(i) 1 1 0 0

(ii) 1 0 1 0

(iii) 0 1 1 1

Solution:
Given:
$$n = 7$$
$$k = 4$$

The generator polynomial should be of the degree $n - k = 3$.

The generator polynomial should be factor of $x^7 + 1$.

$$
\begin{aligned}
(x^7 + 1) &= (x + 1)(x^6 + x^5 + x^4 + x^3 + x^2 + x + 1) \\
&= (x + 1)(x^6 + x^5 + x^4 + x^3 + x^3 + x^3 + x^2 + x + 1) \\
&= (x + 1)(x^6 + x^4 + x^3 + x^5 + x^3 + x^2 + x^3 + x + 1) \\
&= (x + 1)[x^3(x^3 + x + 1) + x^2(x^3 + x + 1) + 1(x^3 + x + 1)] \\
&= (x + 1)(x^3 + x^2 + 1)(x^3 + x + 1)
\end{aligned}
$$

We have two polynomials of order 3, one of which can be selected as generator polynomial.

Let, $\qquad g(x) = x^3 + x^2 + 1$

Now, a code is generated using,

$$c(x) = d(x)\, g(x)$$

(i) 1 1 0 0

$$d(x) = x^3 + x^2$$

$\therefore$
$$
\begin{aligned}
c(x) &= (x^3 + x^2)(x^3 + x^2 + 1) \\
&= (x^6 + x^5 + x^3 + x^5 + x^4 + x^2) \\
&= x^6 + x^4 + x^3 + x^2 \\
&= 1.x^6 + 0.x^5 + 1.x^4 + 1.x^3 + 1.x^2 + 0.x + 0.x)
\end{aligned}
$$

$\therefore \qquad c = [1\,0\,1\,1\,1\,0\,0]$

(ii) 1 0 1 0

$$d(x) = x^3 + x$$

$$c(x) = (x^3 + x)(x^3 + x^2 + 1)$$

COMMUNICATION SYSTEM - II   CHANNEL CODING

$$= x^6 + x^5 + x^3 + x^4 + x^3 + x$$
$$= x^6 + x^5 + x^4 + x$$
$$= 1.x^6 + 1.x^5 + 1.x^4 + 0.x^3 + 0.x^2 + 1.x + 0$$

∴   c = [1 1 1 0 0 1 0]

(iii) 0 0 1 1

$$d(x) = x + 1$$

∴
$$c(x) = (x + 1)(x^3 + x^2 + 1)$$
$$= x^4 + x^3 + x + x^3 + x^2 + 1$$
$$= x^4 + x^2 + x + 1$$
$$= 0.x^6 + 0.x^5 + 1.x^4 + 0.x^3 + 1.x^2 + 1.x + 1$$

∴   c = [0 0 1 0 1 1 1]

It can be observed from above example that the code generated is non-systematic code as message bits and parity bits are not in separate blocks.

Example 5.7:

Find generator polynomial for a (7, 3) cyclic code.

Solution:

Given: n = 7
                  k = 3

∴ The order of generator polynomial will be,

$$n - k = 4$$

g(x) will be a factor of $x^7 + 1$.

$$x^7 + 1 = (x + 1)(x^6 + x^5 + x^4 + x^3 + x^2 + 1)$$
$$= (x + 1)(x^6 + x^5 + x^4 + x^3 + x^3 + x^3 + x^2 + 1)$$
$$= (x + 1) x^3(x^3 + x + 1) + x^2(x^3 + x + 1) + 1(x^3 + x + 1)$$
$$= (x + 1)(x^3 + x^2 + 1)(x^3 + x + 1)$$
$$= (x^4 + x^3 + x + x^3 + x^2 + 1)(x^3 + x + 1)$$
$$= (x^4 + x^2 + x + 1)(x^3 + x + 1)$$

∴ Generator polynomial of order 4 is

$$g(x) = x^4 + x^2 + x + 1$$

5.5.3 Parity Check Polynomial

For linear block code we have seen that there is a generator matrix (G) and a parity check matrix (H) pair used at transmitter and receiver respectively.

A cyclic code can be specified by its generator polynomial g(x). There can be another polynomial called parity check polynomial h(x) such that,

$$[g(x) \cdot h(x)] \bmod [x^n + 1] = 0 \qquad \ldots (5.29)$$

or
$$g(x) \cdot h(x) = x^n + 1 \qquad \ldots (5.30)$$

(Analogous to $GH^T = 0$)

The parity check polynomial is of the order k and is specified as

$$h(x) = 1 + \left(\sum_{i=1}^{k-1} h_i x^i\right) + x^k \qquad \ldots (5.31)$$

Equation (5.30) shows that just like g(x), h(x) is also a factor of $x^n + 1$.

e.g. for (7, 4) cyclic code, let $g(x) = x^3 + x + 1$.

$$\therefore \quad x^7 + 1 = (x + 1)(x^3 + x^2 + 1)(x^3 + x + 1)$$
$$= (x^4 + x^2 + x + 1)(x^3 + x + 1)$$

$$\therefore \quad h(x) = x^4 + x^2 + x + 1$$

5.5.4 Decoding of Cyclic Code

The decoding process of cyclic code is same for both systematic and non-systematic cyclic codes.

Every valid code word polynomial c(x) is a multiple of g(x). When this code word is transmitted, there may be some errors introduced. Hence, the received code word polynomial r(x) may not be same as c(x).

If received code word is same as transmitted code word, then r(x) mod g(x) = 0. Otherwise it will be non-zero polynomial. Consider $\frac{r(x)}{g(x)}$, it can be written as,

$$\frac{r(x)}{g(x)} = q(x) + \frac{s(x)}{g(x)} \qquad \ldots (5.32)$$

where, q(x) is quotient polynomial and s(x) is remainder polynomial also called as syndrome polynomial.

Degree of q(x) will be $k - 1$ and that of s(x) will be $n - k - 1$.

r(x) can be written in terms of c(x) as,

$$r(x) = c(x) \oplus e(x) \qquad \ldots (5.33)$$

where e(x) is an error polynomial decided by the bit error pattern in r(x).

$$\therefore \quad \frac{r(x)}{g(x)} = \frac{c(x) \oplus e(x)}{g(x)} \quad \ldots (5.34)$$

$$= \frac{c(x)}{g(x)} \oplus \frac{e(x)}{g(x)} \quad \ldots (5.35)$$

$$\therefore \quad \text{Remainder}\left[\frac{r(x)}{g(x)}\right] = \text{Rem}\left[\frac{c(x)}{g(x)}\right] + \text{Rem}\left[\frac{e(x)}{g(x)}\right] \quad \ldots (5.36)$$

But remainder after division of c(x) and g(x) will be zero.

$$\therefore \quad \text{Rem}\left[\frac{r(x)}{g(x)}\right] = \text{Rem}\left[\frac{e(x)}{g(x)}\right] \quad \ldots (5.37)$$

Comparing equations (5.32) and (5.37), we can write,

$$s(x) = \text{Rem}\left[\frac{e(x)}{g(x)}\right] \quad \ldots (5.38)$$

Equation (5.38) shows that the syndrome polynomial of error polynomial e(x) is same as received word polynomial.

Thus, the decoding process of a cyclic code will be as below.

If our aim is to only detect errors, then the received code word polynomial is divided by g(x). If the remainder i.e. syndrome polynomial is zero, there will be no error and if it is non-zero, then there will be error. If it is required to correct those errors, then the procedure will be,

    (i) Prepare a table of error patterns and syndromes using relation (5.38).

    (ii) Find syndrome after diving received word polynomial r(x) and g(x).

    (iii) Select the error pattern corresponding to the syndrome.

    (iv) Add error pattern to the received code word.

Example 5.8:

Design (3, 1) cyclic repetition code and its decoding method. Find corrected codewords for –

    (i) 0 1 0

    (ii) 1 1 0

Solution:

Given: n = 3

             k = 1

The generator polynomial g(x) order = 3 – 1 = 2.

Generator polynomial should be factor of $x^3 + 1$.

Now, $(x^3 + 1) = (x + 1)(x^2 + x + 1)$

$\therefore \quad g(x) = x^2 + x + 1$

Since, k = 1, there will be two message words 0 and 1.

(I) Coding:

(i) d = [0]

$$d(x) = 0$$
$$x^{n-k} d(x) = x^2 \cdot 0 = 0$$
$$\therefore \quad p(x) = 0$$
$$\therefore \quad c(x) = x^{n-k} d(x) + p(x)$$
$$= 0 + 0$$
$$= 0$$
$$\therefore \quad c = [0\ 0\ 0]$$

(ii) d = [1]

$$d(x) = 1$$
$$\therefore \quad x^{n-k} d(x) = x^2 \cdot 1$$
$$= x^2$$

To find p(x):

$$
\begin{array}{r}
1 \\
x^2 + x + 1 \overline{\smash{)}\ x^2 } \\
\underline{x^2 + x + 1} \\
x + 1 \leftarrow p(x)
\end{array}
$$

$$\therefore \quad c(x) = x^{n-k} d(x) + p(x)$$
$$= x^2 + x + 1$$
$$\therefore \quad c = [1\ 1\ 1]$$

Hence, code words are

Message	Code
0	0 0 0
1	1 1 1

(II) Decoding:

Since, $d_{min} = 3$, error correcting capability,

$$t_c \leq \frac{d_{min} - 1}{2}$$
$$\leq \frac{3 - 1}{2}$$
$$\leq 1 \text{ error}$$

The error patterns will be,

1 0 0

0 1 0

0 0 1

Find s(x) = e(x) mod g(x) for each error pattern.

(i) For e = 1 0 0

$$e(x) = x^2$$

$$x^2 + x + 1 \overline{\smash{\big)}\ \begin{aligned} & 1 \\ & x^2 \\ & \underline{x^2 + x + 1} \\ & x + 1 \leftarrow s(x) \end{aligned}}$$

∴ s = [1 1]

(ii) For e = 0 1 0

$$e(x) = x$$

$$x^2 + x + 1 \overline{\smash{\big)}\ \begin{aligned} & 0 \\ & x \\ & \underline{0} \\ & x \leftarrow s(x) \end{aligned}}$$

∴ s = [1 0]

(iii) For e = 0 0 1

$$e(x) = 1$$

$$x^2 + x + 1 \overline{\smash{\big)}\ \begin{aligned} & 0 \\ & 1 \\ & \underline{0} \\ & 1 \leftarrow s(x) \end{aligned}}$$

∴ s = [0 1]

Hence, syndrome and error vector table will be as below.

Error Vector	Syndrome
1 0 0	1 1
0 1 0	1 0
0 0 1	0 1

Now, let us decode given received words.

(i) r = 0 1 0

∴ r(x) = x

$$x^2 + x + 1 \overline{\smash{)}\, x} $$
$$\underline{0}$$
$$\,x \; \leftarrow s(x)$$

∴ s = [1 0]

This syndrome corresponds to e = [0 1 0].

∴ Corrected code word c = r ⊕ e

= [0 1 0] ⊕ [0 1 0]

= [0 0 0]

(ii) r = 1 1 0

∴ r(x) = $x^2 + x$

$$x^2 + x + 1 \overline{\smash{)}\, x^2 + x}$$
$$\underline{x^2 + x + 1}$$
$$1 \; \leftarrow s(x)$$

∴ s = [0 1]

This syndrome corresponds to e = [0 0 1]

∴ Corrected code word c = r ⊕ e

= [1 1 0] ⊕ [0 0 1]

= [1 1 1]

5.5.5 Matrix Description of Cyclic Codes

There are two issues related to coding and decoding of cyclic codes.

1. The process of coding one message word is simple, but when it comes to generate all code words in order to study the code, we have to do lot of work.
2. The same is true for decoding. For every error polynomial, we have to relate its syndrome.

In case of linear block code, both these tasks were done by generator matrix and parity check matrix. But then we can show that generator polynomial g(x) and parity check polynomial h(x) can specify generator matrix G and parity check matrix H uniquely. Let us consider generation of cyclic code using,

$$c(x) = d(x) \cdot g(x)$$

Let,
$$d(x) = d_1 x^{k-1} + d_2 x^{k-2} + \ldots + d_k$$

Now,
$$c(x) = (d_1 x^{k-1} + d_2 x^{k-2} + \ldots + d_k) \cdot g(x)$$
$$= d_1 x^{k-1} g(x) + d_2 x^{k-1} g(x) + \ldots + d_k g(x)$$

Thus, any code word can be generated by linear combination of $x^{k-1} g(x)$, $x^{k-2} g(x)$ ... ... $g(x)$. Hence, polynomials can represent the rows of generator matrix.

5.5.6 Encoder for Cyclic Code

Encoding process of an (n, k) systematic cyclic code involves finding remainder after dividing $x^{n-k} d(x)$ by $g(x)$. Hence, a shift register arrangement discussed above can be implemented. $x^{n-k} d(x) \mod g(x)$ involves division of right shifted message polynomial by generator polynomial. The circuit is shown in Fig. 5.8 below for

$$g(x) = x^{n-k} + g_2 x^{n-k-1} + g_3 x^{n-k-2} + \ldots + g_{n-k-1} x^2 + g_{n-k} x + 1$$

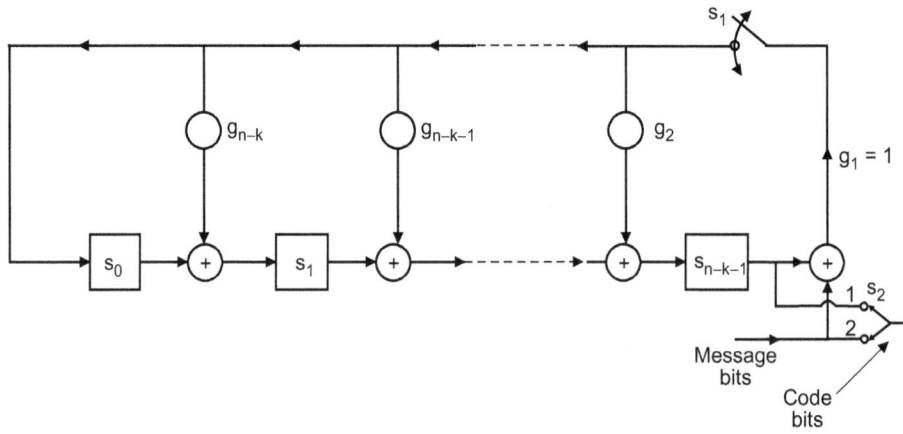

Fig. 5.8

Initially, s_1 is closed and s_2 is in position 2. Hence, all the message bits (k) are shifted out as well as shifted inside the shift registers. When all k bits are over, s_1 is open and s_2 is put in position 1, so that the parity bits available in shift registers can follow message bits.

You must have noticed that this circuit is different from one we discussed earlier shown in Fig. 5.7. In that circuit, we have to wait for feedback till the rightmost stage gets filled. In this circuit, input is loaded from last stage and feedback term in leftmost stage is the sum of input and rightmost stage. Since, g_1 and g_{n-k} are 1, this sum will be surely generated.

Example 5.9:

Design an encoder for an (7, 4) cyclic code for generator polynomial $x^3 + x + 1$.
Show all steps for generating codes for message words :
  (i)   0 1 1 0
  (ii) 1 0 1 1

Solution:

Given:
$$n = 7$$
$$k = 4$$
$$n - k = 3$$
$$g(x) = x^3 + x + 1$$
Comparing with $g(x) = x^3 + g_2 x^2 + g_3 x + 1$
$$g_2 = 0$$
$$g_3 = 1$$

Hence, encoder will be

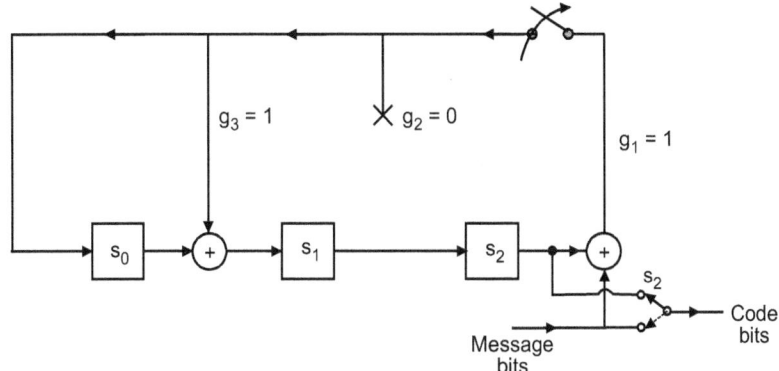

Fig. 5.9

The encoding process for given messages is shown below.

(i) Input message = [0 1 1 0]

Input Message	Shift Number	Shift Registers		
		S_0	S_1	S_2
Initial stage	0	0	0	0
0	1	0	0	0
1	2	1	1	0
1	3	1	0	1
0	4	1	0	0
		↑	↑	↑
		c_7	c_6	c_5

∴ $c_5 = 0$, $c_6 = 0$, $c_7 = 1$

                                Message Parity
Hence, code will be c = [0 1 1 0 0 0 1]

(ii) Input message = [1 0 1 1]

Input Message	Shift Number	Shift Registers		
		S_0	S_1	S_2
Initial stage	0	0	0	0
1	1	1	1	0
0	2	0	1	1
1	3	1	0	1
1	4	0	0	0
		↑	↑	↑
		c_7	c_6	c_5

∴ $c_5 = 0$, $c_6 = 0$, $c_7 = 1$.

∴ Code word will be [1 0 1 1 0 0 0]

5.5.7 Decoder for Cyclic Code

For decoding a cyclic code, we have to divide received code word polynomial r(x) by g(x) and find out remainder. This remainder is syndrome polynomial. Hence, a circuit shown in Fig. 5.9 can be used which is redrawn in Fig. 5.10 below.

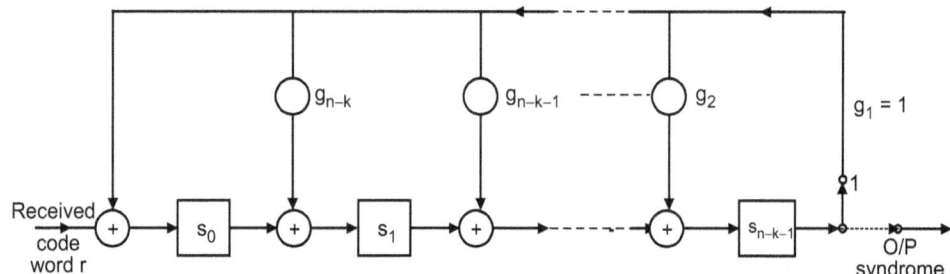

Fig. 5.10: Syndrome Generator for Cyclic Code

Initially, all shift register contents are zero and switch is in position 1. The received code word bits are shifted into register from left side one by one. When all bits are shifted in, the n – k stages of shift register will contain remainder after division of r(x) and g(x) which will be syndrome. The switch is thrown to position 2 and the syndrome bits are shifted out.

Note that this is just a syndrome generator and not complete decoder. The syndrome generated can be further used for detection or correction of errors.

COMMUNICATION SYSTEM - II   CHANNEL CODING

Example 5.10:

Design a syndrome generator for a (7, 4) cyclic code using generator polynomial $g(x) = x^3 + x + 1$.

Also find syndrome for received code words.

   (i)   1 0 0 1 1 0 1

   (ii)   1 0 0 1 0 1 1

   (iii)   1 1 1 1 0 1 1

Solution :

   Given : $g(x) = x^3 + x + 1$

   Comparing it with $g(x) = x^3 + g_2 x^2 + g_3 x + 1$

   We get, $g_2 = 0$, $g_3 = 1$

   The syndrome generator circuit will be as follows.

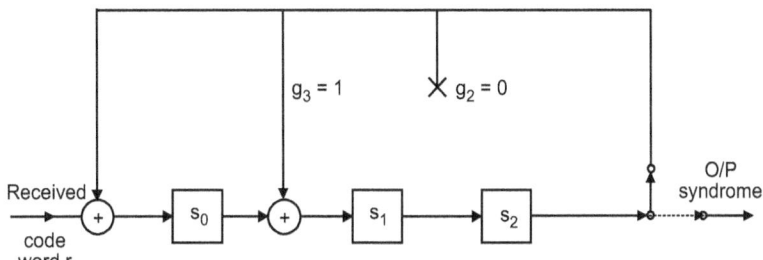

Fig. 5.11: Syndrome Generator for given Code

The steps of syndrome generation are shown below for received code words.

   (i)   r = 1 0 0 1 1 1 0

Received Code Bits	Shift Number	Syndrome		
		S_0	S_1	S_2
Initial stage	0	0	0	0
1	1	1	0	0
0	2	0	1	0
1	3	0	0	1
1	4	0	1	0
1	5	1	0	1
0	6	1	0	0
1	7	1	1	0

∴   Syndrome = [1 1 0]

It shows that received code is in error.

Ch 5 | 5.35

(ii) 1 0 0 1 0 1 1

Received Code Bits	Shift Number	Syndrome		
		s_0	s_1	s_2
Initial stage	0	0	0	0
1	1	1	0	0
0	2	1	1	0
0	3	0	1	1
1	4	0	1	1
0	5	1	1	1
1	6	1	0	1
1	7	0	0	0

∴ Syndrome = [0 0 0]

This shows that received code word is correct.

(iii) 1 1 1 1 0 1 1

Received Code Bits	Shift Number	Syndrome		
		s_0	s_1	s_2
–	–	0	0	0
1	1	1	0	0
1	2	1	1	0
1	3	1	1	1
1	4	0	0	1
0	5	1	1	0
1	6	1	1	1
1	7	0	0	1

Hence, syndrome is [1 0 0].

This shows that received code word is in error.

The complete decoder for the cyclic code will be as shown in Fig. 5.12 below.

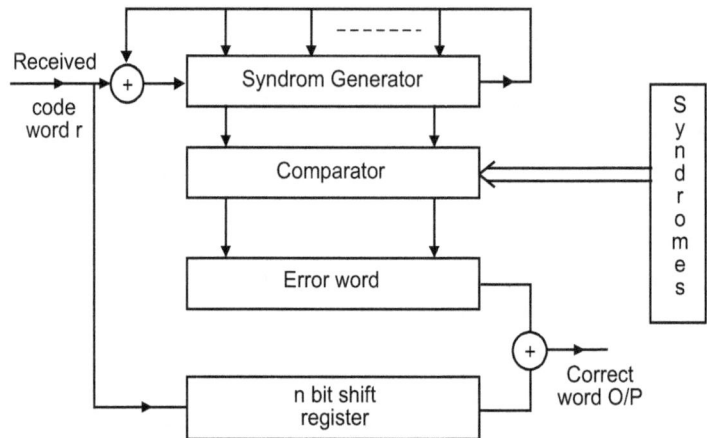

Fig. 5.12: Cyclic Code Decoder

The syndrome generated by syndrome generator is compared with test syndromes which are precomputed. Error pattern is generated by the comparator. The error word is added to received word to generate corrected code word.

5.6 Trellis Coded Modulation (TCM)

TCM schemes use redundant non-binary modulation in combination with finite state machine (encoder) to obtain coding gain without bandwidth expansion. For each symbol interval, a TCM finite state encoder selects one of a set of waveforms and generates sequence of coded waveforms. The received signals corrupted by noise are detected and decoded by a soft-decision maximum likelihood detector/decoder. Note that in TCM system, detection and decoding is done jointly and not separately. The coding gain is achieved at the expense of decoder complexity.

TCM combines a multilevel/phase modulation signalling set with a trellis coding scheme. (A scheme having memory) e.g. a convolutional code. Multilevel/phase signals have multiple amplitude, multiple phase or both types of constellations. A trellis coding scheme can also be characterised with a state transition diagrams, similar to trellis diagrams describing convolutional codes. Viterbi decoding can be used for decoding trellis codes.

5.6.1 Mapping by Set Partitioning (TCM Encoding)

TCM signalling has three basic features.
- (i) For the same data rate, the number of signal points are larger than uncoded format. The additional points add redundancy for forward error-control coding without increasing bandwidth.
- (ii) Convolutional coding is used so that there is certain dependancy between successive signal points and only certain patterns are permitted.
- (iii) Soft-decision decoding is used at the receiver. This decoding involves modeling of permissible sequence of signals as a trellis structure.

The reason for using soft decision decoding at the receiver is use of enlarged signal constellation. Due to enlarged constellation, error probability of symbol increases for a fixed signal-to-noise ratio. If we use hard decision decoding, performance will degrade. Use of soft-decision decoding on TCM takes care of this problem.

In presence of Additive White Gaussian Noise, the maximum likelihood decoding of trellis codes involves finding that particular path through the trellis with minimum squared Euclidean distance to the received sequence. While designing trellis code, the emphasis should be on maximizing the Euclidean distance between code vectors and not on maximizing hamming distance of an error correcting codes.

The approach used to design this type of trellis code is to partition an M-ary constellation into 2, 4, 8, ..., subsets with size $\frac{M}{2}, \frac{M}{4}, \frac{M}{8}$ such that minimum Euclidean distance between their respective signal points is progressively increased. This design approach is called mapping by set partitioning. The concept is illustrated in Fig. 5.13 for 8 PSK signal set.

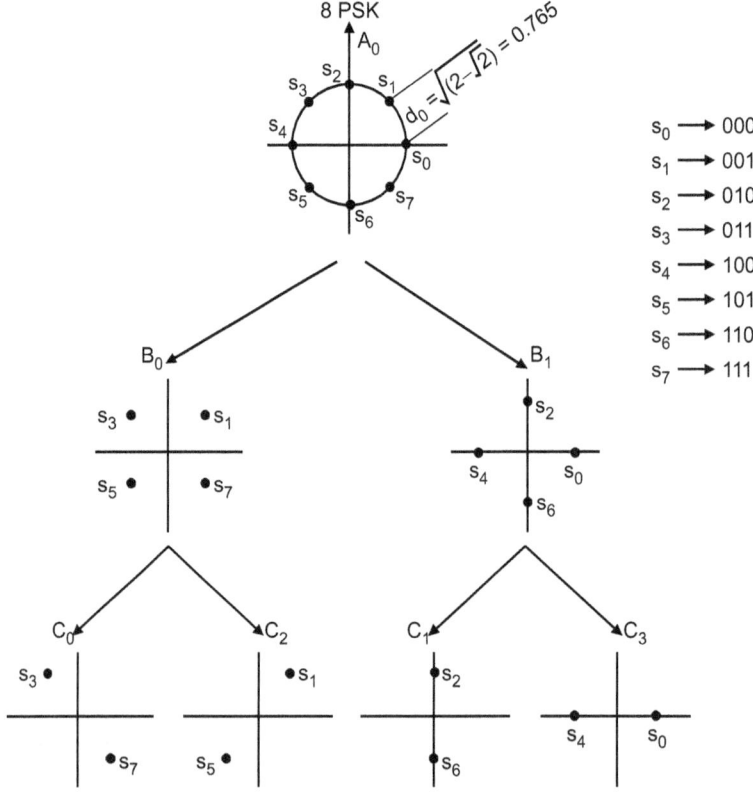

Fig. 5.13: Partitioning of 8-PSK Constellation

The original constellation is labelled A_0 and individual signal points are labelled as $s_0, s_1, s_2, ..., s_7$. If average signal power is chosen equal to E_s, then distance d_0 between any two adjacent signals is

$$d_0 = \sqrt{4E_s \sin^2\left(\frac{\pi}{8}\right)}$$
$$= \sqrt{E_s(2-\sqrt{2})}$$
$$= 0.765\sqrt{E_s}$$

If $E_s = 1$, $\quad d_0 = 0.765 \quad\quad d_0^2 = 0.586$

The first level partitioning results in subsets B_0 and B_1 and the distance d_1 between any two adjacent signals is

$$d_1 = \sqrt{2} \qquad\qquad d_1^2 = 2$$

Further partitioning results into subsets C_0 and C_3, where distance between adjacent signals is

$$d_2 = 2 \qquad\qquad d_2^2 = 4$$

The partitioning can be stopped as soon as minimum distance of subsets is larger than desired minimum Euclidean distance of TCM scheme to be designed.

Using the subsets resulting from partitioning, we can devise simple but highly effective coding schemes.

The block diagram of TCM system is shown in Fig. 5.14.

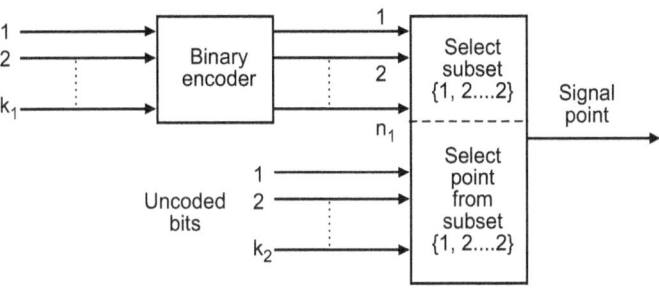

Fig. 5.14: The Block Diagram of a Coded-Modulation System

To send k bits/symbol with quadrature modulation, we start with 2^{k+1} signal points. (e.g. to send 2 bits/symbol using PSK, we start with $2^{2+1} = 8$ signal points). The k input bits are broken into two sub-locks of length k_1 and k_2. The first k_1 bits are applied to (n_1, k_1) convolutional encoder to obtain n_1 bits. These n_1 bits are used to select 2^{n_1} partitions in the constellation.

After constellation is chosen, the remaining k_2 bits are used to select one of the points in chosen constellation. It means each partition has 2^{k_2} points. For TCM encoder, we see that k_2 uncoded bits have no effect on state of convolutional encoder because the input is not changed. Hence, without changing encoder state, we can change last k_2 bits. Thus, we can have 2^{k_2} parallel transitions between states. These parallel transitions are at lowest level in partition tree. This class of trellis codes are known as Ungerboeck Codes.

While doing the partitioning, we see that top level signal points have smaller distances. Hence, errors are more likely in the bits which will be controlling these sets. Hence, we allot coded bits to decide which partition to use. The uncoded bits which cannot correct themselves can be used to at least level to pick the signal transmitted. Thus, Ungerboeck approach leaves most significant bit uncoded and lets it take care of itself via its large Euclidean distance. This is the reason why we get larger coding gain with this approach. Only the bits that decide at the top levels with smaller Squared Euclidean Distance (SED) are coded which reduced the coding rate.

Ungerboeck's TCM Design Rules:
Ungerboeck devised a heuristic set of rules for assigning trellis transition branches to waveforms.
The rules are as below.
1. If k bits are to be encoded per modulation interval, the trellis must allow for 2^k possible transitions from each state to a successor state.
2. More than one transitions may occur between pairs of states.
3. All waveforms should occur with equal frequency and with a fair amount of regularity and symmetry.
4. Transitions originating from same state are assigned waveforms either from state B_0 or B_1 and never a mixture of them.
5. Transitions joining into same state are assigned waveforms either from state B_0 or B_1 and never a mixture of them.
6. Parallel transitions are assigned waveforms either from set C_0 or C_1 or C_2 or C_3 never a mixture of then.

Above rules guarantee that codes constructed in this way will have a regular structure and Euclidean Distance will always be more than minimum distance between signal points of uncoded reference modulation.

Example 5.11:
For the 8 PSK constellation and its partition shown in Fig. 5.15.
The trellis diagram for above scheme is drawn in Fig. 5.16 (b).
The waveform assignments are shown in trellis diagram comply with above rules.
Rule 1 : There are k + 1 = 3 code bits and thus, k = 2 information bits, and there are 2^2 = 4 transitions into and out of each state.
Rule 2 : There are 2 transitions between each pair of states.
Rule 3 : All the 8 waveforms occur with equal frequency = 2 per transition.
Rule 4 : Transition originating from each state is assigned waveforms from B_0 or B_1.

e.g.	state 0 0	Waveforms from B_1	i.e. S_0, S_2, S_4, S_6
	State 1 0	Waveforms from B_0	S_1, S_3, S_5, S_7
	State 0 1	Waveforms from B_1	S_0, S_2, S_4, S_6
	State 1 1	Waveforms from B_0	S_1, S_3, S_5, S_7

Rule 5 : Transitions joining into each state have waveforms, either from B_0 or B_1.

State 0 0	Waveforms from B_0
State 1 0	Waveforms from B_1
State 0 1	Waveforms from B_0
State 1 1	Waveforms from B_1

Rule 6 : Parallel transitions are assigned from C_0 or C_1 or C_2 or C_3.

e.g. first pair in state 00 is from C_0.

The encoder diagram for above scheme is shown in Fig. 5.15 (a). It uses 1/2 convolutional encoder. The output of encoder (2 bits) alongwith first input bit selects 1 out of 8 signal points.

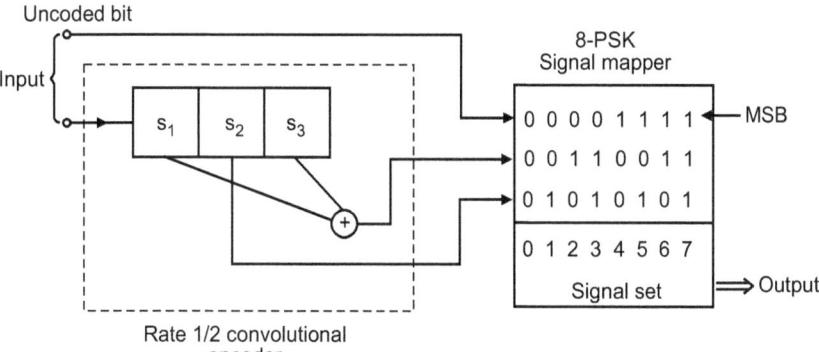

Fig. 5.15

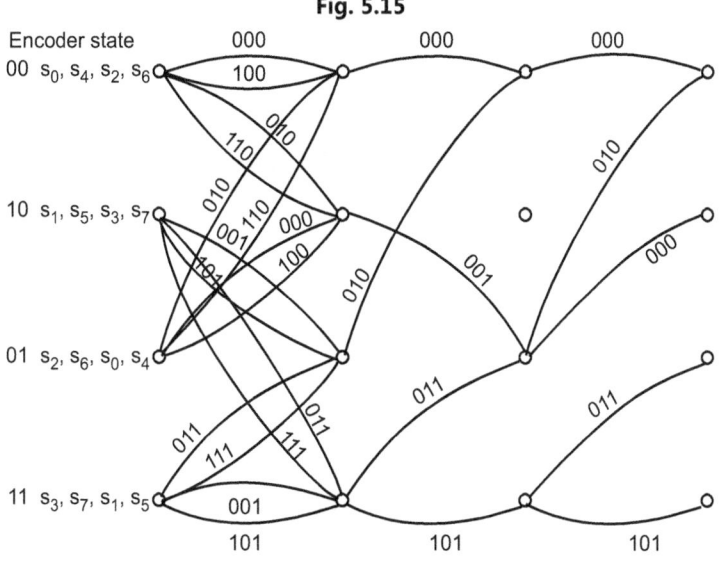

Fig. 5.16

Note that the most significant bit (1st bit) is left uncoded. If this bit is 0, the set B_0 is selected. If this bit is 1, the set B_1 is selected.

The second input bit decides the convolutional encoder output i.e. two bits. These two bits select waveforms from C_0, C_1, C_2 or C_3.

Performance Evaluation

Coding Gain

As defined earlier, the coding gain in dB compared with some encoded reference system is defined as,

$$G_a = 20 \log_{10} \left(\frac{d_{free}}{d_{ref}} \right) \text{ dB}$$

$$= 10 \log_{10} \left(\frac{d_{free}^2}{d_{ref}^2} \right) \text{ dB}$$

where, d_{free} is the free Euclidean distance of the code and d_{ref} is the minimum Euclidean distance of uncoded modulation scheme operating with same signal energy per bit and noise variance.

It is also called asymptotic gain.

For the Ungerboeck 8-PSK code (4 state) discussed earlier, the asymptotic coding gain is calculated as below.

1. From the trellis shown in Fig. 5.16 (b), we have to find a path which is at minimum distance from all-zero path. For this, we have to examine all the paths diverging from all-zero path and remerging into it.

    Let us see two paths and calculate their Euclidean distance.

    $$\text{Path 1} \Rightarrow 010 \ (s_2), \ 001 \ (s_1), \ 010 \ (s_2)$$
    $$d^2 = d^2(s_0, s_2) + d^2(s_0, s_1) + d^2(s_0, s_2)$$
    $$= (\sqrt{2})^2 + (0.765)^2 + (\sqrt{2})^2$$
    $$= 4.585$$

    Let us denote this as d_{free}^2.

    Now, look at the parallel path at t = 0 state 00, we have two parallel pairs first pair s_0 and s_4 and s_2 and s_6. Each pair is 180° phase shift apart. Transition from s_0 to s_4 corresponds to Mean Squared Euclidean Distance (MSED) of 4.0. Let us denote this as d_{min}^2. Note that the parallel transition from s_0 to s_4 can occur due to error in uncoded bit and it is more likely that the uncoded bit will be decoded incorrectly than the two coded bits. Hence, out of the two paths which are having MSED 4.586 and 4.0. The minimum has to be selected.

$$\therefore \quad d_{free}^2 = \min[d_{free}^2 \; d_{min}^2]$$
$$= \min[4.586 \; 4.0]$$
$$= 4.0$$

2. In order to select reference (uncoded) signal set, we know that 8-PSK has 8 message points and we send 2 message bits per point. Hence, uncoded transmission requires a signal constellation of 4 message points. Therefore, uncoded 4-PSK (QPSK) is reference for Ungerboeck 8-PSK code.

   For 4-PSK signal constellation, minimum Euclidean distance is $\sqrt{2}$.

   $$\therefore \quad d_{ref}^2 = 2$$

   $$\therefore \quad \text{Coding gain} = G_a = 10 \log\left(\frac{4}{2}\right)$$
   $$= 3 \text{ dB}$$

   This gain is not as good as 3.6 dB gain, we got for rate 2/3 code. But it is without any increase in bandwidth or symbol rate.

   Why do we get less coding gain in case of rate 1/2 convolutional code ? It is because of single stage error in parallel transition that limits the coding gain. As long as we have parallel transitions, the coding gain is limited to 3 dB. No matter what code we use.

   With four state convolutional code, we cannot do better than that. It is our limiting case. Hence, we have to increase number of states so that there will be no parallel transitions.

   Now let us consider TCM encoding which has 8 states. This can be done by increasing number of memory registers from 2 to 3.

TCM Decoding

TCM decoding is done in two steps. First step is to find most likely signal point in each partition. This is done by finding the point in each partition that is closest in Euclidean distance to received point. This step is called subset decoding. After first step, there will be only one point and one Euclidean distance corresponding to each transition in trellis. The second step of decoding procedure is to use this Euclidean distance to find path through trellis whose total Euclidean distance from received sequence is minimum. This is done by applying Viterbi algorithm. This decision-making criteria is called maximum likelihood decoding.

Since, convolutional code is a group code or linear code, the set of distances that must be examined is independent of which sequence is selected as a test sequence. Hence, all-zero path can be selected as test sequence as shown in Fig. 5.17.

Assuming that all-zero sequence is transmitted, an error event is identified as divergence from all-zero path followed by remerge with the all-zero path. Error events, both start and end in state 00 and they do not return to state 00 anywhere in between.

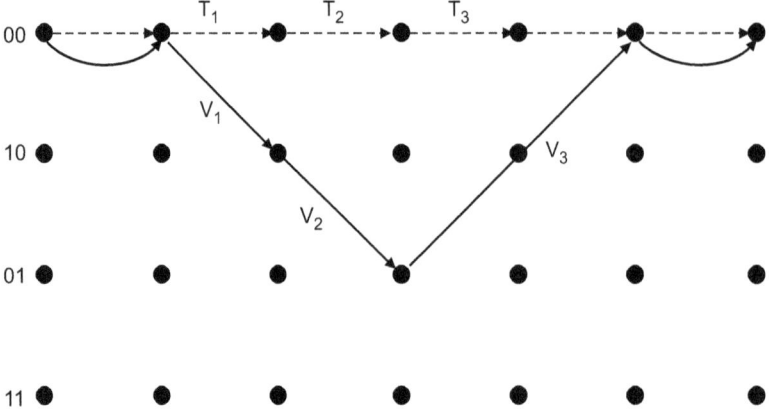

Fig. 5.17: TCM Decoding (Error Event)

As shown in Fig. 5.17, the transmitted all-zero sequence is marked as $T = T_1, T_2, T_3 \ldots$ and an alternate sequence is marked as $V = V_1, V_2, V_3, \ldots$ which is seen to diverge and then remerge with transmitted sequence. Assuming soft decision decoding, an error event occurs whenever the received symbols are closer in Euclidean distance to some alternate sequence V than the actually transmitted sequence T. Thus, the codes for multilevel/multiphase signals should be designed to achieve maximum free Euclidean distance so that error probability will be lower. Assignment of waveforms to trellis transitions at the encoder so that the free Euclidean distance maximized is the key to design the efficient trellis codes.

5.7 BCH Codes

Bose-Choudhary Hocquenghem (BCH) codes are the codes which have the following properties.
1. They are most powerful class of cyclic codes.
2. They can correct multiple errors.
3. They can be easily encoded and decoded.
4. They provide a large selection of block lengths, code rates, alphabet size and error correcting capability.
5. We can design BCH codes for a given error correcting capability.
6. For BCH codes, $n = 2^m - 1$, $k \geq n - mt_c$, $d_{min} \geq 2t_c + 1$.

There is another subclass of BCH codes, called Reed-Solomon Codes (RS codes) that will also be discussed in this chapter.

5.7.1 Generator Polynomial in Terms of Minimal Polynomial (for BCH Codes)

Let, us now look into procedure for constructing generator polynomial for BCH codes, that can correct specified number of errors t_c.

We know that we can factorize $x^n + 1$ in terms of minimal polynomials $f_1(x), f_2(x), f_3(x) \ldots f_p(x)$, where, p is number of primitive/prime polynomials.

Generator polynomial can be formed using these minimal polynomials.

Since, generator polynomial g(x) is factor of $x^n + 1$, it can be written as

$$g(x) = \text{LCM}[f_1(x), f_2(x) \ldots f_p(x)] \qquad \ldots (5.39)$$

where, $f_1(x), f_2(x) \ldots f_p(x)$ are the minimal polynomials of the zeros of g(x).

Thus, steps for designing BCH codes are –

(i) Block length $n = q^m - 1$.

(ii) Select a primitive polynomial of degree m and construct $GF(q^m)$.

(iii) Find minimal polynomial $f_i(x)$ of α^i for $i = 1, 2, \ldots p$.

(iv) Find generator polynomial for error correcting capability t_c using,

$$g(x) = \text{LCM}[f_1(x), f_2(x), \ldots f_{2t_c}(x)]$$

[**Note** that there is no polynomial for (x) corresponding to α^0].

5.6.2 Decoding of BCH Codes

BCH codes can be generated for a given error correcting capability using the same method that was used to generate cyclic codes earlier. Hence, decoding also will be similar to that of cyclic codes. But better and more efficient scheme of decoding is available for BCH codes. Let us discuss this scheme for t_c error correcting BCH codes.

Consider the received vector $r(x) = c(x) + e(x)$ $\qquad \ldots (5.40)$

where, c(x) is code polynomial corresponding to received code and e(x) is error polynomial corresponding to errors introduced.

We know that g(x) is a factor c(x).

$\alpha, \alpha^2, \alpha^3 \ldots \alpha^{2t_c}$ are roots of g(x), where α is primitive element of $GF(2^m)$.

$\therefore \qquad r(\alpha^i) = c(\alpha^i) + e(\alpha^i) \qquad i = 1, 2, \ldots 2t_c \qquad \ldots (5.41)$

$\qquad \qquad = e(\alpha^i) \qquad [\because c(\alpha^i) = 0] \qquad \ldots (5.42)$

But error pattern,

$$e(x) = \sum_{j=1}^{n} e_j x^{j-1} \quad \ldots (5.43)$$

where, $e_j = 1$ or 0 for binary code.

e.g. Suppose there is single error in first bit,

$$e(x) = x^{n-1}$$

or if there is error in first and second bit,

$$e(x) = x^{n-1} + x^{n-2}$$

Hence,
$$r(\alpha^i) = \sum_{j=1}^{n} e_j (\alpha^i)^{j-1} \quad \ldots (5.44)$$

There will be total $2t_c$ equations represented by equation (5.44) as i goes from 1 to $2t_c$. Solving above equations for e_j, we can determine error patterns.

There will be $2t_c$ syndromes corresponding to these error patterns defined as,

$$s_i = r(\alpha^i) \qquad i = 1 \text{ to } 2t_c$$
$$= r_1 + r_2(\alpha^i) + r_3(\alpha^i)^2 + \ldots + r_n(\alpha^i)^{n-1} \quad \ldots (5.45)$$

where, $r_1, r_2, r_3, \ldots r_n$ are coefficients of received polynomial r(x).

$\therefore \qquad s_i = e(\alpha^i)$
$$= e_1 + e_2 \alpha^i + e_3(\alpha^i)^2 + \ldots + e_n(\alpha^i)^{n-1} \quad \ldots (5.46)$$

where atmost t_c coefficients are non-zero.

Let us assume that p errors have occurred in received vector.

Let their locations be $X_1, X_2, \ldots X_p$ and their magnitudes be $Y_1, Y_2, \ldots Y_p$.

Then the syndrome can be written as

$$s_1 = Y_1 X_1 + Y_2 X_2 + \ldots + Y_p X_p$$
$$s_2 = Y_1 X_1^2 + Y_2 X_2^2 + \ldots + Y_p X_p^2$$
$$\vdots$$
$$s_{2t_c} = Y_1 X_1^{2t_c} + Y_2 X_2^{2t_c} + \ldots + Y_p X_p^{2t_c} \quad \ldots (5.47)$$

The above set of equations is difficult to solve as the equations are non-linear. To simplify the solution, following polynomial is used. It is called error locator polynomial.

$$\lambda(x) = 1 + \lambda_1 x + \lambda_2 x^2 + \ldots + \lambda_p x^p \quad \ldots (5.48)$$

This polynomial has zeros at inverse error locations x_l^{-1} for $l = 1, 2, \ldots p$.

$\therefore \qquad \lambda(x) = (1 + y_1 x)(1 + y_2 x) \ldots (1 + y_p x) \quad \ldots (5.49)$

COMMUNICATION SYSTEM - II CHANNEL CODING

If coefficients of λ(x) are determined, then we can find zeros of λ(x) to obtain error locations. These coefficients are related to syndromes of equation (5.47) by matrix equation

$$\begin{bmatrix} S_1 & S_2 & S_3 & \cdots & S_p \\ S_2 & S_3 & S_4 & \cdots & S_{p+1} \\ S_3 & S_4 & S_5 & \cdots & S_{p+2} \\ \vdots & & & & \vdots \\ S_p & S_{p+1} & S_{p+2} & \cdots & S_{2p-1} \end{bmatrix} \begin{bmatrix} \lambda_p \\ \lambda_{p-1} \\ \lambda_{p-2} \\ \vdots \\ \lambda_l \end{bmatrix} = \begin{bmatrix} -S_{p+1} \\ -S_{p+2} \\ \vdots \\ -2_{2p} \end{bmatrix} \quad \ldots (5.50)$$

Using inverse of matrix, we can determine coefficient of λ(z), if matrix is non-singular. For singular matrix, the number of errors will be less than p.

The steps of decoding of BCH code are as follows :

(i) Find syndrome using $GF(2^m)$.

(ii) As a trial, set $p = t_c$ and compute determinant of matrix [M] in equation (5.50). If it is non-zero, then $p = t_c$, else it is $p < t_c$. Then check with $p = t - 1$ and stop when determinant is non-zero.

(iii) Solve λ(z) using matrix inversion of [M] using equation (5.16).

(iv) Find zeros of λ(z) to find error locations. Use trial and error methods known as Chien search. For binary codes locating X_t completes the solution.

Example 5.12 :

Consider (15, 7) double error correcting BCH code with $g(x) = x^8 + x^7 + x^6 + x^4 + 1$.

If $m(x) = (1 + x)$, the transmitted code, i.e. m = [0 0 0 0 0 1 1]

$$c(x) = m(x) \cdot g(x)$$
$$= x^9 + x^6 + x^5 + x^4 + x + 1$$

i.e. c = [1 0 0 1 1 1 0 0 1 1]

Let, $r(x) = x^9 + x^8 + x^6 + x^5 + x^4 + x^3 + x + 1$

i.e. we introduce errors in 3rd and 8th bit.

i.e. r = [1 1 0 1 1 1 1 0 1 1]

Correct the errors.

Solution :

Using $GF(2^4)$ and modulo polynomial,

$$p(x) = x^4 + x + 1$$

the syndromes are as below :

$$s_i = r(\alpha^i)$$
$$= (\alpha^i)^9 + (\alpha^i)^8 + (\alpha^i)^6 + (\alpha^i)^5 + (\alpha^i)^4 + (\alpha^i)^3 + \alpha^i + 1$$

∴ $\quad s_1 = \alpha^9 + \alpha^8 + \alpha^6 + \alpha^5 + \alpha^4 + \alpha^3 + \alpha + 1 = \alpha^8 + \alpha^3 = \alpha^{13}$

$\quad s_2 = \alpha^{18} + \alpha^{16} + \alpha^{12} + \alpha^{10} + \alpha^8 + \alpha^6 + \alpha^2 + 1 = \alpha^{16} + \alpha^6 = \alpha^{11}$

$\quad s_3 = \alpha^{24} + \alpha^9 = 0$

$\quad s_4 = \alpha^{32} + \alpha^{12} = \alpha^7$

Above simplification is made using,

$\alpha^9 + \alpha^6 + \alpha^5 + \alpha^4 + \alpha + 1 = 0$

The determinant,

$$\begin{bmatrix} s_1 & s_2 \\ s_2 & s_3 \end{bmatrix} \neq 0 \qquad [\because p = 2]$$

∴ $\quad M = \begin{bmatrix} \alpha^{13} & \alpha^{11} \\ \alpha^{11} & 0 \end{bmatrix} \qquad \text{Inv}[M] = \dfrac{(\text{cofactor}[M])^T}{\det[M]}$

$$M^{-1} = \dfrac{\begin{bmatrix} 0 & \alpha^{11} \\ \alpha^{11} & \alpha^{13} \end{bmatrix}}{-\alpha^{22}} = \dfrac{\begin{bmatrix} 0 & \alpha^{11} \\ \alpha^{11} & \alpha^{13} \end{bmatrix}}{\alpha^7} = \alpha^{-7} \begin{bmatrix} 0 & \alpha^{11} \\ \alpha^{11} & \alpha^{13} \end{bmatrix}$$

∴ $\quad M^{-1} = \begin{bmatrix} 0 & \alpha^4 \\ \alpha^4 & \alpha^6 \end{bmatrix}$

∴ $\quad \begin{bmatrix} \lambda_2 \\ \lambda_1 \end{bmatrix} = [M^{-1}] \begin{bmatrix} 0 \\ \alpha^7 \end{bmatrix} = \begin{bmatrix} \alpha^{11} \\ \alpha^{13} \end{bmatrix}$

Thus, $\quad \lambda(z) = \alpha^{11} z^2 + \alpha^{13} z + 1 = (\alpha^8 z + 1)(\alpha^3 z + 1)$

Hence, the errors have occurred at 3rd and 8th position.

$\quad e(x) = x^8 + x^3$

∴ $\quad c(x) = r(x) \oplus e(x)$

$\quad\quad\quad = x^9 + x^8 + x^6 + x^5 + x^4 + x^3 + x + 1 + x^8 + x^3$

$\quad\quad\quad = x^9 + x^6 + x^5 + x^4 + x + 1$

5.8 Reed-Solomon Codes (RS Codes)

These are non-binary cyclic codes with symbols having m bit sequences; where m > 2.

An RS (n, k) code such that

$\quad 0 < k < n < 2^m + 2$

where, k is number of data symbols.

n is number of code symbols.

m is number of bits in each symbol.

For (n, k) RS code,
$$n = 2^m - 1$$
$$k = 2^m - 1 - 2t_c$$
where, t_c is symbol correcting capability of the code.
$$n - k = 2t_c \text{ is number of parity symbols.}$$

RS codes achieve largest possible minimum distance for any linear code with same encoder input and output block lengths.

The minimum distance of RS code is given by
$$d_{min} = n - k + 1$$
The erasure correcting capability (Burst Error) of the code is
$$\rho = d_{min} = n - k$$

Let us compare a binary and non-binary code having (n, k) = (7, 3).

The binary code contains $2^7 = 128$ vectors, out of which $2^3 = 8$ are code vectors i.e. 8/128 = 1/16 are code words.

The non-binary code having each symbol m = 3 bits consists of $2^{mn} = 2^{21} = 2097152$ vectors, out of which $2^{km} = 2^9 = 512$ are code words i.e. 1/4096 are code words. This fraction decreases as m increases. Because of this, large d_{min} is created, which in turn increases error correcting capability.

Any linear code is capable of correcting n – k symbol erasure patterns if n – k erased symbols are parity symbols. But RS codes are capable of correcting these erasure patterns occuring anywhere in the code.

The R-S code decoding procedure is such that m bit symbols as a whole can be corrected, hence these codes perform well against burst noise.

5.8.1 Reed-Solomon Encoding

The Reed-Solomon code is specified as
$$(n, k) = (2^m - 1, 2^m - 1 - 2t_c)$$
where, $n - k = 2t_c$ is number of parity symbols and t_c is error correcting capability of the code.

The generator polynomial of RS-code is given by
$$g(x) = g_0 + g_1 x + g_2 x^2 + \ldots + g_{2t_c-1} x^{2t_c-1} + x^{2t_c}$$

RS codes are a subset of BCH code, hence the generator polynomial should have roots as $\alpha, \alpha^2, \alpha^3 \ldots \alpha^{2t_c}$.

i.e. $$g(x) = (x + \alpha)(x + \alpha^2)(x + \alpha^3) \ldots (x + \alpha^{2t_c})$$

If m(x) represents message polynomial, then the non-systematic RS-code is given by
$$c(x) = m(x) g(x)$$

COMMUNICATION SYSTEM - II   CHANNEL CODING

The systematic form of RS-code is given by

$$c(x) = x^{n-k} m(x) + p(x)$$

where,

$$p(x) = \text{Rem}\left[\frac{x^{n-k} m(x)}{g(x)}\right]$$

Example 5.113:
Design a (15, 11) RS code. Find code whose message polynomial is given as $(x + 1)$.

Solution:

Given:
$$n = 15$$
$$k = 11$$
$$n - k = 2t_c$$
$$\therefore t_c = 2$$
$$n = 2^m - 1 = 15$$
$$m = 4 \text{ i.e. each symbol is 4-bit}$$

We require elements from extension field $GF(2^m) = GF(2^4) = GF(16)$.

Sr. No.	Elements of GF(16)	Minimal Polynomial
1.	0	—
2.	$\alpha^0 = 1$	$x + 1$
3.	α^1	$x^4 + x + 1$
4.	α^2	$x^4 + x + 1$
5.	α^3	$x^4 + x^3 + x^2 + x + 1$
6.	$\alpha^4 = 1 + \alpha$	$x^4 + x + 1$
7.	$\alpha^5 = \alpha^2 + \alpha$	$x^2 + x + 1$
8.	$\alpha^6 = \alpha^3 + \alpha^2$	$x^4 + x^3 + x^2 + x + 1$
9.	$\alpha^7 = \alpha^3 + \alpha + 1$	$x^4 + x^3 + 1$
10.	$\alpha^8 = \alpha^2 + 1$	$x^4 + x + 1$
11.	$\alpha^9 = \alpha^3 + \alpha$	$x^4 + x^3 + x^2 + x + 1$
12.	$\alpha^{10} = \alpha^2 + \alpha + 1$	$x^2 + x + 1$
13.	$\alpha^{11} = \alpha^3 + \alpha^2 + \alpha$	$x^4 + x^3 + 1$
14.	$\alpha^{12} = \alpha^3 + \alpha^2 + \alpha + 1$	$x^4 + x^3 + x^2 + x + 1$
15.	$\alpha^{13} = \alpha^3 + \alpha^2 + 1$	$x^4 + x^3 + 1$
16.	$\alpha^{14} = \alpha^3 + 1$	$x^4 + x^3 + 1$
17.	$\alpha^{15} = 1$	$x + 1$

Using the elements, we find the generator polynomial.

$$g(x) = (x + \alpha)(x + \alpha^2)(x + \alpha^3)(x + \alpha^4)$$
$$= \alpha^{10} + \alpha^3 x + \alpha^6 x^2 + \alpha^{13} x^3 + x^4$$
$$m(x) = (1 + x)$$
$$\therefore c(x) = \alpha^{10} + \alpha^{12} x + \alpha^2 x^2 + x^3 + \alpha^6 x^4 + x^5$$
$$\therefore c = \{\alpha^{10}, \alpha^{12}, \alpha^2, \alpha^0, \alpha^6, \alpha^0, 0, 0, 0, 0, 0, 0, 0, 0, 0\}$$

But,
$$\alpha^{10} = \alpha^2 + \alpha + 1 \qquad [0\ 1\ 1\ 1]$$
$$\alpha^{12} = \alpha^3 + \alpha^2 + \alpha + 1 \qquad [1\ 1\ 1\ 1]$$
$$\alpha^6 = \alpha^3 + \alpha^2 \qquad [1\ 1\ 0\ 0]$$
$$\alpha^2 = \alpha^2 \qquad [0\ 1\ 0\ 0]$$

Hence, the code in 15-tuple form is

$$c = \{0\ 1\ 1\ 1, 1\ 1\ 1\ 1, 0\ 1\ 0\ 0, 0\ 0\ 0\ 1, 1\ 1\ 0\ 0, 0\ 0\ 0\ 1, 0\ 0\ 0\ 0,$$
$$0\ 0\ 0\ 0, 0\ 0\ 0\ 0, 0\ 0\ 0\ 0, 0\ 0\ 0\ 0, 0\ 0\ 0\ 0, 0\ 0\ 0\ 0, 0\ 0\ 0\ 0,$$
$$0\ 0\ 0\ 0\}$$

Thus, this code is $(15 \times 4, 11 \times 4) = (60, 44)$.

Note that (15, 11) BCH code accepts 11 bits/message and converts it into 15 bit. Both codes have $d_{min} = 5$. But in RS code, the distance is in terms of 4-tuple symbols. Thus, the rate of transmission of RS code is much higher than BCH code for same error correcting capability.

5.8.2 Decoding of RS-Code

For n-symbol code word, the error pattern can be described as

$$e(x) = \sum_{i=0}^{n-1} e_i x^i$$

For example, if we have 7 symbol code word

$$e(x) = \sum_{i=0}^{n-1} e_i x^i$$

If there is double error,

$$e(x) = 0 + 0x + 0x^2 + \alpha^2 x^3 + \alpha^5 x^4 + 0x^5 + 0x^6$$

This means there is error in 3rd and 4th symbol.

The received code word polynomial will be

$$r(x) = c(x) + e(x)$$

Since, $c(x) = m(x)\, g(x)$, every code word polynomial is multiple of $g(x)$. Hence, roots of $g(x)$ must be roots of $c(x)$.

If r(x) = c(x), then r(x) should be 0 at every root of g(x). i.e. $\alpha, \alpha^2, \alpha^3 \ldots \alpha^{2t_c}$.

If r(x) ≠ c(x), i.e. when there is error, r(x) will be non-zero for one or more roots of g(x).

The values of r(x) at every root of r(x) i.e. $\alpha, \alpha^2, \alpha^3 \ldots \alpha^{2t_c}$ are called syndromes.

i.e. $$s_i = r(x)\big|_{x=\alpha^i}$$
$$= r(\alpha^i) \quad\quad i = 1, 2, \ldots, 2t_c$$

Thus, if any of the s_i is non-zero, there will be error.

To find where exactly the error is and to correct those errors, we have to do some more computations.

Suppose that there are p errors in code word and their locations be $x_1, x_2, \ldots, x_p$ and their magnitudes be $y_1, y_2, \ldots, y_p$.

Hence, the syndromes can be written from

$$s_i = r(\alpha^i) = e(\alpha^i)$$

as,
$$s_1 = r(\alpha) = y_1 x_1 + y_2 x_2 + \ldots + y_p x_p$$
$$s_2 = r(\alpha^2) = y_1 x_1^2 + y_2 x_2^2 + \ldots + y_p x_p^2$$
$$s_3 = r(\alpha^3) = y_1 x_1^3 + y_2 x_2^3 + \ldots + y_p x_p^3$$
$$\vdots$$
$$s_{2t_c} = r(\alpha^{2t_c}) = y_1 x_1^{2t_c} + y_2 x_2^{2t_c} + \ldots + y_p x_p^{2t_c}$$

The above set of equations is difficult to solve as the equations are non-linear. To simplify the solution, following polynomial is used. It is called error locator polynomial.

$$\lambda(x) = (1 + y_1 x)(1 + y_2 x) \ldots (1 + y_p x)$$
$$= 1 + \lambda_1 x + \lambda_2 x^2 + \ldots + \lambda_p x^p$$

The roots of $\lambda(x)$ are $\dfrac{1}{y_1}, \dfrac{1}{y_2} \ldots \dfrac{1}{y_p}$.

The reciprocals of roots of $\lambda(x)$ are the error location numbers of error pattern e(x).

These coefficients $\lambda_1, \lambda_2 \ldots \lambda_p$ are related to syndromes as below.

$$\begin{bmatrix} s_1 & s_2 & s_3 & \ldots & s_{t_c-1} & s_{t_c} \\ s_2 & s_3 & s_4 & \ldots & s_{t_c} & s_{t_c+1} \\ \vdots & & & & & \\ s_{t_c} & s_{t_c+1} & s_{t_c+2} & \ldots & & s_{2t_c-1} \end{bmatrix} \begin{bmatrix} \lambda_{t_c} \\ \lambda_{t_c-1} \\ \vdots \\ \lambda_1 \end{bmatrix} = \begin{bmatrix} -s_{t_c+1} \\ -s_{t_c+2} \\ \vdots \\ -s_{2t_c} \end{bmatrix}$$

To solve above equation to find $\lambda_1, \lambda_2, ..., \lambda t_c$, we take inverse of the matrix.

To find error values, $y_1, y_2, ... y_p$ etc., we write the syndromes as below.

$$s_1 = r(\alpha) = e_1 y_1 + e_2 y_2 + ...$$
$$s_1 = r(\alpha^2) = e_1 y_1^2 + e_2 y_2^2 + ...$$
$$s_3 = r(\alpha^3) = e_1 y_1^3 + e_2 y_2^3 + ...$$
$$\vdots$$
$$s_{2t_c} = r(\alpha^{2t_c}) = e_1 y_1^{2t_c} + e_2 y_2^{2t_c} + ...$$

Solve above equations to find $y_1, y_2, ...$

Hence, the error polynomial will be

$$e(x) = e_1 x_1 + e_2 x_2 + ... + e_p x_p$$

This polynomial is added to r(x) to get corrected code word c(x).

5.9 Convolutional Codes

Convolutional coding uses smaller blocks of message. These blocks are called information frames. Each information frame contains one or more symbols. The code word is obtained using current information frame and few previous information frames. This means convolutional encoders have memory. Decoding of convolutional codes will also require memory as the decision has to be based on past information. Convolutional codes are commonly specified by three parameters (n, k, m).

n is number of output bits.

k is number of input bits.

m is number of memory registers.

The quantity k/n is called code rate (r). It is a measure of code efficiency. Often in commercial specification, the convolutional codes are specified as (r, K) where r is code rate and K is constraint length (memory).

5.9.1 Convolutional Encoder

A convolutional encoder, as shown above, consists of shift registers and modulo-2 adders. Fig. 5.18 shows an encoder with code rate = 1/3 and 3 memory registers. It has 3 output bits. The encoder is specified as $\left(\frac{1}{3}, 3\right)$, where k = 1, n = 3, K = 3. The outputs of encoder are given as :

$$v_1 = s_1 \oplus s_2 \oplus s_3$$
$$v_2 = s_2 \oplus s_3$$
$$v_3 = s_1 \oplus s_3$$

These outputs can also be denoted in terms of generator polynomials as below.

$$g_1 = [1\ 1\ 1]$$
$$g_2 = [0\ 1\ 1]$$
$$g_3 = [1\ 0\ 1]$$

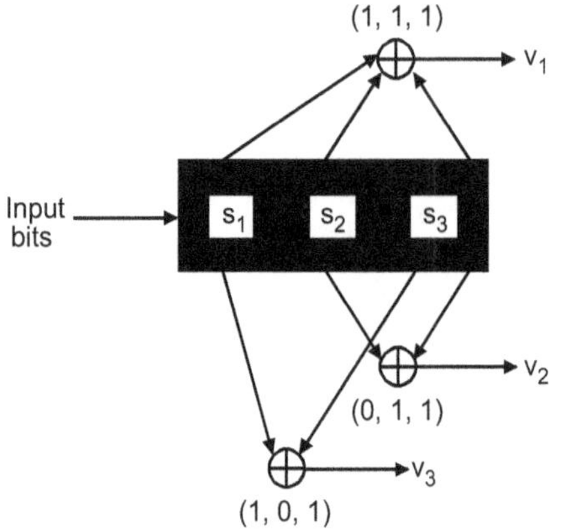

Fig. 5.18 : This $\left(\frac{1}{3}, 3\right)$ Convolutional Code has 3 Memory Registers, 1 Input Bit and 3 Output Bits

The polynomials give the code its unique error protection quality. One $\left(\frac{1}{3}, 3\right)$ code can have completely different properties from another one depending on the polynomials chosen. The various outputs for input 0 1 0 1 0 is shown below for above encoder.

Table 5.2

Input Bit	S_1	S_2	S_3	V_1	V_2	V_3
	0	0	0			
0	0	0	0	0	0	0
1	1	0	0	1	0	1
0	0	1	0	1	1	0
1	1	0	1	0	1	0
0	0	1	0	1	1	0

5.9.2 States of a Code

The convolutional encoders will have different states depending on what bits are there in their memory registers. Fig. 5.19 shows a $\left(\frac{1}{2}, 4\right)$ code having constraint length 4. Since, one bit is input at a time, rest of the three bits decide the state of encoder.

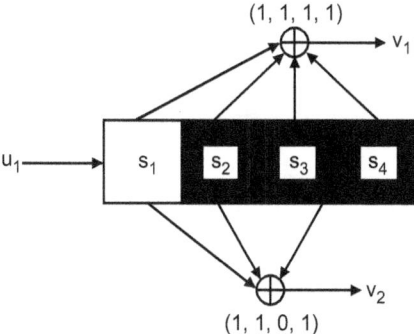

Fig. 5.19: The States of a Code Indicate What is in the Memory Registers

The number of combinations of bits in the shaded registers are called states of the code. Hence, number of states for above encoder will be $2^3 = 8$. The state of an encoder in combination with input bit decides the output bits. e.g. if input bit is 1 and the encoder state is 1 0 1, output bits will be 1 0. The various states of the encoder are (0 0 0, 0 0 1, 0 1 0, 0 1 1, 1 0 0, 1 0 1, 1 1 0, 1 1 1).

5.9.3 Representation of Convolutional Code

Graphically, there are three ways in which we can look at the encoder to gain better understanding of its operation. These are –

1. State diagram.
2. Tree diagram.
3. Trellis diagram.

5.9.3.1 State Diagram

Entire behaviour of encoder can be represented using state diagram. As seen earlier, the encoder can be in different states. Each state of the encoder can be represented by a circle. Whenever, there is a shifting of bits in the encoder, there will be transitions in the states. These transitions are represented by lines to and from the state. Only two events can happen at a time, arrival of bit 1 or bit 0. Each of these events allow encoder to jump into a different state. The look-up, table drawn earlier can be used to draw the state diagram.

The Fig. 5.20 shows the state diagram of $\left(\frac{1}{2}, 4\right)$ code discussed earlier.

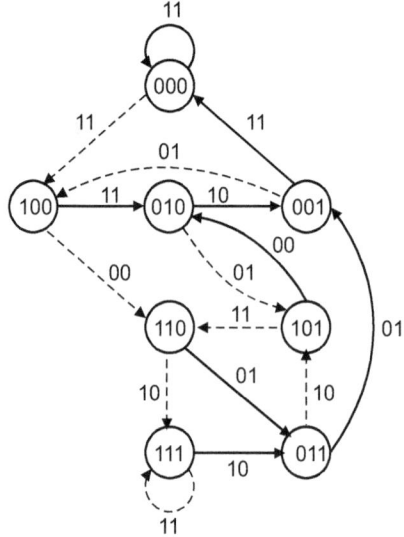

Fig. 5.20: State Diagram of $\left(\frac{1}{2}, 4\right)$ Code

How do we encode the sequence 1011 using the state diagram ?

(1) Let's start at state 0 0 0. The arrival of a 1 bit outputs 1 1 and puts us in state 1 0 0.

(2) The arrival of the next 0 bit outputs 1 1 and puts us in state 0 1 0.

(3) The arrival of the next 1 bit outputs 0 1 and puts us in state 1 0 1.

(4) The last bit 1 takes us to state 1 1 0 and outputs 1 1. So now we have 1 1 1 1 0 1 1 1. But this is not the end. We have to take the encoder back to all zero state.

(5) From state 1 1 0, go to state 0 1 1 outputting 0 1.

(6) From state 0 1 1, we go to state 0 0 1 outputting 0 1, and then

(7) To state 0 0 with a final output of 1 1.

The final answer is : 1 1   1 1   0 1   1 1   0 1   0 1   1 1

This is the same answer as what we got by adding up the individual impulse responses for bits 1 0 1 1 0 0 0.

5.9.3.2 Tree Codes

Fig. 5.21 shows the Tree diagram for the code $\left(\frac{1}{2}, 4\right)$. The tree diagram attempts to show the passage of time as we go deeper into the tree branches. It is somewhat better than a state diagram but still not the preferred approach for representing convolutional codes.

Here instead of jumping from one state to another state, we go down branches of the tree depending on whether a 1 or 0 is received. The first branch in Fig. 5.21 indicates the arrival of a 0 or a 1 bit. The starting state is assumed to be 0 0 0. If a 0 is received, we go up and if a 1 is received, then we go downwards. In Fig. 5.21, the solid lines show the arrival of a 0 bit and the shaded lines show the arrival of a 1 bit. The first 2 bits show the output bits and the number inside the parenthes is the output state.

Let us code the sequence 1 0 1 1 as before. At branch 1, we go down. The output is 1 1 and we are now in state 1 1 1. Now we get a zero bit, so we go up. The output bits are 1 1 and the state is now 0 1 1.

The next incoming bit is 1. We go downwards and get an output of 0 1 and now the output state is 1 0 1. The next incoming bit is 1, so we go downwards again and get output bits 1 1. From this point, in response to a 0 bit input, we get an output of 0 1 and an output state of 0 1 1.

If the sequence were longer, then what ? We have run out of tree branches. The tree diagram now repeats. In fact, we need to flush the encoder, so our sequence is actually 1 0 1 1 0 0 0, with the last 3 bits being the flush bits. We now jump to point 2 in the tree and go upwards for three branches. Now we have the output to the complete sequence and it is

    11 11 01 11 01 01 11

Perhaps you are not surprised that this is also the same answer as the one we got from the state diagram.

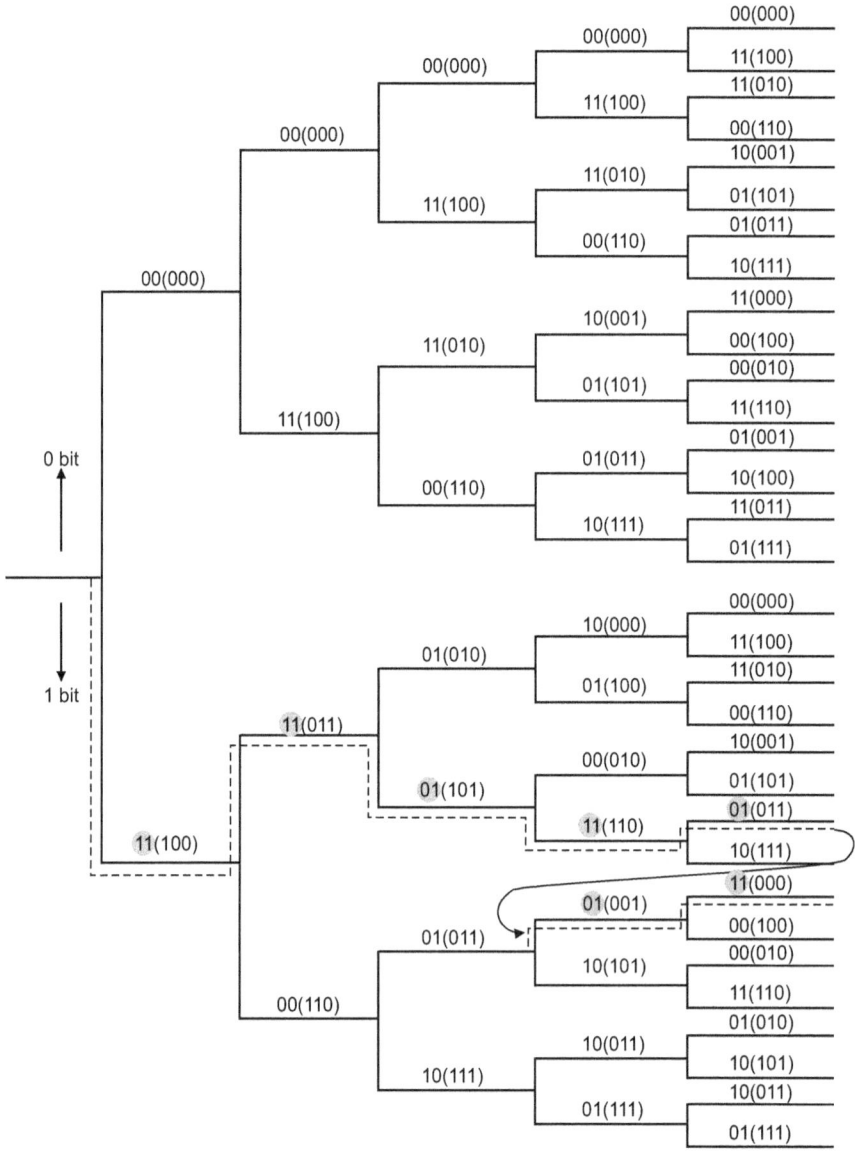

Fig. 5.21: Tree Diagram for $\left(\frac{1}{2}, 4\right)$ Code

5.9.3.3 Trellis Diagram

Trellis diagrams are messy, but generally preferred over both the tree and the state diagrams because they represent linear time sequencing of events. The x-axis is discrete time and all possible states are shown on the y-axis. We move horizontally through the trellis with the passage of time. Each transition means new bits have arrived. The trellis diagram is drawn by lining up all the possible states (2^3) in the vertical axis. Then we connect each state to the next state by the allowable code words for that state. There are only two choices possible at each state. These are determined by the arrival of either a 0 or a 1 bit. The arrows show the input bit and the output bits are shown in parentheses.

The arrows going upwards represent a 0 bit and going downwards represent a 1 bit. The trellis diagram is unique to each code, same as both the state and tree diagrams are. We can draw the trellis for as many periods as we want. Each period repeats the possible transitions. The trellis is preferred over code tree because the number of nodes at any level of trellis does not continue to grow as number of incoming bits increases. The number of levels remain constant at 2^{K-1}, where K is constraint length. We always begin at state 0 0 0. Starting from here, the trellis expands and in L = kK bits becomes fully populated such that all transitions are possible. The transitions then repeat from this point on.

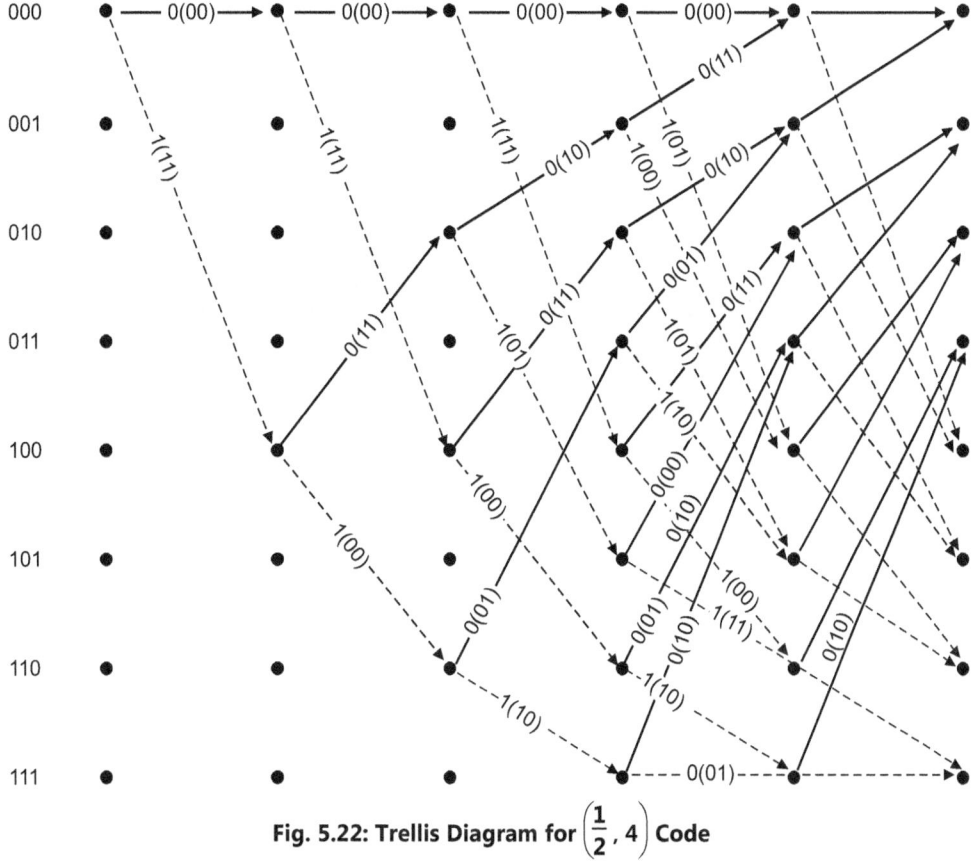

Fig. 5.22: Trellis Diagram for $\left(\dfrac{1}{2}, 4\right)$ Code

5.9.4 Decoding of Convolutional Codes

There are several different approaches to decoding of convolutional codes.

These are grouped in two basic categories.

1. Sequential Decoding
   - Fano algorithm
2. Maximum likely-hood decoding
   - Viterbi decoding

Both of these methods represent two different approaches to the same basic idea behind decoding.

The basic idea behind decoding:

Assume that 3 bits were sent via a rate 1/2 code. We receive 6 bits. (Ignore flush bits for now). These six bits may or may not have errors. We know from the encoding process that these bits map uniquely. So a 3-bit sequence will have a unique 6-bit output. But due to errors, we can receive any and all possible combinations of the 6 bits.

The permutation of 3 input bits results in eight possible input sequences. Each of these has a unique mapping to a 6-bit output sequence by the code. These form the set of permissible sequences and the decoder's task is to determine which one was sent.

Table 5.3: Bit Agreement used as metric to decide between the received sequence and the 8 possible valid code sequences

Input	Valid Code Sequence	Received Sequence	Bit Agreements
0 0 0	0 0 0 0 0 0	1 1 1 1 0 0	2
0 0 1	0 0 0 0 1 1	1 1 1 1 0 0	0
0 1 0	0 0 1 1 1 1	1 1 1 1 0 0	2
0 1 1	0 0 1 1 0 0	1 1 1 1 0 0	4
1 0 0	**1 1 1 1 1 0**	1 1 1 1 0 0	**5**
1 0 1	**1 1 1 1 0 1**	1 1 1 1 0 0	**5**
1 1 0	1 1 0 0 0 1	1 1 1 1 0 0	3
1 1 1	1 1 0 0 1 0	1 1 1 1 0 0	3

Let's say we received 1 1 1 1 0 0. It is not one of the 8 possible sequences above. How do we decode it ? We can do two things.

1. We can compare this received sequence to all permissible sequences and pick the one with the smallest Hamming distance (or bit disagreement).
2. We can do a correlation and pick the sequences with the best correlation.

The first procedure is basically what is behind hard decision decoding and the second the soft decision decoding. The bit agreements, also the dot product between the received sequence and the code word, show that we still get an ambiguous answer and do not know what was sent.

As the number of bits increase, the number of calculations required to do decoding in this brute force manner increases such that it is no longer practical to do decoding this way. We need to find a more efficient method that does not examine all options and has a way of resolving ambiguity such as here where we have two possible answers. (Shown bold in Table 5.3).

If a message of length s bits is received, then the possible number of code words are 2^s. How can we decode the sequence without checking each and everyone of these 2^s code words ? This is the basic idea behind decoding.

5.9.5 Sequential Decoding

Sequential decoding was one of the first methods proposed for decoding a convolutionally coded bit stream. It was first proposed by Wozencraft and later a better version was proposed by Fano.

Sequential decoding is best described by analogy. You are given some directions to a place. The directions consist of some landmarks. But the person, who gave the directions, has not done a very good job and occasionally you do not recognize a landmark and you end up on a wrong path. But since now you do not see any more landmarks, you feel that you may be on a wrong path. You back-track to a point where you do recognize a landmark and then take an alternate path until you see the next landmark and ultimately in this fashion you reach your destination. You may back- track several times in the process depending on how good the directions were.

In sequential decoding similarly you are dealing with just one path at a time. You may give up that path at any time and turn back to follow another path, but important thing is that only one path is followed at any one time.

Sequential decoding allows both forward and backward movement through the trellis. The decoder keeps track of its decisions, each time it makes an ambiguous decision, it tallies it. If the tally increases faster than some threshold value, decoder gives up that path and retraces the path back to the last fork where the tally was below the threshold.

5.9.6 Viterbi Decoding

Viterbi decoding is the best known implementation of the maximum likelihood decoding. Here we narrow the options systematically at each time tick.

The principle used to reduce the choices is.

1. The errors occur infrequently. The probability of error is small.
2. The probability of two errors in a row is much smaller than a single error, that is the errors are distributed randomly.

The Viterbi decoder examines an entire received sequence of a given length. The decoder computes a metric for each path and makes a decision based on this metric. All paths are followed until two paths converge on one node. Then the path with the higher metric is kept and the one with lower metric is discarded. The paths selected are called the survivors.

5.10 ARQ

Error control coding is used for controlling transmission errors. There are two aspects to be taken into account here. If there are too many errors, the coding techniques will not be able to correct them. This will require more overheads. If the errors are corrected at the receiver end, it is called Forward Error Correction (FEC).

If overheads are to be reduced or we want to take care of noisy channels which introduce too many errors, we can only detect errors at the receiver end and if error is found, request the transmitter to retransmit the code again. This is called Automatic Repeat Request (ARQ). A feedback channel is required for signalling back. Error detection codes like CRC codes are used in such techniques.

There are three basic types of ARQ systems.
1. Stop-and-Wait ARQ.
2. Go-back-N ARQ.
3. Selective repeat ARQ.

5.10.1 Stop-and-Wait ARQ

It is simplest ARQ system to implement. Transmitter sends a frame (code word) to receiver. Let the time required to send this frame be T_F. There will be transmission delay between transmitter and receiver before this frame reaches the receiver. Let this time be T_d. The receiver will process this frame and check whether there is an error. Let the time required for this processing be T_{proc}. The receiver will then send a feedback signal to transmitter. If the frame is received without error, it will send positive Acknowledgement (ACK) and if the frame is corrupted, it will send negative acknowledgement (NAK). There will also be time delay in receiving feedback signal which will be same as T_d.

If ACK is received at the transmitter, it will transmit the next frame. But if NAK is received, it will retransmit the previous frame. This means transmitter has to store the previous frame in its buffer. The disadvantage of this system is that the transmitter has to wait for the ACK/NAK signal before transmitting a next frame.

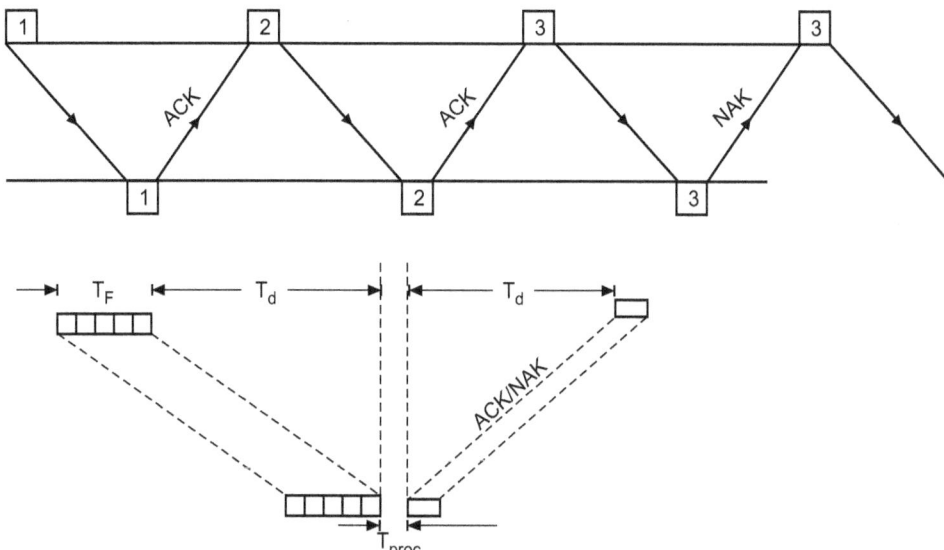

Fig. 5.23: Stop-and-Wait ARQ

5.10.2 Performance of Stop-and-Wait ARQ
Total time required for transmitting the frame = $T_F + T_d + T_{proc.} + T_d + T_{ack} + T_{ack\ proc.}$

where, T_F → Frame time
   T_d → Transmission delay
   $T_{proc.}$ → Processing time for frame at receiver
   T_{ack} → Acknowledgement frame time
   $T_{ack\ proc.}$ → Processing time for acknowledgement at transmitter

We can neglect T_{proc}, T_{ack} and $T_{ack\ proc}$ as they will be small as compared to T_F and T_d. Hence, total time T for transmitting one frame without any error will be

$$T = T_F + 2T_d$$

A frame consists of n code bits which are obtained by encoding k message bits. Hence, we are effectively transmitting k bits.

Hence, efficiency of transmission is defined as 'ratio of average number of information bits accepted at receiver end per unit time' and number of information bits that would be accepted per unit time if ARQ is not used. It is also called throughput (η) of ARQ system. Hence, throughput of Stop-and-Wait ARQ is

$$\eta_{SW} = \frac{T_k}{T}$$

where, $T_k \rightarrow$ Time required to transmit k information bits if ARQ is not used

$T \rightarrow$ Total time required to transmit k information bits if ARQ is used

Now,
$$T_k = \frac{k}{n} T_F$$

$$\therefore \quad \eta_{SW} = \frac{\frac{k}{n} T_F}{T_F + 2T_d}$$

$$= \frac{k}{n} \times \frac{T_F}{T_F + 2T_d}$$

$$= \frac{k}{n} \times \frac{1}{1 + 2\frac{T_d}{T_F}}$$

Let, $2T_d = T_l$ i.e. total delay.

$$\therefore \quad \eta_{SW} = \frac{k}{n} \times \frac{1}{1 + \frac{T_l}{T_F}}$$

Now, consider a case where there are errors in transmission. We do not know how many times a frame will be retransmitted. Hence, we consider average time for transmission of a frame. Let P_A be the probability of receiving frame in single transmission.

Hence, probability that two transmissions will be required is $P_A (1 - P_A)$.

Probability that three transmissions required will be,

$$P_A (1 - P_A)(1 - P_A) = P_A (1 - P_A)^2$$

Hence, average number of successful transmissions of single frame will be

$$\overline{N}_{SW} = 1 \cdot P_A + 2 \cdot P_A(1 - P_A) + 3 P_A(1 - P_A)^2 + \ldots$$

$$= P_A[1 + 2(1 - P_A) + 3(1 - P_A)^2 + \ldots]$$

$$= P_A \sum_{i=1}^{\infty} i(1 - P_A)^{i-1}$$

$$= P_A \times \frac{1}{[1 - (1 - P_A)]^2} \quad \left[\because \sum_{i=1}^{\infty} i x^{i-1} = \frac{1}{(1-x)^2}\right]$$

$$= \frac{1}{P_A}$$

∴ Average number of transmissions required for single successful transmission

$$= \frac{1}{P_A}$$

∴ Average time required for single successful transmissions

= Average number of transmissions × Time required for one transmission

$$T_{avg} = \frac{1}{P_A} \times (T_F + T_l) \qquad \text{[where, } T_l = 2T_d\text{]}$$

∴ Throughput of Stop-and-Wait ARQ with errors in transmission,

$$\eta_{SW} = \frac{T_k}{T_{avg}}$$

$$= \frac{\frac{k}{n} T_F}{\frac{1}{P_A} \times (T_F + T_l)}$$

$$= \frac{k}{n} \times \frac{P_A}{1 + \frac{T_l}{T_F}}$$

If $P_A = 1$, above equation reduces to the case of transmission with no errors.

5.10.3 Go-Back-N ARQ

This system does not wait for the acknowledgement to be received back from receiver. It keeps on sending frames continuously, whereas receiver keeps on sending acknowledgement when negative acknowledgement (NAK) is received for a particular frame, that frame and the N – 1 frames, following it will also be retransmitted. Thus, total N frames are transmitted. This means the receiver should buffer these N frames.

The scheme is shown in Fig. 5.24.

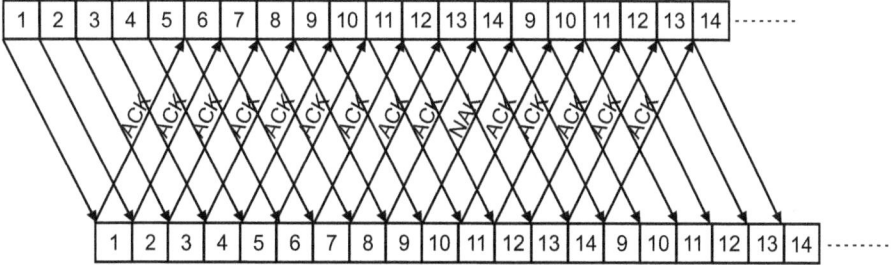

Fig. 5.24: Go-back-N ARQ

This system has improved throughput over stop-and-wait ARQ.

5.10.4 Performance of Go-back-N ARQ

Let us derive the expression for throughput of Go-back-N ARQ with error and then arrive at expression without error. If there is an error in a frame, N − 1 frames following it and that frame are retransmitted. Hence, total number of frames that are retransmitted is N + 1. (Frame in error is transmitted twice). If the frame goes wrong, again we have to transmit N frames again. Hence, number of frames to be transmitted when the frame goes wrong twice is 2N + 1 and so on.

If P_A is probability of error in single transmission. Average number of transmissions required for transmitting a frame successfully is

$$\begin{aligned}\bar{N}_{GCB} &= 1 \cdot P_A + (N+1)P_A(1-P_A) + (2N+1)P_A(1-P_A)^2 + \ldots \\ &= P_A[1 + (N+1)(1-P_A) + (2N+1)P_A(1-P_A)^2 + \ldots] \\ &= 1 + \frac{N(1-P_A)}{P_A}\end{aligned}$$

∴ Average time to successfully transmit one frame will be

$$T_{avg} = T_F \times \left[1 + \frac{N(1-P_A)}{P_A}\right]$$

Note that there is no delay.
Hence, throughput of Go-back-N ARQ is

$$\begin{aligned}\eta_{GBN} &= \frac{T_k}{T_{avg}} \\ &= \frac{\frac{k}{n}T_F}{T_F\left[1 + \frac{N(1-P_A)}{P_A}\right]} \\ &= \frac{k}{n} \times \frac{1}{1 + \frac{N(1-P_A)}{P_A}}\end{aligned}$$

If $P_A = 1$ (transmission without error)

$$\eta_{GBN} = \frac{k}{n}$$

Thus, Go-back-N ARQ has improved the performance over the Stop-and-Wait ARQ.

5.10.5 Selective Repeat ARQ

In this system, transmitter keeps on sending frames without waiting for acknowledgement as in case of Go-back-N ARQ. If there is an error in a frame, that frame will only be requested for retransmission. Hence, this scheme has highest efficiency. But it is complex and costly for implementation. The system is shown in Fig. 5.25.

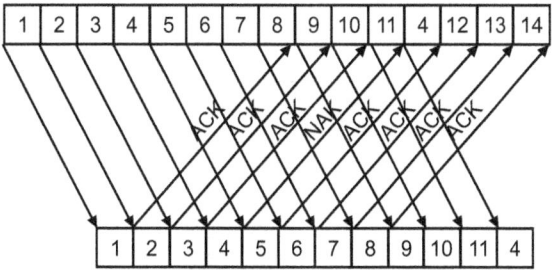

Fig. 5.25: Selective Repeat ARQ

5.10.6 Performance of Selective Repeat ARQ

Selective repeat ARQ retransmits only the frame in error. Hence, it is similar to stop-and-wait ARQ with no delay (T_l) i.e. $T_l = 0$. Hence, if we put $T_l = 0$ in throughput of stop-and-wait ARQ, we can get throughput of selective repeat ARQ.

$$\therefore \quad \eta_{SR} = \frac{k}{n} \times \frac{T_F}{\frac{T_F + 0}{P_A}}$$

$$= \frac{k}{n} \times P_A$$

Example 5.14:

Find throughput of all the three ARQ systems for (1023, 973) BCH code if frame time is 10 μs, probability of single transmission is 0.99. Total delay is 40 μs and N = 4.

Solution:

Given:
$T_F = 10 \times 10^{-6}$
$T_l = 40 \times 10^{-6}$
$P_A = 0.99$
$N = 4$

(i) Stop-and-Wait ARQ:

$$\eta_{SW} = \frac{k}{n} \times \frac{T_F}{T_F + T_l} \times P_A$$

$$= \frac{973}{1023} \times \frac{10 \times 10^{-6}}{(10 + 40) \times 10^{-6}} \times 0.99$$

$$= 0.188$$

(ii) Go-back-N ARQ:

$$\eta_{GBN} = \frac{1}{1 + \frac{N(1-P_A)}{P_A}}$$

$$= \frac{973}{1023} + \frac{1}{1 + \frac{4(0.01)}{0.99}}$$

$$= 0.915$$

(iii) Selective Repeat ARQ:

$$\eta_{SR} = \frac{k}{n} \times P_A$$

$$= \frac{973}{1023} \times 0.99$$

Above example shows that selective repeat ARQ has highest throughput.

EXERCISE

1. Write the characteristics of linear block codes.
2. What is minimum Hamming distance ?
3. Explain –
   (i) Hard decision decoding
   (ii) Soft decision decoding
4. Explain how generator matrix is used to generate (n, k) block code.
5. What is parity check matrix ?
6. What is syndrome decoding ?
7. How minimum Hamming distance is related to parity check matrix ?
8. What are dual codes ?
9. What are perfect codes ?
10. Explain error probability of code after coding ? Compare it with error probability without coding.
11. What are Hamming codes ?

12. What are maximum distance codes ?
13. What are equivalent codes ?
14. Explain properties of cyclic code with suitable example.
15. How are cyclic codes represented using polynomials ?
16. What is generator polynomial ? Why it should be factor of $x^n + 1$?
17. Explain method of generating cyclic code. (Systematic and Non-systematic).
18. Explain the method of decoding cyclic codes.
19. What are fire codes ?
20. Comment on error detection capability of CRC codes.
21. Explain encoder and decoder circuit.
22. How are burst error correcting codes designed ?
23. Explain the features of Golay code.
24. Explain the concept of TCM.
25. What is free Euclidean distance ?
26. What is coding gain ?
27. Explain how mapping by set partitioning is used to design TCM scheme.
28. State and explain Ungerboeck's TCM design rules.
29. Explain TCM decoding process.
30. What is ARQ ? Explain.
31. Explain Stop-and-Wait ARQ.
32. Explain selective repeat ARQ.
33. Explain Go-back-N ARQ.
34. Derive expression for throughput of –
    (i) Stop-and-Wait ARQ
    (ii) Selective repeat ARQ
    (iii) Go-back-N ARQ
35. What is error probability of ARQ system for (n, k) block code ?
36. What is minimal polynomial ?
37. Explain how do you obtain minimal polynomial from primitive polynomial.

38. Explain Encoding procedure of BCH code.
39. Explain Decoding procedure of BCH code.
40. What are the features of BCH code ?
41. What are features of RS code ?
42. How do you carry out encoding in RS code ?
43. Explain decoding process of RS code.
44. Construct GF(9) from GF(3) using primitive polynomial $x^3 + x + 1$.

***

www.ingramcontent.com/pod-product-compliance
Lightning Source LLC
Chambersburg PA
CBHW082036230426
43670CB00016B/2669